SYSTEM EFFECTS

SYSTEM EFFECTS

COMPLEXITY IN POLITICAL AND SOCIAL LIFE

Robert Jervis

PRINCETON UNIVERSITY PRESS   PRINCETON, NEW JERSEY

Copyright © 1997 by Princeton University Press
Published by Princeton University Press, 41 William Street,
Princeton, New Jersey 08540
In the United Kingdom: Princeton University Press, Chichester,
West Sussex
All Rights Reserved

Library of Congress Cataloging-in-Publication Data

Jervis, Robert, 1940–
System effects : complexity in political and social life / Robert Jervis.
p.   cm.
Includes bibliographical references and index.
ISBN 0-691-02624-6 (acid-free paper)
1. Social systems.   2. International relations.   3. Complexity
(Philosophy)   I. Title.
HM131.J44   1997
301—dc21   97-1108   CIP

This book has been composed in Caledonia

Princeton University Press books are printed on acid-free paper and
meet the guidelines for permanence and durability of the Committee on
Production Guidelines for Book Longevity of the Council on Library
Resources

Printed in the United States of America

10 9 8 7 6 5 4 3 2 1

For Kathe, Alexa, and Lisa

_____

Contents

Acknowledgments ⸻

AT LUNCH with younger colleagues a number of years ago, I mentioned that a journal had just rejected my latest article. They could hardly disguise their relief at learning that this doesn't happen just to them. In this spirit I would like to say that several private foundations and public funding agencies declined to support this research.

So my debts are intellectual only. I hope my footnotes indicate some of what I owe to the works of Albert Hirschman, Charles Perrow, Thomas Schelling, Paul Schroeder, Glenn Snyder, and Kenneth Waltz.

I received comments from Charles Cameron, Jack Levy, Gary Marx, Glenn Snyder, Jack Snyder, Marc Trachtenberg, Kenneth Waltz, and Kathryn Yatrakis, and should have taken more of them. I was also assisted by the responses to presentations at Berkeley, Columbia, Harvard, Rutgers, and UCLA. A great many of Columbia's graduate students provided ideas, criticisms (especially), and sources: at the risk of slighting others, let me mention James Davis, Barbara Farnham, Rose McDermott, James McAllister, Jonathan Mercer, and Randall Schweller. Beth Bloodgood compiled the index.

SYSTEM EFFECTS

One

Introduction

When you pick up one piece of this planet, you
find that, one way or another, it's attached to
everything else—if you jiggle over here,
something is going to wiggle over there. . . .
We need this sense of the continuing
interconnectedness of the system as part of the
common knowledge, so that politicians feel it
and believe it, and so that voters feel it and
believe it, and so that kids feel it and believe it,
so that they'll grow up with an ethic.

[To minimize oil spills] we should . . . mandate
double-hulled vessels and compartments in
tankers.
> —Wallace White, "Profiles (Sylvia Earle)" in
> *The New Yorker*

ON THE centennial of the publication of *The Origin of Species*, H. J. Muller
wrote an article entitled "One Hundred Years Without Darwinism Are
Enough."[1] His point was that although the basic ideas of evolution were well
known, people often thought in nonevolutionary terms, a defect he hoped to
correct. My aim is parallel. Although we all know that social life and politics
constitute systems and that many outcomes are the unintended consequence of complex interactions, the basic ideas of systems do not come
readily to mind and so often are ignored.[2] Because I know international

---

[1] H. J. Muller, "One Hundred Years Without Darwinism Are Enough," *School Science and
Mathematics* 59 (April 1959), pp. 304–16; the famous paleontologist George Gaylord Simpson
thought so well of this title that he used it, with acknowledgment, for one of his essays in *This
View of Life: The World of an Evolutionist* (New York: Harcourt, Brace, and World, 1964). For
the argument that many aspects of Darwinism have yet to be incorporated into philosophy, see
Ernst Mayr, "How Biology Differs from the Physical Sciences," in David Depew and Bruce
Weber, eds., *Evolution at a Crossroads: The New Biology and the New Philosophy of Science*
(Cambridge, Mass.: MIT Press, 1986), pp. 43–63.

[2] This may stem from deeply ingrained patterns of thought: Jerome Bruner, Jacqueline
Goodnow, and George Austin, *A Study of Thinking* (New York: Wiley, 1956); also see Nancy
Henley, Robert Horsfall, and Clinton De Soto, "Goodness of Figure and Social Structure,"

politics best, I will often focus on it. But the arguments of the book are more general and I will take examples from many fields. This is not difficult: Systems have been analyzed by almost every academic discipline because they appear throughout our physical, biological, and social worlds.[3] The fact that congruent patterns can be found across such different domains testifies to the prevalence and power of the dynamics that systems display. Much of this constitutes variations on a few themes, in parallel with Darwin's summary remark about the structures of living creatures: "Nature is prodigal in variety, but niggard in innovation."[4]

This is not to promise a systems theory of politics, although some work in this vein has been extremely fruitful. Kenneth Waltz's *Theory of International Politics* is the most important book in the field in the past decade, and I will devote much of chapter 3 to it.[5] My objectives are more modest, however, in part because I have doubts as to whether more ambitious goals can be reached.[6] Few if any realms of human conduct are completely determined at the systems level. Actors' choices are crucial and, as I will discuss later, are influenced by beliefs about how the system operates. We should not expect too much of theorizing here—actors may be able to take advantage of discernable patterns in ways that would destroy at least some of them. But human guile and idiosyncracies are not the only factors that limit our ability to make determinant predictions: Many systems, including inanimate ones, are highly complex and contingent.[7]

Psychological Review 76 (March 1969), pp. 194–204, and Roger Shepard, "Evolution of a Mesh between Principles of the Mind and Regularities of the World," in John Dupré, ed., *The Latest on the Best: Essays on Evolution and Optimality* (Cambridge, Mass.: MIT Press, 1987), pp. 251–75.

[3] The list of works on systems and systems theories is very long. In this book I will cite only those I have found most useful, which I realize excludes many that others consider classics. These, of course, often have influenced other works on which I do draw.

[4] Charles Darwin, *The Origin of Species* (New York: Modern Library, 1936), p. 143.

[5] Kenneth Waltz, *Theory of International Politics* (Reading, Mass.: Addison-Wesley, 1979).

[6] For discussions of what we can—and cannot—expect from theorizing about complex systems see, for example, David Ehrenfeld, "The Management of Diversity: A Conservation Paradox," in F. Herbert Bormann and Stephen Kellert, eds., *Ecology, Economics, Ethics: The Broken Circle* (New Haven, Conn.: Yale University Press, 1991), pp. 26–39; Stuart Kauffman, "Whispers from Carnot: The Origins of Order and Principles of Adaptation in Complex Nonequilibrium Systems," in George Cowan, David Pines, and David Meltzer, eds., *Complexity: Mataphors, Models, and Reality* (Reading, Mass.: Addison-Wesley, 1994), pp. 85–87; David Depew and Bruce Weber, *Darwinism Evolving: Systems Dynamics and the Genealogy of Natural Selection* (Cambridge, Mass.: MIT Press, 1995), pp. 490–91.

[7] Related arguments stem from chaos theory. The standard source for nonexperts—which I assuredly am—is James Gleick, *Chaos Theory* (New York: Penguin, 1988). Also see Roger Lewin, *Complexity: Life at the Edge of Chaos* (New York: Macmillan, 1992); M. Mitchell Waldrop, *Complexity: The Emerging Science at the Edge of Order and Chaos* (New York: Simon and Schuster, 1992); Stephen Kellert, *In the Wake of Chaos: Unpredictable Order in Dynamical Systems* (Chicago: University of Chicago Press, 1993); and David Ruelle, *Chance*

This does not mean an absence of regularities. Indeed, crucial to a systems approach is the belief that structures are powerful and that the internal characteristics of the elements matter less than their place in the system. That is why different kinds of countries often behave similarly, as Waltz has stressed; why the Cold War resembled the rivalry between Athens and Sparta; why the behavior of Frederick the Great in 1756 was not unlike that of Kaiser Wilhelm in 1914; why I can locate parallel processes in realms as diverse as international politics and ecology. As a leading biologist put it: "Whenever I come across a system which is oscillating, whether it be the menstrual cycle or the numbers of hares and lynxes in Canada, I look for delayed feedback. In doing so, I am assuming that . . . the behaviour is determined by the structure, and not by whether the components are electrical circuits, hormones, or animals."[8] In most cases, our first instinct is to explain behavior in terms of the actors' preferences and power. Instead, we should start with how the actors are positioned. For example, the argument that poverty will increase when welfare policy is devolved to individual American states is often rebutted by pointing out that state political leaders are no more heartless than national ones. But a systemic perspective indicates that the focus should be on the fact that because the states compete with one another for national prominence and mobile businesses, their leaders will feel greater pressures to cut welfare benefits, and thereby cut taxes, than will national figures. Furthermore, much about the actor is systemically determined: Many of an individual's preferences stem from her position in the social system, and her power is influenced by its configuration (e.g., a swing voter gains power because the others are evenly divided).

Definitions and Illustrations

Definitions are rarely exciting but rarely can be completely ignored. Perhaps we should simply say about systems what Justice Potter Stewart said about obscenity: "I know it when I see it." Indeed, Garrett Hardin says, "One of the most important ideas in modern science is the idea of a system; and it is almost impossible to define."[9] Hardin continues his excellent essay by defining by examples, which I will do as well. But a little more precision may be

---

and Chaos (Princeton, N.J.: Princeton University Press, 1991). For the importance of contingency in evolution, see Stephen Jay Gould, Wonderful Life (New York: Norton, 1989) and Depew and Weber, Darwinism Evolving. For a critique of the more extreme claims of some theorists, see John Horgan, "From Complexity to Perplexity," Scientific American, June 1995, pp. 104–9.

[8] John Maynard Smith, Did Darwin Get It Right? Essays on Games, Sex, and Evolution (New York: Chapman & Hall, 1989), p. 226.

[9] Garrett Hardin, "The Cybernetics of Competition," Perspectives in Biology and Medicine 7 (Autumn 1963), p. 77.

helpful. We are dealing with a system when (a) a set of units or elements is interconnected so that changes in some elements or their relations produce changes in other parts of the system, and (b) the entire system exhibits properties and behaviors that are different from those of the parts.[10]

As this chapter and the next will show, the result is that systems often display nonlinear relationships, outcomes cannot be understood by adding together the units or their relations, and many of the results of actions are unintended. Complexities can appear even in what would seem to be simple and deterministic situations. Thus over one hundred years ago the mathematician Henri Poincaré showed that the motion of as few as three bodies (such as the sun, the moon, and the earth), although governed by strict scientific laws, defies exact solution: While eclipses of the moon can be predicted thousands of years in advance, they cannot be predicted millions

[10] For similar and overlapping definitions, see Herbert Simon, *The Sciences of the Artificial*, 2d ed. (Cambridge, Mass.: MIT Press, 1981), pp. 195, 209–10; Anatol Rapoport, "Systems Analysis: General Systems Theory," *International Encyclopaedia of the Social Sciences*, vol. 15 (New York: Free Press, 1968), p. 453; Ludwig von Bertalanffy, *General Systems Theory: Foundations, Development, Applications* (New York: Braziller, 1986), p. 55; George Klir, "The Polyphonic General Systems Theory," in Klir, ed., *Trends in General Systems Theory* (New York: Wiley, 1972), p. 1; Howard Odum and Elisabeth Odum, *Energy Basis for Man and Nature*, 2d ed. (New York: McGraw-Hill, 1981), p. 5; Warren Weaver, "Science and Complexity," *American Scientist* 36 (October 1948), pp. 538–39; Kenneth Boulding, *The World as a Total System* (Beverly Hills, Calif.: Sage, 1985), p. 9; W. Ross Ashby, *Design for a Brain*, 2d ed. (New York: Wiley, 1960), p. 16; Thomas Hughes, *Networks of Power: Electrification in Western Society, 1880–1930* (Baltimore, Md.: Johns Hopkins University Press, 1983), pp. 5–6, 20–22; James Miller, *Living Systems* (New York: McGraw-Hill, 1978), pp. 16–19. Also see Ludwig von Bertalanffy and Anatol Rapoport, eds., *Yearbook of the Society for the Advancement of General Systems Theory*, vol. 1 (Ann Arbor: University of Michigan Mental Health Research Institute, 1956), and Robert Flood, *Liberating Systems Theory* (New York: Plenum, 1990), chapter 5. For somewhat different definitions from scholars of international politics, see Inis Claude, *Power and International Relations* (New York: Random House, 1962), p. 42; Stanley Hoffmann, "International Systems and International Law," in Klaus Knorr and Sidney Verba, eds., *The International System* (Princeton, N.J.: Princeton University Press, 1961), pp. 207–8; Morton Kaplan, *System and Process in International Politics* (New York: Wiley, 1957), pp. 4–6; Kaplan, *Towards Professionalism in International Theory* (New York: Free Press, 1979), p. 96; Hedley Bull, *The Anarchical Society* (New York: Columbia University Press, 1977), pp. 8–16; Waltz, *Theory of International Politics*, p. 79; Robert Gilpin, *War and Change in World Politics* (New York: Cambridge University Press, 1981), pp. 25–29. Feedbacks play a vital role in most systems and will be the subject of a later chapter, but one can have a system without them.

For some purposes, it is important to distinguish among systems on such dimensions as organized or disorganized, open or closed, simple or complex, hierarchical or anarchic, or oligopolistic or freely competitive: see, for example, Harlan Wilson, "Complexity as a Theoretical Problem: Wider Perspectives in Political Theory," in Todd La Porte, ed., *Organized Complexity* (Princeton, N.J.: Princeton University Press, 1975), pp. 281–88, and Jack Snyder, "Introduction," in Jack Snyder and Robert Jervis, eds., *Coping with Complexity in the International System* (Boulder, Colo.: Westview Press, 1993), pp. 6–13. But for much of my analysis, these distinctions are not crucial.

of years ahead, which is a very short period by astronomical standards.[11] As a student of mathematical approaches to ecology explains, "It doesn't need any complicating factors to cause complicated behaviour. The very simplest type of self-regulation can . . . account for it."[12] A systems approach shows how individual actors following simple and uncoordinated strategies can produce aggregate behavior that is complex and ordered, although not necessarily predictable and stable.[13] Similarly, biologists stress that highly complex life-forms are composed of elements that, taken individually, are quite simple.

The counterintuitive way systems operate—and the habit of even accomplished systems theorists of lapsing into simpler ways of thinking—can be shown by the quotation that opens this chapter. It seems obvious that if tankers had double hulls, there would be fewer oil spills. But interconnections mean that the obvious and immediate effect might not be the dominant one. The straightforward argument compares two worlds, one with single-hulled tankers and one with double-hulled ones, holding everything else constant. But in a system, *everything else will not remain constant*. The shipping companies, forced to purchase more expensive tankers, might cut expenditures on other safety measures, in part because of the greater protection supplied by the double hulls. The relative cost of alternative means of transporting oil would decrease, perhaps moving spills from the seas to the areas traversed by new pipelines. But even tanker spills might not decrease. The current trade-off between costs and spills may reflect the preferences of shippers and captains, who might take advantage of the greater safety by going faster and taking more chances.[14] If double hulls led to even

[11] For a recent discussion, see Robert Pool, "Chaos Theory: How Big an Advance?" *Science* 245 (July 9, 1989), p. 26.

[12] Karl Sigmund, *Games of Life: Explorations in Ecology, Evolution, and Behaviour* (New York: Oxford University Press, 1993), p. 52.

[13] This is brought out clearly by the studies of "complex adaptive systems": see, for example, Joshua Epstein and Robert Axtell, *Growing Artificial Societies: Social Science from the Bottom Up* (Washington, D.C.: the Brookings Institution, 1996); John Holland, *Adaptation in Natural and Artificial Systems* (Cambridge, Mass.: MIT Press, 1992); Holland, *Hidden Order: How Adaption Builds Complexity* (Reading, Mass.: Addison-Wesley, 1995); Nigel Gilbert and Rosaria Conte, eds., *Artificial Societies: The Computer Simulation of Social Life* (London: University College London Press, 1995); David Lane, "Artificial Worlds and Economics" (unpublished, Santa Fe Institute paper No. 92–09–048). This perspective can be found in Darwin, *Origin of Species*, especially pp. 196–202, 374; also see Thomas Schelling, *Micromotives and Macrobehavior* (New York: Norton, 1978), passim, and especially pp. 147–55.

[14] For a related set of concerns, see Edward Tenner, *Why Things Bite Back: Technology and the Revenge of Unintended Consequences* (New York: Knopf, 1996), p. 89. For a discussion of marine safety in terms of systems effects, see Charles Perrow, *Normal Accidents* (New York: Basic Books, 1984), chapter 6. My thinking has been strongly influenced by this book. For evidence of this effect with automobile safety devices, see below, chapter 2, pp. 68–70.

a slight increase in the price of oil, many other consequences could follow, from greater conservation, to increased uses of alternative fuels, to hardship for the poor.

International history is full of interconnections and complex interactions. Indeed, this one might seem like a parody were it not part of the events leading up to the First World War:

> By the end of the summer of 1913 there was a real danger of yet another Balkan conflict: the King of Greece [said] that Turkey was preparing an expedition to recover the islands in Greek hands, and from Constantinople the German ambassador reported that the Bulgarian minister to the Porte had informed him of a verbal Turco-Bulgarian agreement under which Bulgaria would attack Thrace in the event of a Turco-Greek war. The danger that a Turco-Greek war could spread beyond the Balkans could not be lightly dismissed. If Turkey and Greece came to blows the Bulgarians could be expected to seek revenge for the defeats of the previous summer; so early a repudiation of the Treaty of Bucharest would offend the Rumanians, whilst the Greeks, if attacked by the Bulgarians, could still invoke their treaty with Serbia. If Serbia became involved no-one could guarantee that Austria-Hungary would once again stand aside.[15]

Here part of the complexity arises because we are unfamiliar with the situation, but this is not the entire story. Look, for example, at Paul Kennedy's brief discussion of the multiple relations that interacted with one another in the 1930s:

> It was not simply . . . that [for Great Britain] dealing with "the German problem" involved a constant reference to France and that dealing with "the Japan problem" involved equally close consultation with the United States. An additional complication was that these two triangular relations interacted with each other. For example, British attempts to improve relations with Tokyo would, it was argued, enable a stiffer line to be taken towards Berlin—which would gratify the French; but this "appeasement" of the Japanese would enrage the Americans, possibly with grave consequences, and that would alarm the Dominions. The stiffer tone in Europe might also lead the Germans to settle their differences with that other

[15] R. J. Crampton, *The Hollow Detente: Anglo-German Relations in the Balkans, 1911–1914* (Atlantic Highlands, N.J.: Humanities Press, 1980), p. 131. The late eighteenth century is filled with similar cases: for examples see Paul Schroeder, *The Transformation of European Politics, 1763–1848* (New York: Oxford University Press, 1994), and T. C. W. Blanning, *The Origins of the French Revolutionary Wars* (London: Longman, 1986).

The first scholars who applied ideas from ecology to international politics noted that when elements are interconnected, "any substantial change in one sector of the milieu is nearly certain to produce significant, often unsettling, sometimes utterly disruptive consequences in other sectors." (Harold and Margaret Sprout, *An Ecological Paradigm for the Study of International Politics* [Princeton University, Center for International Studies, Research Memorandum no. 30, March 1968], p. 55.) A more recent study in this vein is James Rosenau, *Turbulence in World Politics* (Princeton, N.J.: Princeton University Press, 1990).

"mystery" state, the Soviet Union. The whole thing worked in the reverse order, too: if Japan threatened aggression in the Far East, the British would need to move closer to the United States; but they would probably also have to "buy off" Hitler in Europe, which might alarm France and its smaller allies.[16]

As these cases show, it is difficult to know what will happen in a system, but at minimum we can say that a change at one point will have wide-ranging effects. Thus when the European settlers in North America made friends or enemies of a native tribe or gave it modern tools and weapons, they affected relations between that tribe and its neighbors, setting in motion a ripple effect that affected the behavior of others hundreds of miles away.[17]

Ripples move through channels established by actors' interests and strategies. When these are intricate, the ramifications will be as well, and so the results can surprise the actor who initiated the change. The international history of the late nineteenth and early twentieth centuries, centered on maladroit German diplomacy, supplies several examples. Dropping the Reinsurance Treaty with Russia in 1890 simplified German diplomacy, as the Kaiser and his advisors had desired. More important, though, were the indirect and delayed consequences, starting with Russia's turn to France, which increased Germany's need for Austrian support, thereby making Germany hostage to its weaker and less stable partner. In 1902, the Germans hoped that the Anglo-Japanese Alliance, motivated by Britain's attempt to reduce its isolation and vulnerability to German pressure, would worsen British relations with Russia (which was Japan's rival in the Far East) and France (which sought British colonial concessions).[18] There were indeed ramifications, but they were not to Germany's liking. The British public became less fearful of foreign ties, easing the way for ententes with France and Russia.

[16] Paul Kennedy, "The Logic of Appeasement," *Times Literary Supplement*, May 28, 1982, p. 585.

[17] As one historian has noted, "A tribe whose enemies had the weapons which it lacked had few alternatives, and all of them were unpleasant. It inevitably made war upon the competitor. So quickly did such hostilities arise after the entry of the Europeans, and so fiercely did they continue, that observers were prone to consider war as the usual intertribal relationship, not knowing how they themselves had transformed these relations" (George Hunt, *The Wars of the Iroquois* [Madison: University of Wisconsin Press, 1940], p. 19). For the argument that the explanation for why lions encountered by the European settlers in East Africa had a propensity to eat humans can be traced to ecological changes brought about by earlier European activities elsewhere on the continent, see Craig Packer, "Coping with a Lion Killer," *Natural History* 105 (June 1996), p. 16. Ecologists sometimes try to trace relations by removing the members of a species from an area, although the extent to which these experiments can mimic natural processes is not entirely clear: See, for example, Stuart Pimm, *The Balance of Nature? Ecological Issues in the Conservation of Species and Communities* (Chicago: University of Chicago Press, 1991), chapter 12.

[18] P. J. V. Rolo, *Entente Cordiale* (New York: St. Martin's, 1969), p. 121.

Furthermore, Japan, assured of Britain's benevolent neutrality, was able to first challenge and then fight Russia. The Russian defeat, coupled with the strengthening of the Anglo-Japanese treaty, effectively ended the Russian threat to India and so facilitated Anglo-Russian cooperation, much against Germany's interests and expectations.

The interwar period also reveals the way changes in bilateral relations both ramify through the system and are conditioned by it. Great Britain, realizing that the strength of its potential enemies outran its resources, was unable to act on the sensible impulse to conciliate Japan because doing so would have alienated the United States. But, in the end, American hostility to Japan turned out to serve Britain well: Without the attack on Pearl Harbor, Britain might have lost the Second World War. Indeed, Japan attacked the American naval base as well as Malaya and the Dutch East Indies in the questionable belief that the U.S. and U.K. were so closely linked that the former would respond with force to an attack on the latter's empire. Furthermore, the U.S. was spared a terrible dilemma when Hitler, Japan's ally, responded by declaring war on the U.S. despite the fact that he had previously taken great care not to match the American provocations in the Atlantic.[19] These processes do more than reflect established interests: Alliances often derive their influence less from norms or the value that states place on their reputations for living up to their commitments than from the way interconnections expand and alter states' concerns.[20]

We Can Never Do Merely One Thing

In a system, the chains of consequences extend over time and many areas: The effects of action are always multiple. Doctors call the undesired impact of medications "side effects." Although the language is misleading—there is no criterion other than our desires that determines which effects are "main" and which are "side"—the point reminds us that disturbing a system will produce several changes. Hardin again gets to the heart of the matter in pointing out that, contrary to many hopes and expectations, we cannot develop or find "a highly specific agent which will do only one thing. . . . *We can never do merely one thing.* Wishing to kill insects, we may put an end to the singing of birds. Wishing to 'get there' faster we insult our lungs with smog."[21] Seeking to protect the environment by developing nonpolluting

[19] The reasoning behind Hitler's decision is still unclear: for a brief summary of recent research, see Justus Doenecke, "U.S. Policy and the European War, 1939–1941," *Diplomatic History* 19 (Fall 1995), pp. 682–83.

[20] For further discussion, see Glenn Snyder and Paul Diesing, *Conflict Among Nations* (Princeton, N.J.: Princeton University Press, 1977), pp. 426–27 and chapter 6 below.

[21] Hardin, "The Cybernetics of Competition," pp. 79–80, emphasis added. John Dewey would not have been surprised: "It is willful folly to fasten upon some single end of conse-

sources of electric power, we build windmills that kill hawks and eagles that fly into the blades; cleaning the water in our harbors allows the growth of mollusks and crustaceans that destroy wooden piers and bulkheads; adding redundant safety equipment makes some accidents less likely but increases the chances of others due to the operators' greater confidence and the interaction effects among the devices; placing a spy in the adversary's camp not only gains valuable information but also leaves the actor vulnerable to deception if the spy is discovered; eliminating rinderpest in East Africa paved the way for canine distemper in lions because it permitted the accumulation of cattle, which required dogs to herd them, dogs which provided a steady source for the virus that could spread to lions; releasing fewer fine particles and chemicals into the atmosphere decreases pollution but also is likely to accelerate global warming; pesticides often destroy the crops that they are designed to save by killing the pests' predators; removing older and dead trees from forests leads to insect epidemics and an altered pattern of regrowth; allowing the sale of an antibaldness medicine without a prescription may be dangerous because people no longer have to see a doctor, who in some cases would have determined that the loss of hair was a symptom of a more serious problem; flying small formations of planes over Hiroshima to practice dropping the atomic bomb accustomed the population to air raid warnings that turned out to be false alarms, thereby reducing the number of people who took cover on August 6.[22]

In politics, connections are often harder to discern, but their existence guarantees that here too most actions, no matter how well targeted, will have multiple effects. For example, William Bundy was correct to worry that putting troops into Vietnam might not make that country more secure be-

---

quence which is liked, and permit the view of that to blot from perception all other . . . consequences" (*Human Nature and Conduct* (New York: Henry Holt, 1922), pp. 228–29).

[22] Jonathan Weisman, "Tilting at Windmills," *Wildlife Conservation* 97 (January/February 1994), pp. 52–57; Lindsey Gruson, "Problem with Clean Harbor: Creatures Devour Waterfront," *New York Times*, June 27, 1993; Aaron Wildavsky, *Searching for Safety* (New Brunswick, N.J.: Transaction Books, 1988); Perrow, *Normal Accidents*; the classic case of "turned" agents was revealed in J. C. Masterman, *The Double-Cross System in the War of 1939 to 1945* (New Haven, Conn.: Yale University Press, 1972); Packer, "Coping with a Lion Killer," pp. 14–17; William Stevens, "Acid Rain Efforts Found to Undercut Themselves," *New York Times*, January 27, 1994; Richard Kerr, "Study Unveils Climate Cooling Caused by Pollutant Haze," *Science* 268 (May 12, 1995), p. 802; Kerr, "It's Official: First Glimmer of Greenhouse Warning Seen," ibid. 270 (December 8, 1995), pp. 1565–67; Nancy Langston, *Forest Dreams, Forest Nightmares: The Paradox of Old Growth in the Inland West* (Seattle: University of Washington Press, 1995), pp. 148–50, 292–94; "You Want Hair, Get a Prescription," *Aspen Daily News*, July 28, 1994 (in the end, the FDA decided to permit freer sale of the medication: "Hair-Growth Drug to Be Sold over the Counter," *New York Times*, February 13, 1996); Leon Sigal, *Fighting to a Finish: The Politics of War Termination in the United States and Japan, 1945* (Ithaca, N.Y.: Cornell University Press, 1988), pp. 215–16. Those who believe that it is healthy to eat food that has not been treated with pesticides will be interested in Jane Brody, "Strong Views on Origins of Cancer," *New York Times*, July 5, 1994. But as we will discuss in chapters 2 and 7, not all unintended consequences are undesired.

cause deployment could not only lead the North to escalate, but also might "(1) cause the Vietnamese government and especially the army to let up [and] (2) create adverse public reactions to our whole presence on 'white men' and 'like the French' grounds."[23] It seems that the American development of nuclear weapons simultaneously restrained Stalin by increasing his fear of war and made him "less cooperative and less willing to compromise, for fear of seeming weak."[24] Indeed, it is now widely accepted that mutual second strike capability not only decreased the chance of nuclear war but also made it safer for either side to engage in provocations at lower levels of violence.[25] (Similarly, providing security guarantees to the countries of East Europe might lead them to take harsher stances toward minority ethnic groups and make fewer efforts to maintain good relations with their neighbors.)

To mention three more surprising cases, in the fall of 1948 General Lucius Clay warned that American budget deficits would be seen in Europe as a forerunner of inflation and so would undermine morale in West Berlin; the American pressure on the Europeans to rearm more rapidly in response to the North Korean attack on the South produced squabbles that encouraged the USSR "to believe that contradictions in the enemy camp ultimately would tear apart the enemy coalition. . . . [and so] undermined U.S. bargaining power"; in 1994 the dollar strengthened after President Clinton hired a powerful lawyer to defend him against charges of sexual harassment: As one currency trader put it, "We were starting to lose faith in him and that helped turn things."[26]

We should now return to what is meant by the claim that the system has properties distinct from those of its parts and then give a more extended discussion of how interconnections knit systems together.

Emergent Properties

The phrase "The whole is greater than the sum of its parts" can call up images of metaphysical "holism" and organic metaphors. That is not what I have in mind. If we are dealing with a system, the whole is *different from*,

[23] Quoted in Larry Berman, "Coming to Grips with Lyndon Johnson's War," *Diplomatic History* 17 (Fall 1993), p. 525.

[24] David Holloway, *Stalin and the Bomb* (New Haven, Conn.: Yale University Press, 1994), p. 272.

[25] Glenn Snyder, "The Balance of Power and the Balance of Terror," in Paul Seabury, ed., *The Balance of Power* (San Francisco: Chandler, 1965), pp. 184–201.

[26] Walter Millis, ed., *The Forrestal Diaries* (New York: Viking, 1951), p. 526; William Stueck, *The Korean War* (Princeton, N.J.: Princeton University Press, 1995), p. 6; quoted in Thomas Friedman, "It's a Mad, Mad, Mad, Mad World Money Market," *New York Times*, May 8, 1994. As these examples show, people's expectations—based in part on their beliefs about others' expectations—are central to the dynamics of systems.

not *greater than*, the sum of the parts.[27] Reductionism—seeking to understand the system by looking only at the units and their relations with one another—is not appropriate. Many academic disciplines have come to this conclusion, although often using different terminologies. Economics rests in part on an understanding of the "fallacy of composition." Biologists who study entire organisms see the world differently than their colleagues who work on the level of cells or molecules.[28] Interactional psychology rests on

[27] For a good—and critical—discussion and review of the literature, see D. C. Phillips, *Holistic Thought in Social Science* (Stanford, Calif.: Stanford University Press, 1976).

Also relevant are discussions of self-organizing systems: See, for example, Heinz Von Foerster and George Zopf, Jr., eds., *Principles of Self-Organization* (New York: Pergamon Press, 1962); Ilya Pregogine and Isabelle Stenger, *Order out of Chaos: Man's New Dialogue with Nature* (New York: Bantam Books, 1984); Per Bak and Kan Chen, "Self-Organized Criticality," *Scientific American*, January 1991, pp. 46–53; Stuart Kauffman, *The Origins of Order: Self-Organization and Selection in Evolution* (New York: Oxford University Press, 1993); more accessible is Kauffman's *At Home in the Universe: The Search for Laws of Self-Organization and Complexity* (New York: Oxford University Press, 1995). A good general discussion of the meaning and development of complexity in organisms is John Bonner, *The Evolution of Complexity* (Princeton, N.J.: Princeton University Press, 1988); For some of the literature in economics, see Paul Krugman, *The Self-Organizing Economy* (Cambridge, Mass.: Blackwell, 1966). Some of these arguments resemble standard defenses of the free market (e.g., the writings of Friedrich Hayek), but the formation and maintenance of markets in fact requires strong authority and conscious efforts.

[28] It is not surprising that a number of scholars who went on to develop systems theories, like Anatol Rapoport and Ludwig von Bertalanffy, started their careers as biologists. See, for example, Arthur Koestler and J. R. Smythies, eds., *Beyond Reductionism: New Perspectives in the Life Sciences* (Boston: Beacon Press, 1969); Francisco Ayala and Theodosius Dobzhansky, eds., *Studies in the Philosophy of Biology: Reduction and Related Problems* (Berkeley: University of California Press, 1975); Richard Levins and Richard Lewontin, *The Dialectical Biologist* (Cambridge, Mass.: Harvard University Press, 1985); Michael Ruse, *Philosophy of Biology Today* (Albany: State University of New York Press, 1988), chapter 3; Depew and Weber, eds., *Evolution at a Crossroads*, especially the chapters by Ayala and Mayr; Timothy Allen and Thomas Hoekstra, *Toward a Unified Ecology* (New York: Columbia University Press, 1992), pp. 195–200. Also see C. Dyke, *The Evolutionary Dynamics of Complex Systems* (New York: Oxford University Press, 1988); Stanley Salthe, *Development and Evolution: Complexity and Change in Biology* (Cambridge, Mass.: MIT Press, 1993), pp. 200–218; John Searle, "The Mystery of Consciousness," *New York Review of Books* 42 (November 2, 1995), pp. 60–66. For arguments about holism and reductionism in other disciplines, see Ernest Nagel, "Whole, Sums, and Organic Unities," *Philosophical Studies* 3 (February 1952), pp. 17–32; Kyriakos Kontopoulos, *The Logics of Social Structure* (New York: Cambridge University Press, 1993), passim, and especially pp. 14–41; Alan Garfinkel, *Forms of Explanation: Rethinking the Questions in Social Theory* (New Haven, Conn.: Yale University Press, 1981), chapter 2; Daniel Little, *Varieties of Social Explanation* (Boulder: Westview, 1991), chapter 8; Frank Golley, *A History of the Ecosystem Concept in Ecology: More Than the Sum of the Parts* (New Haven, Conn.: Yale University Press, 1993), passim, and especially pp. 190–95; John Bennett, *The Ecological Transition: Cultural Anthropology and Human Adaptation* (New York: Pergamon, 1976); Geoffrey Hodgson, *Economics and Evolution: Bringing Life Back into Economics* (Ann Arbor: University of Michigan Press, 1993), passim, and especially chapter 15. An earlier critique of economics for ignoring systems approaches is Sidney Schoeffler, *The Failures of Eco-*

the parallel sense that what seem to be immutable personality traits are in fact formed by the interaction between the individual and her surroundings, including, if she is in therapy, the behavior of the therapist, which in turn, is influenced by her.[29]

Much of sociology is similarly built on the idea that societies cannot be reduced to the sum of the individuals who compose them. Indeed, many sociologists draw the analogy between society and a living creature, although this need not imply organic unity. As Emile Durkheim put it:

> Whenever certain elements combine and thereby produce, by the fact of their combination, new phenomena, it is plain that these new phenomena reside not in the original elements but in the totality formed by their union [or interaction]. The living cell contains nothing but mineral particles, as society contains nothing but individuals. Yet it is patently impossible for the phenomena characteristic of life to reside in the atoms of hydrogen, oxygen, carbon and nitrogen.[30]

As a social psychologist explains: "The whole might be symmetric in spite of its parts being asymmetric, a whole might be unstable in spite of its parts being stable in themselves. . . . Properties of a social group, such as its orga-

---

nomics: A Diagnostic Study (Cambridge, Mass.: Harvard University Press, 1995). For reductionism and chaos, see Kellert, In the Wake of Chaos, pp. 88–90, 114–18.

[29] See, for example, Paul Watzlawick, Janet Beavin, and Don Jackson, Pragmatics of Human Communication: A Study of Interactional Patterns, Pathologies, and Paradoxes (New York: Norton, 1967); Paul Watzlawick and John Weakland, eds., The Interactional View (New York: Norton 1977); George Vaillant, Adaptation to Life (Boston: Little, Brown, 1977); David Magnusson and Norman Endler, eds., Personality at the Crossroads (Hillsdale, N.J.: Earlbaum, 1977); David Magnusson, "Personality Development from an Interactional Perspective," in Lawrence Pervin, ed., Handbook of Personality: Theory and Research (New York: Guilford Press, 1990), chapter 8; Albert Bandura, Social Foundations of Thought and Action (Englewood Cliffs, N.J.: Prentice Hall, 1986); Sandra Scarr, "Developmental Theories for the 1990s: Development and Individual Differences," Child Development 63 (February 1992), pp. 1–19.

[30] Emile Durkheim, The Rules of Sociological Method (Glencoe, Ill.: Free Press, 1938), p. xlvii. Quite different kinds of work in sociology share this general perspective: See, for example, Walter Buckley, Sociology and Modern Systems Theory (Englewood Cliffs, N.J.: Prentice Hall, 1967); Jonathan Turner, A Theory of Social Interaction (Stanford, Calif.: Stanford University Press, 1988); Tamotsu Shibutani, Social Processes (Berkeley: University of California Press, 1986); David Knoke, Political Networks: The Structural Perspective (New York: Cambridge University Press, 1990). Sociology is also the home discipline for dialectics, an approach—or set of approaches—similar to systemic analysis: See Kenneth Boulding, A Primer on Social Dynamics (New York: Free Press, 1970), chapters 3 and 4, and Louis Schneider, "Dialectic in Sociology," American Sociological Review 36 (August 1971), pp. 667–78. Also relevant are many of the studies of the "micro-macro link"—see, for example, the volume of that title edited by Jeffrey Alexander and others (University of California Press, 1987). More recently, studies of artificial life and artificial worlds have focused on how seemingly uncoordinated individual acts create and are influenced by emergent properties: See the literature cited in footnote 13, above.

nization, its stability, its goals, are something different from the organization, the stability, and the goals of the individuals in it."[31]

In some cases the concepts we apply to a system (e.g., polarity) cannot be applied to the units that compose it, and in other cases the description of a unit, such as a state being nonaligned, an actor being centrally positioned, or a person playing multiple roles, only makes sense in systemic terms. More strikingly, from the hypothetical fact that everyone in the system possesses a given characteristic, we cannot infer that the system can be so described. Thus the whole may be symmetric, peaceful, or stable only if the parts are not, and a reliable system can be formed from unreliable components.[32] This view is not an intuitive one and many people undoubtedly would agree with Margaret Thatcher that "you get a responsible society when you get responsible individuals" or with Charles Kindleberger that "for the world economy to be stabilized, there has to be a stabilizer."[33] But this simply is not true when the units interact to form a system that has quite different characteristics than they do. As James Madison put it in Federalist No. 55, "In all very numerous assemblies, of whatever characters composed, passion never fails to wrest the sceptre from reason. Had every Athenian citizen been a Socrates; every Athenian assembly would have been a mob."[34]

The difference between the parts and the system is often put in terms of the latter's "emergent properties," and the question of whether they exist does not have to involve metaphysics:

> Can the properties of complex systems be inferred from knowledge of the properties that their component parts have in isolation? For example, can the properties of benzene be predicted from knowledge about oxygen, hydrogen, and carbon? Or, at a higher level of complexity, can the behavior of a cheetah chasing a deer be predicted from knowledge about the atoms and molecules making up these animals? . . . No matter how exhaustively an object is studied in isolation, there is usually no way to ascertain all the properties that it may have in association with any other object.[35]

As Reuben Ablowitz explained over fifty years ago, in a system we find

---

[31] Kurt Lewin, *Resolving Social Conflicts* (New York: Harper & Brothers, 1948), p. 73.

[32] See the critical discussion in Scott Sagan, *The Limits of Safety: Organizations, Accidents, and Nuclear Weapons* (Princeton, N.J.: Princeton University Press, 1993), pp. 19–21.

[33] Quoted in R. J. Apple, Jr., "Margaret Thatcher: A Choice, Not an Echo," *New York Times Magazine*, April 29, 1979, p. 36; Kindleberger, *The World in Depression* (Berkeley: University of California Press, 1973), p. 305. For a sophisticated demonstration of how increasing the number of whites who are tolerant of minorities in their neighborhood can lead it to become segregated, see Schelling, *Micromotives*, pp. 162–64; for the argument that "order may prevail without an orderer," see Waltz, *Theory of International Politics*, p. 77; also see p. 64.

[34] *The Federalist Papers* (London: Penguin, 1987), p. 336.

[35] Francisco Ayala, "Biological Reductionism: The Problem and Some Answers," in F. Eugene Yates, ed., *Self-Organizing Systems* (New York: Plenum, 1987), p. 318.

a characteristic that could not possibly have been deduced from the nature of its components; it is a *new* characteristic that is attributable only to the structural organization. . . . of its component parts [and which can be called] "emergent." . . . I can tell precisely what the volume or loudness of the new sound [of the piano] will be if I know how loud each note is, ... [but] if I play two notes together. . . , there is an aspect or quality of this sound which is *not* the property of either of the notes taken separately. The chord has the characteristic of "chord-ness"; the harmonious combination of sounds has a new attribute which no one of its individual components had.[36]

More recently, Charles Perrow analyzed "error-inducing systems" whose problems cannot be traced to faults in any particular element or to the relationships between any of them.[37]

This argument is not teleological: The system is driven by the behavior of individual actors who are moved by their own incentives, goals, and calculations. But local predictability, if not simplicity, produces a high degree of complexity and unpredictability as the outcomes and patterns are formed interactively. Moving from actors' intentions and behavior to results (and to the environment the actors face at later periods of time) is extremely difficult, in part because behavior is influenced by the actors' own estimates of the consequences of alternative courses of action. In other words, the approach outlined here has firm microfoundations despite its rejection of the reductionist claim that the system is "nothing but" the behaviors of individuals.[38]

The system also can influence the characteristics of its elements. It is often said that Indira Gandhi and Margaret Thatcher refute the claims that world politics would be more peaceful if women played larger roles. But although this conclusion may be correct, the reasoning is not. The kind of women who would be selected as leaders in a world of sexual equality could be very different from those who now come to the fore. Indeed, much about actors can be explained in terms of their positions in the system. The state's place in the international economic system affects its internal arrangements, and a state is more likely to be democratic if its international environment

---

[36] Reuben Ablowitz, "The Theory of Emergence," *Philosophy of Science* 6 (January 1939), pp. 2–3.

[37] Perrow, *Normal Accidents*, p. 172. For a lucid discussion of how an understanding even of individual characteristics requires an appreciation of the attributes of the system as a whole, see Stephen Jay Gould, *Full House* (New York: Harmony Books, 1996).

[38] I am grateful to Mark Blyth for discussion on this point. Waltz's systems theory also has microfoundations and disagreement on whether his analysis is focused on the system or on the individual actors thus does not take us far: See the exchange between Martin Hollis and Steve Smith and Alexander Wendt in *Review of International Studies* 17 (October 1991), pp. 383–410 and 18 (April 1992), pp. 181–85.

permits it the luxuries of internal tolerance and diffusion of power.[39] (Of course, democracies and dictatorships may also have different predispositions toward war, thus influencing the environments in which both they and others live.) Many of the characteristics of individuals are formed interactively as well. We all know couples of whom we could say: "Why did he marry her? He's so kind, sensitive, and helpful and she is cold and self-centered." But each of them may have developed in this way in part because of the relationship with the other.

The study of life-forms brings out the reciprocal relations between units and the context which they form and by which they are constrained. Darwin's formulation is hard to improve:

> [T]he structure of every organic being is related, in the most essential yet often hidden manner, to that of all the other organic beings, with which it comes into competition for food or residence, or from which it has to escape, or on which it preys. This is obvious in the structure of the teeth and talons of the tiger; and in that of the legs and claws of the parasite which clings to the hair on the tiger's body. But in the beautifully plumed seed of the dandelion, and in the flattened and fringed legs of the water-beetle, the relation seems at first confined to the elements of air and water. Yet the advantage of plumed seeds no doubt stands in the closest relation to the land being already thickly clothed with other plants; so that the seeds may be widely distributed and fall on unoccupied ground. In the water-beetle, the structure of its legs, so well adapted for diving, allows it to compete with other aquatic insects, to hunt for its own prey, and to escape serving as prey to other animals.[40]

Interconnections

Emergent properties are less central to my analysis than is "interconnectedness"—in a system, the fates of the units and their relations with others are strongly influenced by interactions at other places and at earlier periods of time. When the interconnections are dense, it may be difficult to trace the impact of any change even after the fact, let alone predict it ahead of time, making the system complex and hard to control.[41] Many years ago, Harry (the Hat) Walker spoke for many of us when he opposed changes in the rules of baseball: "I think it is dangerous to fool around with fundamentals because they can have a chain effect on other parts. Every move in that

[39] Peter Gourevich, "The Second Image Reversed," *International Organization* 32 (Autumn 1978), pp. 881–912.

[40] *Origin of Species*, p. 61.

[41] This is the theme of Perrow, *Normal Accidents*.

direction should be taken with extreme caution because the consequences could be disastrous."[42]

As Walker implies, interconnections can defeat purposive behavior. Not only can actions call up counteractions, but multiple parties and stages permit many paths to unanticipated consequences. Thus Jay Forrester posits dynamics by which obvious ways to help the urban poor may fail to do so: Building subsidized housing attracts more poor people to the city and increases the tax rate, thereby making the city less attractive to business and so decreasing employment.[43] The obvious question of how—and indeed whether—people can act effectively in the face of systems effects will be addressed in the concluding chapter.

Interconnections are highlighted when a system is disturbed by the introduction of a new element. The study of ecology provides numerous examples:

Some keen gardener, intent upon making Hawaii more beautiful than before, introduced a plant call "Lantana Camera," which in its native home of Mexico causes no trouble to anybody. Meanwhile, someone else had also improved the amenities of the place by introducing turtle-doves from China, which, unlike any of the native birds, fed eagerly upon the berries of Lantana. The combined effects of the vegetative powers of the plant and spreading of the seeds by the turtle-doves were to make the Lantana multiply exceedingly and become a serious pest on the grazing country. Indian mynah birds were also introduced, and they too fed on the Lantana berries. After a few years the birds of both species had increased enormously in numbers. But there is another side to the story. Formerly the grass-lands and young sugar-cane plantations had been ravaged yearly by vast numbers of army-worm caterpillars, but the mynahs also fed on these caterpillars and succeeded to a large extent in keeping them in check, so that the outbreaks became less severe. About this time certain insects were introduced in order to try and check the spread of Lantana and several of them . . . did actually destroy so much

[42] Quoted in Arthur Daley, "Out of the Hat," *New York Times*, March 26, 1969; also see Lewis Thomas, "On Meddling," in Thomas, *The Medusa and the Snail* (New York: Viking, 1979), pp. 110–11. The same point is made in the title of a recent news story: R. W. Apple, Jr., "Line-Item Veto Would Begin Voyage into a Vast Unknown," *New York Times*, March 27, 1995. This perspective is common in ecology: "The more managers alter a forest, the less they can predict the paths that succession will take. . . . [although] the changes managers have made to forests have all been done with the goal of making succession *more* predictable" (Langston, *Forest Dreams*, p. 227).

[43] Jay Forrester, *Urban Dynamics* (Cambridge, Mass.: MIT Press, 1969). The argument has several flaws, most notably in the systems context the treating of an individual city as a self-enclosed universe; in fact the results of what one city does influence and are influenced by the policies of others. (On this point, see Schelling, *Micromotives*, p. 69.) Forrester's general approach has spawned a cottage industry, which can be followed in the journal *Systems Dynamics Review*. Its best-known and most controversial application is Donella Meadows et al., *The Limits to Growth* (New York: Universe Books, 1972).

seed that the Lantana began to decrease. As a result of this, the mynahs also began to decrease in numbers to such an extent that there began to occur severe outbreaks of army-worm caterpillars. It was then found that when the Lantana had been removed in many places, other introduced shrubs came in, some of which are even more difficult to eradicate than the original Lantana.[44]

Because most systems have either been designed to cope with adversity or have evolved in the face of it, breakage or overload at one point rarely destroys them. It will, however, produce disturbances at other points. Thus the argument that the German railroad system in World War II was invulnerable because it had so much excess capacity appears to have been an oversimplification. While military traffic was only a small percentage of the total, German industry depended on power generated almost exclusively by coal. Coal, in turn, had to be moved in enormous quantities over the railroad net, which meant that the system's capacity did not have to be reduced to anything like the point at which only military material could be carried in order to cripple the German war effort. Furthermore, while the extensive interconnections in the system made it flexible, it also meant that disruptions could spread throughout the system. As one set of marshaling yards was disabled, traffic had to be shifted to other areas, creating burdens, bottlenecks, and obstacles for even a sophisticated command and control system. In response, individual ministries, sectors, and industries tried to design their own solutions, usually by hoarding coal and sequestering boxcars. While at the beginning these kept the system going, past a certain point they paralyzed it.[45] Tightening the connections between elements will increase efficiency when everything works smoothly but will spread any problems that arise, as air travelers discover when they sit in a plane that is awaiting passengers from a delayed connecting flight and wonder if their own connecting flight will be held for them.[46]

Some arrangements of connections will make a system resistent to change and others can facilitate instability. When one element or relation cannot

[44] Charles Elton, *Animal Ecology* (New York: Macmillan, 1927), pp. 54–55, as quoted in Hardin, "The Cybernetics of Competition," p. 77. See Tenner, *Why Things Bite Back*, chapters 6–7 for a review of many cases in which species have been introduced into an area.

[45] The postwar debates about the effects of the Allied bombing campaign and alternatives to it are almost as heated as the contemporary arguments were. Here I am relying on Alfred Mierzejewski, *The Collapse of the German War Economy* (Chapel Hill: University of North Carolina Press, 1988). He observes that the leading proponent of attacking the German transportation net was Solly Zuckerman, a zoologist who "looked at problems as wholes and considered their individual components as parts of a complete organism" (ibid., p. 81). For a discussion of vulnerability and the transmission of disturbances throughout an organization, see Chris Demchak, *Military Organizations, Complex Machines: Modernization in the U.S. Armed Services* (Ithaca, N.Y.: Cornell University Press, 1991).

[46] For a general discussion of loose and tight coupling, see Perrow, *Normal Accidents*, pp. 89–96.

change unless several others do, small and slow adjustments will not be possible; each element has a veto over all the others. In international politics the most important case is that each state might be glad to abandon a preoccupation with power and narrow self-interest if its rivals did. But for anyone to change everyone must change, which means that Realism may exist because it exists: Once it is in place, no individual state can alter it.[47] To turn to domestic society, many experts believe that the U.S. would have a much more efficient transportation system if it relied more on rail (including streetcars in urban areas) and less on airplanes and automobiles. The difficulty is that such a change would require not only enormous investments of capital, but also coordinated changes in attitudes, municipal codes, tax laws, and subsidy policies. To take an example from university life, the increasing costs of books coupled with decreasing library budgets has created a crisis in many areas of scholarly publishing as university presses cannot afford to publish many excellent monographs. An obvious alternative is to move to cheaper electronic forms of dissemination for books that contain important scholarship but will never attract many buyers. But doing so would require large and almost simultaneous adjustments of policies and attitudes on the part of such disparate but interrelated actors as publishers, libraries, individual scholars, departmental hiring committees, and the authorities that grant tenure.[48]

In other cases, one element controls another, which in turn controls a third, thereby producing great indirect influence. Thus in the 1920s, if the U.S. had been willing to guarantee Britain's security, Britain would have been willing to guarantee France's, which would have generated a very different pattern of international politics. Under still other circumstances, a small change in any one of several elements can set off other changes in the same direction, leading to drastic alterations in the system and its elements.[49]

Sometimes the interconnections are relatively obvious because the chains are short or the processes involved are familiar. For example, the danger of the spread of nuclear weapons as each country arms in response to its neighbor's program is relatively straightforward: Pakistan's desire to acquire nuclear weapons was in significant measure a response to India's program; India's was partly triggered by China's; China's program was in part a reaction to the nuclear weapons of the U.S. and the USSR; the latter's program

---

[47] For a nice appreciation, see Schroeder, *Transformation of European Politics*, especially pp. 10, 48. This dynamic also means that we cannot infer desires from behavior: Any or all statesmen could prefer a world governed by norms and justice to one dominated by power politics and yet act according to the precepts of the latter.

[48] For parallel examples in ecology and international political economy, see Langston, *Forest Dreams*, p. 277, and Giulio Gallarotti, *The Anatomy of an International Monetary Regime: The Classical Gold Standard, 1880–1914* (New York: Oxford University Press, 1995) respectively.

[49] Chapter 4 will discuss the related topic of feedbacks.

was accelerated by U.S. success.[50] In the domestic arena, the connection between rent control and housing shortages is now so clear that even ardent liberals shun this policy. Indeed, the foreseeability of consequences is often an element in determining legal responsibility. Thus in New York State a person who commits a crime but does not kill anyone can be tried for murder if the crime leads to a death in a way that a reasonable person could have expected; more questionably, "Five teen-agers were charged with murder . . . after authorities said their effort to flee a crime scene had caused two police vehicles to crash, killing an officer."[51]

When chains of interconnections are long and intricate, the results are more likely to be surprising. Charles Darwin provides a nice example:

> Humble-bees are almost indispensable to the fertilization of the heartsease [and some kinds of clover]. . . . as other bees cannot reach the nectar. . . . The number of humble-bees in any district depends in great measure on the number of field-mice, which destroy their combs and nests. . . . Now the number of mice is largely dependent, as everyone knows, on the number of cats. . . . Hence . . . the presence of feline animals in large numbers might determine, through the intervention first of mice and then of bees, the frequency of certain flowers in that district![52]

But even this account may underestimate the complexity of the chains. With fewer cats, other animals might move into the district. Even without a predator, the mouse population might stabilize due to increased competition for territory or the spread of disease. Furthermore, cats probably have a number of effects on the environment, and introducing or removing them could set off several other changes, some of which would affect the fates of the bees and the flowers, others of which would alter other aspects of the environment.

Kinds of Interconnections

Interconnections can be of several kinds.[53] Most obviously, the parts may be locked together so that one change literally requires, prohibits, or constrains

[50] Some second-order considerations are not as obvious: The invocation of the Pressler amendment prohibiting U.S. aid to Pakistan if that country developed nuclear weapons may have decreased India's incentives to reach a nonproliferation agreement with Pakistan, thereby making it more likely that the latter will continue its program.

[51] See Jan Hoffman, "Court Weighs Expanding Scope of Murder Charge," *New York Times*, January 9, 1994; Joseph Fried, "5 Charged With Murder in Crash Fatal to Officer," ibid., April 29, 1994 (also see Joe Sexton, "Parolee Faces Murder Charge in Queens Fire," ibid., January 2, 1996). For an interesting discussion of related issues, see Linda Greenhouse, "High Court Narrows Definition of What 'Using' a Gun Means," ibid., December 7, 1995.

[52] *Origin of Species*, p. 59. Darwin similarly explains how "in several parts of the world insects determine the existence of cattle" (ibid., p. 58); also see the story of the sources of canine distemper in Tanzanian lions in Packer, "Coping with a Lion Killer."

[53] For related classifications of linkages, see Ernst Haas, "Why Collaborate: Issue-Linkage

others. This is true in some biological systems and in technologically advanced projects. Thus military aircraft developers have found to their dismay that changing one part is likely to call for a series of cascading alterations that consume much time and money.[54] The adoption of one weapon similarly often requires changes in other weapons, in tactics, and—in some cases—in strategies and interests.

The linkages that confronted France in the 1920s were not quite physical, but were so embedded in the laws of economics that they might as well have been. France had two basic objectives: to extract reparations from Germany and to keep that country weak. "Only a prosperous Germany could pay reparations and buy French goods, but a prosperous Germany would pose a renewed threat, and if French recovery became narrowly dependent on Germany prosperity, the Germans would have the leverage to throw off reparations entirely."[55] Even if the U.S. had loaned Germany money to enable it to trade with France, it is hard to see how France could have prospered if Germany had remained impoverished. The understanding of this linkage paved the way for very different policies after the next war.

The laws of politics are also hard to evade. The importance of "strategic interests" will lead states to try to gain or at least neutralize those areas that, if controlled by an adversary, could menace them.[56] Thus when coal replaced sail as the force propelling their warships, the British had to acquire and protect coaling stations around the world. The subsequent shift to oil led Britain to acquire oil fields—and commitments—in Persia and the Middle East. Once Great Britain occupied Egypt in the late 1880s (partly to protect the route to India), it not only gained a new territory to defend, but also menaced the colonial aspirations of other European states. The process

---

and International Regimes," *World Politics* 32 (April 1980), pp. 357–405; Kenneth Oye, *Economic Discrimination and Political Exchange: World Political Economy in the 1930s and the 1980s* (Princeton, N.J.: Princeton University Press, 1992); Arthur Stein, *Why Nations Cooperate: Circumstance and Choice in International Politics* (Ithaca, N.Y.: Cornell University Press, 1990), chapter 2. Also see Kenneth Boulding, *Ecodynamics: A New Theory of Societal Evolution* (Beverly Hills, Calif.: Sage, 1978); John Kroll, "The Complexity of Interdependence," *International Studies Quarterly* 37 (September 1993), pp. 321–48; Thomas Schelling, "A Framework for the Evaluation of Arms-Control Proposals," *Daedalus* 104 (Summer 1975), pp. 187–200.

[54] Michael Brown, *Flying Blind: The Politics of the U.S. Strategic Bomber Program* (Ithaca, N.Y.: Cornell University Press, 1992). Earlier weapons also formed a system and so were also constrained: See Stanley Sandler, *The Emergence of the Modern Capital Ship* (Newark: University of Delaware Press, 1979), pp. 154–55, 234–35.

[55] Walter McDougall, *France's Rhineland Diplomacy, 1914–1924* (Princeton, N.J.: Princeton University Press, 1978), pp. 128–29.

[56] Glenn Snyder, *Deterrence and Defense* (Princeton, N.J.: Princeton University Press, 1961), pp. 31–40. For a recent discussion, see Michael Desch, *When the Third World Matters: Latin America and the United States Grand Strategy* (Baltimore, Md.: Johns Hopkins University Press, 1993).

of dividing Africa then fed on itself as there were few natural barriers behind which the colonial possessions could be secure.[57] This dynamic was at
work on a smaller scale when the British established outposts in South Africa and Malaya that required protective belts, which in turn created a new
frontier that had to be defended.[58] A similar process operated when new
laws dealing with corruption and racketeering made illegal behavior that
could only be detected by undercover agents, thereby requiring new kinds
of police practices.[59]

In deterrence theory it is reputation, commitments, and others' expectations that create interconnections. As Schelling put it, "Our threats are interdependent. Essentially we tell the Soviets that we have to react here because, if we did not, they would not believe us when we say that we will
react there."[60] This line of reasoning is not unique to the era of bipolarity
and nuclear weapons: At the turn of the century a British statesman argued
that "if we have rights and interests in any quarter of the world and are
unprepared to defend them, it is certain that foreign nations will know how
to take advantage of our weakness."[61] Underlying these arguments is the
belief that the actor's behavior is attributable to its stable internal characteristics or dispositions and therefore that its behavior will be the same from
one situation to the next. Even if this view is false, the actor must be guided
by it if others believe it.[62]

The inferences others draw may therefore require that a state's foreign
policy have a kind of perceived unity. Thus the admonition to the British
foreign minister in the spring of 1938:

Foreign policy must be regarded as a whole. It is not possible to take a strong line
in one quarter and an apparently weak one in another indefinitely. There is some
danger, it seems to me, that our policy in Spain may react eventually and unfavora-

[57] Ronald Robinson and John Gallagher with Alice Denny, *Africa and the Victorians* (New
York: St. Martin's, 1967).

[58] John Galbraith, "The 'Turbulent Frontier' as a Factor in British Expansion," *Comparative
Studies in Society and History* 2 (October 1968), pp. 150–68. Similar processes can entrap
statesmen and produce deeper involvement in ventures than they had originally intended,
although the old belief that American policy in Vietnam was largely to be explained in this way
probably is not correct. For some Israeli decision-makers, this process was at work during the
invasion of Lebanon in 1982: Avner Yaniv, *Dilemmas of Security: Politics, Strategy, and the
Israeli Experience in Lebanon* (New York: Oxford University Press, 1987), pp. 110–27. Related
are the more benign linkages discussed later that can be triggered by limited regional
integration.

[59] Gary Marx, *Undercover: Police Surveillance in America* (Berkeley: University of California Press, 1988).

[60] Thomas Schelling, *Arms and Influence* (New Haven, Conn.: Yale University Press, 1966),
p. 55.

[61] Quoted in J. L. Garvin, *The Life of Joseph Chamberlain*, vol. 3, *Empire and World Policy*
(London: Macmillan, 1934), pp. 213–14.

[62] For a further discussion of the domino theory, see chapter 4 below.

bly upon our policy in central Europe and in the Far East. . . . In the Far East the
Japanese are watching us closely. If we appear to them to be kicked about by the
Italians and Germans over Spain, they must be expected to start doing the same
with British shipping and interests, etc., in China and the China Seas. If we can
follow up our initial success in Czechoslovakia and also put a stop to the attacks on
our shipping in Spain, the Japanese will view us with the more respect.[63]

According to this view, it is hard to treat issues separately: Disputes that
would be small if they could be isolated are highly consequential because
the world is tightly interconnected.

During the Cold War, perceived interconnectedness not only forced a
worldwide role on the U.S., it also made it possible. The obvious difficulty
was that the credibility of American threats to protect allies was undercut by
the disparity between the great costs and risks of doing so and the slight
inherent value of these countries to the U.S. But if everyone believed that
permitting a limited defeat would have widespread consequences, they
would expect the U.S. to pay a high price in order to defend even a small
country. Indeed, the U.S. reinforced this perception by promising to protect
these countries: Commitment is a tactic that increases the unity of foreign
policy by tying the state's reputation for living up to its word to its behavior
in a designated area.[64] The degree to which and the ways in which world
politics is interconnected then are not entirely forced on the state by the
laws of international relations or the perceptions of others, but can be altered by statesmen.[65]

The kinds of interconnections believed to be present strongly influence
policy preferences. Some people think that economic integration is so great
that each state must be concerned with all economic issues everywhere;
others argue that the behavior of one state in one area will set a precedent
for others; those who believe that peace is indivisible will have to prevent

[63] John Harvey, ed., *The Diplomatic Diaries of Oliver Harvey, 1937–1940* (New York: St.
Martin's, 1970), pp. 425–26. Henry Kissinger made a similar argument on somewhat different
grounds: "A conceptual framework—which 'links' events—is an essential tool [of foreign pol-
icy]. The absence of linkage produces exactly the opposite of freedom of action; policy makers
are forced to respond to parochial interests, buffeted by pressures without a fixed compass"
(*White House Years*, [Boston: Little, Brown, 1979], p. 130).

[64] The classic discussion of commitment is Thomas Schelling, *The Strategy of Conflict*
(Cambridge, Mass.: Harvard University Press, 1960).

[65] Secretary of State Vance explains that the Carter administration was careful to deal with
the invasion of the Shaba province in Zaire "as an African—not an East-West—problem":
Cyrus Vance, *Hard Choices: Critical Years in America's Foreign Policy* (New York: Simon and
Schuster, 1983), pp. 70–71. On the general subject of the decoupling of signals, see Robert
Jervis *The Logic of Images in International Relations*, 2d ed. (New York: Columbia University
Press, 1989), pp. 142–65. In some cases, consistency develops because people think they and
others *should* be consistent; thus arguments about "slippery slopes."

wars throughout the world in order to keep their own country safe.[66] Because Metternich believed that revolution—and even liberalism—was contagious, he concluded that the sovereignty of states had to be limited: "Any false or pernicious step taken by any state in its internal affairs may disturb the repose of another state. . . . Therefore, every state—or rather, every sovereign of a great power—has the duty, in the name of the sacred rite of independence of every state, to supervise the governments of smaller states and to prevent them from taking false and pernicious steps in their internal affairs."[67] He then saw connections that enforced a sort of unity in outcome as the entire world would remain conservative or become revolutionary. Both the U.S. and USSR had similar beliefs during the Cold War. The "Brezhnev Doctrine" declared that decisions of socialist countries "must damage neither socialism in their own country nor the fundamental interest of other socialist countries nor the worldwide workers' movement. . . . This means that every Communist Party is responsible not only to its own people but also to all the socialist countries and the entire communist movement."[68]

The U.S. also saw the world as interconnected not only by American reputation and credibility, but by developments within countries as well. As Dean Acheson told students at the National War College in December 1947: "I remember when it was accepted doctrine to say in the United States, 'We don't care if another country wants to be communist, that is all right, that is an internal matter, that is a matter for them to decide.'" But then the U.S. concluded that a communist regime "had the inescapable consequence of inclusion in the system of Russian power" and that neighbors were affected through contagion and subversion.[69]

By contrast, critics of American policy during the Cold War argued that the U.S. vastly overestimated the degree to which events were interconnected. For them, the causes and outcomes of local disputes lay in the ac-

---

[66] Precedents and beliefs about them have received insufficient attention: see Elizabeth Kier and Jonathan Mercer, "Setting Precedents in Anarchy: Military Intervention and Weapons of Mass Destruction," *International Security* 20 (Spring 1996), pp. 77–106. For the claim that allowing Norway to use a loophole in international treaties to kill whales will lead to the slaughter of wildlife in Africa, see the political advertisement "The Next Victim of Norway's Whale Slaughter?" *New York Times*, May 8, 1993. For a balanced discussion of when and where interconnections require American intervention today, see James Davis and Jack Snyder, "Projecting Power Abroad: An Indirect Approach," in Charles Hermann, ed., *American Defense Annual, 1994* (Lexington, Mass.: Lexington Books, 1994), pp. 129–45.

[67] Paul Schroeder, *Metternich's Diplomacy at its Zenith, 1820–1823* (Westport, Conn.: Greenwood Press, 1969), p. 126; also see pp. 89–90.

[68] Quoted in Charles Gati, *The Bloc That Failed: Soviet-East European Relations in Transition* (Bloomington: Indiana University Press, 1990), p. 47.

[69] Quoted in John Lewis Gaddis, *Strategies of Containment* (New York: Oxford University Press, 1982), pp. 63–64.

tions of indigenous actors, these incidents were not tests of American resolve, and the effects would not reverberate throughout the international system. Other critics made arguments quite different in content but similar in their denial of interconnections: The sources of Soviet conduct were internal as Soviet leaders followed the dictates of their ideology, if not of a plan. It was then foolish to worry that American efforts might provoke the USSR since it would seek to expand when and only when it was ready.[70]

This is not to say that everything in the world is connected to everything else. Even in today's international system, not all countries influence one another. A book on Afghan-Bolivian relations would be short (although politics in Afghanistan affects how much opium grows there, which in turn affects the drug trade in Bolivia), and few changes in the relations between Argentina and Brazil would affect anyone outside of the Western Hemisphere. Domestically, in recent years the Supreme Court has looked with favor on arguments that many federal laws, such as those banning guns in the vicinity of schools, are unconstitutional because the effects on interstate commerce are inconsequentially remote.

Appearances are not sufficient to determine whether actors are reacting to each other, however. For example, when two states sequentially increase their arms, they may be responding similarly to technological opportunities, domestic politics, or bureaucratic bargaining, not racing against each other. In other areas as well, actors may be responding to the same objective situation rather than to the other's actions. Thus James Joll argues that in July 1914 "although each government claimed that its own mobilization was ordered as a reaction to the preparation of others, the respective military machines were set in motion largely independently of each other once the gravity of the crisis was realized."[71] Similarly, we need to ask the extent to which waves of social fashion and protest reflect contagion and the extent to which they represent parallel responses to similar conditions. For example, was 1968 a turbulent year in some countries because there had been disturbances in others, or were an unusual number of societies independently unstable, perhaps because they were feeling the same tensions?

The fact that interconnections are not always present is not inconsistent with the argument that they may be overlooked. Actors are often caught in a wider web than they realize. Thus before World War I, both American and German statesmen thought that the main threats to their relations were bilateral and neither side focused on what turned out to be the eventuality that unfolded. In 1918, the French supported the Japanese intervention in

---

[70] See, for example, George Kennan quoted in ibid., p. 20. As Gaddis notes, "The extent to which Soviet behavior would be determined by Western attitudes was the most consistent single theme in wartime analyses of Soviet-American relations undertaken by the Office of Strategic Services" (ibid., p. 19).

[71] James Joll, *The Origins of the First World War* (London: Longman, 1984), p. 82.

Siberia but "tended to ignore the obvious consequences of this policy on their relations with the Bolsheviks, or preferred to treat European Russia and Siberia as two separate theaters of action."[72] Japan's policy in the 1920s and the 1930s was similarly flawed as it failed to see that its attempt to dominate China would greatly increase conflict with the U.S. and Britain. "From the Japanese point of view, China and America were separate problems."[73] More recently, Nixon and Kissinger did not expect the rapprochement with China to adversely affect American relations with India.

Games against Nature Are Not Games against Nature

While the human attempt to anticipate and thwart others' behavior underlies some of the dynamics discussed in this book, more fundamental is the simpler capacity to react. The phrase "playing a game against nature" generally is used to designate a situation in which the other side is unchanging. But this misunderstands the natural world: Nature *does* react to what people do—or, more precisely, the elements in nature compose a system. While William McNeill may go too far when he talks of "the tendency towards the conservation of catastrophe," he is certainly correct to point out that many attempts to "tame" natural forces have unleashed if not more then at least different kinds of disasters. Writing four years before the great floods of 1993, he took

> a simple example from water engineering [to] make this situation obvious. In my lifetime the Army Corps of Engineers began to control Mississippi floods by building an elaborate system of levees along the river's lower course. This had the undesired effect of concentrating sediment on the river bottom between the levees. As a result, the water level now rises each year, and the levees have to be raised higher from time to time. Under this regimen, sooner or later the mighty Mississippi will break its banks and inflict far greater damage on the surrounding landscape than if there were no levees and the river were free to overflow each spring and deposit sediment across the breadth of its natural floodplain, as it did in my childhood.[74]

[72] Michael Carley, "French Intervention in Russia," *Journal of Modern History* 48 (September 1976), p. 432.

[73] Akira Iriye, "The Role of the United States Embassy in Tokyo," in Dorothy Borg and Shumpei Ikamoto, eds., *Pearl Harbor as History* (New York: Columbia University Press, 1973), p. 126; also see Iriye, *After Imperialism* (New York: Atheneum, 1969), pp. 87–88, 222–23. Iriye argues that in the 1920s the U.S. as well believed that its policies toward China would not affect its relations with Japan and that East Asian affairs could be isolated from the rest of world politics: ibid., pp. 185, 259.

[74] William McNeill, "Control and Catastrophe in Human Affairs," *Daedalus*, Winter 1989, pp. 1–2. As an expert notes, "River systems have a way of adjusting themselves in response to

Attempts to control beach erosion also magnify the problem. To preserve the sand on their beach, people build groins to trap sand moving laterally along the shore. But this creates severe erosion on the other side of the groin, and those living there have to build their own groins to prevent that area from being completely stripped. And so it goes all the way down the beach. Other communities, seeing what the individualistic approach produces, have tried to cope collectively by constructing barriers that weaken the power of the waves and stabilize the beach. These rarely work: The beach is indeed prevented from migrating inland as it would have without intervention, but slow erosion is replaced by periods of temporary stability interrupted by catastrophic failures when the waves, no longer able to dissipate their energy on a beach shaped by natural forces, break through the barriers.[75]

Recent work in ecology also indicates that change—often unpredictable change—is much more common than equilibrium. Even without human intervention, old forests rarely attain a stable configuration and predators and prey may neither reach a plateau nor change their numbers in a regular cycle. As one expert noted, "When you introduce a population to a new area it goes up and then crashes, and it doesn't remain constant. The long-term numbers vary." Indeed, in a number of cases, predators wiped out the prey and then themselves starved.[76]

Interconnections and emergent properties define systems, whether or not humans are part of them. The general kinds of effects that are produced are the subject of the next chapter, after which we will review the systems literature in international politics, analyze feedbacks, discuss the dynamics of bargaining and alliances, and close with the puzzle of how people can act effectively in the face of processes that generate outcomes that are so hard to control and even foresee.

---

human manipulation . . . in ways that can never be entirely foreseen": James Tripp quoted in William Stevens, "The High Risks of Denying Rivers Their Flood Plains," *New York Times*, July 20, 1993.

[75] See Wallace Kaufman and Orrin Pilkey, Jr., *The Beaches Are Moving* (Durham, N.C.: Duke University Press, 1983); Robert Dolan, "Barrier Dune System along the Outer Banks of North Carolina," *Science* 176 (April 21, 1972), pp. 286–88.

[76] William Stevens, "New Eye on Nature: The Real Constant Is Eternal Turmoil," *New York Times*, July 31, 1990; Daniel Botkin, *Discordant Harmonies: A New Ecology for the Twenty-first Century* (New York: Oxford Univerity Press, 1990); Allen and Hoekstra, *Toward a Unified Ecology*; Pimm, *Balance of Nature?*, chapter 6; also see Andrew Read and Paul Harvey, "Evolving in a Dynamic World," *Science* 260 (June 18, 1993), pp. 1760–62; Alan Hastings and Kevin Higgins, "Persistence of Transients in Spatially Structured Ecological Models," ibid. 263 (February 25, 1994), pp. 1133–36; Anne Simon Moffat, "Biodiversity Is a Boon to Ecosystems, Not Species," ibid. 271 (March 15, 1996), p. 1497.

Two

System Effects

THE PREVIOUS chapter explained that we cannot understand systems by examining only the attributes and goals of the interconnected elements. Here I will outline the basic results that follow: Many crucial effects are delayed and indirect; the relations between two actors often are determined by each one's relations with others; interactions are central and cannot be understood by additive operations; many outcomes are unintended; regulation is difficult. I will close by showing that many of the methods that actors and social scientists use to understand the world are not suited to dealing with systems.

Indirect and Delayed Effects

Because of interconnections, many effects are indirect, mediated, and delayed. Thus people who oppose the use of a synthetic hormone that would induce cows to produce more milk do not argue that the milk would be different, but that the greater milk flow would lead to udder infections, which would require increased use of antibiotics, which would accelerate the spread of drug-resistant bacteria. When what happens influences events in places or times far removed, prediction and even post-hoc explanation are very difficult, as students of ecology stress. For example, surviving a mass extinction does not guarantee the future of a life-form. Although it is likely to thrive initially as it moves into the spaces previously occupied by defunct competitors and is freed from predators now wiped out, eventually it will have to cope with the new competitors and predators who will develop in the new environment. Indeed, a species may make a similar immediate recovery in two different geographical areas and yet have different fates in the long run depending on what other forms of life develop.[1]

Indirect effects may be more important than direct ones.[2] Researchers

---

[1] Richard Kerr, "Who Profits From Ecological Disaster?" *Science* 266 (October 7, 1994), pp. 28–30. Similarly, the fact that the proportion of "greenhouse gases" in the atmosphere has been increasing for over a hundred years without much increase in world temperature may be attributable to the delays in the effect working its way through the system rather than to the basic scientific argument being incorrect: see Stephen Schneider, "Detecting Climatic Change Signals: Are There Any 'Fingerprints'?" ibid. 263 (January 1994), pp. 341–43.

[2] Indeed, for individuals, some of the most important values in life—happiness, self-esteem, self-fulfillment—can be reached only indirectly, as the by-product of other goals and activities.

have found that certain kinds of compost suppress undesired microorganisms not by killing them, "but by encouraging such a rich diversity of other organisms that the bad bugs can't compete."[3] Less happily, introducing new species in order to control a pest often has a greater impact on the ecology through consequences that are less immediate: destroying vegetation that nontargeted animals not only eat, but use for nests; altering moisture runoff and thus the amount of dirt in streams; affecting the distribution of parasites and therefore the fates of many other species. In natural ecosystems, "two species with non-overlapping diets which are preyed upon by a common predator may nonetheless have a net negative effect on each other's population density: as one becomes less abundant, the predator turns its attentions more to the alternative prey."[4] Indeed, it appears that if an area is inhabited by multiple predators, it will be more susceptible to invasion from outside prey species because the indigenous population is kept under control.[5] Even harder to locate were the links between dead wood in a forest, carpenter ants, woodpeckers, and pests that destroyed trees. When foresters removed fallen timber, they were surprised but initially not disturbed by the decrease of woodpeckers, which followed because they lived on carpenter ants, which in turn subsisted on fallen trees: "Pileated woodpeckers did not eat spruce budworm or tussock moths, so no one thought they were important in regulating pest populations. But pileated woodpeckers did excavate cavities in dead trees, and these cavities provided nests and roost sites for birds that did eat spruce budworm and Douglas-fir tussock moth."[6] As a result, pest infestations greatly increased, which of course was an undesirable outcome.

Not unlike these cases is the possibility that one reason the network coverage of the 1992 election was particularly cynical was the need for these outlets to distinguish themselves from CNN and C-SPAN, which provided the kind of factual reporting that the networks previously had monopolized.[7] To take a case from the American economic system, while most of Clinton's 1993 tax increase directly affected those earning over $200,000, as these people change their behavior, there will be ramifications throughout the entire economy. To mention just the simplest possible ones, if the rich spend

---

[3] William Bryant Logan, "Rot Is Hot," *New York Times Magazine*, September 8, 1991, p. 51.

[4] R. J. Putman and S. D. Wratten, *Principles of Ecology* (Berkeley: University of California Press, 1984), p. 142; also see Stuart Pimm, *The Balance of Nature? Ecological Issues in the Conservation of Species and Communities* (Chicago: University of Chicago Press, 1991), pp. 181–88, 346–53.

[5] Pimm, *Balance of Nature?*, pp. 213–14, 219–21, 229–32.

[6] Nancy Langston, *Forest Dreams, Forest Nightmares: The Paradox of Old Growth in the Inland West* (Seattle: University of Washington Press, 1995), pp. 151–52.

[7] Tom Rosenstiel, *Strange Bedfellows: How Television and the Presidential Candidates Changed American Politics, 1992* (New York: Hyperion Press, 1993).

less, people who are selling goods and services to them may suffer, in which case they will have less money to spend. Furthermore, if incomes decline there will be a corresponding decrease in taxes and therefore in government revenue, and if unemployment increases, government spending will have to increase. Of course favorable effects are also possible: An expected decrease in the federal deficit can increase consumer and investor confidence and so increase prosperity and government revenues. But the central point is that the direct impact of a change in the tax rate may be less important than the indirect effects and that the total influence is certain to be quite different than if all other activity stayed constant. Similarly, Daniel Patrick Moynihan argues that the most important consequence of a line-item budget veto might not be to increase the president's power or decrease federal spending, but to undercut congressional log-rolling because the president could untie packages that, under current rules, have to be accepted or rejected in their entirety.[8]

In some cases actors understand the system well enough to set their policy by the expected indirect effects. Thus in World War I Winston Churchill called for attacking the enemy around the peripheries: "The Decisive theatre is the theatre where a vital decision may be obtained at any given time. The Main theatre is that in which the main armies or fleets are stationed. This is not at all times the Decisive theatre. . . . In any hostile combination, once it is certain that the strongest Power cannot be directly defeated itself, but cannot stand without the weakest, it is the weakest that should be attacked."[9]

Had the attack on the Dardenelles been pressed to a successful conclusion, he argued, the war would have been greatly shortened: The Eastern Front would have been secured and the Balkan states would have been united against Austria-Hungary, which would have brought that empire down and made Germany sue for peace. Hitler similarly hoped that by destroying the USSR, he would force Britain to surrender because Churchill would see that assistance would not be forthcoming from either the USSR or from the U.S., which would have to face a Japan made even stronger by

[8] R. W. Apple, Jr., "Line-Item Veto Would Begin Voyage Into a Vast Unknown," *New York Times*, March 27, 1995.

[9] Winston Churchill, *The World Crisis*, abridged ed. (New York: Scribner's, 1931), p. 308; also see p. 577. The course of many battles in World War I was determined by indirect or unraveling effects. A military unit was often forced to retreat not because it was hard-pressed, but because a neighboring unit pulled back and exposed the first unit's flanks. Since the units had to try to keep close connections with one another, what happened in one part of the battlefield was often strongly influenced by events elsewhere. For a good discussion, see Tim Travers's treatment of the German offensive of March 1917: Travers, *How the War Was Won: Command and Technology in the British Army on the Western Front, 1917–1918* (London: Routledge, 1992), pp. 70–91. For a diplomatic example, see Paul Schroeder, "World War I as Galloping Gertie," *Journal of Modern History* 44 (September 1972), pp. 337–38.

the elimination of Soviet power in the Far East.[10] States have also started a war, as Egypt did in 1973, in order to pull others in, either militarily or diplomatically.

When it takes time for actors to adjust to what others have done, the short-term impact of behavior will be quite different from what will result later, and it is hard to know when to declare a policy a success or a failure. For the same reason, the delays may make the causal relations hard to discern even in retrospect. Thus it took a close observer almost a decade to determine that the shift from a territorial to a nonterritorial mating system in a herd of pronghorn antelope was rooted in a change in the age structure of the animals, which stemmed from the harsh winter three years before he began his investigation.[11]

Similarly, even if forest managers had been more sensitive to delayed effects and interactions, it would have been hard to have quickly estimated how changes in cattle grazing, deer and elk browsing, timber harvesting, and fire suppression would alter a forest many years later or to have seen that moderate insect damage would encourage forest regeneration.[12] Turning to politics, although for many Americans Vietnam and Watergate are at best dim memories, these experiences may have helped shape attitudes and structures that strongly influence the current American political scene.

Relations Are Often Not Bilaterally Determined

Dwight D. Eisenhower noted that "anyone who becomes immersed in international affairs soon realizes that no important issue exists in isolation; rarely is it only bilateral."[13] Not only is the issue likely to affect others, but policy toward one state will have implications for and effects on several others.[14]

---

[10] Alan Bullock, *Hitler and Stalin: Parallel Lives* (New York: Knopf, 1992), p. 682.

[11] John Byers, "Pronghorns in—and Out of—a Rut," *Natural History* 98 (April 1989), pp. 39–48. Social scientists have been exploring this phenomenon under the rubric of path-dependent development (see chapter 4, pp. 155–61, below). For a discussion of the fact that in chaotic physical systems what happens is determined not only by the state of the variables at the current time but also by where they were earlier, see Stephen Kellert, *In the Wake of Chaos: Unpredictable Order in Dynamical Systems* (Chicago: University of Chicago Press, 1993), pp. 93–96.

[12] Langston, *Forest Dreams*, pp. 244–45, 149–50. Indeed, one study found that an Amazon forest was still marked by a drought four hundred years ago: M. Keller et al., "If a Tree Falls in the Forest . . ." *Science* 273 (July 12, 1996), p. 201.

[13] Dwight D. Eisenhower, *The White House Years*, vol. 1, *Mandate for Change: 1953–1956* (Garden City, N.Y.: Doubleday, 1963), p. 409. For an application to a recent case, see Steve Yetiv, *America and the Persian Gulf: The Third Party Dimension in World Politics* (Westport, Conn.: Prager, 1995).

[14] Because the South American system in the nineteenth century was tightly interconnected, it provides many examples of the dynamics discussed here: see Robert Burr, *By Reason or Force: Chile and the Balance of Power in South America, 1830–1905* (Berkeley: University

Indeed, the others may be more important than the state that is the direct object of the action. As Secretary of State Robert Lansing wrote in his diary regarding policy toward Mexico in 1915, "It comes down to this: Our possible relations with Germany must be our first consideration; and our intercourse with Mexico must be regulated accordingly."[15] In some cases, others will draw significant inferences about how the state is likely to behave toward them from how it acts toward a third party. More generally, as we will discuss in chapters 5 and 6, changes in relations between two states affect each state's stance toward third parties, and the distribution of bargaining power between two states is strongly influenced by existing and possible relations with others. Countries can then benefit from or be endangered by changes in relations among others over which they have no control. Israel in the 1950s was a beneficiary: As relations between Nasser and the West soured, the latter saw fewer costs and more advantages in supporting Israel. But Israel was menaced by this process as well: Part of the reason why Nasser took an anti-Israeli position was that he believed this would help him gain the leadership of the Arab states and the Third World.[16]

It follows that observers will often misunderstand the state's policy if they examine it only in local terms. In the late nineteenth century, British behavior on Indian border issues was largely regulated by its policy toward Russia, which in turn was conditioned by calculations of European politics. Thus when Russia asked Britain to put pressure on Japan to moderate its peace terms in the wake of Japan's victory over China in 1885, British statesmen were placed in a difficult position as they sought to offend neither party. Their response was to compensate for rejecting the Russian request by conciliation on Indian issues—a connection that escaped contemporary observers and later historians who examined the border question through the perspective of the seemingly most relevant documents in the India Office. As Gordon Martel points out, "Foreign secretaries were not in the habit of explaining their Moroccan policy to the Viceroy of India, nor were they in the habit of showing their Ambassador at Paris how events in the north of India influenced negotiations in Nigeria."[17] More generally, if we focus on

---

of California Press, 1965). "Spin-off crises" are what Richard Ned Lebow calls cases in which two states collide because of the conflict one of them has with a third party: *Between Peace and War* (Baltimore, Md.: Johns Hopkins University Press, 1981).

[15] Quoted in P. Edward Haley, *Revolution and Intervention: The Diplomacy of Taft and Wilson with Mexico, 1910–1917* (Cambridge, Mass.: MIT Press, 1970), p. 184.

[16] Jonathan Shimshoni, *Israel and Conventional Deterrence: Border Warfare from 1953 to 1970* (Ithaca, N.Y.: Cornell University Press, 1988), p. 94.

[17] Gordon Martel, "Documenting the Great Game: 'World Policy' and the 'Turbulent Frontier' in the 1880s," *International History Review* 2 (April 1980), p. 291. Similarly, Paul Schroeder argues that scholars have misunderstood Britain's German policy in the early and mid–nineteenth century because they have focused on Britain's direct interests toward Germany rather than on its concern for balancing against France or Russia: Schroeder, "'System' and Systemic Thinking in International History," *International History Review* 15 (February 1993),

bilateral relations it seems strange that states go to war with those with whom they have few direct conflicts, as was the case for many of the participants in World War I.[18]

Interactions, Not Additivity

We cannot understand systems by summing up the characteristics of the parts or the bilateral relations between pairs of them.[19] This is not to say that such operations are never legitimate, but only that when they are we are not dealing with a system.[20] More precisely, actions often interact to produce results that cannot be comprehended by linear models. "Linearity involves two propositions: 1) changes in system output are proportional to changes in input . . . and 2) system outputs corresponding to the sum of two inputs are equal to the sum of the outputs arising from the individual inputs."[21]

---

pp. 120–22. For other cases where understanding requires seeing obscure links between events, see Reynolds Salerno, "Multilateral Strategy and Diplomacy: The Anglo-German Naval Agreement and the Mediterranean Crisis, 1935–1936," *Journal of Strategic Studies* 17 (June 1994), pp. 39–74; Trevor Hope, "French and British Diplomacy, 1895–1899: The Fashoda Crisis," in Andrew Cordier, ed., *Columbia Essays in International Affairs*, vol. 5 (New York: Columbia Univerity Press, 1969), pp. 13–18.

[18] For further discussion, see chapter 6.

[19] Kenneth Waltz, *Theory of International Politics* (Reading, Mass.: Addison-Wesley, 1979), p. 64. Also see Randolph Siverson and Harvey Starr, *The Diffusion of War* (Ann Arbor: University of Michigan Press, 1991); Gary Goertz, *Contexts of International Politics* (New York: Cambridge University Press, 1994); Benjamin Most and Harvey Starr, *Inquiry, Logic, and International Politics* (Columbia: University of South Carolina Press, 1989). For parallel discussions in social psychology, organization theory, and ecology, see respectively Paul Watzlawick, Janet Beavin, and Don Jackson, *Pragmatics of Human Communication: A Study of Interactional Patterns, Pathologies, and Paradoxes* (New York: Norton, 1967), pp. 125–26, 135–39; Charles Perrow, *Normal Accidents* (New York: Basic Books, 1984); Pimm, *Balance of Nature?*, pp. 249–56.

[20] Linearities are common when interconnections are absent or weak enough to disregard. Indeed, people often underestimate the power of simple linear models and incorrectly believe that they can improve on them by detecting interaction effects: For a summary, see Robyn Dawes and Bernard Corrigan, "Linear Models in Decision-Making," *Psychological Bulletin* 81 (February 1981), pp. 95–106.

[21] Alan Beyerchen, "Nonlinear Science and the Unfolding of a New Intellectual Vision," in Richard Bjornson and Marilyn Waldman, eds., *Papers in Comparative Studies*, vol. 6 (Columbus: Center for Comparative Studies in the Humanities, Ohio State University Press, 1989), p. 30; also see John Holland, *Hidden Order: How Adaptation Builds Complexity* (Reading, Mass.: Addison-Wesley, 1995), pp. 15–23. Nonlinear relations in sociology are reviewed in Michael Faia, *Dynamic Functionalism: Strategy and Tactics* (Cambridge, Mass.: Cambridge University Press, 1986), chapter 4; in political science see Courtney Brown, *Serpents in the Sand: Essays on the Nonlinear Nature of Politics and Human Destiny* (Ann Arbor: University of Michigan Press, 1995), and L. Douglas Kiel and Euel Elliott, eds., *Chaos Theory in the Social*

Intuitively, we often expect linear relationships. If a little foreign aid slightly increases economic growth, then more aid should produce greater growth. But in a system a variable may operate through a nonlinear function. That is, it may have a disproportionate impact at one end of its range. Sometimes even a small amount of the variable can do a great deal of work and then the law of diminishing returns sets in, as is often the case for the role of catalysts.[22] In other cases very little impact is felt until a critical mass is assembled. For example, women may thrive in a profession only after there are enough of them so that they do not feel like strangers.[23] Clausewitz noted a related effect:

> The scale of a victory does not increase simply at a rate commensurate with the increase in size of the defeated armies, but progressively. The outcome of a major battle has a greater psychological effect on the loser than the winner. This, in turn, gives rise to additional loss of material strength [through abandonment of weapons in a retreat or desertions from the army], which is echoed in loss of morale; the other two become mutually interactive as each enhances and intensifies the other.[24]

Similarly, the effect of one variable or characteristic can depend on which others are present. Thus even if it is true that democracies do not fight each other in a world where other regimes exist, it would not follow that an entirely democratic world would necessarily be a peaceful one: Democracies might now be united by opposition to or the desire to be different from autocracies and once triumphant might turn on one another. (The other side of this coin is that many of the characteristics of democracies that classical

Sciences (Ann Arbor: University of Michigan Press, 1966). For an application of nonlinear dynamics to international politics, see Murray Wolfson, Anil Puri, and Mario Martelli, "The Nonlinear Dynamics of International Conflict," *Journal of Conflict Resolution* 36 (March 1992), pp. 119–49, and, less formally, Alan Beyerchen, "Clausewitz, Nonlinearity, and the Unpredictability of War," *International Security* 17 (Winter 1992/93), pp. 59–90. Also see the discussion of feedbacks in chapter 4. For a discussion of how nonlinearity affects the search for and indeed the meaning of simplicity, generalization, and understanding, see Kellert, *In the Wake of Chaos*, pp. 106–18, 136–47.

[22] For a discussion of catalysts in ecology, see Pimm, *Balance of Nature?*, pp. 248–56.

[23] Gerhard Sonnert, with the assistance of Gerald Holton, *Gender Differences in Science Careers* (New Brunswick, N.J.: Rutgers University Press, 1995). For examples from ecology, see Timothy Allen and Thomas Hoekstra, *Toward a Unified Ecology* (New York: Columbia University Press, 1992), pp. 72–74; Langston, *Forest Dreams*, pp. 134–36. For a lucid discussion of the spread of diseases and crime from this perspective, see Malcolm Gladwell, "The Tipping Point," *The New Yorker*, June 3, 1996, pp. 32–38. For another example, see Ronald Burt, *Structural Holes: The Social Structure of Competition* (Cambridge, Mass.: Harvard University Press, 1992), pp. 94–97.

[24] Carl von Clausewitz, *On War*, edited and translated by Michael Howard and Peter Paret (Princeton, N.J.: Princeton University Press, 1976), p. 253. For a general discussion of war from the perspective of systems effects, see Roger Beaumont, *War, Chaos, and History* (Westport, Conn.: Praeger, 1994).

Realists saw as undermining their ability to conduct foreign policy—the tendency to compromise, heed public opinion, and assume others are reasonable—may serve them well when most of their interactions are with other democracies.)

The direction as well as the size of the effect can be reversed as the stimulus increases. This was understood by the Israeli official in charge of immigration who said about the influx of Soviet Jews in the late 1980s: "I'm very worried if immigration goes up 10 or 20 percent. But if it goes up 300 percent I'm not worried at all" because the U.S. would provide massive assistance.[25] Other curvilinear relations are more familiar. Up to a certain point, stress seems to increase the quality of decision making; additional pressure decreases it.[26] More recently, Edward Mansfield has shown that war is least likely when power is either highly concentrated or highly dispersed, with intermediate degrees of concentration being more dangerous.[27] Reversals also can occur when two influences, either of which alone works in one direction, push in the opposite direction when they operate together. For example, material incentives for good behavior, far from adding to the influence of moral ones, may undercut them.[28]

Related to the lack of proportionality is the failure of "second best" conditions to automatically yield "second best" outcomes. That is, common sense indicates, and many scholars used to believe, that if the best result would be produced by the presence of variables $A \ldots Z$, and if Z were absent, the next best result would be produced by the presence of $A \ldots Y$. When the variables interact, however, this is not necessarily the case.[29] Because

[25] Joel Brinkly, "Soviet Jews Finding Israel Short of Jobs and Housing," *New York Times*, September 17, 1989. Walter Ulbricht apparently stimulated the flow of refugees from East Germany in 1961 in order to increase the pressure on Khrushchev to support sealing the border between the two halves of Berlin: Hope Harrison, "The Bargaining Power of Weaker Allies in Bipolarity and Crisis: The Dynamics of Soviet–East German Relations, 1953–1961" (unpublished dissertation, Columbia University, 1993), pp. 213–26.

[26] Ole Holsti, "Crisis Decision Making," in Philip Tetlock et al., eds., *Behavior, Society, and Nuclear War*, vol. 1 (New York: Oxford University Press, 1989), pp. 85–173. More strangely, the introduction of radar on ships reduced collisions when only a few of them were so equipped, "but when several ships could peer at the cathode ray tube, problems appeared" as the captain could no longer assume that the other would continue on a steady course: Perrow, *Normal Accidents*, p. 204.

[27] Edward Mansfield, *Power, Trade, and War* (Princeton, N.J.: Princeton University Press, 1994).

[28] See the discussion in Amitai Etzioni, *The Moral Dimension: Toward a New Economics* (New York: Free Press, 1988), pp. 242–43; for additional examples, see David Lumsdaine, *Moral Vision in International Politics: The Foreign Aid Regime, 1949–1989* (Princeton, N.J.: Princeton University Press, 1993), pp. 254–55.

[29] The classic article is Richard Lipsey and Kelvin Lancaster, "The General Theory of Second Best," *Review of Economic Studies* 24 (October 1956), pp. 11–32.

the trajectory being followed is not unilinear, moving toward a goal may bring one further from it rather than closer to it. This means that a policy that would be the right one in a perfect world may be worse than alternatives in an imperfect one and that conditions that would be desirable if all else were in good order may not be beneficial if it is not. For example, many people jump from the premise that we are seeking a color-blind society to the conclusion that government policies should be color-blind. The logic is flawed: While such a stance would be appropriate in a world without bigotry, when many people and groups in fact do respond to others in terms of their skin color, compensatory color-aware policies may have many beneficial effects, including bringing us closer to a society in which color plays a much smaller role.

In a system, not only addition but also multiplication will be inappropriate when the order in which variables act influences the outcome.[30] That is, it can matter a great deal whether the expansion of suffrage or the development of modern governmental institutions comes first; who in the game of chicken moves first; and, even today, whether a baby precedes or follows a marriage. Timing can be very important in politics, as the impact of a bit of information, a new proposal, or a strong plea will depend in part on the stage of the processes at which it is received.[31] In international politics, two policies that have the same mix of concessions and threats can produce very different outcomes depending on whether the threats are made before or after the concessions, thus complicating the choice between deterrence and tension-reduction strategies.[32] Many processes then can be hard if not impossible to reverse: Forests that have been drastically altered by logging may not return to their original states even if left undisturbed for one hundred years; fires that served to maintain the ecology in the past may have a very different impact on today's landscapes.[33] Similarly, a British policy of con-

---

[30] In mathematical terms, the operations then are not commutative. For a discussion of the importance of temporal order in biology, see Stephen Jay Gould, *Ontogeny and Phylogeny* (Cambridge, Mass.: Harvard University Press, 1977); in ecology, see Allen and Hoekstra, *Toward a Unified Ecology*, chapter 6.

[31] For a good example, see Richard Harris, *Decision* (New York: Dutton, 1971), esp. pp. 116–17, 170–72, and 192–93.

[32] When Gorbachev and his colleagues deliberated easing the terms of Sakharov's confinement, they were concerned that if a decision were announced near the time of summit meetings with Western leaders, "it will be seen as a concession, which is undesirable" ("Meeting of Politburo of CPSU, August 29, 1985," translated by Loren Utkin, *Cold War International History Project Bulletin*, no. 4 [Fall 1994], p. 83). Abraham Lincoln similarly felt that he had to wait for a Union victory on the battlefield before issuing the Emancipation Proclamation lest it be seen as motivated by desperation: David Donald, *Lincoln* (New York: Simon and Schuster, 1995), pp. 364–66.

[33] Langston, *Forest Dreams*, pp. 260–63; George Johnson, "In Sick, Crowded Ponderosa Forests of West, Seeds of Infernos Lie Ominously in Wait," *New York Times*, May 11, 1996.

ciliation toward Germany that might have reduced tensions in 1906 could have threatened British security in later years; had Germany not started the naval race with Britain, relations might not have broken down, but the end of the race in 1913 could not return the two countries to the terms they enjoyed earlier. In other words, a factor that is the cause of important effects can induce changes so that when it is removed, the effects continue: Most institutions are easier to maintain than to establish; high levels of homelessness may persist after the circumstances that produced them disappear.[34]

The status of a system at a particular point then depends not only on the state of particular variables, but also on how that state was reached. In physical science, this is known as hysteresis, and an example from everyday life is that "for a single position on the handle, water flows differently out of a faucet depending on whether you have turned it slowly from the 'off' position or slowly decreased the pressure from the 'full on' position."[35] The fact that most African countries are worse off today in terms of wealth and social order than they were when they gained their independence does not mean that they benefited from colonialism: They might have developed more swiftly—and quite differently—had they never fallen under foreign rule that altered their societies in ways that made progress much more difficult when the Europeans departed. Ecology again provides examples. Earlier I noted that a change in the age structure within an antelope herd caused a shift from a territorial to a nonterritorial mating system. What is significant here is that when time passed and the previous age distribution returned, the territorial system was not reestablished. It could not develop incrementally: Even the largest male can defend his territory and harem only if many of the other males are tied to their areas and females; if many males are free to be intruders, no territory can be defended even under conditions that previously supported a territorial system.[36] This kind of complexity means that if we find that changing a variable does not change the outcome, the inference may be not that the variable is unimportant, but that change requires that at least two of them be altered.

Nonlinearities create problems with the classic conservative argument that changes should proceed only incrementally: "By a slow but well-

[34] Robert Keohane, *After Hegemony* (Princeton, N.J.: Princeton University Press, 1984); Brendan O'Flaherty, *Making Room: The Economics of Homelessness* (Cambridge, Mass.: Harvard University Press, 1996), chapter 6. For a brief discussion of the difficulties for standard economics posed by irreversibility, see Henry Aaron, "Public Policy, Values, and Consciousness," *Journal of Economic Perspectives* 8 (Spring 1994), pp. 6–10; also see below, chapter 4, pp. 146–65.

[35] Kellert, *In the Wake of Chaos*, p. 94.

[36] Byers, "Pronghorns in—and Out of—a Rut." Also see John Maynard Smith, *Did Darwin Get It Right? Essays on Games, Sex, and Evolution* (New York: Chapman and Hall, 1989), pp. 55–57, and Stephen Jay Gould, "Reversing Established Orders," *Natural History* 104 (September 1995), pp. 12–16.

sustained progress, the effect of each step is watched; the good or ill success of the first gives light to us in the second; and so, from light to light, we are conducted safely through the whole series."[37]

But this prescription ignores several facts: Jumps rather than smooth progressions often characterize operations of systems; some goals can only be reached by quick and drastic changes; the direct response to a small alteration in a policy or input may tell us very little about either the delayed effects or those that would follow from a large change. Similarly, many people, especially but not exclusively conservatives, believe that problems develop slowly and that it is wise to alter policy and behavior only after difficulties have revealed themselves rather than trying to anticipate long-run consequences, which would require relying on speculative theories and evidence. Unfortunately, however, when variables interact in a non-linear manner, changes may not be gradual. Instead, for a prolonged period there may be no apparent deterioration, followed by sudden collapse or transformation.

To further explore interactions it is useful to start with the basic point that the results cannot be predicted from examining the individual inputs separately. I will then move on to the ways in which the effect of one actor's strategy depends on those of others, after which I will discuss how the actors and their environments shape each other, sometimes to the point where we should make the interaction itself the unit of analysis.

First Interactions: Results Cannot Be Predicted from the Separate Actions

The effect of one variable frequently depends on the state of another, as we often see in everyday life: Each of two chemicals alone may be harmless, but exposure to both could be fatal; patients have suffered from taking combinations of medicines that individually are helpful.[38] So research tries to test for interaction effects, and much of modern social science is built on the understanding that social and political outcomes are not simple aggregations of the actors' preferences because very different re-

---

[37] Edmund Burke, *Reflections on the Revolution in France* (New York: Everyman's Library, 1967), pp. 19–20.

[38] The "Gulf War Syndrome" may have been caused by "simultaneous exposure to two or more of the insecticides and drugs used by Gulf War soldiers . . . even though none of the chemicals causes problems by itself": Elizabth Pennisi, "Chemicals Behind Gulf War Syndrome?" *Science* 272 (April 20, 1996), pp. 479–80. The other side of this coin is that medications that have little impact when taken individually can be very effective in combination, as may be the case in the treatment of AIDS: See the special issue of *Science* 272 (June 28, 1996).

sults are possible depending on how choices are structured and how actors move strategically.[39]

Turning to international politics, Shibley Telhami argues that while pan-Arabism and pro-Palestinian sentiment worked to enhance Egyptian influence when Egypt was strong, they made it more dependent on other Arab states when Egypt was weak.[40] From the fact—if it is a fact—that nuclear weapons stabilized Soviet-American relations we cannot infer that they would have a similar impact on other rivalries because variables that interact with nuclear weapons may be different in these cases (and of course may vary from one pair of rivals to another). Within the military domain one finds interaction effects as well: Two weapons or tactics can work particularly well together and indeed most analysts stress the value of "combined arms" techniques that coordinate the use of infantry, artillery, armor, and aircraft. Events that occur close together also can have a different impact than they would if their separate influences were merely summed. The Soviet invasion of Afghanistan affected American foreign policy very deeply in part because it came on the heels of the Iranian revolution, which undercut American power, disturbed public opinion, and frightened allies.[41]

When elements interact it is difficult to apportion the responsibility among them as the extent and even the direction of the impact of each depends on the status of the others. Thus in the example of combined arms tactics, the answer to the question of how we might best invest any additional dollar of defense spending might vary depending not only on the enemy we expect to fight, but also on the existing levels of each kind of arms. Robert Kaufman explains the American navy's failure to explore the potentialities of aircraft carriers during the 1920s and 1930s by the interaction of extreme budgetary pressures, the navy's conservatism, and the restraints imposed by arms control agreements. To develop aviation the navy would have had to experiment with different types of carrier designs. This could have

---

[39] A good introduction is William Riker, *The Art of Political Manipulation* (New Haven, Conn.: Yale University Press, 1986).

[40] Shibley Telhami, *Power and Leadership in International Bargaining: The Path to the Camp David Accords* (New York: Columbia University Press, 1990), pp. 12, 92–106. A recent explanation for the height of nontariff barriers involves interactions among macroeconomic conditions, state size, and state strength: Edward Mansfield and Marc Busch, "The Political Economy of Nontariff Barriers," *International Organization* 49 (Autumn 1995), pp. 723–49; also see David Epstein and Sharyn O'Halloran, "The Partisan Paradox and the U.S. Tariff, 1877–1934," ibid. 50 (Spring 1996), pp. 301–24. For an interaction effect in economic development, see Newman Kwadwo Kusi, "Economic Growth and Defense Spending in Developing Countries," *Journal of Conflict Resolution* 38 (March 1994), pp. 152–59.

[41] For examples from the origins of the Spanish-American War, see John Offner, *An Unwanted War: The Diplomacy of the United States and Spain Over Cuba, 1895–1898* (Chapel Hill: University of North Carolina Press, 1992), pp. 125, 134.

been done within the limits set by the Washington Naval Treaty only if the navy had had more money and desire to innovate; experimentation would have been easier without the treaty restraints even if funds and interest had been low.[42] The result might then have been different had any one of the three elements been different. One could argue that all three conditions were necessary, but this is too simple because the elements were not independent. That is, naval conservatism was reinforced by lack of funds; the arms control agreements contributed to both budgetary stringency and conservatism; the desire to save money was a major motivation for the treaties.

In a parallel fashion, Charles Perrow finds that complex systems often fail because of the failure of several components, each of which would have been harmless had the others not occurred, and that in many cases "improving or changing any one component will either be impossible because some others will not cooperate, or inconsequential because some others will be allowed more vigorous expression."[43] When we are dealing with biological systems like human beings we cannot attribute a certain percentage of the behavior to one variable (like genetic endowment) and the rest to another (such as the environment): We are not dealing with "a separable amalgam (like shuffling two decks of cards with different backs), but [with] a . . . new entity that cannot be decomposed."[44] On a larger scale, people often think that evolution proceeds through the spread of superior traits without recognizing that a trait has survival value only in a particular context, as what gives a plant or animal an advantage in one environment can harm it in another. Similarly, people may form a particularly effective team despite—or even because of—their being quite ordinary individually; a person may be very productive when working with one set of colleagues and do little when she interacts with others; even the greatest of national leaders might have had a

[42] Robert Kaufman, *Arms Control During the Pre-Nuclear Era: The United States and Naval Limitation Between the Two World Wars* (New York: Columbia University Press, 1990), p. 86; also see Thomas Hone, "Spending Patterns in the United States Navy, 1921–1941," *Armed Forces and Society* 8 (Spring 1982), pp. 443–62.

[43] Perrow, *Normal Accidents*, p. 173. Similar arguments have been made about the difficulty of attributing causes in ecological systems, in one case by a scholar who noted the similarity between this realm and the one Perrow describes: David Ehrenfeld, "The Management of Diversity: A Conservation Paradox," in F. Herbert Bormann and Stephen Kellert, eds., *Ecology, Economics, Ethics: The Broken Circle* (New Haven, Conn.: Yale University Press, 1991), pp. 26–39. For relevant discussions of simplicity and complexity, see Lawrence Slobodkin, *Simplicity and Complexity in Games of the Intellect* (Cambridge, Mass.: Harvard University Press, 1992), chapter 10, and Robert Flood and Ewart Carson, *Dealing with Complexity*, 2d ed. (New York: Plenum, 1993).

[44] Stephen Jay Gould, "The Monster's Human Nature," *Natural History* 103 (July 1994), p. 20; also see Stuart Kauffman, *The Origins of Order: Self-Organization and Selection in Evolution* (New York: Oxford University Press, 1993), pp. 40–45, 255–56, and Pimm, *Balance of Nature?*, pp. 249–56.

different or lesser influence in other circumstances.[45] Analogously, one bit of evidence may have enormous impact if and only if several other pieces of data, themselves inconclusive, are kept in mind. The key piece to a jigsaw puzzle matters more than others, but does so only because they are in place, and which piece is the key depends in part on which others have already been fit together.

A focus on interactions also reminds us that the "good cop–bad cop" routine is not restricted to law enforcement officers, and the fact that the criminal does what the former asks does not mean the latter was unimportant. Thus nonsytemic reasoning underlies the common claim that the relatively conciliatory posture taken by many European countries toward difficult Third World regimes during the Cold War was more successful than the American "hard line." In the same way, there is a problem with Rolf Steininger's argument that John Foster Dulles's "mixture of threats and alarmist predictions" was ineffective if not counterproductive in dealing with France over the European Defense Community and that the flexible British policy was more constructive.[46] Similarly, much of the influence over the USSR that the European states gained through their policies of detente was made possible by the less conciliatory American stance: Not only did the latter make the former safe, it gave greater value to what the Europeans could offer.

In explaining outcomes, we also are prone to examine one side's behavior and overlook the stance of the other with which it is interacting. Although deterrence theory is built on the idea of interdependent decisions, most explanations for why deterrence succeeds in some cases and fails in others focus on differences in what the defender did while ignoring variation in the power and motivation of the challenger, just as much policy analysis in general starts—and often ends—with the strengths and weaknesses of the policies contemplated and adopted.[47] But one hand cannot clap; we need to

[45] For a summary of the literature, see Dean Simonton, "Personality and Politics," in Lawrence Pervin, ed., *Handbook of Personality: Theory and Research* (New York: Guilford Press, 1990), pp. 684–85.

[46] Rolf Steininger, "John Foster Dulles, the European Defense Community, and the German Question," in Richard Immerman, ed., *John Foster Dulles and the Diplomacy of the Cold War* (Princeton, N.J.: Princeton University Press, 1990), p. 98. (For a somewhat different view, see Hans Jürgen Grabbe, "Konrad Adenauer, John Foster Dulles, and West German–American Relations," in ibid., pp. 118–19.) For the argument that the PLO was receptive to Israeli proposals in the summer of 1993 in part because of the effectiveness of the previous earlier Israeli unyielding stance, see William Safire, "The Separate Peace," *New York Times*, September 2, 1993.

[47] For correctives, see Alexander George and Richard Smoke, *Deterrence in American Foreign Policy* (New York: Columbia University Press, 1974), and Robert Jervis, Richard Ned Lebow, and Janice Stein, *Psychology and Deterrence* (Baltimore, Md.: Johns Hopkins Univer-

look at the goals, resources, and policies of those with whom the actor is dealing. Teachers are prone to make the parallel error of not exploring how shortcomings in our students' performances on tests may be attributable to the questions we ask.[48]

Intuitive analysis of changes in outcomes also is often flawed by a focus on a single factor on the assumption that others are constant. Thus a newspaper account of the causes of the peace agreement in the former Yugoslavia notes that the American stance

> represented the evolution of Mr. Christopher's . . . thinking. Even before he was confirmed as Secretary of State, he was skeptical that diplomacy could bring peace to Bosnia. But he later came to the conclusion that the only way for the parties to make peace was if the United States seized control of the negotiations from the Europeans and pressured all the parties.[49]

But this ignores the role of the successful Croatian offensive in leading Christopher—and many others—to believe that negotiations now had a good chance to succeed. We should not be too quick to laugh: Many professionals are confused when people react badly to practices that have worked for years. The problem is not that they have changed, but that they have not changed while those they are dealing with have. Professors who received favorable teaching evaluations for being direct and well organized in the early 1960s were reported as being authoritarian by students at the decade's end. Managers who maintain the manner of mentoring female subordinates that was effective twenty years ago are likely to fail today, if not to be guilty of sexual harassment. Even at one point in time, what is good practice for managers, doctors, and teachers will depend on the needs and expectations of those they are trying to direct and help. One reason why the rankings of colleges is a foolish guide to choice is that, as most students (but fewer of

sity Press, 1985). As Kissinger remarked of Napoleon in 1805: "He had forgotten, if he ever knew, that his great victories had been due as much to the ease which his opponents had accepted defeat as to the success of his arms" (Henry Kissinger, *A World Restored* [New York: Grosset and Dunlap, 1964], p. 63). John Mueller examines the American victory in the Gulf War in similar terms: "The Perfect Enemy: Assessing the Gulf War," *Security Studies* 5 (Autumn 1995), pp. 77–117 (an alternative, but still interactional, account is Stephen Biddle, "Victory Misunderstood: What the Gulf War Tells Us about the Future of Conflict," *International Security* 21 [Fall 1966], pp. 139–79). For a good analysis of the need to take the difficulty of the task into account when judging the success of a policy, see David Baldwin, *Economic Statecraft* (Princeton, N.J.: Princeton University Press, 1985).

[48] A humorous but deeply insightful analysis is E. S. Chill and Julian Franklin, "Prolegomenon to any Future Examination in C.C." (unpublished manuscript, Columbia University, n.d.); also see Herbert Spencer, *The Study of Sociology* (Ann Arbor: University of Michigan Press, 1961) (originally published, 1880), pp. 87–88.

[49] Elaine Siolino, "All Sides Make Concessions to End 4 Years of Conflict," *New York Times,* November 22, 1995.

their parents) realize, learning and thriving do not occur in proportion to any characteristic of the institution but are products of the fit between it and the student.

Second Interactions: Strategies Depend on the Strategies of Others

Further complexities are introduced when we look at the interactions that occur between strategies when actors consciously react to others and anticipate what they think others will do. Obvious examples are provided by many diplomatic and military surprises: A state believes that the obstacles to a course of action are so great that the adversary could not undertake it; the state therefore does little to block or prepare for that action; the adversary therefore works especially hard to see if it can make it succeed. As an eighteenth-century general explained, "In war it is precisely the things which are thought impossible which most often succeed, when they are well conducted."[50] Conversely, a threat may be minimized only because the actor is prepared to meet it. Thus in the fall of 1940, Winston Churchill believed that the threat of invasion had decreased, but he resisted the suggestion that England should therefore send more troops to other fronts. It was the very presence of these troops that was responsible for the decreased threat, he insisted.[51] In the war in Vietnam, the U.S. Air Force missed this dynamic and stopped patrolling sections of the North's supply lines when reconnaissance revealed that the number of targets had greatly diminished: After the attacks ceased, the enemy resumed use of the route.[52]

An actor's policies can make possible or foreclose the adversary's strategies. One side can conduct a limited nuclear war only if the other side is willing to fight in this way; a preemptive strategy makes no sense against an adversary who will launch its forces if it sees an attack coming. Conversely, the deterrent strategy that the state selects will influence what the adversary can do: If a state communicates its plans to launch its forces on warning, then the adversary cannot successfully threaten or carry out preemption; if a state plans to retaliate only after receiving the first blow, then it is not vulnerable to the adversary's provocations.

Because strategies interact, our judgment about the wisdom of the policy followed by one actor often implies—and follows from—judgments about those adopted by others. Thus people who fault President Kennedy for hav-

---

[50] Quoted in Reed Browning, *The War of the Austrian Succession* (New York: St. Martin's, 1993), p. 123; also see Edward Luttwak, *Strategy* (Cambridge, Mass.: Harvard University Press, 1987), pp. 7–8.

[51] John Colville, *The Fringes of Power: 10 Downing Street Diaries, 1939–1955* (New York: Norton, 1985), pp. 283–84.

[52] Barry Watts, "Unreported History and Unit Effectiveness," *Journal of Strategic Studies* 12 (March 1989), p. 98.

ing been excessively bellicose toward the USSR must believe that Khrushchev was not an expansionist and that his menacing moves like placing missiles in Cuba were reactions to Kennedy's misguided actions; defending Kennedy (or saying he should have been tougher) necessitates or flows from a very different picture of the Soviet leader as not pushed by the U.S., but pulled by ideology and the belief that American weakness gave him opportunities for expansion.

Just as the success of policies is determined interactively, so too errors are likely to be interrelated. This means that many cases of intelligence failure are mutual—i.e., they are failures by the side that took the initiative as well as by the state that was taken by surprise. Indeed, an actor's anticipation of what others will do stems in part from its estimate of what the other thinks the actor will do. In many cases of surprise, a state sees that a certain move by the adversary cannot succeed and therefore does not expect the other to take it: The U.S. did not expect the Russians to put missiles into Cuba or Japan to attack Pearl Harbor because American officials knew that the U.S. would thwart these measures if they were taken. These judgments were correct, but because the other countries saw the world and the U.S. less accurately, the American predictions were also inaccurate.[53]

Actors sometimes fail to appreciate both the degree to which their strategies are sensitive to those of others and the ability of the adversary to change its behavior in reaction to what the actor is doing. For example, proponents of President Reagan's Strategic Defense Initiative often matched their proposed system against the existing Soviet missile deployment, ignoring the ways in which the latter could be altered to foil the former. But the opponents ignored the ways in which the possibility of an SDI, and the American technological advantage that it represented, could undermine Soviet faith in the powers of communism and the ability of the USSR to compete. Even without prior awareness, interaction can produce shifting pairs of strategies. This was the case in Vietnam. The American conventional offensives that worked well when the North Vietnamese thought they could win by large-scale battles failed when the latter reverted to guerrilla warfare; the weakness of the American effort against unconventional warfare led the North to seek more decisive conventional battles in late 1972, which in turn made their forces vulnerable to the kind of American air strikes that had yielded so few results previously; the return to unconventional war forced the South to disperse its army and thus facilitated the success of the North Vietnamese offensive in 1975.[54]

[53] Klaus Knorr, "Failures in National Intelligence Estimates: The Case of the Cuban Missiles," *World Politics* 16 (April 1964), pp. 455–67; for a related discussion, see James Wirtz, *The Tet Offensive* (Ithaca, N.Y.: Cornell University Press, 1991).

[54] Robert Pape, Jr., "Coercive Air Power in the Vietnam War," *International Security* 15 (Fall 1990), pp. 134–45; Mark Clodfelter, *The Limits of Air Power: The American Bombing of*

In some cases, then, actors can succeed by selecting the same policy that others do and in other cases must adopt one that differs from theirs.[55] In buying and selling stocks, you want to do what others will do—only do it first; if I believe that others will heed warnings of exceptionally heavy traffic and stay off the roads on special occasions like the Olympics, I can use my car; in a game of chicken, you can stand firm if and only if you believe that your opponent will not do so; congressmen often vote for a bill because they know the president will veto it (indeed, sometimes the point is not to take a particular position, but to take a position different from others);[56] Pakistan can proclaim a willingness to sign the Non-Proliferation Treaty if India signs largely because it knows that India will not sign; Japan's ability to be a "trading state" and neglect its military security is feasible because the U.S. follows a very different policy.[57] During the Cold War the U.S. granted asylum to all those who could leave a communist country. But this policy required that

---

North Vietnam (New York: Free Press, 1989), pp. 172–76; Rod Paschall, "Low-Intensity Conflict Doctrine: Who Needs It?" *Parameters* 15 (Autumn 1985), pp. 33–45. For an oscillating measure-countermeasure struggle during World War II, see Alfred Price, *Instruments of Darkness: The History of Electronic Warfare* (New York: Scribner's, 1978).

[55] For a good survey from biology of the conditions under which actors—including genes— are advantaged by doing the same as others and when they gain by doing or being the opposite, see Karl Sigmund, *Games of Life: Explorations in Ecology, Evolution and Behavior* (New York: Oxford University Press, 1993), pp. 108–11, 120–21, 135–36, 148–51, 165–70; also see David Depew and Bruce Weber, *Darwinism Evolving: Systems Dynamics and the Genealogy of Natural Selection* (Cambridge, Mass.: MIT Press, 1995), pp. 386–88; John Dupré, ed., *The Latest on the Best: Essays on Evolution and Optimality* (Cambridge, Mass.: MIT Press, 1987), part 2; John Thompson, *The Coevolutionary Process* (Chicago: University of Chicago Press, 1994), pp. 189–91, 214–16. The classic analysis is John Maynard Smith, *Evolution and the Theory of Games* (Cambridge: Cambridge University Press, 1982); also see Malte Andersson, *Sexual Selection* (Princeton, N.J.: Princeton University Press, 1994), chapter 16; Verne Grant, *The Evolutionary Process*, 2d ed. (New York: Columbia University Press, 1991), chapter 13; David Rowe, *The Limits of Family Influence: Genes, Experience, and Behavior* (New York: Guilford Press, 1994), pp. 213–16. For applications to economics, see Geoffrey Hodgson, *Economics and Evolution: Bringing Life Back into Economics* (Ann Arbor: University of Michigan Press, 1993), pp. 207–9, 229–32; for an example see Russell Cooper and Andrew John, "Coordinating Coordination Failures in Keynesian Models, *Quarterly Journal of Economics* 103 (August 1988), pp. 441–64. The seminal study of how the incentives to cooperate vary with the number of cooperators and defectors is Thomas Schelling, "Hockey Helmets, Daylight Savings, and Other Binary Choices," in Schelling, *Micromotives and Macrobehavior* (New York: Norton, 1978), chapter 7.

[56] Although much of Richard Nixon's approach to politics was built on defining himself by who his enemies were, his chief of staff reports this idea as new to him when John Connally suggested it: H. R. Haldeman, *The Haldeman Diaries* (New York: Putnam, 1994), p. 232.

[57] Actors often understand but rarely acknowledge this: Bosnia's president was unusually candid when he said about a peace plan offered by the Western powers: "If we evaluate that the Serbs will say no, then we will say yes" (quoted in Roger Cohen, "Bosnia's Map: A Bitter Pill," *New York Times*, July 7, 1994).

the communists sharply restrict emigration; as we now see, being willing to let people in when others are willing to let them out is not attractive.[58]

To take a multilateral case, a person will benefit from saving bottle caps or baseball cards only if most others do not, which means that those of us who berate our parents for having thrown out our collections should remember that it would have made sense for them to save them only if other parents had not. Indeed, the very meaning of behavior can be influenced by what others do: Being one of the few people to wear an AIDS ribbon is very different from joining the majority who are so attired.

In other cases, actors want to adopt the same approach or strategy that others do. In games of coordination there is no conflict of interest, as any solution to which all actors conform works equally well for each of them. Thus it does not matter if we drive on the left or right side of the road as long as we all do the same. And if in some cases I will vote for a bill only if I think it will lose, in others, I will vote for it only if I expect many others to do so, if not enough for it to pass, then at least enough to make my position seem reasonable.[59] As we will discuss in chapter 4, positive feedback sets in here as the greater the number of actors who adopt a form of behavior, the more others are likely to.

The interaction of strategies helps explain the paradoxical fact that, because of others' reactions, some attributes or behavior that would seem to harm the actor in fact work to its advantage. A classic case comes from a controversial argument in biology. Because the genes of animals who produce multiple offspring will drive out the genes of those who cannot, evolution depends in part on the criteria by which mates are selected. Thus some characteristics have evolved not because they help the animal get food or avoid predators, but because they attract mates. The peacock's tail is the best-known example, and it now appears that very large antlers on deer and elk may be more important for attracting females than for defeating competitors. The paradox is that these appendages place the animal at a disadvantage because they increase its vulnerability to predators (it is hard for a

---

[58] See the discussion in Myron Weiner, "Security, Stability, and International Migration," *International Security* 17 (Winter 1992/93), pp. 91–126.

[59] For a fascinating case study of the Senate's rejection of Nixon's attempt to elevate Harrold Carswell to the Supreme Court that sees this dynamic as central, see Harris, *Decision*. The dynamics here are related to self-fulfilling prophecies. The classic modern statement is Robert Merton, "The Self-Fulfilling Prophecy," *Antioch Review*, Summer 1948, pp. 193–210; for summaries of the literature, see Russell Jones, *Self-Fulfilling Prophecies* (Hillsdale, N.J.: Erlbaum, 1977), and Mark Snyder, "When Belief Creates Reality," in Leonard Berkowitz, ed., *Advances in Experimental Social Psychology*, vol. 18 (New York: Academic Press, 1984), pp. 248–305. For the ways in which neurotics create environments that justify their styles of coping, see David Shapiro, *Neurotic Styles* (New York: Basic Books, 1965). Prophecies can be self-denying as well, as we will discuss in chapters 4 and 7.

peacock with a large and ostentatious tail to hide) and the food and muscle that went into them could have made the animal stronger or faster. For this very reason, however, females may choose these males on the grounds that any potential mate who can waste so many resources must be healthy and strong, desirable traits that will increase the chances that its offspring will thrive.[60] States may similarly waste resources—for example by procuring unnecessary arms—in order to show that they are so rich and powerful that they can afford to be careless.[61] In cases like these, we could observe a correlation between the behavior and measures of success, but it would be an error to infer that the behavior, by itself, strengthened the actor. On the contrary, it is the very fact that the behavior weakens it that produces success in the context of the system.

Third Interactions: Behavior Changes the Environment

Initial behaviors and outcomes often influence later ones, producing powerful dynamics that explain change over time and that cannot be captured by labeling one set of elements "causes" and other "effects." Although learning and thinking play a large role in political and social life, they are not necessary for this kind of temporal interaction. Indeed, it characterizes the operation of evolution in nature. We usually think of individuals and species competing with one another within the environment, thus driving evolution through natural selection. In fact, however, there is coevolution: Plants and animals not only adapt to the environment, they change it.[62] As a result, it becomes more hospitable to some life-forms and less hospitable to others.

[60] The argument is not that the animals reason in this way, but that selection produces the result. For summaries of the issues and recent findings, see Matt Ridley, "Swallows and Scorpionflies Find Symmetry Is Beautiful," *Science* 257 (July 17, 1992), pp. 327–28; Randy Thornhill, "The Allure of Symmetry," *Natural History* 102 (September 1993), pp. 30–36; Niles Eldredge and Marjorie Grene, *Interactions: The Biological Context of Social Systems* (New York: Columbia University Press, 1992); Andersson, *Sexual Selection.* Jared Diamond, "Kung Fu Kerosene Drinking," *Natural History* 99 (July 1990), pp. 20–24) argues that the human propensity to ingest toxic chemicals (e.g., alcohol and tobacco) can represent the same mechanism. To put this in terms I have used elsewhere, doing something harmful is an index to strength which cannot be used for deception: Jervis, *The Logic of Images in International Relations*, 2d ed. (New York: Columbia University Press, 1993), pp. 26–65.

[61] Ibid., p. 93.

[62] For surveys, see John Thompson, *Interaction and Coevolution* (New York: Wiley, 1982); Thompson, *The Coevolutionary Process*; Geerat Vermeij, *Evolution and Escalation: An Ecological History of Life* (Princeton, N.J.: Princeton University Press, 1987); Kauffman, *Origins of Life*, chapters 6 and 9; also see Charles Darwin, *The Origin of Species* (New York: Modern Library, 1936), pp. 58–61, 161, 362. A classic application to human history is William McNeill, *Plagues and Peoples* (Garden City, N.Y.: Doubleday, 1976). Insightful if sometimes polemical are Richard Levins and Richard Lewontin, *The Dialectical Biologist* (Cambridge, Mass.: Harvard University Press, 1985); Lewontin, *Biology and Ideology* (New York: HarperCollins,

Nature is not likely to "settle down" to a steady state as the development or growth of any life-form will consume—and be consumed by—others, closing some ecological niches and opening others, which in turn will set off further changes. To some extent, organisms create their own environments, not only by direct actions (e.g., digging burrows, storing food, excreting waste products), but as their very existence alters the microclimates, nutrients, and feeding opportunities that will affect them and others.

> When plants put down roots, they change the physical nature of the soil, breaking it up and aerating it. They exude organic molecules . . . that change the soil's chemical nature as well. They make it possible for various . . . fungi to live. . . . They alter the humidity in their immediate neighborhood, and the upper leaves of a plant change the amount of light that is available to the lower leaves. . . . Earthworms through their castings completely change the local topology. Beavers have had at least as important an effect on the landscape in North America as humans did until the beginning of the last century.[63]

Indeed, not only does the amount of rainfall influence the vegetation that grows, but the latter affects the former as well. To take a more readily visible example, elephants thrive on acacia trees. But the latter can only develop in the absence of the former. After a while, the elephants destroy the trees, drastically changing the wildlife that the area can sustain and even affecting the physical shape of the land. In the process, they render the area uncongenial to themselves, and they either die or move on. The land is adapting to the elephants just as they are to it. One Maasai put it well: "Cows grow trees, elephants grow grasslands."[64] Most consequentially, the very atmosphere that supports current life was produced by earlier forms, many of which could not survive in the new environment: Long before humans, species of

---

1993); and Lewontin, "Gene, Organism, and Environment," in Derek Bendall, ed., *Evolution from Molecules to Men* (Cambridge: Cambridge University Press, 1983), pp. 273–85. For a good example, see the discussion of the genetic modifications that flourish among people who live in areas where malaria is prevalent and the changes in mosquitoes induced by the human efforts to control the disease by containing its carriers: Ronald Nagel, "Malaria's Genetic Billiards Game," *Natural History* 100 (July 1991), 59–61.

[63] Lewontin, *Biology as Ideology*, p. 113. Also see Langston, *Forest Dreams*. For a documentation of the impact of beavers, see Robert Naiman, Carol Johnston, and James Kelley, "Alteration of North American Streams by Beaver," *BioScience* 38 (December 1988), pp. 753–62; see the other articles in that issue for additional case studies of the influence of animals on plants and landscapes. Because of these kinds of effects, we could not calculate how many people the earth can support without taking account of the impact of all sorts of human activities, which are in part a function of population size.

[64] Quoted in David Western, "The Balance of Nature," *Wildlife Conservation* 96 (March/April 1993), p. 54. For more technical discussions, see Roger Lewin, "In Ecology, Change Brings Stability," *Science* 234 (November 28, 1986), pp. 1071–73, and S. J. McNaughton, R. W. Ruess, and S. W. Seagle, "Large Mammals and Process Dynamics in African Ecosystems," *BioScience* 38 (December 1988), pp. 794–800.

bacteria were so successful and generated so much pollution that they poisoned themselves.

Politics, like nature, rarely settles down as each dispute, policy, or action affects others and reshapes the political landscape, inhibiting some behaviors and enabling others. Campaign financing reforms generated new actors in the form of PACs, new issues in the form of arguments about what PAC activities should be permitted, new debates about the meaning of the First Amendment, and new groups that track the flow of money and services. These in turn not only affect how funds are solicited and given, but also change the allies and adversaries that are available to political actors and the ways in which a variety of other issues are viewed. Political maneuvers create niches for new actors and disputes, often in ways that no one had anticipated. William Miller's fascinating study of the southern attempt to control—indeed choke off—the debate about slavery in the 1830s points out that by passing a "gag rule" prohibiting congressional discussion of petitions asking for the end of the slave trade in the District of Columbia, the South called up "petitions against the gag rule itself" and made a new issue of the right to petition the government.[65] Indeed, many protest movements grow as people previously unsympathetic are offended by the way the authorities respond. Each added issue may mobilize the population in a different way than did the original one—and of course the new dispute in turn changes the political environment.

Turning to individual behavior, we should note the possible interactions between battered children and those who are bringing them up. It is well known that those who abuse their children are likely to have been abused themselves. Less well known is the fact that some abused children may behave in ways that make abuse more likely, which helps explain why in these cases only one child in a family is abused and some children are subject to repeated abuse as they move from one foster home to another, even though the foster parents had no previous problems.[66] Similar dynamics

---

[65] William Lee Miller, *Arguing About Slavery* (New York: Knopf, 1996), p. 278. The classic treatments of these processes are E. E. Schattschneider, *Politics, Pressures and the Tariff* (New York: Prentice-Hall, 1935), and Schattschneider, *The Semisovereign People* (New York: Holt, Rinehart, and Winston, 1960); also see Norton Long, "The Local Community as an Ecology of Games," *American Journal of Sociology* 44 (November 1958), pp. 251–61; George Tsebelis, *Nested Games: Rational Choice in Comparative Politics* (Berkeley: University of California Press, 1990); and Edward Carmines and James Stimson, *Issue Evolution: Race and the Transformation of American Politics* (Princeton, N.J.: Princeton University Press, 1989).

[66] Kenneth Bowers, "There's More to Iago than Meets the Eye: A Clinical Account of Personal Consistency," in David Magnusson and Norman Endler, eds., *Personality at the Crossroads* (Hillsdale, N.J.: Earlbaum, 1977), pp. 76–77; also see Gerald Patterson, *Coercive Family Process* (Eugene, Ore.: Castalia Press, 1982). For the mutual training of parents and aggressive children, see Harold Kelley and Greg Schmidt, "The 'Aggressive Male' Syndrome: Its Possible Relevance for International Conflict," in Paul Stern et al., eds., *Perspectives on Deterrence* (New York: Oxford University Press, 1989), pp. 272–79.

were used to help "problem students" in a California junior high school. Instead of giving them incentives for good behavior or even training their teachers to elicit better behavior from them, researchers taught the students how to elicit better behavior from their teachers, e.g., by making eye contact, sitting up straight in their chairs, and praising the teacher when things went well. As a result, not only did the students behave better and receive better grades, but they also developed greater confidence in their ability to control their lives.[67]

This example seems extreme and the previous one is pathological, but the underlying processes are the way everyday life is constituted:

> Two people meet for the first time. They do things to and with each other. They speak, they gesture, they touch. In the process, each forms a conception of the other, and of self in relation to the other. Mutual feelings arise. Each affects the other in some way [and this in turn influences how they will interact at the start of their next meeting].[68]

We know that some people bring out the best in us and others the worst just as we seem to be able to elicit desired behavior from some of our acquaintances and not from others. (People who fail to understand this are surprised when they find that they and their friends have quite different impressions of third parties.) Of particular interest to students of interactional politics is the experiment by Kelley and Stahelski in which trusting and distrusting subjects played prisoner's dilemma games. Not only did the former tend to elicit cooperative responses and the latter uncooperative ones, thereby creating different environments in which they acted, but each type was also confirmed in its beliefs about how people behave.[69]

What each actor does affects not only how others react but also the number and type of others with which it has to deal, which in turn affects both the actor's behavior and the results during later periods. A common tactic for an actor who is losing a conflict is to increase the number of participants

[67] Farnum Gray, Paul Graubard, and Harry Rosenberg, "Little Brother Is Changing You," *Psychology Today*, March 1974, pp. 42–46.

[68] Donald Peterson, "A Functional Approach to the Study of Person-Person Interactions," in Magnusson and Endler, eds., *Personality at the Crossroads*, pp. 306–7. Indeed, one scholar has defined social psychology as "the study of the reactions of individuals to the reactions of other individuals": Gregory Bateson, *Naven*, 2d ed. (Stanford: Stanford University Press, 1958), pp. 175–76. For an interactionist discussion of the finding that identical twins reared apart display striking similarities, see Sandra Scarr and Kathleen McCartney, "How People Make Their Own Environments," *Child Development* 54 (April 1983), pp. 424–35. For an excellent summary and synthesis of social psychological studies of the interaction between personality and situation, see Lee Ross and Richard Nisbett, *The Person and The Situation* (New York: McGraw-Hill, 1991), passim, and especially pp. 19, 152–58. Also see the literature cited in note 29, chapter 1 above.

[69] Harold Kelley and Anthony Stahelski, "The Social Interaction Basis of Cooperators' and Competitors' Beliefs about Others," *Journal of Personality and Social Psychology* 16 (September 1970), pp. 66–91.

involved, which can change the outcome without altering any individual actor's characteristics or resources; in other cases, actors prefer to interact with those of like kind, thereby increasing their number and power.[70] But while creating or mobilizing like-minded supporters often brings success, it is not always the case that actors will thrive if others adopt their way of life or code of behavior. For example, the spread of trust can make it easier for exploiters to thrive. But as the latter become more numerous they will find fewer victims and more resistance—i.e., this success as well will generate an environment that will be conducive to a new mix of strategies.[71]

The capabilities, preferences, and beliefs of actors can also be changed by interaction. Conflict often hardens attitudes and drives people to extreme positions in addition to mobilizing those who had not been previously involved. Thus the Supreme Court's ruling that school segregation was illegal both drove southern politics to the right and helped build the civil rights movement, developments that in turn led to demonstrations and violence which greatly increased the pressure for civil rights legislation.[72] Just as conflict spirals can be understood as changing the environment in which each actor finds itself and which its behavior creates, so biologists stress that the environment of each species includes others with which it interacts; this is why we should not be surprised that coevolutionary processes include arms races between predators and prey.[73] Of course humans have some ability to guide the way they change others, their situation, and themselves: The Cuban Missile Crisis led to a subsequent easing of tensions (which may have made American intervention in Vietnam possible) as Kennedy and Khrushchev altered the environment that they had previously created and that now seemed intolerably dangerous.

Interaction and experience can produce deeper changes in our values and thus determine our later behavior. Trying an activity, we may find not only that we like it (i.e., that it gratifies our existing tastes), but also that it leads us

[70] Schattschneider, *Semisovereign People*; Robert Axelrod, *The Evolution of Cooperation* (New York: Basic Books, 1984); Hendrik Spruyt, *The Sovereign State and its Competitors* (Princeton, N.J.: Princeton University Press, 1994); W. Richard Scott, John Meyer, and Associates, *Institutional Environment and Organizations: Structural Complexity and Individualism* (Thousand Oaks, Calif.: Sage, 1994).

[71] See, for example, Maynard Smith, *Evolution and the Theory of Games*.

[72] Michael Klarman, "How *Brown* Changed Race Relations: The Backlash Thesis," *Journal of American History* 81 (June 1994), pp. 81–118.

[73] R. Dawkins and J. Krebs, "Arms Races Between and Within Species," *Proceedings of the Royal Society, London* B 205 (September 21, 1979), pp. 489–511; Leigh Van Valen, "A New Evolutionary Theory," *Evolutionary Theory* 1 (July 1973), pp. 1–30. For an intriguing application of this theory to conflict between mates, see William Rice, "Sexually Antagonistic Male Adaptation Triggered by Experimental Arrest of Female Evolution," *Nature* 381 (May 16, 1996), pp. 232–34. For the argument that these effects are limited by the development of evolutionary stable strategies, see Nils Stenseth and John Maynard Smith, "Coevolution in Ecosystems: Red Queen Evolution or Stasis?" *Evolution* 38 (July 1984), pp. 870–80.

to develop new skills, appreciations, and judgments of what is important. Because people tend to intertwine their self-images with their behavior and engage in self-justification, beliefs and values can follow from as well as produce behavior.[74] People not only seek what they want, but also often come to want what they have gained.[75] Through these processes, acting can accustom the person to the behavior and the values it embodies and can lead to its continuation if not intensification. It is not likely that the subjects in Milgram's famous experiments on obedience would have been able to bring themselves to deliver shocks that they believed were dangerous if not fatal had they not started out giving small jolts.[76] This is true as well for most of the doctors in Nazi Germany who conducted barbaric experiments and murdered the mentally retarded: As Robert Lifton has shown, their participation grew slowly and few would have committed these crimes had they been asked to do so initially.[77]

It is clear that, for better and for worse, people change as they are affected by experiences, including those that they have chosen. Personal development does not mean that the person simply turns into what was latent in him. Instead, we need to take account of the situations in which he was placed. To take some examples familiar to academics, when we think about whether a bright undergraduate would do well in a Ph.D. program, we are likely to ask whether she enjoys and does well at independent research. But the right question may be whether she will enjoy and do well at it after she has experienced two or three years of graduate school. It is also a mistake to point to the lackluster career of a person who failed to get into a major

---

[74] The psychological processes at work are cognitive dissonance and self-perception. For the former see, for example, Jack Brehm and Arthur Cohen, *Explorations in Cognitive Dissonance* (New York: Wiley, 1962); for an application to international politics, see Robert Jervis, *Perception and Misperception in International Politics* (Princeton, N.J.: Princeton University Press, 1976), chapter 11. For self-perception, see Daryl Bem, "Self-Perception Theory," in Leonard Berkowitz, ed., *Advances in Experimental Social Psychology*, vol. 6 (New York: Academic Press, 1972), pp. 1–61; for an application to international politics see Deborah Larson, *Origins of Containment: A Psychological Explanation* (Princeton, N.J.: Princeton University Press, 1985).

[75] This is called the "endowment effect": see Richard Thaler, "Toward a Positive Theory of Consumer Choice," *Journal of Economic Behavior and Organization* 1 (March 1980), pp. 39–60; Daniel Kahneman, Jack Knetsch, and Richard Thaler, "The Endowment Effect, Loss Aversion, and Status Quo Bias," *Journal of Economic Perspectices* 5 (Winter 1991), pp. 193–206. I have applied this theory to international conflict in "Political Implications of Loss Aversion," in Barbara Farnham, ed., *Avoiding Losses/Taking Risks: Prospect Theory and International Conflict* (Ann Arbor: University of Michigan Press, 1994), pp. 23–40.

[76] Stanley Milgram, *Obedience to Authority* (New York: Harper and Row, 1974).

[77] Robert Lifton, *The Nazi Doctors: Medical Killing and the Psychology of Genocide* (New York: Basic Books, 1986); Ervin Staub, *The Roots of Evil: The Origins of Genocide and Other Group Violence* (Cambridge: Cambridge University Press, 1989). The processes involved can be seen as a form of feedback, which is discussed in chapter 4.

graduate school or to receive tenure at a top school as justification for these decisions because we do not know how well she would have done in a more stimulating and demanding setting. Similarly, only transforming interactions can explain why on this sunny Sunday afternoon I am not only revising this chapter, but also enjoying the effort: forty years ago I had quite different activities in mind. In a marriage, one partner sometimes wonders about what would have happened had she married someone else. Hearing this, her husband is likely to become upset, thinking she might have preferred someone else to him. But this is not the point: With a different spouse, she might have been quite a different person, with different preferences. Indeed, one cannot readily ask which husband or life "she" would prefer because there is no single individual who could make this choice. Similar reasoning explains the limitations of the common argument that international institutions do not matter because states will ignore them "when push comes to shove" and vital interests are at stake. Although the statement is correct, it misses the role institutions can play in shaping interests and seeing that push does not come to shove.

Many of the ways in which deterrence can fail reflect interactions in which the state's behavior changes its environment. Thus it might seem obvious that for Pakistan to build nuclear weapons could not but decrease the likelihood of an Indian attack. But this would overlook both the danger that India would feel increased pressures to preempt and the likely Indian judgment that world public opinion would be less censorious of an attack against a nuclear-armed Pakistan. Furthermore, the deterrence tactics that bring success at one point can change the other side and make future deterrence more difficult, most obviously by increasing the challenger's dissatisfaction with the status quo and giving it incentives to "design around" the defender's threats that previously had been adequate.[78] A version of this process may have been at work in Vietnam in the late 1950s. The standard account is that the American advisors erroneously feared a conventional attack from the North and so trained the South Vietnamese army to meet a fictitious danger.[79] But the reason Diem's enemies turned to guerrilla warfare may have been that he had succeeded in foreclosing the option of fighting a conventional war. The American policy was still in error in failing to

[78] George and Smoke, *Deterrence in American Foreign Policy*, pp. 522–30. For a good example, see Janice Stein, "Calculation, Miscalculation, and Conventional Deterrence I: The View from Cairo," in Jervis, Lebow, and Stein, *Psychology and Deterrence*, pp. 34–59. Paul Nitze worried that the success of American deterrence in Europe and Asia in the early 1950s would increase the danger in the Middle East: Robert McMahon, *The Cold War on the Periphery: The United States, India, and Pakistan* (New York: Columbia University Press, 1994), pp. 145–46; also see Frank Ninkovich, *Modernity and Power: A History of the Domino Theory in the Twentieth Century* (Chicago: University of Chicago Press, 1994), pp. 181–83.

[79] See, for example, Andrew Krepinevich, Jr., *The Army and Vietnam* (Baltimore, Md.: Johns Hopkins University Press, 1986), pp. 16–26.

anticipate the response it could trigger, but not in having been misconceived from the start.

Because actions change the environments in which they operate, identical but later behavior does not produce identical results. Indeed, history is about the changes produced by previous thought and action as people and organizations confront each other through time. The final crisis leading to World War II provides an illustration of some of these processes. Hitler had witnessed his adversaries give in to pressure; as he explained, "Our enemies are little worms. I saw them at Munich."[80] But they had changed because of Hitler's behavior. So had Poland. As A. J. P. Taylor puts it, "Munich cast a long shadow. Hitler waited for it to happen again; Beck took warning from the fate of Benes."[81]

Hitler was not the only leader to fail to understand that his behavior would change his environment. Like good linear social scientists, many statesmen see that their actions can produce a desired outcome, all other things being equal, and project into the future the maintenance of the conditions that their behavior will in fact undermine. This in part explains the Argentine calculations preceding the seizure of the Falklands/Malvinas. Their leaders could see that Britain's ability to protect its position was waning, as evinced by the declining naval presence, and that Argentina's claim to the islands had received widespread international support. But what they neglected to consider was the likelihood that the invasion would alter these facts, unifying British opinion against accepting humiliation and changing the issue for international audiences from the illegitimacy of colonialism to the illegitimacy of the use of force.[82]

A similar neglect of the transformative power of action may explain why Saddam Hussein thought he could conquer Kuwait. Even if the U.S. wanted to intervene, it could do so only with the support and cooperation of other Arab countries, which had sympathized with Iraq's claims and urged American restraint. But the invasion of Kuwait drastically increased the Arabs' perception of threat and so altered their stance. Furthermore, their willingness to give credence to Iraqi promises was destroyed by the deception that had enabled the invasion to take everyone by surprise.[83] Germany's mis-

[80] Quoted in Glenn Snyder and Paul Diesing, *Conflict Among Nations* (Princeton, N.J.: Princeton University Press, 1977), p. 187.

[81] A. J. P. Taylor, *The Origins of the Second World War* (Greenwich, Conn.: Fawcett, 1966), p. 242. Russell Leng found that the state that lost one diplomatic encounter usually was the first to threaten to use force in the next one: "When Will They Ever Learn? Coercive Bargaining in Recurrent Crises," *Journal of Conflict Resolution* 27 (September 1983), pp. 379–420. Also see the discussion of path-dependence, chapter 4, pp. 155–61, below.

[82] Lawrence Freedman and Virginia Gamba-Stonehouse, *Signals of War: The Falklands Conflict of 1982* (Princeton, N.J.: Princeton University Press, 1991), pp. 14–15.

[83] For a related argument, see Shibley Telhami, "Arab Public Opinion and the Gulf War," *Political Science Quarterly* 108 (Fall 1993), pp. 442–44.

calculation in 1917 was based on a related error: Although unrestricted submarine warfare succeeded in sinking more British ships than the Germans had estimated would be required to drive Britain from the war, the American entry (which Germany expected) led the British to tolerate shortages that otherwise would have broken their will because they knew that if they held out, the U.S. would rescue them.[84] Escalation can also alter behavior since to retreat after having contested an issue is usually more costly than never having resisted at all, which is one reason why actors may find it rational to continue escalating although doing so would not have made sense in the absence of the initial move.[85]

The failure to appreciate the fact that the behavior of the actors is in part responsible for the environment which later impinges on them can lead observers—and actors as well—to underestimate actors' influence. Thus states caught in a conflict spiral believe that they have little choice but to respond in kind to the adversary's hostility. This may be true, but it may have been the states' earlier behavior that generated the situation that now is compelling. In parallel, one reason why Neville Chamberlain and his colleagues felt that they had no choice but to make concessions to Germany in the late 1930s was that Britain was militarily weak, but one reason for the weakness was Chamberlain's earlier resistance to rearmament.[86] That the current environment may have been in part created by the actor without his knowing it is the burden of Lewis Dexter's analysis of congressmen and lobbyists:

A congressman very largely gets back what he puts out. In his limited time, he associates more with some kinds of people than with others, listens to some kinds of messages more than to others, and as a result hears from some kinds of people more than from others. He controls what he hears both by his attention and by his attitudes. He makes the world to which he thinks he is responding. Congressmen, indeed, do respond to pressures, but they generate the pressures they feel.[87]

[84] Fred Charles Iklé, *Every War Must End* (New York: Columbia University Press, 1971), pp. 42–48.

[85] For a discussion of dynamics of this type, see Zeev Moaz, *Paradoxes of War* (Boston: Unwin Hyman, 1990), chapter 4; also see Joel Brockner and Jeffrey Rubin, *Entrapment in Escalating Conflicts* (New York: Springer, 1985).

[86] For a good discussion, see Donald Kagan, *On the Origins of War and the Preservation of Peace* (New York: Doubleday, 1995), chapter 4.

[87] Raymond Bauer, Ithiel de Sola Pool, and Lewis Anthony Dexter, *American Business and Public Policy* (New York: Atherton, 1963), p. 420. Similar perspectives have been employed by those who explain voting behavior by what the candidates are saying and doing: "Even the most discriminating popular judgment can reflect only ambiguity, uncertainty, or even foolishness if those are the qualities" of the political campaign (V. O. Key, *The Responsible Electorate* [Cambridge: Harvard University Press, 1966], pp. 2–3); "Congressional voters behave the way they do because politicians behave the way they do" (Gary Jacobson, *The Politics of Congressional Elections* [Boston: Little, Brown, 1987], p. 139). More recently, this argument has been applied

Robert McNamara complains about how he was misled by faulty military reporting but similarly fails to consider whether his style and pressure might have contributed to what he was being told.[88] Lawrence Tribe more perceptively argues that recent Supreme Court decisions that deny the appropriateness of judicial remedies for "private" wrongs are in error because they similarly neglect the role of laws, courts, and the state in generating the forces that brought about the problems.[89] More cunning actors are able to reach their goals by manipulating their environment so that it changes in a way that enables or requires them to reach their goals.[90]

Observers and actors then go astray if they believe that people and institutions will be unaffected by the new environment in which their new behavior will place them. Novels tell these stories particularly well, but real cases are also instructive. One analyst argues that John Maynard Keynes

> underestimated the need for government control because he assumed that, unlike the men on the street, the captains of industry had motives considerably loftier than self-interest [because] . . . so many of [them] came from the British aristocracy, for whom, as a class, the pursuit of profit was a bit crass. . . . Here Keynes was guilty of the same mistake made by Adam Smith. He assumed that the social and moral fabric of his society was a part of the natural order of things. He failed to realize that the very act of participation in the market system would turn his lofty aristocrats—if not them, then their children—into self-seeking egoists no different in motivation from the people they employed.[91]

As actions combine to constitute the environment in which the actors are situated and actors in turn change as the environment alters, the language of

---

to how the media first shape and then respond to what people find important and interesting in political campaigns: Graham Ramsden, "Media Coverage of Issues and Candidates: What Balance Is Appropriate in a Democracy?" *Political Science Quarterly* 111 (Spring 1996), pp. 69–70.

[88] Robert McNamara, *In Retrospect: The Tragedy and Lessons of Vietnam* (New York: Times Books, 1995); Deborah Shapley, *Promise and Power: The Life and Times of Robert McNamara* (Boston: Little Brown, 1993), pp. 149–52. "'Ah, les statistiques!' one of the Vietnamese generals exclaimed to an American friend. 'Your Secretary of Defense loves statistics. We Vietnamese can give him all he wants. If you want them to go up, they will go up. If you want them to go down, they will go down": Roger Hilsman, *To Move a Nation* (Garden City, N.Y.: Doubleday, 1967), p. 523.

[89] Lawrence Tribe, "The Curvature of Constitutional Space: What Lawyers Can Learn from Modern Physics," *Harvard Law Review* 103 (November 1989), pp. 1–39.

[90] See, for example, George Kennan's analysis of Franklin Roosevelt in Warren Kimball, *The Juggler: Franklin Roosevelt as Wartime Statesman* (Princeton, N.J.: Princeton University Press, 1991), p. 18; for further discussion of this phenomenon, see chapter 7, pp. 282–91, below.

[91] Barry Schwartz, *The Battle for Human Nature* (New York: Norton, 1986), p. 294 (I am grateful to Kenneth Waltz for reminding me that Adam Smith in fact did not make this error); for a general analysis, see Albert Hirschman, *Rival Views of Market Society and Other Recent Essays* (New York: Viking, 1986), chapter 5.

dependent and independent variables becomes problematic. As one psychologist puts it, "The interaction paradigm has little truck for hard and fast distinctions between antecedent conditions and behavioral outcomes. Behavioral outcomes are the antecedents for subsequent perception and behavior."[92] This may not correspond to our initial impressions: At first glance, it often seems obvious that the behavior of a powerful person is determining the reaction of others. But we need to probe more deeply for interactions. Furthermore, although a system's perspective can show us that a person may in part create the situations to which he later reacts, reciprocally it stresses that the behavior, characteristics, and dispositions of individuals may be the product of the previous environment. This reminder may be especially needed in a society like ours that holds each person accountable for his own fate. Thus one analyst argues:

> In America today certain norms are widely held. First, children are expected to study hard and complete at least high school. Second, young people are expected to refrain from conceiving children until they have the personal and financial resources to support them. . . . Third, adults are expected to work at a steady job. . . . Fourth, everyone is expected to obey the laws . . . The problem is too many people who are not fulfilling their end of the bargain; these people constitute the underclass. Have such people failed society, or has society failed them?[93]

Put this way, the answer is clear. But the question excludes the possibility that most of these people disobey the norms because society has failed them—or has failed their parents: They grew up in surroundings in which these norms were not valued, partly because they did not seem to provide the means to a decent life. To blame the individual misses the processes at work and leads to inadequate prescriptions for change. Similarly, students of international politics have utilized an interactionist perspective to criticize theories that see states as driven by their external circumstances while ignoring the extent to which these environments are themselves the products of state behavior.[94]

[92] Bowers, "There's More to Iago Than Meets the Eye," in Magnusson and Endler, eds., *Personality at the Crossroads*, p. 76. Another psychologist notes, "Once we attend to interactions, we enter a hall of mirrors that extends to infinity": Lee Cronbach, "Beyond the Two Disciplines of Scientific Sociology," *American Psychologist* 30 (February 1975), p. 119.

[93] Isabel Sawhill, "An Overview," *The Public Interest*, Summer 1989, p. 5.

[94] See, for example, Alexander Wendt, "The Agent-Structure Problem in International Relations Theory," *International Organization* 41 (Summer 1987), pp. 335–70; David Dessler, "What's at Stake in the Agent-Structure Debate?" ibid. 43 (Summer 1989), pp. 441–74; Nicholas Onuf, *World of Our Making: Rules and Rule in Social Theory and International Relations* (Columbia: University of South Carolina Press, 1989), chapter 2. This argument is proposed as a contrast to Waltz's perspective, but in fact the difference is easy to exaggerate: see Waltz, *Theory of International Politics*, pp. 74, 78.

PRODUCTS OF INTERACTION AS THE UNIT OF ANALYSIS

Interaction can be so intense and transformative that we can no longer fruit-fully distinguish between actors and their environments, let alone say much about any element in isolation.[95] We are accustomed to referring to roads as safe or dangerous, but if the drivers understand the road conditions this formulation may be misleading: The knowledge that, driving habits held constant, one stretch is safe or dangerous will affect how people drive—they are likely to slow down and be more careful when they think the road is dangerous and speed up and let their attention wander when it is "safe." It is then the road-driver system that is the most meaningful unit of analysis. In the wake of the sinking of a roll-on, roll-off ferry, an industry representative said: "With roro's, the basic problem is that you have a huge open car deck with doors at each end. But people are well aware of this, and it is taken into account in design and operation. You don't mess around with them. There have not been too many accidents because they are operated with such care."[96]

Similarly, we often refer to international situations as precarious, unsta-ble, or dangerous. But, again, if statesmen perceive them as such and fear the consequences, they will act to reduce the danger—one reason why the Cuban Missile Crisis did not lead to war was that both sides felt this could be the outcome if they were not very careful. Nuclear weapons generally have this effect. Because statesmen dread all-out war, international politics is safer than it would otherwise be, and probably safer than if war were less destructive. Conversely, like drivers on a "safe" stretch of road, decision makers can behave more recklessly in calmer times because they have more freedom to seek unilateral gains as well as needing to generate risk to put pressure on others. For example, the relaxation of Anglo-German tensions after 1911 may have misled both countries into believing that they could afford dangerous tactics in 1914.[97]

[95] For similar arguments in biology, see Thompson, *Coevolutionary Biology*; Depew and Weber, *Darwinism Evolving*, pp. 376–81, 409–10; Maynard Smith, *Did Darwin Get It Right?*, pp. 110–13; in social psychology see Watzlawick, Beavin, and Jackson, *Pragmatics of Human Communication*, pp. 54–59, 134–46, 156–57.

[96] Quoted in Stephen Kenzer, "Little Hope for 800 Lost in Sinking of Baltic Sea Ferry," *New York Times*, September 29, 1994. Similarly, a stair architect explains: "It used to be as-sumed that circular stairs were automatically more dangerous [than straight ones], but statistics show they're actually safer. That's because they're a little more difficult to walk on, so you're more cautious": quoted in Richard Wolkomir, "An Architect Who Takes Stairs One Step at a Time," *Smithsonian*, June 1993, p. 57.

[97] See Sean Lynn-Jones, "Détente and Deterrence: Anglo-German Relations, 1911–14," *International Security* 11 (Fall 1986), pp. 121–50. For the argument that the Soviet-American détente contributed to the Middle East crisis in 1973, see Richard Ned Lebow and Janice Gross Stein, *We All Lost the Cold War* (Princeton, N.J.: Princeton University Press, 1994), pp. 220–25.

CIRCULAR EFFECTS

Systems can produce circular effects as actors respond to the new environments their actions have created, often changing themselves in the process. In international politics, perhaps the most important manifestation of this dynamic is the large-scale operation of the security dilemma—i.e., the tendency for efforts to increase a state's security to decrease the security of others.[98] Because states know that they cannot rely on others in the unpredictable future, they seek to protect themselves against a wide range of menaces, and these actions may create new dangers. Thus in the 1930s Japan, which was heavily dependent on resources from outside its borders, sought to expand the area it controlled. Immediate economic needs generated by the worldwide depression increased but did not create this impulse. Nor was it brought on by specific conflicts with the Western powers. Rather, what was driving it was the fear that conflict might be forced upon Japan in the future, which meant that to remain secure it needed raw materials and larger markets. The result was the conquest of Manchuria, followed by a larger war with China, and then by the occupation of Indochina. Each move generated resistance that made the next action seem necessary, and the last move triggered the American oil embargo, which in turn pushed Japan into attacking the West before it ran out of oil. Had Japan been secure, its aggression would not have been necessary; it was the fear of an eventual war with the West that required policies that moved Western enmity from a possibility to a reality. (Of course a further irony is that World War II led to the reconstruction of international politics and the Japanese domestic system that brought Japan security, economic dominance of Southeast Asia, and access to markets around the world.)

In summary, much of our world is unintelligible without attending to three kinds of interactions which form and generate a system. Two or more elements produce results that cannot be understood by examining each alone; the fate of an actor's policy or strategy depends on those that are adopted by others; behavior alters the environment in ways that affect the trajectory of actors, outcomes, and environments. These kinds of interactions explain much of the otherwise puzzling behavior to which we will now turn: Intentions and outcomes often are very different, regulation is prone to misfire, and our standard methodologies are not likely to capture the dynamics at work.

[98] John Herz, "Idealist Internationalism and the Security Dilemma," *World Politics* 2 (January 1950), pp. 157–80; Herbert Butterfield, *History and Human Relations* (London: Collins, 1951), pp. 19–20; Arnold Wolfers, *Discord and Collaboration* (Baltimore, Md.: Johns Hopkins University Press, 1962), pp. 84–85; Jervis, *Perception and Misperception*, chapter 3.

Outcomes Do Not Follow from Intentions

In a system, actions have unintended effects on the actor, others, and the system as a whole, which means that one cannot infer results from desires and expectations and vice versa.[99] The most obvious reason for this is competition.[100] As actors seek advantage and try to outstrategize one another, some of them—if not all—must be surprised. But competition is not necessary for many consequences to be unintended because the phenomenon is a basic product of complex interconnections. Indeed, interventions to ameliorate natural disasters can increase their damage.[101] Competition also was peripheral to the reasons why the Reagan administration's population control program that aimed at decreasing abortions in the Third World probably increased them. Cutting off funds to organizations that performed abortions indeed put many of them out of business. But since they also provided

[99] Albert Hirschman notes that the idea of unintended consequences is as old as the Greek Hubris-Nemesis sequence and that the "reconnaissance and systematic description of . . . unintended consequences have ever since [the eighteenth century] been a major assignment, if not the raison d'être, of social science": Hirschman, *The Rhetoric of Reaction* (Cambridge, Mass.: Harvard University Press, 1991), pp. 36–37. The classic is Robert Merton, "The Unanticipated Consequences of Purposive Social Action," *American Sociological Review* 1 (December 1936), pp. 894–904; also see Spencer, *Study of Sociology*. Recent summaries are Edward Tenner, *Why Things Bite Back: Technology and the Revenge of Unintended Consequences* (New York: Knopf, 1996); Philippe Van Parijis, "Perverse Effects and Social Contradictions: Analytical Vindication of Dialectics?" *British Review of Sociology* 33 (December 1982), pp. 589–603; Raymond Boudon, *The Logic of Social Action* (London: Routledge & Kegan Paul, 1978); Jon Elster, *Logic and Society* (London: Wiley, 1978); Sam Sieber, *Fatal Remedies: The Ironies of Social Intervention* (New York: Plenum, 1981); Patrick Baert, "Unintended Consequences: A Typology and Examples," *International Sociology* 6 (June 1991), pp. 201–10. Much of Schelling, *Micromotives* deals with aspects of these questions. Also see Thomas Sowell's interesting but overdrawn distinction between "constrained" and "unconstrained" visions (the former being sensitive to the prevalence of unintended consequences and the latter believing that human affairs can be benevolently engineered): Thomas Sowell, *A Conflict of Visions* (New York: Morrow, 1987). This is not to say that unintended consequences occur only within systems (we do not need a systems approach to deal with the fact that I might trip and fall down the stairs), but only that systems dynamics almost always lead to at least some consequences that are unintended. In some cases, consequences may be unintended without being unanticipated, as with the known "side effects" of medications.

[100] Competition is stressed in Waltz, *Theory of International Politics*. For a broader survey of unintended consequences in world politics, see Andrew Scott, *Dynamics of Interdependence* (Chapel Hill: University of North Carolina Press, 1982), chapter 2.

[101] Surveying the impact of the measures taken to clean up oil spills (e.g., washing beaches with hot water, applying toxic solvents), Sylvia Earle, the marine biologist quoted at the beginning of the previous chapter, said: "Sometimes the best . . . thing to do in the face of an ecological disaster is to do nothing" (quoted in Richard Kerr, "A Lesson Learned, Again, at Valdez," *Science* 252 [April 10, 1991], p. 371).

birth control supplies, unwanted pregnancies and abortions increased.[102] More obviously, laws that mandate life imprisonment for a third felony conviction can increase violent crime by those who have been convicted twice and decrease the proportion of those who are willing to plea-bargain. In international politics, not only are the expectations of states often thwarted by the actions of others, but many outcomes are mutually undesired: Thus it is not correct to claim that "the absence of superpower war is puzzling only if at least one of the superpowers was expansionist and aggressive."[103]

In these cases the results were the reverse of the intention; in others they may be orthogonal to it, as with the side effects of medications. Thus through a multistep interaction, the decrease in the demand for electric power in the early 1980s complicated antiproliferation efforts as manufacturers responded to decreased sales of nuclear power reactors by offering Third World countries sensitive technologies and paths around international safeguards.[104]

It might seem that unintended consequences would not arise when we deal directly with the actor, for example, by increasing the resources at its disposal. But good Samaritans have found that people may not respond to such interventions by increasing the valued activities, as they would in a linear world. One reason for the failure of massive intervention to assist children who were at risk for delinquency and unemployment may be that families in the program substituted it for the use of friends, clergy, and others to whom they otherwise would have turned.[105] Similarly, if foreign aid allows a poor country to procure the essentials of government without developing a powerful state to guide and extract resources from its society, the result will be decreased effectiveness, lower rates of economic growth, and instability.[106] In a parallel manner, states may decrease their efforts in support of a common cause when their allies do more.[107] In a less well

[102] Constance Holden, "U.S. Abortion Policy May Increase Abortions," ibid. 238 (November 27, 1987), p. 1222.

[103] Lebow and Stein, *We All Lost the Cold War*, p. 357.

[104] For a brief discussion, see Judith Miller, "Effort to Halt Spread of A-Arms Said to Falter," *New York Times*, June 21, 1982.

[105] Ross and Nisbett, *Person and Situation*, pp. 214–19. Of course other factors may have been at work, such as the children and their families developing low self-images and expectations of failure.

[106] For overstated arguments to this effect, see Edward Banfield, "Foreign Aid Doctrines," in Melvin Laird, ed., *The Conservative Papers* (Garden City, N.Y.: Anchor Books, 1964), pp. 77–95, and Peter Bauer, *Reality and Rhetoric: Studies in the Economics of Development* (Cambridge, Mass.: Harvard University Press, 1984), p. 43. For the related argument that American assistance to governments beset by insurgency did more harm than good see William Odom, *On Internal War: American and Soviet Approaches to Third World Clients and Insurgents* (Durham, N.C.: Duke University Press, 1992).

[107] Buck-passing is analyzed in Barry Posen, *The Sources of Military Doctrine: France, Britain, and Germany Between the World Wars* (Ithaca, N.Y.: Cornell University Press, 1984);

known case, when the Chinese provided arms to insurgent movements throughout Southeast Asia to divert the U.S. from its fight in Vietnam, the rebels "fell to squabbling among themselves."[108] As these cases show, when the values and objectives of those receiving assistance differ from those providing it, the behavior of the former may also diverge from what the latter intended.[109]

These problems cannot be avoided by giving people simple incentives and orders. In fact, these easily misfire, not because people disregard them, but because following them leads to undesired behavior. Thus centrally planned economies failed because orders were obeyed too well: Having been told to maximize production, factories rationally turned out a high volume of shoddy goods with great waste; having been given incentives for production with minimum waste, clothing factories produced nothing but large sizes.[110] While at first glance the ability to direct behavior would seem to lead to perfect control, it simply is not possible to design incentives that can guide people through a multitude of unforeseen situations in a way that is desired by those establishing the rules.[111] Thus a welfare reform typical of the 1990s gives a flat rate to an agency for placing foster children in homes rather than paying a certain amount for each day the child is in its care. The admirable objective is to give the agency incentives to resolve the child's future as quickly as possible; the danger is that speed rather than the child's best interests will guide the agency's behavior.[112] Even more disturbingly, it appears that laws designed to deter illegal immigration by holding ships' crews accountable for anyone they bring to port have led them to murder stowaways.[113]

Overlapping with these processes, problems are created when the effects of incentives cannot be limited to the target population. Most obviously, ameliorating the plight of unfortunates may make it worthwhile for others to

also see Douglas Macdonald, *Adventures in Chaos: American Interventions for Reform in the Third World* (Cambridge, Mass.: Harvard University Press, 1992).

[108] Harvey Nelsen, *Power and Insecurity: Beijing, Moscow, and Washington, 1949–1988* (Boulder, Colo.: Lynne Rienner, 1989), p. 89.

[109] For related problems, see the discussion of regulation below, pp. 68–73.

[110] The classic study is Joseph Berliner, *Factory and Manager in the USSR* (Cambridge, Mass.: Harvard University Press, 1957).

[111] See, for example, Theodore Groves and Martin Loeb, "Incentives and Public Inputs," *Journal of Public Economics* 4 (August 1975), pp. 211–26; Duncan Black, *Theory of Committees and Elections* (Cambridge: Cambridge University Press, 1985); James Buchanan and Gordon Tullock, *The Calculus of Consent* (Ann Arbor: University of Michigan Press, 1962). Principal-agent relations also raise some of these problems.

[112] Kimberly McLarin, "Foster Care Model Attracts New York—But Only in Part," *New York Times*, November 20, 1995; for the perverse effects on foster care created by the new welfare incentives, see Nina Bernstein, "Foster Care System Wary of Welfare Cuts," ibid., November 19, 1995.

[113] "Did a Taiwan Ship Hurl Stowaways Overboard?" ibid., May 29, 1996.

assume that status. Supply creates its own demand in what economists call the "moral hazard" problem, as people who know that they will be helped if they are in need do not struggle as hard to avoid this outcome.[114] For example, supplying housing to the homeless or even improving shelters leads some people who are housed dreadfully to abandon their accommodations;[115] giving first priority for housing to those living in unsafe conditions provides incentives for people to temporarily move into such quarters;[116] decent welfare payments make it monetarily irrational to take low-paying jobs.[117] In the same way, developing plans to rescue people who get lost in the wilderness or who reject hurricane warnings can encourage them to take foolish risks or call for help prematurely,[118] and feeding starving refugees will draw others to the camps, sometimes delaying the planting of new crops as farmers remain away from their fields and foresee low prices for any harvest they could bring in.[119] People then respond to orders and incen-

[114] For summaries of the literature, see Yair Aharoni, *The No-Risk Society* (Chatham, N.J.: Chatham House, 1981), chapter 7; David Kreps, *A Course in Microeconomic Theory* (Princeton, N.J.: Princeton University Press, 1990), chapters 16–17; Steven Shavell, "On Moral Hazard and Insurance," *Quarterly Journal of Economics* 93 (November 1979), pp. 541–62. Schelling's treatment, although brief, is—as usual—insightful in noting "the clash between equity and incentives": *Choice and Consequence* (Cambridge, Mass.: Harvard University Press, 1984), pp. 6–9.

[115] How the head of the New York City Office on Homelessness learned this is described in Celia Dugger, "Memo to Democrats: Housing Won't Solve Homelessness," *New York Times*, July 12, 1992. For the changes in New York's policy in response to those dynamics, see Dugger, "Tough Help for Homeless," ibid., September 25, 1992, and Dugger, "New Rules Tighten Access to Shelter in New York City," ibid., August 11, 1993. Also see Robert Ellickson, "The Homelessness Muddle," *The Public Interest*, no. 99 (Spring 1990), pp. 45–60.

[116] Dan Barry, "Chinatown Alarms May Be Hoax to Get Quick Housing," *New York Times*, November 29, 1995.

[117] The stronger—and I think unconvincing—argument is that the welfare system changes the attitudes and values of the recipients, undermining their work ethic. This would be an example of the third level of interaction discussed earlier. This argument fits well with classical conservatism; the claim for the power of incentives fits with free-market conservatism. Much of the current debate about the effect of reducing welfare payments revolves around the question of the extent to which people's behavior will be altered by changed incentives. Those who favor reduction believe that the harm done to some people who remain on welfare—and their children—will be outweighed by the large number of people who will respond by getting a job and/or refraining from having children they cannot support. Opponents reply that these behaviors are more constrained and inelastic and so the response to the new incentives will be slight. For a good discussion of the magnitude of the effect of monetary incentives as they affect homelessness, see O'Flaherty, *Making Room*, chapter 10.

[118] Timothy Egan, "2 Parks to Require Rescue Insurance for Climbers," *New York Times*, September 14, 1993; Tenner, *Why Things Bite Back*, pp. 224–27.

[119] See, for example, Jane Perlez, "Disease Joins Death and Famine in Somali Tragedy," *New York Times*, September 13, 1992, and Alison Mitchell, "A New Question in Somalia: When Does Free Food Hurt?" ibid., January 13, 1993. These perverse effects are recognized by many activists in the field: See, for example, Donatella Lorch, "Refugees' Return Home Called Only Real Solution to Crisis," ibid., July 7, 1994. For a general discussion, see Jean Drèze and

tives, but the results are not what was intended because in a system you cannot do just one thing.

Historians are familiar with these phenomena, which they call "the ironies of history," as time and again they see behavior taking people to unexpected and often undesired destinations.[120] Indeed, the general course of human history may have been set in motion by the unintended consequences of people forming tribes and growing food, thereby providing both the ability and the incentives for large-scale violence.[121] John Gaddis begins his discussion of "the long peace" between the superpowers by presenting the paradox that after World War I the statesmen set out to establish arrangements to keep the peace only to find themselves at war a generation later, while after World War II there was no such design, and yet there followed years of peace and stability among the great powers.[122] But while the fates of the two international systems do call for an explanation, it is not strange that the one that lasted was not designed and the one that was designed worked in a very different way than anyone expected. Interconnections and interactions create sufficient complexity so that it would be surprising if the results conformed to statesmen's anticipations.

Unintended consequences need not be undesired. Indeed, economic growth may fit in this category, springing from the psychological tensions generated by Protestantism and sustained by the desire of individuals to enrich themselves which, although usually unsuccessful, enriches society

---

Amartya Sen, *Hunger and Political Action* (Oxford: Clarendon Press, 1989). The issue of the wisdom of supplying food aid to poor countries has long been debated, with critics arguing that the good is outweighed by the disincentives created: For a balanced review, see Paul Isenman and Hans Singer, "Food Aid: Disincentive Effects and Their Policy Implications," *Economic Development and Cultural Change* 25 (January 1977), pp. 205–37. The original studies were Theodore Schultz, "Value of U.S. Farm Surpluses to Underdeveloped Countries," *Journal of Farm Economics* 42 (December 1960), pp. 1019–30, and Mordecai Ezekiel, "Apparent Results in Using Surplus Food for Financing Economic Development," *Journal of Farm Economics* 40 (November 1958), pp. 915–23.

[120] For the argument that a number of historians have misread British policy during the Napoleonic Wars because of an excessive focus on intentions, see Paul Schroeder, "Old Wine in New Bottles: Recent Contributions to British Foreign Policy and European International Politics, 1789–1848," *Journal of British Studies* 26 (January 1987), pp. 1–25.

[121] Jared Diamond, "The Worst Mistake in the History of the Human Race," *Discover* 8 (May 1987), pp. 63–66; Bard Schmookler, *The Parable of the Tribes: The Problem of Power in Social Evolution* (Berkeley: University of California Press, 1984).

[122] John Lewis Gaddis, *The Long Peace* (New York: Oxford University Press, 1987), pp. 215–16. Kissinger similarly errs when he says, "We will never be able to contribute to building a stable and creative world order unless we first form some conception of it": Henry Kissinger, *American Foreign Policy*, 2d ed. (New York: Norton, 1974), p. 97. A more subtle treatment of the relation between seeking stability and obtaining it is Paul Schroeder, *The Transformation of European Politics, 1763–1848* (New York: Oxford University Press, 1994).

through the operation of Adam Smith's invisible hand.[123] To take an example from international politics, Sadat's trip to Jerusalem, which was applauded by President Carter and most Americans, was at least in part motivated by the Egyptian leader's desire to derail the Soviet-American Joint Communiqué calling for a Geneva meeting with a significant role for the Soviet Union.[124] Carter may also have benefited from the unintended consequences of his pledge to remove American troops from Korea. Although he soon backed away from it, the anxiety it created brought Japan and Korea closer together.[125]

States may need and be able to exploit the fact that not only others but they themselves cannot be sure of the outcome of their actions. Most dramatically, this figures in Schelling's "threat that leaves something to chance," as the state coerces its adversary by threatening to do something that could lead to great violence even though no one wants it to.[126] The threat to take such actions can be credible even when the threat to actually start a major war would not be because the action *might not* lead to war; the threat can be effective because the action *could* lead to war. Thus the commonsense claim that a "credible policy of [nuclear] first use implies an ability . . . to control the process of escalation" has it backwards.[127] A high degree of control would defeat deterrence since it would mean that all-out war would occur only if the state sought it; it is the other side's knowledge that escalation is not completely controllable that gives the threat of limited military use great potency.

British leaders in 1914 and 1938 both feared and utilized the chance of

[123] Max Weber, *The Protestant Ethic and the Spirit of Capitalism* (New York: Scribner's, 1976). In somewhat the same way, many of the most profitable enterprises are run by people who are motivated less by the desire to maximize profit than by pride in serving and doing a good job. More broadly, many of the procedures and institutions of politics in pluralist societies are designed to produce outcomes that are not desired by any individual participant: see chapter 7, pp. 282–83, below.

[124] For a somewhat different explanation, but one that still involves unintended consequences, see William Quandt, *Camp David: Peacemaking and Politics* (Washington, D.C.: the Brookings Institution, 1986), pp. 123–48. For cases of desired but unintended consequences in ecology, see Les Line, "A Summer Without Bobolinks," *Wildlife Conservation*, July/August 1994, p. 42; Gary Noel Ross, "Winged Victory," ibid., pp. 60–67; Michael Killion and S. Bredleigh Vinson, "Ants with Attitude," ibid., January/February 1995, p. 49.

[125] Victor Cha, *Alignment Despite Antagonism: The United States–Korea–Japan Security Triangle* (Stanford, Calif.: Stanford University Press, forthcoming).

[126] Schelling, *The Strategy of Conflict* (Cambridge, Mass.: Harvard University Press, 1960), chapter 8; Schelling, *Arms and Influence* (New Haven, Conn.: Yale University Press, 1966), chapter 3. I have argued that the failure to appreciate this dynamic underlies the central flaw in much of American strategic nuclear policy: Jervis, *The Illogic of American Nuclear Strategy* (Ithaca, N.Y.: Cornell University Press, 1984), chapter 5; Jervis, *The Meaning of the Nuclear Revolution* (Ithaca, N.Y.: Cornell University Press, 1989), chapter 3.

[127] Leon Sloss, "The Roles of Strategic and Theatre Nuclear Forces in NATO Strategy: Part II," in *Power and Policy: Doctrine, the Alliance and Arms Control: Part I* (London: International Institute of Strategic Studies), Adelphi Papers no. 205, Spring 1986, p. 64.

undesired consequences. Although they have been criticized for not taking a firm position in the former case, they did indicate that if war started, no one could be sure where it would end. According to the German ambassador, the British foreign secretary told him that "the British Government . . . could stand aside as long as the conflict remained confined to Austria and Russia. But if we and France should be involved, then the situation would be immediately altered, and the British Government would . . . find itself forced to make up its mind quickly." Chamberlain took a similar line at the start of the crisis over Czechoslovakia in March 1938, telling the House of Commons: "If war broke out . . . . it would be quite impossible to say where it might end and what Governments might become involved."[128]

Unfortunately, British leaders in the 1930s and German leaders before World War I neglected the more general operation of dynamics that can draw states in deeper than they intend. British defense policy was based on the concept of "limited liability" which involved sending only a small ground force to Europe in the event of war, and in the first decade of this century most German leaders conceived of their *Weltpolitik* as "a policy of limited risks and limited aims."[129] But in both cases statesmen failed to realize that their policies would have to work themselves out in the context of others' behavior, which could undo the limits they were trying to set. American decision-makers fell into a similar trap in the fall of 1964. They favored gradual escalation in Vietnam in the belief that it maximized their control and foreclosed fewest choices for the future, but they did not see that once they were committed, it would be the adversary's actions that would drive their subsequent policy.[130]

A Qualification

While the complex interactions in a system mean that some of the consequences will be unintended and undesired, it is hard to measure their fre-

---

[128] Quoted in Imanuel Geiss, ed., *July 1914: The Outbreak of the First World War, Selected Documents* (New York: Scribner's, 1967), p. 289; Chamberlain is quoted in Keith Middlemas, *The Strategy of Appeasement: The British Government and Germany, 1937–39* (Chicago: Quadrangle Books, 1972), p. 202. For a similar statement by the American ambassador to France during the Munich Crisis, see John Haight, Jr., "France, the United States, and the Munich Crisis," *Journal of Modern History* 32 (December 1960), p. 345.

[129] Michael Howard, *The Continental Commitment: The Dilemma of British Defence Policy in the Era of Two World Wars* (Harmondsworth, Middlesex, England: Pelican, 1974), and Brian Bond, *British Military Policy Between the Two World Wars* (Oxford: Clarendon Press, 1980); David Kaiser, "Germany and the Origins of World War I," *Journal of Modern History* 55 (September 1983), p. 451. A Soviet analyst acknowledged that his country failed to appreciate how difficult it would be to control the course of the 1973 Mideast war: Lebow and Stein, *We All Lost the Cold War*, p. 224.

[130] VanDeMark, *Into the Quagmire*, pp. 28–37; one reason why George Ball dissented was that he believed that the escalatory process would be hard to control: ibid., pp. 88–89.

quency. As Albert Hirschman has stressed, straightforward effects are common and often dominate perverse ones.[131] If this were not the case, it would be hard to see how society, progress, or any stable human interaction could develop. The successes of concerted action should not be glossed over: Food stamps have greatly diminished hunger, public-health measures have decreased disease, and the federal highways have vastly increased commerce and travel, although at the expense of a number of undesired and at least initially unexpected side effects. To take the classic case, Malthus was wrong: A rising standard of living decreases rather than increases the birth rate and so is self-sustaining. In our era, if the War on Poverty did not meet all its proponents' expectations, it still accomplished a great deal.[132] Disproportionate attention may be drawn to cases in which the consequences are unanticipated and unwanted because these will be dramatic policy failures that call out for explanation. As a result, books like this select a biased sample of cases; when things work out, we do not study or even notice them.

Regulation

When governments seek to restrain undesired behavior through laws and regulation, the results are often unintended. The problem is not so much that laws are difficult to enforce, but more that, as noted in chapter 1, in a system "we can never do merely one thing."[133] When the British government was considering traffic regulations in the 1930s, the secretary of the Cyclists' Touring Club argued that "if rear lamps became compulsory on bicycles the mortality among cyclists would immediately go up enormously" because people who were driving at night would expect to see the bicyclists more easily and so would drive faster and hit more of them, especially those whose lights had gone out.[134] Although this argument seems so far-fetched as to discredit systems thinking, it turns out to have a significant measure of truth. John Conybeare found that when seat belts were made mandatory in Australia, deaths and injuries declined for the occupants of automobiles but

[131] Hirschman, *Rhetoric of Reaction*.

[132] Irving Bernstein, *Promises Kept: John F. Kennedy's New Frontier* (New York: Oxford University Press, 1991); Bernstein, *Guns or Butter: The Presidency of Lyndon Johnson* (New York: Oxford University Press, 1966). For a general discussion of how systems effects need not defeat purposive action, see chapter 7, below.

[133] Garrett Hardin, "The Cybernetics of Competition," *Perspectives in Biology and Medicine* 7 (Autumn, 1970), p. 80.

[134] William Plowden, *The Motorcar and Politics: 1896–1970* (London: Bodley Head, 1971), p. 241. More recently, riders of mountain bikes opposed a U.S. Forest Service plan to improve a trail in Colorado on the grounds that this will "make it more dangerous because it will allow for increased speed by bikers" ("Bikers, USFS in a Rails-to-Trails Battle," *Aspen Times*, July 19–20, 1993, p. 4C).

went up for pedestrians.[135] In a classic study, Samuel Peltzman argued that safety devices like seat belts and energy-absorbing steering columns did not produce the expected effects because drivers, knowing that they had a greater margin of safety, drove faster and less carefully.[136] This offsetting behavior leads to what can be called the "Titanic effect," after the ship whose captain took fewer precautions because he felt that he had such a great margin of safety that it made sense to reduce it slightly in order to make a speedier trip. As noted earlier, people who are given resources may use them for their own purposes, which may not be the same as those of the people who established the regulations. Gerald Wilde outlines the logic at work as it applies to auto safety:

> It is assumed that the introduction of [a] new measure gives rise to road users forming an opinion of the intrinsic effect that such a measure would have upon the accident rate. By "intrinsic" is meant the effect that would occur *ceteris paribus* (i.e., if the amount or manner of mobility would not change). However, risk homeostasis theory predicts that the ceteris paribus clause does not hold and that, in fact, the road users would adjust their behavior such that the level of perceived risk will match the level of target risk.[137]

[135] John Conybeare, "Evaluation of Automobile Safety Regulations: The Case of Compulsory Seat Belt Legislation in Australia," *Policy Sciences* 12 (June 1980), pp. 27–39. For a related discussion, see chapter 7, pp. 275–82 below.

[136] Samuel Peltzman, "The Effects of Automobile Safety Regulation," *Journal of Political Economy* 83 (August 1975), pp. 677–725. Also see Perrow, *Normal Accidents*, pp. 179–80. The empirical analyses necessary to tease out the influence of regulations from the multiplicity of other factors at work is extremely difficult and so the studies are controversial. Two reviews argue that safety regulations in fact have had at least some desired effect: Robert Crandall, *Regulating the Automobile* (Washington, D.C.: the Brookings Institution, 1986), pp. 56–84; Leonard Evans, *Traffic Safety and the Driver* (New York: Van Nostrand Reinhold, 1991), chapters 4–5, 10–11. Also see Steven Peterson, George Hoffer, and Edward Millner, "Are Drivers of Air-Bag-Equipped Cars More Aggressive? A Test of the Offsetting Behavior Hypothesis," *Journal of Law and Economics* 38 (October 1995), pp. 251–64; Robert Chirinko and Edward Harper, Jr., "Buckle Up or Slow Down? New Estimates of Offsetting Behavior and Their Implications for Automobile Safety Regulation," *Journal of Policy Analysis and Management* 12 (Spring 1993), pp. 270–96; Barry O'Neill, "A Decision-Theory Model of Danger Compensation," *Accident Analysis and Prevention* 9 (September 1977), pp. 157–65; William Evans and John Graham, "Risk Reduction or Risk Compensation? The Case of Mandatory Safety-Belt Use Laws," *Journal of Risk and Uncertainty*, Spring 1991, pp. 61–73. Ruth Schwartz Cowan, *More Work for Mothers* (New York: Basic Books, 1983), argues that, as the title suggests, labor-saving devices have not saved women time, largely because their introduction led people to increase their standards and demands.

[137] Gerald J. S. Wilde, "The Theory of Risk Homeostasis: Implications for Safety and Health," *Risk Analysis* 2 (December 1982), p. 213; also see Wilde, *Target Risk* (Toronto: PDE Publications, 1994). This line of reasoning led me to expect that when batting helmets were introduced into baseball, batters would take advantage of the protection to dig in more and pitchers would respond by brushing them back more often. While this may have occurred, Robert Amdur and his colleagues could find no corresponding increase in the number of bat-

Similarly, the attempt to increase the safety of nuclear power reactors by implementing numerous protective routines and devices seems to have failed in at least some instances: "There were so many duplicated procedures in the safety system that some workers felt that ignoring individual items would not compromise overall safety."[138]

While regulators believe that controlling one element will allow them to change behavior as desired, in fact this would be the case only if everything else in the system were constrained. But usually it is not. Thus we should not be surprised that the attempt to protect civil liberties by limiting police behavior (e.g., by excluding evidence gathered in violation of the Fourth Amendment) created new and undesired practices (e.g., police perjury about how they found the evidence).[139] As Gary Marx explains: "Restrict police use of coercion, and the use of deception increases. Restrict investigative behavior after an offense, and increased attention will be paid to anticipating an offense."[140] Because criminals also react to changes in their environments, a drastic increase in car-jacking in Nairobi followed the introduction of measures to prevent the more normal form of car theft: "As insurance companies insisted that their clients install car alarms and electronic devices that can immobilize engines, it made more sense to just steal the car when in motion."[141] In a related dynamic, civilian attempts to gain control of the military by means of detailed orders may erode its professionalism and faith in the civilian leadership, thereby making it less responsive to civilian goals and commands than it was before.[142]

That attempts at regulation, broadly construed, can produce undesired activities is well known from arms control. Money and ingenuity that can no

---

ters hit by pitched balls (personal communication). For a review of the evidence in other sports, see Tenner, *Why Things Bite Back*, chapters 10–11.

[138] "U.S. Affirms Errors at Hanford Nuclear Plant," *New York Times*, November 26, 1986; also see Aaron Wildavsky, *Searching for Safety* (New Brunswick, N.J.: Transaction, 1988), chapter 6. In his acute analysis of the motives that drive all participants in the system, Perrow (*Normal Accidents*) correctly stresses the importance of pressures from the top of the organization generated by the need to maximize profit.

[139] Sarah Terry, "Experts Try to Pin Down Extent of Police Misconduct," *New York Times*, November 19, 1995.

[140] Marx, *Undercover*, p. 47. In much the same way, tightening the legal controls on discharging toxic wastes into the air and surface water led to land disposal and deep-well injection, which contaminated aquifers: William Goldfarb, "Groundwater: The Buried Life," in Borman and Kellert, eds., *Ecology, Economics and Ethics*, pp. 126–27

[141] Donatella Lorch, "In Nairobi, Car-Jacking is a Bitter Fact of Life," *New York Times*, December 19, 1993; similarly it is now generally believed that harsh sentences for drug dealers greatly increased the number of teenagers in the drug trade.

[142] This analysis is drawn from Samuel Huntington, *The Soldier and the State* (Cambridge, Mass.: Harvard University Press, 1957) and Peter Feaver, *Guarding the Guardians: Civilian Control of Nuclear Weapons in the United States* (Ithaca, N.Y.: Cornell University Press, 1992), especially pp. 251–53.

longer be put into some military programs are likely to be displaced onto others, as when the ABM agreement led to research on forms of missile defense that were arguably legal. Furthermore, restrictions can increase an actor's incentives to engage in the forbidden activity.[143] Thus a particular weapon might not do a state much good if many others had it, but could be potent if they did not. Even more perversely, the very banning of an activity may make it more attractive, not only through a noninstrumental psychological reaction,[144] but also by a reasonable, if strained, inference. Several years after bacteriological warfare was prohibited by the 1925 Geneva Protocol, "a Japanese army major . . . returned home from a European tour convinced that biological weapons were an effective means of fighting a war: with flawless logic he concluded that they must be, otherwise the statesmen at Geneva would not have gone to the trouble of banning them."[145]

The most extreme argument is that regulation is always futile or counterproductive:[146] One cannot improve on market-driven outcomes; order arises spontaneously; the resultants of separate decisions by individuals who are focused on their own interests will produce better outcomes for society than will the decisions of benign rulers seeking the common interest.[147] A

[143] For a discussion of how the incentives to abide by an agreement change as the numbers of cooperators and cheaters change, see Schelling, "Hockey Helmets, Daylight Savings, and Other Binary Choices," in Schelling, *Micromotives*; also see pp. 44–48 above.

[144] See Jack Brehm, *Responses to Loss of Freedom: A Theory of Psychological Reactance* (Morristown, N.J.: General Learning Press, 1972); Sieber, *Fatal Remedies*, pp. 136–40.

[145] Robert Harris and Jeremy Paxman, *A Higher Form of Killing: The Secret Story of Gas and Germ Warfare* (London: Chatto & Windus, 1982), p. 75.

[146] As Hirschman notes, although the "futility thesis" and the "perversity thesis" are often conjoined, they actually represent quite different beliefs about the ways in which systems defeat attempts to alter them: Hirschman, *Rhetoric of Reaction*, pp. 71–74.

[147] It is not surprising that many of those who doubt the efficacy of imposed change are economists, for whom *regulation* is a dirty word. See, for example, Richard Gilbert, ed., *Regulatory Choices: A Perspective on Developments in Energy Policy* (Berkeley: University of California Press, 1991). A similar treatment by a systems theorist who, although an engineer by training, approached problems much as an economist, is Jay Forrester, *Urban Dynamics* (Cambridge, Mass.: MIT Press, 1969). For a balanced view by an economist, see Charles Schultze, *The Public Use of Private Interest* (Washington, D.C.: the Brookings Institution, 1977). Thomas McGarity, *Reinventing Rationality: The Role of Regulatory Analysis in the Federal Bureaucracy* (Cambridge: Cambridge University Press, 1991), presents good case studies but is theoretically confused. For a critique of organization theory from the antiregulatory perspective, see Raymond Bauer, "N + 1 Ways Not to Run a Railroad," *The American Psychologist* 15 (October 1960), pp. 650–55. For a skeptical analysis of the ability of international authorities to manage problems from a scholar strongly influenced by neoclassical economics, see Giulio Gallarotti, "The Limits of International Organization," *International Organization* 45 (Spring 1991), pp. 183–220. Of course the assumption that existing markets are free and competitive and maximize social efficiency is rarely warranted. Even Western property rights, on which so much of our prosperity rests, had to be designed and do not automatically produce the best possible incentives: see Yoram Barzel, *Economic Analysis of Property Rights* (Cambridge: Cambridge University Press, 1989).

good example is the claim that minimum-wage legislation will create inefficiencies and unemployment because businesses will no longer find it profitable to hire certain people.[148] More recently, conservatives have opposed a wide range of regulations on the grounds that they increase costs and thereby produce undesired effects. Thus President Bush argued that "if government mandates make ladders more and more costly to customers [by requiring safety features], . . . more people will turn to cheaper substitutes. And they'll climb up on chairs or step stools, which are far less safe."[149] Following this line of reasoning, the Bush administration sought to have occupational health regulations incorporate second-order effects on the grounds that by increasing the costs to business, the new rules could lead employers to cut wages or fire workers, which in turn would endanger their health: "Better-off workers tended to use their higher wages for more leisure, more nutritious food, and more preventative health care, as well as extending their longevity by smoking and drinking less than former workers."[150]

But this rejection of regulation pretends to more precision than is possible. While the complexity of the interconnections means that we cannot be certain that the proposed rules will work as intended (indeed, even after the fact it would be extremely difficult to tell), neither can we be confident that the dire predictions are correct.[151] To claim that we can be certain of how each actor will respond, how the different behaviors will interact, and how people will then adjust to the changed circumstances goes beyond the knowledge we can have. On the other hand, it is also an error to stop the analysis too soon and look only at direct effects. Thus the same people who supported Bush's calculation of the indirect effects of mandating greater safety for ladders argued that only unfounded speculation could lead one to conclude that cutting welfare would push children into poverty or that reducing college loans would force many students to drop out.

For regulation, as for systems effects in general, there is no simple way to say how far an analyst or actor should go in projecting expected effects. We

[148] See, for example, Milton Friedman, *Capitalism and Freedom* (Chicago: University of Chicago Press, 1962), p. 180.

[149] Andrew Rosenthal, "Outsider Steals Bush's Rose Garden Scene," *New York Times*, April 30, 1992.

[150] Robert Hershey, Jr., "Citing Cost, Budget Office Blocks Work Place Health Proposal," ibid., March 16, 1992; also see Adam Clymer, "Budget Office Retreats on Work Health," ibid., March 30, 1992.

[151] Hirschman, *Rhetoric of Reaction*, p. 28; also see George Stigler, "The Economics of Minimum Wage Legislation," *American Economic Review* 36 (June 1946), pp. 358–65. For a recent empirical study showing that, contrary to the predictions of standard neoclassical economics, an increase in the minimum wage was followed by an increase in the employment rate of low-wage earners, see David Card and Alan Krueger, *Myth and Measurement: The New Economics of the Minimum Wage* (Princeton, N.J.: Princeton University Press, 1995).

cannot even say that uncertainties will grow with time because forces could operate to bring the system toward equilibrium. So disagreements are not surprising. Thus to those who argue that airlines should mandate the use of safety seats for infants, opponents reply that while this would mean fewer babies killed in crashes, more would be killed overall because some parents would make the trip by car rather than pay for the extra seat, and driving is a more dangerous mode of transportation.[152] In the absence of reliable guidelines, people then are likely to carry the analysis to that point, but only to that point, at which the conclusions support their preferences if not their prejudices.[153] Thus Republicans argued for incorporating indirect effects into the analysis of safety regulations, as previously discussed, while simultaneously rejecting democratic claims for the beneficial second-order effects of pollution reduction on public health.

In summary, although changing whatever arrangements have evolved can be beneficial, regulation will alter the incentives and opportunities of many actors and, through interconnections and interactions, produce multiple consequences. Because only some activities are constrained, behavior is likely to move in unanticipated directions, especially because while the purpose of regulation is to block actors' paths, actors will seek ways around them.

Implications for Testing and Method

It is common to test the validity of propositions by making comparisons between two situations that are identical except for one variable. When we are dealing with systems, however, things cannot change one at a time—everything else cannot be held constant.[154] To try to estimate the role of one

---

[152] Matthew Wald, "Jet Crash Revives Debate About Child Safety Seats," *New York Times*, April 6, 1995; Wald, "Study Attacks F.A.A. on Child Safety Seats," ibid., May 4, 1995.

[153] As New York's mayor Giuliani said when disputing a critic's study of the impact of the mayor's proposed budget cuts: "When you start dealing with secondary and indirect analysis, it very much is guided by the predisposition of the person who does the analysis" (quoted in Steven Lee Myers, "Comptroller Says Cuts May Prove Costly," *New York Times*, May 17, 1995).

[154] For related arguments, see Jørgen Randers, ed., *Elements of the System Dynamics Method* (Cambridge, Mass.: MIT Press, 1980); Daniel Luecke and Noel McGinn, "Regression Analyses and Education Production Functions: Can They Be Trusted?" *Harvard Educational Review* 45 (August 1975), pp. 325–50; A. Glazer, "The Advantages of Being First," *American Economic Review* 75 (June 1985), pp. 473–80; Gary King, Robert Keohane, and Sidney Verba, *Designing Social Inquiry* (Princeton, N.J.: Princeton University Press, 1994), pp. 128–37; and Thomas Homer-Dixon, "Strategies for Studying Causation in Complex Ecological Political Systems," The Project on Environment, Population, and Security (Washington, D.C.: American Association for the Advancement of Science), 1995. For a parallel discussion of the use of counterfactuals, see Nelson Goodman, "The Problem of Counterfactual Conditionals," *Journal*

element or action, we have to understand complex interactions, and as we will demonstrate shortly, these present a series of challenges to standard comparative methods. In many cases, functional substitutes could arise. That is, if one element that played a vital role had not been present, the forces and interests at work could have generated another one that would have produced a similar effect. When the outcome emerges from the interaction of several elements, it may not be possible to determine the contribution of each taken separately. Neither can we readily determine the effects of a policy by comparing a case in which an actor followed one policy with another case in which it adopted a different one: it is likely that the actor chose to behave differently because it saw the two situations as being different. Furthermore, because actors are part of the system, it may not be possible to judge progress or the success of a policy by using a fixed yardstick. We can, however, try to trace the ramifications of an action and detect the operations of the system's dynamics.[155]

Power

Related methodological difficulties arise in the conceptualization and measurement of power. As many scholars have noted, simple and straightforward ways of proceeding will rarely suffice because power constitutes a relationship among actors who formulate goals on the basis of what they think is possible and who act on estimates of how they think others will respond.[156]

---

of Philosophy 44 (February 1947), pp. 113–38; Philip Nash, "The Use of Counterfactuals in History: A Look at the Literature," SHAFR Newsletter 22 (March 1991), pp. 2–12; James Fearon, "Counterfactuals and Hypothesis Testing in Political Science," World Politics 43 (January 1991), pp. 192–94. The classic set of imaginative essays is J. C. Squire, ed., If it Had Happened Otherwise (London: Longmans Green, 1932) (and especially Churchill's "If Lee Had Not [sic] Won the Battle of Gettysburg"); a recent social science treatment is Philip Tetlock and Aaron Belkin, eds., Counterfactual Thought Experiments in World Politics (Princeton, N.J.: Princeton University Press, 1996), and I have discussed the uses and abuses of counterfactuals from a systems perspective in my contribution to that volume, "Counterfactuals, Causation, and Complexity."

[155] Thus ecologists sometimes remove one species from an isolated area and see what happens: Pimm, Balance of Nature?, pp. 277–93, 306–12.

[156] See, for example, the discussions in Peter Bachrach and Morton Baratz, "The Two Faces of Power," American Political Science Review 56 (December 1962), pp. 947–52; Steven Lukes, Power: A Radical View (London: Macmillan, 1974); Baldwin, Paradoxes of Power; Carl Friedrich, Constitutional Government and Democracy (Boston: Ginn and Company, 1937), pp. 589–91. Ecologists have similarly found that judging the influence of a species by its direct impact on the environment is rarely adequate. Instead, they have developed the concept of "keystone" species, which are central to the ecology because of the number and importance of the indirect consequences that flow from their activities: see, for example, Yvonne Baskin, "Ecologists Dare to Ask: How Much Does Diversity Matter?" Science 264 (April 8, 1994), pp. 202–3; Sigmund, Games of Life, pp. 60–63; Norman Myers, "Biological Diversity and

Most obviously, various forms of anticipation, strategic behavior, and inter-active preference formation mean that we cannot judge power by noting the parties' initial claims and seeing which was closer to the final outcome. Fur-thermore, because an actor's bargaining power over another depends in part on the alternatives each has, it is affected by the actual and potential rela-tions of each with third parties, which in turn are influenced by the relation-ships among those third parties.[157]

The fact that the state's behavior changes the environment in which it acts further complicates matters. It is often misleading to use the term *strength* in politics. If a weight lifter gets stronger, he can lift heavier weights; in politics, the actor's efforts change not only its own capabilities, but the capa-bilities and/or intentions of others in ways that influence what its capabilities can accomplish—i.e., behavior changes the weights. In dynamics linked to the security dilemma and the balance of power, if a state tries to maximize its power by increasing the resources that would enable it to menace others if everything else remained constant, the others are likely to seek to neutral-ize or counterbalance the state's efforts with the result that its power will not, in fact, be maximized. The exercise of power may also give others le-verage and so diminish the actor's later ability to gain its goals. Thus acquir-ing colonies gives the state new lines of communication to be protected, new neighbors to fear, and new commitments to honor; more recently, when Britain and France put forces into Croatia and Bosnia, they gave the dispu-tants hostages and thereby reduced their own freedom of action.[158]

Since Waltz is a systems theorist, it is not surprising that he assumes that states seek to maximize not power but security.[159] Indeed, since power de-pends on what others think and do, the idea of seeking to maximize power unilaterally makes no sense, although statesmen at times fail to realize

---

Global Security," in Bormann and Kellert, eds., *Ecology, Economics, Ethics*, pp. 13–15; Pimm, *Balance of Nature?*, chapter 15. For a nice application, see William Stevens, "Wolf's Howl Heralds Change for Old Haunts," *New York Times*, January 31, 1995.

[157] See chapter 5 below.

[158] An actor's assertion of leadership similarly gives leverage to others: For a discussion in the context of Arab politics, see Malcolm Kerr, *The Arab Cold War: Gamal abd al-Nasir and His Rivals, 1958–1970* (London: Oxford University Press, 1971).

[159] Waltz, *Theory of International Politics*, pp. 126–27; Waltz, "Reflections on *Theory of International Politics*: A Response to My Critics," in Robert Keohane, ed., *Neorealism and Its Critics* (New York: Columbia University Press, 1986), p. 334. The importance of this distinction is often missed, even by those who note what Waltz has said: See Bruce Bueno de Mesquita and David Lalman, *War and Reason: Domestic and International Imperatives* (New Haven, Conn.: Yale University Press, 1992), pp. 182–86. In many formulations power and security are seen as directly related and as flowing from the level of resources the actor controls. See, for example, Emerson Niou and Peter Ordeshook, "Stability in Anarchic International Systems," *American Political Science Review* 84 (December 1990), pp. 1207–34.

this.[160] Waltz would then appreciate Paul Schroeder's two-fold argument that in the nineteenth and early twentieth centuries Austria could not improve its international position by focusing on relative gains because doing so would induce dangerous reactions by its neighbors, and that a key to the Austrians' success was the degree to which they understood this.[161]

The interactive nature of power is one reason why the disintegration of the USSR and the concomitant increase in America's share of the world's political, economic, and military resources may not increase American power. During the Cold War, others followed the American lead in part because they needed security against the Soviet Union, which the U.S. was willing to provide because of the Soviet threat. Without a pressing adversary, there is now less reason for others to accommodate the U.S., and less reason for the U.S. to exert itself to see that they do.

Causes and Effects

A biologist objected to the movie *Arachnophobia* on the grounds that without spiders we would be overwhelmed by insects.[162] This prediction is certainly correct if spiders were to disappear and everything else remained constant. But in a system it would not, and the claim shows the perils of using the ceteris paribus assumption. Although even experts cannot predict what a spiderless world would be like, even a nonexpert can say that in the absence of one of the insects' prime predators other kinds would flourish and the world would be different in many ways. In the end, perhaps life would be much worse for human beings (although it also could be better), but the simple extrapolation is inappropriate. Similarly, during the Cold War many analysts tried to determine the American vulnerability to economic boycotts by examining the percentages of various vital raw materials that the

[160] In 1946 Maksim Litvinov, the former Soviet foreign minister, is reported to have said with regret that there had been "a return in Russia to the outmoded concept of security in terms of territory—the more you've got the safer you are": quoted in David Holloway, *Stalin and the Bomb* (New Haven, Conn.: Yale University Press, 1994), p. 167.

[161] Schroeder, "'System' and Systemic Thinking in International History," pp. 116–34. For a discussion of relative and absolute gains, see David Baldwin, ed., *Neorealism and Neoliberalism* (New York: Columbia University Press, 1993).

[162] "Spider Expert Accuses Hollywood of Spinning Web of Deceit," *Aspen Daily News*, July 26, 1990. Similarly, a leading economist argued that global warming is not likely to have a major impact on the American economy because "agriculture, the part of the economy that is sensitive to climate change, accounts for just 3% of national output." But since the demand for food is relatively inelastic, if agricultural production were badly disrupted, it could require a much larger percentage of GNP to supply national needs: Herman Daly, "Ecological Economics," *Science* 254 (October 18, 1991), p. 358; Schelling's analysis does not take this into account: Thomas Schelling, "Some Economics of Global Warming," *American Economic Review* 82 (March 1992), p. 5.

U.S. imported either from the entire world or from unsecured parts of it. Many of these numbers were high, and the implication was that America was at the mercy of its suppliers. What was neglected, however, was that many other changes would be put in train if the primary source of a material were cut off: Prices would increase sharply, leading to conservation, development of substitutes, and the search for new supplies. Although the outcomes of these processes is uncertain, one cannot make sense of what would happen without considering them. Similarly flawed are the standard recitations of how many jobs are at stake in trade disputes: Knowing how many people are producing exports to a country does not tell us how many jobs would be lost if trade were restricted because the consequences of restriction would be multiple, including some that would increase employment, most obviously the demand for products previously imported from the other country.

The three kinds of interactions discussed earlier raise different difficulties for analyzing causation. When two elements interact, we will be misled if we sum up the impact that each factor would have were it to act by itself. Herman Kahn estimated the efficacy of civil defense in the event of a nuclear war by examining what had happened to communities that had suffered various natural disasters in the past.[163] But in a nuclear attack, all these plagues would arrive simultaneously and visit the entire nation. Similarly, during the interwar period the Royal Navy underestimated the threat posed by air power to battleships by looking at each mode of attack separately—e.g., torpedo bombs, high-altitude bombing, dive-bombing—without taking into account either the fact that the damage from one attack would reduce the ship's ability to cope with subsequent ones or that the tactics appropriate to deal with one threat would increase vulnerability to others.[164] To take a larger-scale example, although British strategists tended to debate the merits of two types of grand strategy—using Continental allies and relying on sea power—as alternatives, in fact the latter worked so well because it was combined with the former: As Paul Kennedy has shown, without a Continental enemy, Britain's adversary would be free to pour resources into a navy and defeat Britain at sea.[165]

This means that a strategy can succeed at one time or place and fail in

[163] Herman Kahn, *On Thermonuclear War* (Princeton, N.J.: Princeton University Press, 1960), pp. 109–16.

[164] Geoffrey Till, "Air Power and the Battleship in the 1920s," in Brian Ranft, ed., *Technical Change and British Naval Policy: 1860–1939* (New York: Holmes and Meier, 1977), p. 119.

[165] Paul Kennedy, *The Rise and Fall of British Naval Mastery* (London: Macmillan, 1983). For a smaller-scale case, see Ralph Erskin, "Naval Enigma: A Missing Link," *International Journal of Intelligence and Counter Intelligence* 3 (Winter 1989), p. 503. For the difficulties of assuming other variables remain constant in ecology, see, for example, Langston, *Forest Dreams*, pp. 34–35.

another not because of any difference in the actor's resources or skill, but because others are behaving differently. Thus the failure of British policy in the war that started with the rebellion of the American colonies is not traceable to Britain's following a strategy different from that which earlier had yielded success. As before, Britain sought allies to check France; the difference was that this time the French placated their potential enemies.[166] In a parallel manner, in the 1930s the democracies' liberal and conciliatory approach to world politics, which may be optimal today, failed because it interacted with the very different strategy of the dictatorships, which in turn ceased to bring success when the democracies were forced to change their outlook.

Of course each actor not only reacts, but also anticipates what the other is likely to do in light of its estimates of what the other expects it to do, as we discussed in the second kind of interaction presented earlier. The effect of a change in one variable may then be counterintuitive. Thus George Tsebelis reminds us of the basic game theory principles which show that in certain situations, changes in the incentives for one person will alter, not his behavior, but the behavior of the other. If the penalty for speeding increases, common sense would indicate that drivers will slow down. But this conclusion is reached by assuming that enforcement practices remain unchanged, which might be true in the short run. But as fewer people speed, the police are likely to shift some of their resources from traffic enforcement to other duties, thus allowing speeders to take greater liberties.[167] Barry O'Neill shows that the claims for the advantages of relatively unambiguous arms control verifications schemes are similarly flawed in treating as independent the decisions of whether or not to cheat and whether or not to accuse the other of cheating. "The problem is that all the factors interact. . . . because the two [sides'] decisions-makers know each other's outlooks and know that their interests are in partial opposition."[168] The inspector knows that the inspectee is now less likely to cheat because the latter realizes that a more effective system is in place. This lowers the inspector's initial estimate of the

---

[166] John Brewer, *Sinews of Power: War, Money and the English State, 1688–1783* (New York: Knopf, 1989), pp. 176–77. Tucker and Hendrickson argue that Jefferson and his colleagues attributed their success in the Louisiana Purchase to their policy alone and so tried to repeat it toward Spain in order to gain the Floridas without realizing that the circumstances were no longer propitious: Tucker and Hendrickson, *Empire of Liberty*, chapter 15.

[167] George Tsebelis, "The Abuse of Probability in Political Analysis: The Robinson Crusoe Fallacy," *American Political Science Review* 83 (March 1989), pp. 77–91. For a critique, see Jack Hirshleifer and Eric Rasmusen, "Are Equilibrium Strategies Unaffected by Incentives?" *Journal of Theoretical Politics* 4 (July 1992), pp. 353–56. For a parallel debate in ecology, see Pimm, *Balance of Nature?* pp. 290–92.

[168] Barry O'Neill, "Why a Good Verification Scheme Can Give Ambiguous Evidence," York Centre for International and Strategic Studies, Working Paper #8, York University, Toronto, April 1991, p. 19.

likelihood of cheating, which means that more evidence is required before he will accuse the other side of cheating. A good inspection scheme then may not provide better grounds for decisions because of the way both sides react to it.

When we deal with the third kind of interaction, we need to track the circular processes at work as actors respond to changes in their environments, which are in part a product of what they and others did earlier. In thought experiments we often ask what would have happened if one element in our world were different. Living in New York, I hear people speculate that traffic would be unbearable (as opposed to merely terrible) had Robert Moses not built his highways, bridges, and tunnels. But estimates cannot merely subtract these structures from present-day Manhattan. The traffic patterns, the location of businesses and residences, and the number of automobiles now on the streets are in significant measure the product of Moses' road network. Had it not been built, or had it been built differently, many other things would have been different. Traffic might now be worse, but it might also be better if a more efficient public transportation system had been developed. Alternatively, traffic might be light because the city would not have grown so large and prosperous. In any event, the thought experiment cannot be carried out in a simple way.

Quite often, we look at a series of negotiations or interactions and, noting that the final one produced a satisfactory result while the earlier ones did not, give credit to the tactics or conditions that were present later but not earlier. While this may be correct, it overlooks the possible role of the previous rounds and the parties' behavior in them in paving the way for the subsequent success. Sometimes actors make it a principle to never agree at first; sometimes a stiff position is necessary to convince the other side to accept a later compromise; conversely, friendly discussions may be the prerequisite for hard bargaining. The comparative method, valuable as it is, assumes that the cases are independent in a way that often is not the case with continuing interactions.

Because systemic outcomes are the product of the interaction of multiple factors, a commonsense method of probing the environment cannot be trusted. It seems obvious that we could try several tactics and adopt the one that works best. But the possibility that adversaries could learn to thwart the tactic is not the only problem. Unless the areas are completely isolated, the tactic's success could be attributable to the entire ensemble that had been employed: The use of those that had apparently failed might have been necessary for the success of the others. Most obviously, police tactics that appear to be effective may have pushed crime to other areas rather than reducing it, just as bilateral free trade zones may divert rather than increase worldwide trade. In Vietnam, critics argued for shifting resources from large search-and-destroy operations, which had yielded few results, to the pacification program, which had established government control where it was put in place. But the army's reply may have been valid: Pacification worked only because conventional offensives contained the enemy's most effective forces, which would destroy the program if American policy changed. More recently, the costs of medical care have been growing more slowly under private plans than under Medicare. This does not mean the success could be duplicated, however. Not only may the two populations have different characteristics, but the private plans have been able to use their bargaining power to pay doctors and hospitals less, forcing them to recoup their expenses by charging Medicare more.[169]

Many policy prescriptions are flawed by the nonsystemic assumption that the new course of action will leave untouched the environment with which it interacts. Thus because they thought in static terms during World War I, the British navy opposed meeting the German submarine menace by instituting convoys. Such tactics were merely defensive, it argued; only tracking down the U-boats could put an end to the menace. But this overlooked the fact that protecting merchant ships would force the U-boats to either abandon their attacks or come to the convoys where they could be destroyed by the naval escorts.[170]

This case is odd in that the adversary's response improved the policy's prospects. More often, the response will be undesired. But the basic line of nonsystemic thinking is the same: An actor sees that an action will be in its interest, all other things being equal, and neglects the fact that the adversary is likely to react and so things are not likely to remain equal. For example, if we were not in a system, then lifting the arms embargo on Bosnia during the recent war would have strengthened that state. But Serbia and Croatia probably would have reacted by buying more arms and increasing their aggression. Similarly, if all things remained equal, a regime faced by guerrilla opposition could safely employ repression or outside intervention. But doing so might alienate previously neutral citizens and lead to even greater support for the rebels.[171] For the same reasons, tactics or exogenous changes that increase an actor's incentives to stand firm in bargaining may

[169] This point is missed, for example, in Milt Freudenheim, "Medicare, Jot This Down," *New York Times*, May 31, 1995, which moves from the basic facts to the conclusion that "business has a lot to teach the Government about controlling medical costs."

[170] The standard account is Arthur Marder, *From the Dreadnought to Scapa Flow* vol. 4, *1917: Year of Crisis* (London: Oxford University Press, 1969), chapters 4–7, 10. This was not the most egregious of the navy's miscalculations, most of which were rooted in the desire to preserve its traditional ways of doing things.

[171] Biology teaches the same lesson: If we looked at the evolution of animals in nonsystemic terms, we would think that as a species improves, its members will catch more prey. But this would disregard the fact that the prey's defenses are also improving under the pressures of natural selection: Dawkins and Krebs, "Arms Races Between and Within Species"; Van Valen, "A New Evolutionary Law."

not increase its ability to prevail if the other's incentives are symmetrically increased as well (e.g., an adversary will gain more in terms of reputation by defeating a state that has committed itself to its position than by prevailing against one that has not done so).[172]

Broader analyses of security policies have fallen into similar traps in ignoring connections among variables. In rebuttal to the argument that one of the causes of World War I was the participants' faith in offensive strategies, some scholars have argued that the need to protect allies would have produced war even in a defense-dominant world.[173] The conclusion may be correct, but one cannot try to judge the role of offense-dominance by comparing the world of July 1914 with one that would have been identical except for the belief that the defense was stronger because the war plans, alliance configurations, and general ideas that characterized the pre–World War I era arose in part out of the belief that the offense would prevail. With different expectations, the countries would have felt less need for allies, might not have believed that war was inevitable, and would have been less likely to think that the only alternative to decline was competitive growth.

Testing Propositions

Testing the validity of propositions is difficult in a system because we cannot readily hold all other factors constant when the variable on which we are focusing influences the composition of the set of cases we are studying.[174] While this phenomenon is most prevalent and interesting when actors' calculations are involved, all that is required is for elements to be interconnected in a way that undercuts straightforward comparisons. Take, for example, the claim by Richard Lewontin, a noted biologist who usually thinks in systemic terms: "Scientific medicine has done little to add years to people who have already reached their maturity. In the last 50 years only about four months have been added to the expected lifespan of the person who is already 60 years old."[175] But the reasoning is incorrect because the world that modern medicine has helped to shape is a very different one from that

[172] Robert Jervis, "Bargaining and Bargaining Tactics," in J. Roland Pennock and John Chapman, eds., NOMOS, vol. 14, Coercion (Chicago: Aldine Atherton, 1972), pp. 279–84; also see Peter Liberman, "The Spoils of Conquest," International Security 18 (Fall 1993), p. 152.

[173] Scott Sagan, "1914 Revisited: Allies, Offense, and Instability," ibid. 11 (Fall 1986), pp. 151–76; also see the exchange between Jack Snyder and Scott Sagan in ibid. 11 (Winter 1986–87), pp. 187–98.

[174] We should also note that statistical techniques appropriate for the analysis of cases that are independent of each other will be faulty if the occurrence, course, and outcome of one incident influences those that follow, as historical reasoning suggests. Not only can actors learn, but each case changes the environment within which strategies are chosen and outcomes are produced. For a similar argument, see Siverson and Starr, The Diffusion of War.

[175] Lewontin, Biology as Ideology, pp. 42–43.

which existed earlier. Lewontin's data refer only to those who live past sixty, and if health science has saved people who otherwise would have died young—people who are not as strong and healthy as others—then the fact that life expectancy after sixty has grown a bit indicates, not the weakness of modern medicine, but its potency.

The situation poses more hurdles for testing propositions when at least one actor calculates the expected impact of the variable in question. To extend the example in the previous paragraph, people may engage in more health-threatening activities because of their faith in the health system, in which case medicine would have heightened the challenges it faces and any increase in life expectancy would show that health care had improved greatly. To put this in the terms used earlier, the validity of obvious tests is undermined by the ability of people to use resources for their own purposes, which may differ from those who provided them. Thus McKenzie and Tullock note that if we introduced a new way of teaching economics and found no increase in the students' learning, we could not infer that the experiment had failed: The students might have been able to learn the required material more quickly but chose to use the liberated time not to study more economics but to do better in other subjects or to go to the movies.[176]

Actors' anticipations and choices can then disguise the influence of variables that actually are quite powerful.[177] To take a simple case of a "game against nature" where the actor does not have to worry about how an adversary expects him to behave, we might try to estimate the efficacy of flood control measures by comparing the incidence of flooding in areas where embankments had and had not been constructed. But if we found no difference, we could not conclude that the levees had been ineffective: People may have built them in areas that were especially prone to flooding.[178]

In politics as well, our tests have to be sensitive to the possibility that the impact of a variable may be reflected in the actors' choices, and therefore may not be apparent in the outcomes. For example, one central argument of deterrence theory is that in situations resembling the game of chicken, an actor can increase his chance of prevailing by showing the other side that he

[176] Richard McKenzie and Gordon Tullock, *The New World of Economics: Explorations into the Human Experience*, rev. ed. (Homewood, Ill.: Irwin, 1978), pp. 285–88. For a discussion of how we are to evaluate programs in light of complications like this, see Irwin Deutscher, "Toward Avoiding the Goal-Trap in Evaluation Research," in Francis Caro, ed., *Readings in Evaluation Research*, 2d ed. (New York: Russell Sage, 1977), pp. 229–31.

[177] For a parallel discussion, see George Downs and David Rocke, *Optimal Imperfection? Domestic Uncertainty and Institutions in International Relations* (Princeton, N.J.: Princeton University Press, 1995), pp. 130–31.

[178] A further complication is that constricting the river's flow in one area can increase the chance of flooding elsewhere.

is committed to standing firm.[179] The obvious way to test this proposition would be to compare the outcomes of two sets of crises, one in which an actor had committed itself and another in which it had not. But situations in which crises occur when the defender has made a commitment are likely to be different from those that occur in the absence of such a pledge, which means that we cannot construct comparisons in which all variables save one are either the same or are randomly different. To be specific, a challenger will move in the face of a commitment only when he is either unable to understand the situation or is extremely strongly motivated to prevail. In either case, he is likely to be particularly difficult to dissuade. Commitment thus might decrease the number of challenges, but not allow the defender to beat back those that do occur.[180] This does not mean that commitment is irrelevant in the latter cases: The challenger might have been even bolder in its absence. But a comparison of success rates will not be revealing. Similarly, to see whether deterrence is easier than compellence, the obvious thing to do is look at how often these policies succeed. But if statesmen believe that compellence is very difficult, they will resort to it only under unusual circumstances, circumstances not unrelated to the likely outcomes.[181]

When actors choose a course of action on the basis of what they think it will produce, we cannot employ comparisons appropriate to a laboratory experiment in which actors were randomized and assigned their behaviors. Yet this is what we do in almost all studies of the effectiveness of alternative policies.[182] To take a hypothetical example, what could we make of a com-

---

[179] Schelling, *Strategy of Conflict*.

[180] To use Morgan's terms, commitment may then be positively correlated with the success of general deterrence and negatively correlated with the success of immediate deterrence. See Patrick Morgan, *Deterrence: A Conceptual Analysis* (Beverly Hills, Calif.: Sage, 1977), pp. 25–45. For further discussion, see Jervis, "Systems: Dynamics and Effects," in Richard Zeckhauser, ed., *Strategy and Choice* (Cambridge, Mass.: MIT Press, 1991), pp. 121–22; James Fearon, "Signaling versus the Balance of Power and Interests," *Journal of Conflict Resolution* 38 (June 1994), pp. 236–69, and, for a similar analysis of the effectiveness of alliances, Alastair Smith, "Alliance Formation and War," *International Studies Quarterly* 39 (December 1995), pp. 405–26.

[181] For a study that takes account of some of these difficulties, see Walter Petersen, "Deterrence and Compellence: A Critical Assessment of Conventional Wisdom," *International Studies Quarterly* 30 (September 1986), pp. 269–94; for a good study that makes use of selection effects, see Scott Gartner and Randolph Siverson, "War Expansion and War Outcome," *Journal of Conflict Resolution* 40 (March 1996), pp. 4–15.

[182] To merely take examples from the most recent journal I have seen, see William Dixon, "Third-Party Management Techniques for Preventing Conflict Escalation and Promoting Peaceful Settlement," *International Organization* 50 (Autumn 1966), pp. 653–81, and Paul Diehl, Jennifer Reifschneider, and Paul Hensel, "United Nations Intervention and Recurring Conflict," ibid., pp. 683–700.

parison that revealed that the success rate of threats was higher than that of conciliation? Because the state selected its approach by estimating how alternative policies would work in the particular circumstances it faced, we could not infer that the state would have done better to have used the more successful tactic in the other cases. The tactic that failed more often may have been applied in cases that were more difficult or that were not suited to the more successful approach. Of course we can try to control for as many situational factors as possible, but the statesmen may well look at more subtle cues than we do. Furthermore, the more effective approach might not work so well were it used all the time.

To take a case from domestic politics, it may simultaneously be true that congressmen can increase their chances of reelection by doing extensive work for their constituencies and that a comparison of congressmen who do a great deal of such work with those who do not would reveal no correlation with electoral success because congressmen may undertake these activities only when their positions are weak.[183] Similarly, we cannot readily judge the effectiveness of White House lobbying with Congress by comparing the outcomes of cases in which the president used many resources with cases in which he did not: He will exert himself only when he thinks that the bill will not otherwise pass. Thus it is not surprising that although an unpopular tax increase was passed just weeks before the 1990 elections, very few who voted for it were defeated: Most of those who supported it were not running or held safe seats.[184]

Standard methods of testing propositions are even more problematic when each actor knows that its behavior is believed to reveal characteristics that are linked to what it will do later in the interaction.[185] Thus common sense would indicate that big and strong men are more likely to try to fight back against a mugger than are women or smaller men. But the situation is unlike an experiment not only because muggers do not pick their victims at random, but also because victims know this. Thus if a person who appears able to defend himself is attacked, he may realize that only a particularly strong, vicious, or highly motivated mugger would attack him and therefore conclude that fighting back would be especially foolish. The resistance rates among various kinds of victims then would not vary. It is similarly difficult to determine the influence of nuclear weapons by looking for differences in the course of conflicts according to whether either side had them. Daniel

[183] Douglas Rivers and Morris Fiorina, "Constituency Service, Reputation, and the Incumbency Advantage," in Morris Fiorina and David Rohde, eds., *Home Style and Washington Work: Studies of Congressional Politics* (Ann Arbor: University of Michigan Press, 1989), pp. 17–45.

[184] Gary Jacobson, "Deficit Cutting Politics and Congressional Elections," *Political Science Quarterly* 108 (Fall 1993), pp. 375–402.

[185] Jervis, *Logic of Images*.

Geller tries and concludes that "in conflicts between nuclear and non-nuclear states, the possession of nuclear weapons has no apparent inhibitory effect on the escalatory behavior of the opponent."[186] The first problem is one we have seen before: A nation without nuclear weapons is likely to enter into a dispute with a nuclear power only if the stakes are very important to it and/or if it believes that there are especially good reasons why it should be able to prevail. One could try to deal with this possibility by holding constant the objective situation. But this is not only hard to do, it is also conceptually faulty because the statesman's judgment of the situation which strongly influences his behavior includes his estimate of the likely reaction of the other side, and each state's initial behavior gives the other information about the situation and how the state sees it. The very fact that a non-nuclear state is willing to join a confrontation with a nuclear one sends a powerful message to the latter, thereby shaping the case and undermining comparisons to cases in which everything is the same except for nuclear weapons.

It is then a mistake to apply a decision-theoretic rather than a game-theoretic framework to cases in which actors' behavior is based on their expectations of what others will do. That is, we cannot look at one side while holding the other side constant because even to explain one side's decisions, we need to capture its estimate of the other side's likely response, which in turn is influenced by what it thinks the other thinks the state will do. Thus it would be an error to argue that war will result if a state can increase its expected utility by attacking without considering whether in these circumstances the other side would make preemptive concessions, whether a rational state would anticipate that these concessions will be forthcoming, and whether it should or would change its expectations if they are not.[187] Similarly, arguments about the likely frequency of international conflicts at various points in the cycle of the rise and fall of hegemons will be flawed if they hold constant the behavior of one state and the other's expectations of it.[188] Despite the fact that the basic ideas of game theory are well known, the literature is filled with propositions such as: "The more favorable the balance of military capabilities for the challenger, the higher the probability

[186] Daniel Geller, "Nuclear Weapons, Deterrence, and Crisis Escalation," *Journal of Conflict Resolution* 34 (June 1990), p. 302.

[187] For a related argument, see James Fearon, "Rationalist Explanations for War," *International Organization* 49 (Summer 1995), pp. 379–414, and Gartner and Siverson, "War Expansion and War Outcome," pp. 13–14.

[188] A. F. K. Organski and Jacek Kugler, *The War Ledger* (Chicago: University of Chicago Press, 1980), chapter 1; K. Edward Spiezio, "British Hegemony and Major Power War, 1815–1939: An Empirical Test of Gilpin's Model of Hegemonic Governance," *International Studies Quarterly* 34 (June 1990), pp. 165–82. This kind of problem is discussed in Benjamin Most and Harvey Starr, *Inquiry, Logic, and International Politics* (Columbia: University of South Carolina Press, 1989), chapters 3–4.

that it will initiate a militarized dispute against a rival."[189] But a state that is facing a challenger with very great military capabilities is likely to make more concessions than one facing a weaker adversary. Furthermore, as discussed earlier, cases in which a weak state does not do so are likely to be special and the fact of its refusing to compromise may tell the other side something. It is then not surprising that Jack Levy's review of the literature finds that "the dyadic balance of power between two states is a poor predictor of the probability of war between them."[190]

In domestic politics as well, conditions, actors, their expectations, and the outcomes can be interconnected in ways that shape the relations between any two of these factors. This is nicely shown by a re-analysis of data on public opinion, party control of legislatures, and policy outcomes in American states. For a number of years, scholars have known that there is little correlation between how liberal or conservative opinion is in a state and whether the Democrats or Republicans dominate the legislature and between which party is in power and how liberal or conservative the laws are. These findings would seem to imply either that the parties lack distinctive ideologies or that parties have little impact on policy and that, understanding this, people do not vote according to their ideologies. But a recent study has shown that parties both matter and have known ideologies. The explanation is a dynamic one: The parties in each state adjust their positions to the general orientation of public opinion, with the Republican party becoming more liberal in liberal states and the Democratic party moving to the right when opinion is conservative. So although states with more liberal opinions do have more liberal laws, they are not more likely to be governed by Democrats and the policy outputs are not sensitive to which party controls the legislature. Because the "result is achieved by a circuitous process," matched comparisons at each stage will not be revealing.[191] Here as else-

[189] Paul Huth, D. Scott Bennett, and Christopher Gelpi, "System Uncertainty, Risk Propensity, and International Conflict Among the Great Powers," *Journal of Conflict Resolution* 36 (September 1992), p. 489. Problems of this type are recognized in Donald Wittman, "How a War Ends: A Rational Model Approach," ibid. 23 (December 1979), pp. 743–63; Paul Huth and Bruce Russett, "General Deterrence Between Enduring Rivals: Testing Three Competing Models," *American Political Science Review* 87 (March 1993), pp. 62–63; D. Scott Bennett, "Security, Bargaining, and the End of Interstate Rivalry," *International Studies Quarterly* 40 (June 1996), pp. 164–65.

[190] Jack Levy, "The Causes of War: A Review of Theories and Evidence," in Philip Tetlock et al., eds., *Behavior, Society, and Nuclear War*, vol. 2 (New York: Oxford University Press, 1991), p. 242; see pp. 231–58 for a good discussion of the literature and arguments on this general subject. Selection effects are discussed in this context in James Fearon, "Domestic Political Audiences and the Escalation of International Disputes," *American Political Science Review* 88 (September 1994), p. 578.

[191] Robert Erikson, Gerald Wright, Jr., and John McIver, "Political Parties, Public Opinion, and State Policy in the United States," *American Political Science Review* 83 (September 1989), pp. 729–50; the quotation is from p. 743.

where, the apparent lack of a relationship disguises powerful effects that work throughout the system.

Yardsticks and Indicators

Actors and analysts often use an indicator or yardstick to compare two cases, or one case over time, in order to measure progress. But the interactions in the system may alter the meaning of the yardstick, bending it if you will. For example, many academic programs use the yield rate as a measure of their perceived quality: If this year 40 percent of the people who we accept enroll in our program, we must be doing worse than we were five years ago when 60 percent enrolled. But the data do not rule out an alternative explanation —the program's reputation may have improved, thus attracting better applicants who will also be admitted to other excellent programs. Indeed, the total number of applicants might not increase as weaker ones no longer apply. Similarly, interactions may render problematic the attempt to determine which professors are easy and hard graders by looking at the distribution of marks they give: Once students know who is lenient and who is tough, those less motivated and able will be attracted to the former, thereby destroying the relationship between a professor's standards and the number of As and Cs she gives. For the same reason, one cannot judge the competence of a doctor or hospital by the rate at which patients survive if excellent physicians and facilities attract sicker people.[192]

In these cases, a consistent reading of the yardstick is undercut by the processes set in motion by the actor's behavior without anyone seeking to manipulate the results. But often this will occur as well: Giving an actor incentives to do well according to an indicator can be self-defeating because people who are aware of how they are being judged may behave in ways that alter or sever the connection between the indicator and what it used to measure. If I value the (hypothetical) fact that my daughter keeps her room neat because I think this shows admirable values and I tell her how glad I am for it, her future neatness may reflect not these values but her desire to please me.

More frequently, motive remains constant, but an appreciation of the yardstick leads to strategic manipulation of varying degrees of subtlety. Thus

[192] When the government rated the providers of medical services it sought to control for this effect, but there are limits to how well this can be done: See Elisabeth Bumiller, "Death-Rate Rankings Shake New York Cardiac Surgeons," *New York Times*, September 6, 1995. Similarly, if a bank makes special efforts to attract mortgage applications from minority areas, it may reject a higher percentage of applicants than would a less biased institution: Steven Holmes, "All a Matter of Perspective," ibid., October 11, 1995. For a parallel discussion of affirmative action programs in the funding of scientific research, see Eliot Marshall, "Congress Finds Little Bias in System," *Science* 265 (August 12, 1994), p. 863.

even if the skill of health care providers initially was reflected in the survival rates of patients, dispensing rewards and punishments on this basis would give the former incentives to avoid hard cases. This effect is widespread: Since colleges are now rated on such measures as SAT scores and graduation rates, they have changed their counting rules; teachers and schools that are judged by their students' scores on standardized tests often "teach to the test," which can raise scores without increasing the learning that they were designed to measure; companies judged by the profits they report are likely to find ways of making the "bottom line" appear quite healthy even if the business is not doing well.[193] To take an important international case, Soviet statements about the value of nuclear superiority ceased shortly after American defense analysts argued that they showed that the USSR was aggressive. Did the Soviets change their views or did they change the way they talked because they saw that their speeches were having an undesired effect? On a lighter note, because people who design web sites want to attract as many visitors as possible, they try to discern the rules used by the people who are developing search engines: One "client selling mole traps tried to sneak the word 'sex' repeatedly into his site."[194]

Distortion can occur even in the absence of the motive to deceive. This is sometimes the case with the use of surrogate markers or end points in medical research. When it is impractical to measure what one cares most about—mortality rates and quality of life—researchers must judge the efficacy of treatments by markers, such as the number of CD4 cells in people who are HIV-positive, or cholesterol counts in heart patients. But even if these markers were originally correlated with the matters of concern, treatments aimed at affecting them may do so without producing the health benefits that are desired—i.e., judging success by the progress with the surrogate may reduce if not destroy the correlation that originally made it a useful indicator.[195] Charles Goodhart of the Bank of England identified what he calls Goodhart's law which, with the indicated modification, has much validity: "If an economic statistic becomes the focus of attention [and if actors have the ability to affect the statistic, then] that statistic is likely to distort."[196]

[193] Steve Strecklow, "Colleges Inflate SATs and Graduation Rates in Popular Guidebooks," *Wall Street Journal*, April 5, 1995; Iris Rotberg, "Myths about Test Score Comparisons," *Science* 270 (December 1, 1995), pp. 1446–48; Reed Abelson, "Truth or Consequences? Hardly," *New York Times*, June 23, 1996.

[194] Laurie Flynn, "Desperately Seeking Surfers: Web Programmers Try to Alter Search Engines' Results," ibid., November 11, 1996.

[195] Rachel Nowak, "Problems in Clinical Trials Go Far Beyond Misconduct," *Science* 264 (June 10, 1994), pp. 1540–41.

[196] Jim Barge, "Goodhart's Law Strikes Again," *The Banker*, July 1985, p. 31; for further discussion of this problem, see Jervis, *Logic of Images*, chapter 3 ("The Manipulation of Indices"). For the related way people can fool themselves and change their behavior when they act as though an indicator of a trait is a cause of it, see George Quattrone and Amos Tversky,

The meaning of a yardstick is especially vulnerable when two sides are in conflict. As each alters its behavior to try to defeat the other, many of the standard indicators of success will be drained of meaning even if neither side intends this effect. For example, because the U.S. and South Vietnam established the strategic hamlet program in order to provide security for the rural population, they kept careful track of how many hamlets were overrun. But when the initial success of the program forced the Viet Cong to change its tactics and work by infiltration, inducements, and intimidation, the continuing decrease in the number of hamlets conquered or even attacked no longer provided evidence for the government's control of the countryside.[197] Similarly, Israel's use of air power in the War of Attrition produced success as measured by a reduction in Egyptian artillery fire, but this impression is misleading because the Egyptians reacted by shifting to small-arms fire.[198]

As this case shows, looking at a single yardstick to measure success in a complex system is likely to mislead because it fails to capture the multiple and indirect effects that will become increasingly important as the system reacts to the actor's behavior. Both the difficulties and some ways of coping with them appear when military organizations seek to establish how well their weapons and tactics are working. Because effectiveness can rarely be gauged directly, surrogate measures are required. Usually, these take the form of enemy forces that have been destroyed or shortfalls in enemy military production. But looking only at these obvious effects ignores "virtual attrition"—the reduction in effectiveness of enemy forces or the diversion of resources that is required for the enemy to cope with your efforts. For example, the value of an air defense cannot be calculated only by the number of bombers shot down or even raids deterred because reacting to defenses usually imposes significant but more elusive costs on the enemy. The enemy may put armor on its bombers, which reduces the payloads they can carry, build more fighter planes and therefore fewer bombers, fly the bombers on circuitous routes (thereby requiring them to carry more fuel and fewer bombs), and forgo precision. The success of the Allied bombing offensive against Germany similarly cannot be captured by a single measure. After the war, the U.S. Strategic Bombing Survey noted that "it was to the lowering of the level of Germany's finished munitions output that the Allied

"Self-Deception and the Voter's Illusion," in Jon Elster, ed., *The Multiple Self* (Cambridge: Cambridge University Press, 1986), pp. 35–58. This is not unlike the classic question of how the prospect of salvation, if given by God on the basis of divine grace rather than good behavior, can influence behavior: Weber, *Protestant Ethic*.

[197] See Krepinevich, *Army and Vietnam*, pp. 87–88.

[198] Shimshoni, *Israel and Conventional Deterrence*, pp. 154–55; for a similar case see Walter Enders and Todd Sandler, "The Effectiveness of Antiterrorism Policies," *American Political Science Review* 87 (December 1993), pp. 829–44.

Strategic Bombing Offensive was in the main addressed" and that, by this measure, the offensive failed.[199] But this account neglects the fact that the German reaction to the bombing campaign consumed resources that otherwise would have been devoted to defending Germany or killing Allied soldiers. For example, aircraft plants had to be dispersed, which not only put additional strains on the already overburdened transportation system, but also "caused a 'tremendous dilution' of German supervisory and technical talent, increased the size of the workforce the aircraft industry required (by an estimated 20 percent), [and] made efficient engineering and program changes 'practically impossible.'"[200] Furthermore, the bombing forced the German fighters to rise to the attack, and their destruction by the American escorts depleted Germany's pool of skilled pilots.[201]

The American bombing of Tokyo in April 1942 (the "Doolittle Raid") did very little direct damage. But this does not mean that it did little damage. I cannot improve on Roche and Watts' analysis, and so will quote it at length:

> The loss of face the raid inflicted on the Japanese military was, by far, the raid's most important psychological effect because of its impact on subsequent Japanese operations, deployments, and strategy. Some 53 battalions of the Japanese Army were dispatched on a punitive expedition through Chekiang province, where most of the American B-25s landed [and]. . . . four army fighter groups were brought home to provide air defense of the Japanese cities. . . .
>
> Even more critically, the bombing of Japan's "sacred home soil" affected Japanese strategy. [Japanese military leaders] were so mortified by the raid that they committed themselves to a course of military action in the Pacific that culminated in major defeats. Not only was any lingering resistance to Yamamoto's proposed Midway operation quelled by Doolittle's B-25s, but the Japanese high command additionally resolved to forestall any further raids on Japan by Admiral Shigeru Fukudome's drive to Fiji and New Caledonia aimed at cutting off Australia from America. As a result the Japanese committed themselves to attempting two major operations in widely separated locations [which] . . . prevented concentration of Japan's full strength in either.[202]

[199] Quoted in James Roche and Barry Watts, "Choosing Analytic Measures," *Journal of Strategic Studies* 14 (June 1991), p. 176.

[200] Ibid., p. 178; the internal quotations are from Carl Norcross et al., *Aircraft Division Industry Report* (Washington, D.C.: Government Printing Office, 1st ed., November 2, 1945), p. 26. For an analysis of the same kind of effect on the tactical level, see Ian Gooderson, "Allied Fighter-Bombers Versus German Armour in North-West Europe, 1944–1945: Myths and Realities," *Journal of Strategic Studies* 14 (June 1991), pp. 210–31. For an excellent discussion of the broader subject of "the strategy of inflicting costs" on the adversary, see Schelling, *Choice and Consequence*, chapter 12.

[201] It is also important to remember that in a system effects cannot be attributed to any single factor. The Germans would have been able to react quite differently had they not simultaneously been under great pressure from Allied ground forces.

[202] Roche and Watts, "Choosing Analytic Measures," pp. 186–87.

The concept of virtual attrition applies more broadly. An overture toward an adversary's ally may require the adversary to divert attention and resources to this new problem; raising issues that embarrass the adversary may require it to spend precious political capital; failed diplomatic initiatives can call forth costly countermeasures. Because in a system it is impossible to do just one thing, measurements of success will rarely be unidimensional and static.

This chapter has outlined many of the effects that characterize systems. Additive and linear operations cannot capture what happens because the impact of one variable or strategy depends on others as actors both shape and are shaped by their environments. The complexity involved helps explain why the results of actions are often unintended and why regulations often misfire: Actors can rarely be fully constrained and will react in ways that those who seek to influence them are unlikely to foresee or desire. If systems are troublesome for actors, they also pose methodological problems for analysts by complicating the concepts of power and causation, confounding standard tests of many propositions, and undermining the yardsticks or indicators of the success of policies.

So far I have not focused on systems theories in international politics, having wanted first to outline the general phenomena of interest. But now I should turn to this literature from which I have heavily drawn and partly dissent.

Three

Systemic Theories of International Politics

To REVIEW all the literature on international systems could take a book in itself, but to ignore what others have said would be perverse. I will strike an uneasy compromise and analyze the issues closest to my own concerns, paying special attention to Waltz's seminal *Theory of International Politics*.[1]

We can separate the theories by whether the dependent variables, the independent variables, or both are on the system level, putting aside the fourth box in the accompanying table that designates studies in which both causes and effects are at the unit level. Some placements are problematic, in part because a scholar can sustain more than one kind of analysis. Thus Waltz and Snyder and Diesing[2] span two boxes because while the bulk of their attention is directed toward phenomena in which both the independent and the dependent variables are systemic, they also analyze the system's impact on states' foreign policies.[3]

Another complication is that some independent variables are difficult to classify. Stanley Hoffmann stresses the importance of transnational technol-

---

[1] Kenneth Waltz, *Theory of International Politics* (Reading, Mass.: Addison-Wesley, 1979). A good review of the earlier literature is John Weltman, *Systems Theory in International Relations* (Lexington, Mass.: D.C. Heath, 1973).

[2] Glenn Snyder and Paul Diesing, *Conflict Among Nations* (Princeton, N.J.: Princeton University Press, 1977), especially chapter 6; for an extension of the argument, see Snyder, "The Security Dilemma in Alliance Politics," *World Politics* 36 (July 1984), pp. 461–95; also see chapter 5, below.

[3] He is at pains to stress that his is not a theory of foreign policy: Waltz, *Theory of International Politics*, pp. 48–49, 72, 78, 87, 121–23; Waltz, "Reflections on *Theory of International Politics*: A Response to My Critics," in Robert Keohane, ed., *Neorealism and its Critics* (New York: Columbia University Press, 1986), pp. 328, 339–40, 343. But many people, including some of his students, have treated it very much like one: See, for example, Barry Posen, *The Sources of Military Doctrine: France, Britain, and Germany between the World Wars* (Ithaca, N.Y.: Cornell University Press, 1984). For an analytical discussion, see Colin Elman, "Why *Not* a Neorealist Theory of Foreign Policy?" *Security Studies* 6 (Autumn 1996), pp. 7–51, and the exchange between Elman and Waltz, ibid., pp. 52–59. One can also argue about whether Waltz's approach really is systemic rather than unit-level because the systemic constraint is formed by the behavior of other actors. It is not clear, however, that this dispute is a fruitful one: See Alexander Wendt, "Bridging the Theory/Meta-Theory Gap in International Relations," *Review of International Studies* 17 (October 1991), pp. 383–92; Martin Hollis and Steve Smith, "Beware of Gurus: Structure and Action in International Relations," ibid., pp. 393–410; Wendt, "Levels of Analysis vs. Agents and Structures: Part III," *Review of International Studies* 18 (April 1992), pp. 181–85.

	Dependent Variable		
	System		*Unit*
System	Singer	Snyder & Diesing Waltz	Posen Dependency Theory
Independent *Variable*			
Unit	Rosencrance Hoffmann Aron Kaplan		X

ogies, norms, and beliefs.[4] While these are located within individual states, they often cross national boundaries. Similarly, elsewhere I have argued that the degree to which the security dilemma operates is strongly influenced by whether the offense has the advantage over the defense and whether offensive military and political postures can be distinguished from defensive ones.[5] Are these variables unit-level or systemic?

What Are the Variables?

Theorists usually focus on stability. But this dependent variable has been defined badly and may not provide the best avenue into understanding international politics. Also alarming is the paucity of independent variables. Waltz lays out three dimensions on which the system's structure can be characterized, but in international politics one of them is constant (the organizing principle is always anarchical) and so a second (the differentiation of the units) drops out. As a result, systems can be only multipolar, which was the case before 1945, or bipolar, which it became after then, possibly reverting to multipolarity after 1991.[6] Kaplan and Hoffmann develop more causal factors, but they are ad hoc rather than being theoretically grounded.[7]

[4] Stanley Hoffmann, "International Systems and International Law," in Klaus Knorr and Sidney Verba, eds., *The International System* (Princeton, N.J.: Princeton University Press, 1961), pp. 205–37.

[5] Robert Jervis, "Cooperation Under the Security Dilemma," *World Politics* 30 (January 1978), pp. 168–214. Also see George Quester, *Offense and Defense in the International System* (New York: Wiley, 1977), and Kenneth Oye, ed., *Cooperation Under Anarchy* (Princeton, N.J.: Princeton University Press, 1985). For a further discussion of variables that do not easily fit the unit/structure distinction, see below, pp. 107–10.

[6] For Waltz's views of the current structure, see Kenneth Waltz, "The Emerging Structure of International Politics," *International Security* 18 (Fall 1993), pp. 44–79.

[7] Morton Kaplan, *System and Process in International Politics* (New York: Wiley, 1957); Hoffmann, "International Systems and International Law."

Stability

Although much attention has been paid to the stability of the intentional system, the concept is used differently by different scholars and the most common definition is problematic.[8] Dina Zinnes develops a mathematical model and so must provide a precise definition: "Stability here is simply a shorthand term to denote a situation in which an attack will not occur, i.e., here 'stability' = 'peace.'"[9] Many other scholars do the same. The reason presumably is that wars are likely to produce a great deal of change, and do so with violence and speed. John Herz's definition makes this thinking explicit: "A system is (relatively) stable where changes are relatively slow, gradual, and peaceful; unstable, where they tend to be sudden, far-reaching in impact, and frequently violent."[10]

These definitions are troublesome. *Peace* is a perfectly good word. Why do we need another one that means the same thing?[11] In common parlance stability has to do with the system's ability to ward off or cope with radical change and the links between this and war need to be explored empirically, not posited by definition. Although balance of power theory argues that wars often are the instrument by which stability is produced, the history of the twentieth century may explain the propensity to equate stability with peace. It is hard to see the two world wars as either exemplifying a stable system or

[8] Students in other fields have also wrestled with the appropriate definition of stability and similarly deploy alternative formulations: see, for example, R. J. Putman and S. D. Wratten, *Principles of Ecology* (Berkeley: University of California Press, 1984), chapter 13; Stuart Pimm, *The Balance of Nature? Ecological Issues in the Conservation of Species and Communities* (Chicago: University of Chicago Press, 1991), pp. 13–14.

[9] Dina Zinnes, *Contemporary Research in International Relations: A Perspective and a Critical Appraisal* (New York: Free Press, 1976), p. 315. She puts it slightly differently when she defines a stable system as one that is "peaceful, or [in which] the status quo will be maintained": "Coalition Theories and the Balance of Power," in Sven Groennings, E. W. Kelley, and Michael Leiserson, eds., *The Study of Coalition Behavior: Theoretical Perspectives and Cases from Four Continents* (New York: Holt, Rinehart, and Winston, 1970), p. 352.

[10] John Herz, "The Impact of the Technological-Scientific Process on the International System," in Abdul Said, ed., *Theory of International Relations* (Englewood Cliffs, N.J.: Prentice-Hall, 1968), p. 115. Quincy Wright similarly defines stability as "the absence of sudden change": Quincy Wright, *A Study of War* (Chicago: University of Chicago Press, 1942), p. 257; also see pp. 387–92.

[11] Waltz has recently both noted this error and acknowledged that he made it earlier: Waltz, "Emerging Structure," p. 45. Also see Jack Levy, "The Polarity of the System and International Stability: An Empirical Analysis," in Alan Ned Sabrosky, ed., *Polarity and War: The Changing Structure of International Conflict* (Boulder, Colo.: Westview, 1985), pp. 43–45; R. Harrison Wagner, "The Theory of Games and the Balance of Power," *World Politics* 38 (July 1986), pp. 546–47; Emerson Niou, Peter Ordeshook, and Gregory Rose, *The Balance of Power: Stability in International Systems* (New York: Cambridge University Press, 1989). For a related issue in ecology, see Putman and Wratten, *Principles of Ecology*, pp. 349–50.

as stabilizing it, even though one could indeed make such an argument, and in the Cold War the connection between peace and stability was even tighter. But definitions that seek to help us understand at least three hundred years of history should not be skewed by the most obvious features of the current era.

At first glance, Herz's formulation seems acceptable because it includes not only peacefulness, but also the speed and consequences of changes. But these may not go together. Change can be peaceful without being slow and gradual, as the events in East Europe in 1989 remind us, and peaceful changes can be "far-reaching in impact." One example, which also shows that even if wars could be equated with instability, peace could not be equated with stability, is the model of regional integration. Ernst Haas and others have shown that relatively small steps toward regional integration can have "spillover effects" that lead to more integration, which in turn introduces even more problems, opportunities, and pressures that lead to still more integration. The system then will be radically transformed, but the process is both peaceful and gradual.[12]

Other scholars use definitions that are related to peace. To Richard Rosecrance, "an international system is conceived to be stable if its outcomes fall within limits generally 'accepted' by the major participants in the system," and for Robert Gilpin, "a stable system is one in which changes can take place if they do not threaten the vital interests of the dominant states and thereby cause a war among them."[13] But these definitions conflate instability with its causes, or at least with the causes of war. It is reasonable (although not necessarily correct) to argue that states are likely to fight when their vital interests are at stake or when the outcomes will be unacceptable if they do not resist. But it is not helpful to transform these propositions into a definition.

Deutsch and Singer avoid some of these pitfalls, but dig a new one:

> Stability may . . . be considered from the vantage point of both the total system and the individual states comprising it. From the broader, or systemic, point of view, we shall define stability as the probability that the system retains all of its essential characteristics; that no single nation becomes dominant; that most of its members continue to survive; and that large-scale war does not occur. And from the more limited perspective of the individual nations, stability would refer to the

---

[12] Ernst Haas, *The Uniting of Europe* (Stanford, Calif.: Stanford University Press, 1958). For further discussion, see chapter 4, below.

[13] Richard Rosecrance, *Action and Reaction in World Politics* (Boston: Little, Brown, 1963), p. 231; Robert Gilpin, "The Theory of Hegemonic War," in Robert Rotberg and Theodore Rabb, eds., *The Origin and Prevention of Major Wars* (New York: Cambridge University Press, 1988), p. 16. For similar views, see Henry Kissinger, *A World Restored* (New York: Grosset and Dunlap, 1964), p. 5, and Hoffmann, "International Systems and International Law," p. 208.

probability of their continued political independence and territorial integrity without any significant probability of becoming engaged in a "war for survival."[14]

But it is not clear whether it is useful to define stability from the standpoint
of individual actors. One can easily imagine a system in which individual
units did not last long—some dying, others replacing them—while the international configuration is retained.[15] For Deutsch and Singer, such a system would be unstable from the vantage point of units and stable from the
vantage point of the system. But why not just say that it is stable although
the actors are insecure and unhappy?

It may be better to turn to the classic definition of stability in terms of the
operation of negative feedback. In the words of Ross Ashby, the theorist of
biology and cybernetics who influenced many early social science systems
theorists, "Every stable system has the property that if displaced from a state
of equilibrium and released, the subsequent movement is so matched to the
initial displacement that the system is brought back to the initial state of
equilibrium."[16] Similarly, for Brian Barry and others, "A system is called
'homeostatic' if it contains mechanisms capable of changing its performance
so as to keep a certain variable or certain variables within some limits."[17]
The example most often given is a thermostat: If the temperature in a house
exceeds established boundaries, sensors signal the heating or cooling mechanism to turn on until the temperature reaches the opposite boundary.
Waltz argues that this is a poor analogy to the international system because it
is hierarchical—i.e., one portion of the system (the heating or cooling mechanism) controls the rest.[18] But this difference may be less important than
the basic idea that a system is stable if it is characterized by negative feedback that keeps essential variables within prescribed limits and is unstable if

[14] Karl Deutsch and J. David Singer, "Multipolar Power Systems and International Stability," *World Politics* 16 (April 1964), pp. 390–91. They stress the probabilistic nature of this
concept of political stability, but it does not play a central role in their argument and so it will be
put aside here.

[15] Waltz argues that this description frequently characterizes international politics: *Theory
of International Politics*, p. 162.

[16] W. Ross Ashby, *Design for a Brain*, 2d ed. (London: Chapman & Hall, 1960), p. 54, also
see pp. 48–49, 80–99, 171–75, 205–14. More recent complexity theorists also draw on Ashby:
See, for example, Stuart Kauffman, *The Origins of Order: Self-Organization and Selection in
Evolution* (New York: Oxford University Press, 1993). The mechanisms by which animals main-
tain their bodies are not limited to feedbacks: For a good discussion see Aaron Wildavsky,
Searching for Safety (New Brunswick, N.J.: Transaction, 1988), chapter 7.

[17] Brian Barry, *Sociologists, Economists and Democracy* (Chicago: University of Chicago
Press, 1978), pp. 169–70. Also see Ernest Nagel, *Logic Without Metaphysics* (Glencoe, Ill.:
Free Press, 1956), pp. 247–83.

[18] Waltz, *Theory of International Relations*, pp. 56–57. Social scientists are not of one mind
on whether the concept of feedback applies when control is absent: George Richardson, *Feedback Thought in Social Sciences and Systems Theory* (College Station: University of Pennsylvania Press, 1991), chapter 3.

a change in one direction sets off positive feedback—i.e., is self-reinforcing by calling up forces that produce further motion in the same direction, as in the model of regional integration mentioned earlier.

Thinking about stability in terms of the ability of a system to contain disturbances shows that stability and durability are not the same, although Waltz's claim that multipolarity is less stable than bipolarity needs to confront the fact that the former lasted for three hundred years.[19] A system could be stable and short-lived if it had the bad luck to be quickly confronted by a large or unusual shock.[20] Conversely, a system could last a long time, not because it was stable, but because it happened to exist during propitious times. But talking of exogenous shocks has some difficulties in international politics since the policies of the states can both challenge and determine the stability of the system. Thus threats to stability may have been rare during the Cold War because the superpowers deterred each other. Indeed, the actors' behavior often is influenced by their beliefs about the systems' stability. Similarly, while negative feedback is usually equated with mechanisms that insulate the organism from its environment, for example as a warm-blooded animal keeps its temperature within a narrow range despite wide variations in the weather, it is not clear what the international system's environment is. In some cases, we can think of technical and perhaps transnational social change as being outside the system and disturbing it. But such forces operate mainly through the policies of states. This means that we could conceive of a system's environment as being the states that compose it. This reverses the normal approach and so seems strange, yet it might prove helpful.[21]

Perhaps we could judge stability by the relative ease with which one system could be transformed into another. Thus we could ask whether a bipolar system is more likely to become multipolar than a multipolar system is to become bipolar, assuming similar disturbances. But this assumption may be conceptually troublesome because the kinds of disturbances that are likely to arise may not be unrelated to the system's polarity. It may be more than hindsight that leads to the conclusion that bipolar systems are particularly vulnerable to transformation through the collapse of a superpower. Not only is the competition severe under bipolarity, but other states have neither the

---

[19] Waltz says that the international system is stable if "it remains anarchic . . . [and] no consequential variation takes place in the number of principal parties that constitute the system" (*Theory of International Politics*, pp. 161–61). But this lacks the dynamic system-maintaining element and so is better called durability (ibid., p. 135; also see pp. 172–73, 176–77). Furthermore, by this definition the pre-1914 system was stable, although war prone.

[20] For an example, see Paul Schroeder, "The Lost Intermediaries: The Impact of 1870 on the International System," *International History Review* 6 (February 1984), pp. 20–22.

[21] Waltz disagrees and criticizes Kaplan for a similar suggestion: *Theory of International Politics*, p. 54.

incentives to provide support should a superpower weaken nor the strength to replace it.

Other difficulties appear when we try to determine the identities and boundaries of the essential variables. For Waltz, there is a new system only when the polarity changes. For Rosecrance, the system changes whenever the configuration of power alters significantly.[22] The theoretical question is what aspects of the system should be considered vital. Do rapid and large changes in the power of individual states constitute instability? Do we have a new system when established diplomatic practices fall out of favor or new areas are considered permissible targets of state activity, for example when it is believed that states can legitimately object to human rights violations in other nations? Should we consider the essential variables of the system to include the actors' conceptions of self-interest and the structure of the pay-offs for cooperating with others? If so, then the balance of power and the concert are different systems.[23] Obviously, there are no objectively correct answers here. Rather the question is what conceptions of the defining characteristics of systems are most useful.

In the next chaper I will discuss the positive and negative feedbacks that are powerful drivers of systems. But here I will stay closer to the formulation used in most of the literature being reviewed and consider a system as un-stable if its dynamics make it prone to experience changes—especially wars—that are so large that they will alter such basic characteristics as the number, arrangement, and goals of the states that in turn affect many pat-terns of behavior.

Both Dependent and Independent Variables Systemic

The work of J. David Singer and his colleagues in the Correlates of War project looks to the system for both the dependent variables (stability in the form the incidence of war) and the independent variables (alliance aggrega-

---

[22] Rosecrance, *Action and Reaction*. Also see Michael Haas, *International Conflict* (Indi-anapolis: Bobbs-Merrill, 1974). For Kaplan's approach to this problem, see *System and Process*, chapter 2; for Hoffmann's, see "International Systems and International Law," pp. 206–9. Stu-dents of ecology have found that what is necessary to maintain the viability of specific species may not be the same as what is required to maintain the stability of the broader system: Joe Alper, "Everglades Rebound from Andrew," *Science* 257 (September 25, 1992), pp. 1852–54. An understanding of human interaction patterns stresses that stability often resides not in the content of the exchanges but in how they are generated: Paul Watzlawick, Janet Beavin, and Don Jackson, *Pragmatics of Human Communication: A Study of Interactional Patterns, Pa-thologies, and Paradoxes* (New York: Norton, 1967), chapter 5.

[23] See Jervis, "Security Regimes," *International Organization* 36 (Spring 1982), pp. 357–78, and Jervis, "From Balance to Concert: A Study of International Security Cooperation," *World Politics* 38 (October 1985), pp. 58–79.

tion and the concentration of power).[24] Evaluating this project would be a digression and only four points are necessary here, the first three of which are familiar. First, the work is primarily inductive; theorizing takes a backseat to the attempt to mine the data. Second, as the project's name indicates, the results are correlations without great concern for whether they also represent causation. Third, the way the variables are measured often produces codings that are at variance with what contemporary observers see and creates divergences between the way we normally conceive of concepts and how they are captured in the studies.[25]

Partly as a result of the first two problems, a fourth one is created: We cannot rule out the possibility that the correlations on the systemic level are spurious and that the more important independent (and possibly dependent) variables reside within the units. A correlation between high aggregation of alliances or polarization on the one hand and a high level of war on the other might mean not that highly polarized systems are war prone, but rather that both polarization and war are produced by a high degree of aggressiveness on the part of particular states or by high conflict of interest between pairs of states. Similarly, if we find that cross-cutting alliances correlate with a relatively peaceful international system, the former variable may not be doing much independent work: Both it and the lack of armed conflict may reflect the absence of issues that sharply divide countries.

System as the Dependent Variable

In other theories, only the effect is at the systems level. Thus despite Richard Rosecrance's discussion of the presence or absence of regulators of international conflict, for him the main determinant of the system's stability is the security of elites. Waltz calls this analysis reductionist; it is in its focus on independent variables, but not in its concern with systemic effects.[26]

Aron and Hoffmann see different unit-level causes as central to stability. More interestingly in the context of this book, their reasoning is not systemic. This does not mean that it is invalid, but examining it in some detail and explicating the differences between it and Waltz's mode of analysis will help us understand what systems theory is all about. Aron and Hoffmann argue that heterogeneous systems tend to be unstable while homogeneous ones tend to be stable. Because the former consist of actors of very different types—i.e., differing in their internal compositions, conceptions of proper

[24] For a review of this literature, see David Dessler, "Beyond Correlations: Toward a Causal Theory of War," *International Studies Quarterly* 35 (September 1991), pp. 337–55.

[25] See, for example, William Wohlforth, "The Perception of Power: Russia in the Pre-1914 Balance," *World Politics* 39 (April 1987), pp. 353–81.

[26] Rosecrance, *Action and Reaction*; Waltz, *Theory of International Politics*, pp. 41–43.

international conduct, and visions of the future—the actors' inability to find common ground means that they are likely to destroy themselves. The most obvious example is the international system of the 1930s, composed of liberal democracies, fascist regimes, and a Bolshevik Soviet Union. Homogeneous systems are composed of units alike in crucial domestic characteristics and usually are moderate in their international politics because understandings and compromises are possible and any wars that result from the limited disagreements will remain regulated.[27]

This argument is plausible, although scholars have not attempted to verify it. When states are founded on very different principles, not only are they likely to seek to spread their values, but the very existence of dissimilar states makes them insecure by casting doubt on their legitimacy.[28] Heterogeneity also creates misunderstandings and inhibits bargains that would be in the states' common interests. For example, World War II might have been avoided had the democracies and the USSR been able to form a common front, as they should have if balance of power considerations had dominated.

There are three problems with this line of argument, however. First, it may be too systemic: It is not clear whether it is really the heterogeneity of the system as opposed to the nature of particular regimes that produces the instability. A system composed entirely of Nazi states would have been homogeneous but I doubt if conflict would have been limited. The other side of the coin is that Fascist Italy, the communist Soviet Union, and Western democracies might have produced a fairly moderate international system in the absence of Hitler.

Second, the argument is antisystemic in the core claim for the importance of heterogeneity.[29] Waltz argues that differences in ideologies and founding principles, although striking, rarely generate system-affecting international behavior.[30] The failure of the USSR and the Western democracies to work together before the war was unfortunate but easily explicable in systemic terms because each state was seeking to make others pay the price for op-

[27] Raymond Aron, *Peace and War*, translated by Richard Howard and Annette Baker Fox (Garden City, N.Y.: Doubleday, 1966), pp. 99–124, 373–403; Hoffmann, "International Systems and International Law," pp. 207–9. Also see Henry Kissinger, "Domestic Structure and Foreign Policy," *Daedalus*, Spring 1966, pp. 503–6. For Waltz's critique of Aron and Hoffmann, see *Theory of International Politics*, pp. 43–49.

[28] In a parallel argument, Henry Kissinger perceptively notes that revolutionary states are prone to disturb the system not so much because they seek expansion as because they cannot be reassured: *A World Restored*, pp. 2–3; also see Stephen Walt, *Revolution and War* (Ithaca, N.Y.: Cornell University Press, 1996).

[29] The fact that the argument is unsystemic does not make it incorrect. In fact, there is much to be said for it, at least as far as the Cold War is concerned: see pp. 103–04 below for discussion in the context of the level of analysis question.

[30] Waltz, *Theory of International Politics*, pp. 127–28.

posing Hitler. Indeed, relations between the Western democracies and the USSR were not so different from those among the former. Britain and France had great frictions and could not collaborate; attempts to involve the U.S. in the common effort worked no better than the attempts to draw in the USSR; Chamberlain's private remarks about the U.S. were almost as bitter as those about the Soviet Union. Furthermore, although Hitler's ambitions were extreme and his motivations bizarre, it can be argued that his foreign policy was not particularly Hitlerian or Nazi; it was just German.[31] Revanchism was to be expected of any country that had been deprived of territory but not of its power. A Waltzian would not have been surprised when the opening of the private papers of Gustav Stresemann, the leading statesman of the Weimar era, revealed that, far from being a "good European," he was bent on overthrowing the Versailles regime.[32] Thus even had the system remained homogeneous, it might not have been moderate.

It is even harder to credit the conflicts before 1914 to the heterogeneity of the system. Indeed, it is far from clear whether the pre-1914 system was heterogeneous.[33] Although empires, republics, and aristocracies coexisted, foreign policies and disputes were not primarily caused by differences in founding principles. Perhaps domestic similarity helped draw Germany and Austria-Hungary together, but the two countries whose sources of legitimacy were most different from each other—republican France and imperial Russia—allied because of external pressures. The European system in the late eighteenth century was even more clearly homogeneous and yet was riven by wars so destructive that they might have led to revolutionary changes even in the absence of the French Revolution.[34]

Most importantly, the Aron-Hoffmann position is unsystemic in the links it posits between the level of conflict and the existence of a revolutionary or a moderate international system. As I discussed earlier, in analyzing a system, additive operations are inappropriate. Yet addition is the logic of the Aron-Hoffmann argument: If the conflicts among the states are high, the system cannot be moderate. As a student of Morton Kaplan says: "A system of merely growth-seeking actors would obviously be unstable; there would be no provision for balancing or restraint."[35] But this is not correct. Or, to put it more precisely, if one can determine the stability of the system by

[31] A. J. P. Taylor, *The Origins of the Second World War* (New York: Atheneum, 1961).

[32] Manfred Enssle, "Stresemann's Diplomacy Fifty Years After Locarno: Some Recent Perspectives," *Historical Journal* 20 (December 1977), pp. 937–48.

[33] Some of the ambiguities are discussed in Aron, *Peace and War*, pp. 101–3.

[34] See Paul Schroeder, *The Transformation of European Politics, 1763–1848* (New York: Oxford University Press, 1994).

[35] Donald Reinken, "Computer Explorations of the 'Balance of Power,'" in Morton Kaplan, ed., *New Approaches to International Relations* (New York: St. Martin's, 1968), p. 469; also see Morton Kaplan, *Towards Professionalism in International Theory* (New York: Free Press, 1979), p. 136.

adding up either the aggressiveness of individual countries or the extent of conflicts between pairs of countries, then we can dispense with systems theories and use simpler modes of analysis.

But usually we are dealing with a system, which means that even if conflict between nations is greater in a heterogeneous system than in a homogeneous one, it does not follow that the former is less stable than the latter. As I will discuss in the next chapter, balance of power theorists argue that even if each state seeks to grow (and so creates conflict), self-interest will lead them to work together to prevent the domination of any would-be hegemon. There may be a high level of violence, but this is the very means by which the system is maintained.

The other side of this coin is that relatively low conflict of interest can lead to large wars and significant changes in the system. In pre-1914 Europe the goals of all the major states were limited. Germany wanted greater prestige and economic penetration of underdeveloped areas; Russia wanted greater influence in the Balkans; Britain, France, and Austria-Hungary sought to maintain their positions; and while France would have liked to regain Alsace and Lorraine, it was not willing to pay a high price to reach this goal.[36] All the states wanted to maintain if not increase their security. But this was the problem. In part because of beliefs about military technology, in part because of the alliance structure (discussed below), and in part because of the expectations of war, the states' foreign policies interacted in a way that led to war. None of the bilateral conflicts or internally generated impulses to expand would have produced a war on this scale; an additive method of analysis is misleading.

System as the Independent Variable

Other theories see the system as the cause and the behavior or characteristics of the state as the effect. Dependency theory is of this type.[37] Although the behavior of the dominant state arises internally, the fates of the weaker peripheral powers are systemically driven. Furthermore, the influence of the international system on these states goes beyond their foreign behavior to their domestic politics and social structures as individuals and classes who are allied with worldwide capitalism gain power and privilege. The nature of these states, then, far from determining the foreign policies followed and

[36] An excellent study of French foreign policy in this period is John F. V. Kreiger, *France and the Origins of the First World War* (London: Macmillan, 1983).

[37] The literature on this subject is enormous. See the summary and critique in Robert Packenham, *The Dependency Movement: Scholarship and Politics in Development Studies* (Cambridge, Mass.: Harvard University Press, 1992). For a general discussion of the impact of the external environment on states' domestic structures and politics, see Peter Gourevitch, "The Second Image Reversed," *International Organizations* 32 (Autumn 1978), pp. 881–912.

the international system that results, is a product of the system and the place of the states in it.

This approach has been subject to vigorous criticism, in part because of its lack of precision. But all that is relevant here is the reply that it underestimates the power and autonomy of even weak states: It is too systemic in its view of the degree to which external forces control the fate of states. Underdeveloped countries do not follow the same policies or develop the same internal structures. Some seek an integrated, although not necessarily compliant, role in the international capitalist system (the NICs), others break away by revolution (Cuba), still others isolate themselves (Myanmar). That a high price may be paid for the latter choices does not mean that states cannot and have not made them.

Waltz

The previous sections of this chapter have illustrated the three types of systems theories, separating them by whether the cause, the effect, or both were at the system level. Because Waltz's work is so influential, I wish to give it more attention, although rather than offering a comprehensive critique I will focus on the aspects that are most relevant to the arguments in this book.

The most basic objection to Waltz and any systems theory is that variables at the system level rarely determine the nature of international politics, let alone the foreign policies of individual states. As Hoffmann puts it: "Nothing is more mistaken than to assume that the international system is a sort of monster with an implacable will of its own, that the variable elements interact so as to determine the outcome, that the participants are dominated by the system in such a way that their moves are either mere responses to its dictates or exercises in irrelevance or self-defeat when they go against the system's logic."[38] Because these levels of analysis issues encompass too much of international politics to be fully treated here,[39] I will select only a few central points. To begin with, although Waltz seeks to explain interna-

---

[38] Stanley Hoffmann, *Gulliver's Troubles, or the Setting of American Foreign Policy* (New York: McGraw-Hill, 1968), p. 12; also see p. 32. Thus Hoffmann strongly rejects the argument that intra-European politics will be dangerous in the post–Cold War era because of the system's demands: Hoffmann, "Correspondence," *International Security* 15 (Fall 1990), pp. 191–92. For a similar stance, see Zeev Maoz, *National Choices and International Processes* (Cambridge: Cambridge University Press, 1990), pp. 547–65. Note, however, that Waltz argues for the importance, not of the international system in general, but of its structure (see below, pp. 107–10).

[39] For further discussion, see Robert Jervis, *Perception and Misperception in International Politics* (Princeton, N.J.: Princeton University Press, 1976), pp. 13–28.

tional outcomes, not states' foreign policies,[40] it is not clear exactly how much and what kind of variation of state behavior is compatible with his ideas. There certainly would be difficulties if crucial states did not recognize their place in the structure—for example, if the U.S. had failed to understand that it was a superpower after World War II and decided that it did not need to counterbalance the Soviet Union. Indeed, it can be argued that an isolationist triumph after 1945 was far from inconceivable—and Waltz replies that the very fact that the U.S. broke with its traditions and assumed worldwide responsibilities in the face of strong domestic opposition shows the power of systemic imperatives.[41]

An alternative reductionist approach to this case brings up the related general question of the role of states' domestic systems: Would bipolarity have produced anything like the Cold War had the Soviet Union been a democracy or Britain and France been dictatorships?[42] Much of Stalin's grasping but self-defeating policies and the American reaction to them can be explained by the nature of the Soviet regime.[43] Similarly, is it an accident that the Cold War ended only after revolutionary change within one of the superpowers?[44] Waltz denies consistent and powerful connections between the characteristics of the units and the dominant international outcomes and stresses the continuity of international politics as long as structure remains the same. His critics see more variability and change, much of it stemming from domestic sources.

Waltz argues that the international system directs state behavior through socialization and natural selection, which reinforce each other: statesmen learn because they see the misfortunes of those who do not conform.[45] A

[40] Waltz, *Theory of International Politics*, pp. 48–49, 78, 87, 121–23; Waltz, "Reflections," pp. 327–28, 343.

[41] Waltz, *Theory of International Politics*, p. 125.

[42] For discussions of relations among democracies, see, for example, Michael Doyle, "Kant, Liberal Legacies, and Foreign Affairs," parts 1 and 2, *Philosophy and Public Affairs* 12 (Summer and Fall 1983), pp. 205–35, 323–53; Doyle, "Liberalism and World Politics," *American Political Science Review* 80 (December 1986), pp. 1151–61; Bruce Russett et al., *Grasping the Democratic Peace: Principles for a Post–Cold War World* (Princeton, N.J.: Princeton University Press, 1993); William Dixon, "Democracy and the Peaceful Settlement of International Conflict," *American Political Science Review* 88 (March 1994), pp. 14–32; John Owen, *Liberal Peace, Liberal War: Ideology, Institutions, and Democratic Foreign Policy* (Ithaca, N.Y.: Cornell University Press, forthcoming); Spencer Weart, *Never at War: Why Democracies Will Not Fight One Another* (New Haven, Conn.: Yale University Press, forthcoming).

[43] William Taubman, *Stalin's American Policy* (New York: Norton, 1982); John Lewis Gaddis, *The Long Peace* (New York: Oxford University Press, 1987), pp. 34–6; Thomas Patterson, *Meeting the Communist Threat* (New York: Oxford University Press, 1988), chapter 1.

[44] Indeed, Waltz notes that "structural change begins in a system's unit" ("Emerging Structure," p. 49), although he seems to have in mind its power more than its ideology.

[45] Waltz, *Theory of International Politics*, pp. 74–77, 92, 118–19, 127–28; for discussions of natural selection in other fields of social science see, for example, Herbert Simon, *The Sciences*

new regime may initially make drastic alterations in the state's foreign policy, but if it is to survive, let alone thrive, it will have to return to the normal pattern.[46] For example, contrary to their ideology, the Bolsheviks soon donned frock coats and followed a foreign policy that was difficult to distinguish from their czarist predecessors. Rapallo, the Soviet-German military cooperation, and the alliance of World War II typified the effects of the pressure of common enemies on antipathetical states; the Nazi-Soviet pact resembles the partitions of Poland in the late eighteenth and early nineteenth centuries; during the Cold War American and Soviet "actions were similar."[47] These patterns are not expected by reductionist accounts.

But one may entertain doubts as to how easily internally driven states are tamed. The Comintern was more than a minor adjunct to Soviet diplomacy and, in conjunction with the communist ideology and domestic system, was one reason for the bad relations between the USSR and the West. Revolutionary France was eventually socialized, but not before a generation of wars had changed the face of domestic and international politics alike.[48] Hitler could not be socialized; he had to be destroyed. Even after Khomeini's death, Iran's deviationist behavior, while not affecting the structure of the system, continues to affect its relations with the U.S. and the pattern of regional politics.

For Waltz, states that are not socialized pay the penalty of "falling by the wayside."[49] But is this correct? At the time of Waltz's writing, few modern nations had died.[50] Although it is not fanciful to attribute the subsequent breakup of the USSR, if not of Yugoslavia and Czechoslovakia, to the failure to meet the international competition, in general it is hard to see much natural selection working in this way. More potent is falling by the wayside

---

of the Artificial, 2d ed. (Cambridge, Mass.: MIT Press, 1981), pp. 52–56; Douglass North, Institutions, Institutional Change, and Economic Performance (New York: Cambridge University Press, 1990), pp. 18–22; Richard Nelson and Sidney Winter, An Evolutionary Theory of Economic Change (Cambridge, Mass.: Harvard University Press, 1982). For a good discussion of the relationships between theories that stress rationality and those that rely on natural selection, see Barry Schwartz, The Battle for Human Nature (New York: Norton, 1986).

[46] For conflicting views on the ease and speed with which revolutionary regimes are socialized, see David Armstrong, Revolution and World Order: The Revolutionary State in International Society (New York: Oxford University Press, 1993), and Walt, Revolution and War.

[47] Waltz, "Emerging Structure," p. 47; also see Waltz, Theory of International Politics, pp. 127–28.

[48] The wars following the French Revolution were partly caused by the interplay of domestic politics in France and its adversaries and the latter's misreading of the significance of events within France. See Kyung-Won Kim, Revolution and International System (New York: New York University Press, 1970). For a general treatment, see Walt, Revolution and War.

[49] Waltz, Theory of International Politics, pp. 71, 91, 118–19.

[50] Waltz so notes: ibid., pp. 95, 137; "Reflections," pp. 330–31. Of course most of the states that currently exist were formed out of smaller units, but it is not clear that Waltz's theory seeks to account for this process.

in the sense not of physical extinction, but of loss of power and influence. As Stalin put it: "Those who lag behind are beaten."[51] Certainly, over time individual states have risen and fallen. Two questions need to be asked, however. The first involves something of a value judgment and may not be central to Waltz's argument. Sweden is no longer a great power, but in what sense is this a failure? Swedish citizens, if not the abstraction of the Swedish state, probably are better off for this. They are rich and have been spared several wars. Similarly, postwar Japan was shorn of its empire and armed forces and is no longer a complete great power. But it is hard to say that the country and its citizens are the poorer for this loss of role and status. Sitting on the sidelines, although only possible under special circumstances of geography and the interests of other important states, can be a fine place to watch (and benefit) as the great power parade goes by.

The second question goes more directly to Waltz's theory: Is the fall of great powers to be explained by their failure to conform to the imperatives of their external environments? Many books have been written on the rise and fall of nations,[52] and readers should not expect much of an answer here. In many cases foreign policy errors are at least in part responsible for decline as the state collects too many obligations, clients, and enemies. What Kennedy calls "imperial overstretch" is not the product of rash or revolutionary states, however. These policies are followed by mature states and cannot be explained by a lack of socialization; indeed, if Kennedy is correct, these states decline *because* they are responding to systemic pressures. By contrast, Jack Snyder points to domestic politics as causing excessive expansion. Log-rolling coalitions allow each faction to pursue its goals at the expense of the best interests of the country as a whole. Furthermore, coalitional dynamics encourage fears and hopes that support belligerence and discourage learning about the effects of the state's policies.[53] Although tracing overexpansion to domestic sources is inconsistent with Waltz's perspective, the fact that these domestically generated policies are foolish and eventually fail supports Waltz.

But in fact faulty foreign policy usually is a less important cause of great powers' decline than is slow economic growth. Perhaps in some cases this can be attributed to the state's role in the international system. As Stein has shown, even though a hegemon will gain from an open economic system, others will gain even more, thereby undermining the hegemon's domi-

---

[51] Quoted in Isaac Deutscher, *Stalin* (New York: Oxford University Press, 1949), p. 328.

[52] See, for example, Robert Gilpin, *War and Change in World Politics* (New York: Cambridge University Press, 1981); Paul Kennedy, *The Rise and Fall of the Great Powers: Economic Change and Military Conflict from 1500 to 2000* (New York: Random House, 1987). Most of the numerous rebuttals to Kennedy have focused on whether and why America is declining rather than on his more general argument.

[53] Jack Snyder, *Myths of Empire* (Ithaca, N.Y.: Cornell University Press, 1991).

nance.[54] But most of the sources of economic growth and decline are internal, even if they are hard to determine (and harder to change). Countries seem to go through cycles of faster and slower growth as infrastructure and behavior that served the country well at one point inhibit growth at later stages, dominant industries obsolesce, consumption squeezes out investment, and self-indulgence if not decadence takes hold. Thus it is hard to attribute most of Great Britain's decline to the international system, let alone to Britain's inability or unwillingness to conform to the rules of proper international behavior. German and American growth was facilitated by England's helpful economic hegemony, but these countries would have developed rapidly in any event. While Britain was weakened by the need to defend imperial commitments and fight two world wars, these burdens only accelerated Britain's decline because the difference in growth rates would have eroded its position in time without them.

In summary, it is only partly correct to argue that states are socialized by the international system, that those who behave discrepantly "fall by the wayside," and therefore that domestic characteristics can be put aside. Few states are eliminated, some gain in many important ways by sacrificing their great power status, and the rise and fall of leading states cannot be understood apart from the internal sources of economic growth.

Waltz's Concept of Structure

For Waltz, the crucial independent variable is the structure of the system: "how [units] stand in relation to one another (how they are arranged or positioned)."[55] Because all international systems are anarchical, the units cannot afford to engage in a division of labor and so structure is determined by the distribution of power among the units, particularly whether the system is bipolar or multipolar.[56] This definition of structure is an austere one.

---

[54] Arthur Stein, "The Hegemon's Dilemma: Great Britain, the United States, and the International Economic Order," *International Organization* 38 (Spring 1984), pp. 355–86.

[55] Waltz, *Theory of International Politics*, p. 80; for a defense of this conception, see Waltz, "Reflections," pp. 323–30, and Waltz, "Realist Thought and Neorealist Theory," *Journal of International Affairs* 44 (Spring/Summer 1990), pp. 30–32; also see Robert Powell, "Anarchy in International Theory: The Neorealist-Neoliberal Debate," *International Organization* 48 (Spring 1994), pp. 321–26. For other claims for the importance of structure, defined in somewhat different ways, see Theda Skocpol, *States and Social Revolutions* (New York: Cambridge University Press, 1979); Ronald Burt, *Structural Holes: The Social Structure of Competition* (Cambridge, Mass.: Harvard University Press, 1992); John Maynard Smith, *Did Darwin Get It Right? Essays on Games, Sex, and Evolution* (New York: Chapman & Hall, 1989), part 5.

[56] One might also agree with Waltz that the crucial element in a system's structure is the distribution of power but argue that, contrary to his position, power cannot be treated as unitary. These arguments raise three major theoretical and empirical issues which are not

Waltz has chosen it to rigorously separate systemic from unit attributes. But the cost is to leave little space for factors of considerable explanatory power. First, many have argued that Waltz's dichotomy between hierarchical and anarchical systems is excessively simplified.[57] While the international system lacks a sovereign, we should neither exaggerate the role of superordinate authority in domestic society nor assume that hierarchy is the only way a system can be nonanarchically ordered. To a significant extent, states may form an anarchical *society*, with many shared values, principles, norms, and practices. Indeed, rather than conceiving of the states and the international system as separate levels and taking the existence of states for granted, theories should recognize that the latter are actually brought into being by the standing and legitimacy given them by other actors and the system they constitute. We may then require "structurationist ontologies [which will] replace the 'dualism' of agency and social structure that pervades individualist and collectivist ontologies with a perspective that recognizes the 'codetermined irreducibility' of these two fundamental units of social analysis."[58] These issues are complex and important, but I will be content merely to flag them because they not only have been discussed at length (although often without much clarity) but also are peripheral to the systems dynamics of concern here. Indeed, my approach, being strongly interactionalist, shares some of the structurationist perspective.[59]

Another line of objection to Waltz's conception of structure also is not central here. For Waltz, the second dimension of structure—differentiation among the units—can be ignored: Because the international system is anarchical and states must be prepared for war with one another, there can be little international division of labor, which means that the states must resemble one another in crucial ways. Some scholars have noted that this analysis

---

central here and so only need to be noted. First, how do we characterize countries that are economically strong, yet militarily weak (Japan today) or states for which the reverse is true (Prussia in the eighteenth century)? Second, is world politics composed of "issue-areas" which are separate from each other? These questions in part turn on a third one: the fungibility of power—i.e., the extent to which the same resources can be deployed across a range of issues. If power is completely fungible, then Waltz's approach is appropriate; if it is not fungible at all, then one could apply a Waltzian analysis to each issue area, but could not characterize the system as a whole.

[57] See John Ruggie's review of Waltz, "Continuity and Transformation in World Polity: Toward a Neorealist Synthesis," *World Politics* 35 (January 1983), pp. 261–85; Daniel Deudney, "The Philadelphian System: Sovereignty, Arms Control, and Balance of Power in the American States-Union, 1787–1861," *International Organization* 49 (Spring 1995), pp. 191–228.

[58] Alexander Wendt and Raymond Duvall, "Institutions and International Order," in Ernst Otto Czempiel and James Rosenau, eds., *Global Changes and Theoretical Challenges* (Lexington, Mass.: Lexington Books, 1989), p. 59.

[59] In fact, where Waltz draws heavily on Watzlawick, Beavin, and Jackson, *Pragmatics of Human Communication*, his approach is not so different: *Theory of International Politics*, pp. 74, 78.

assumes the kind of states that have existed since the treaty of Westphalia. When we look back to the medieval world, and perhaps ahead to the "post-modern" era, we find conceptions of sovereignty and internal structures that are neither similar to today's nor uniform, which shows that this second dimension can meaningfully take on different states—i.e., that it is a variable, not a constant.[60] But even if this argument is correct, it does not dispute the utility of Waltz's notion of structure in explaining modern international politics.

A third line of objection is that Waltz's structure leaves no room for variables and arrangements that are important but are neither at the level of the unit nor the system.[61] It is not clear how we are to categorize such factors as technology, including the damage states can do to one another; the balance between offensive and defensive postures; widely shared empirical and normative beliefs; the degree and kind of international interdependence and institutionalization; whether the situation is more or less conducive to cooperation; and the extent and type of prevailing nationalisms, which can tear some units apart, weld others together, lead to an elevated sense of honor, and invest value in what otherwise would be trivial areas and disputes.[62] In many eras there are one or two dominant lines of cleavage produced by geography, previous wars, or differences in religion or ideology. These, too, are neither systemic (in Waltz's sense) nor unit-level characteristics. Yet they provide much of the explanation not only for individual states' foreign policies, but also for such outcomes as the ease with which states can change alliance partners, the height of the barriers to cooperation, and whether or not the system becomes divided into two camps. Thus for many purposes it

[60] Ruggie, "Continuity and Transformation"; Ruggie, "International Structure and International Transformation: Space, Time, and Method," in Czempiel and Rosenau, eds., *Global Changes*, pp. 21–35; and Waltz's reply in "Reflections," pp. 323–30. Also see Barry Buzan, Charles Jones, and Richard Little, *The Logic of Anarchy: Neorealism to Structural Realism* (New York: Columbia University Press, 1993).

[61] I am indebted to Arthur Stein and Glenn Snyder for discussions on this point. See Stein, *Why Nations Cooperate* (Ithaca, N.Y.: Cornell University Press, 1990), and Snyder, "Process Variables in Neorealist Theory," *Security Studies* 5 (Spring 1996), pp. 167–92; and *Alliance Politics* (Ithaca, N.Y.: Cornell University Press, forthcoming). Also see Buzan, Jones, and Little, *Logic of Anarchy*, section 1; Keohane and Nye, *Power and Interdependence*; Kaplan, *System and Process*, part 2; Edward Mansfield, *Power, Trade, and War* (Princeton, N.J.: Princeton University Press, 1994); Maoz, *National Choices*. For Waltz's reply, see "Realist Thought and Neorealist Theory," pp. 29–32, 37.

[62] See, for example, Jervis, "Cooperation Under the Security Dilemma"; Stephen Van Evera, *Causes of War* (Ithaca, N.Y.: Cornell University Press, forthcoming); Ted Hopf, "Polarity, the Offense-Defense Balance, and War," *American Political Science Review* 85 (June 1991), pp. 475–95; Thomas Christensen and Jack Snyder, "Chain Gangs and Passed Bucks: Predicting Alliance Patterns in Multipolarity," *International Organization* 44 (Spring 1990), pp. 137–68. Hoffmann considers some of these variables to be systemic: "International Systems and International Law," pp. 207–8.

may be appropriate to sacrifice some parsimony in order to develop a level of analysis for variables that fit between structural and unit characteristics.

Even if state behavior and the shape of the system are driven by the external environment, the structure of the system (aside from its anarchy) may not be central. Traditionally, states have been seen as billiard balls, to borrow Arnold Wolfers' analogy, their behavior being determined not by their internal composition, but by the forces they exert on one another.[63] This analysis is not structural, however: Polarity is not the main independent variable and attention is centered on detailed aspects of the state's external environment rather than on its place in the system. Indeed, this focus can reveal the limits of structural analysis. Thus elsewhere I have argued that many of the characteristics of the Cold War—high defense budgets, the militarization of NATO, extreme Sino-American hostility, and global alliance commitments—were products of the Korean War.[64] Bipolarity did not by itself yield much of the behavior that we have come to associate with it. Furthermore, this war was not structurally determined, which means that the hardening of much of the globe into two hostile and well-armed camps cannot be entirely explained by bipolarity. The structure of the system fails to catch a large portion of the external environment that determines patterns of state action.

What Waltz's Theory Can Explain

The main conclusion of Waltz's theory is that bipolar systems are more stable than multipolar ones, being less likely to produce major wars and more likely to manage common problems.[65] There are three reasons for this. Waltz and those who have followed him have paid most attention to the third, and I will do so as well.

First, under bipolarity each superpower knows that the other is the only state that can seriously menace it. In a multipolar system, by contrast, it is

---

[63] Arnold Wolfers, *Discord and Collaboration* (Baltimore, Md.: Johns Hopkins University Press, 1961), p. 19. Also see Kenneth Waltz, *Man, the State and War* (New York: Columbia University Press, 1954).

[64] Robert Jervis, "The Impact of the Korean War on the Cold War," *Journal of Conflict Resolution* 24 (December 1980), pp. 563–92.

[65] For a recent critique, see Dale Copeland, "Neorealism and the Myth of Bipolar Stability," *Security Studies* 5 (Spring 1996), pp. 29–47. For related arguments about the superiority of bipolarity, see John Mearsheimer, "Back to the Future: Instability in Europe After the Cold War," *International Security* 15 (Summer 1990), pp. 13–18, 22–27. The best quantitative studies are Levy, "The Polarity of the System and International Stability," and Mansfield, *Power, Trade, and War*. For summaries of the findings, see John Vasquez, *The War Puzzle* (New York: Cambridge University Press, 1993), pp. 249–55, 343–44, and Patrick James, "Structural Realism and the Causes of War," *Mershon International Studies Review* 39 (October 1995), pp. 181–208.

hard for each state to determine which of the others is the greatest threat because they are roughly the same size.[66] Thus for a number of years after World War I, Britain worried more about France than about Germany and saw the increasing power of the latter as helping balance against the potential French threat. Aggressors may then be able to make major accretions of power before the defenders of the status quo see that they must react. When the system is bipolar this cannot happen: Because each superpower knows that the other is a potential if not an actual threat, it will guard against the other making gains anywhere. Dean Acheson was able to persuade senators to overcome their isolationist sympathies and provide aid to Europe in 1947 by explaining that "only two great powers remained in the world. . . . For the United States to . . . strengthen countries threatened with Soviet aggression or Communist subversion . . . was to protect the security of the United States."[67] As Waltz notes in a related context, Truman and his colleagues "could not very well echo Neville Chamberlain's words in the Czechoslovakian crisis by claiming that [any menaced country was inhabitated by] a people far away . . . of whom Americans knew nothing."[68] Although later shown to be incorrect, Chamberlain's analysis could not be dismissed in a multipolar world.

Second and relatedly, under bipolarity each superpower knows that it cannot evade its responsibility for keeping the peace in the expectation that others will take up the slack. Containing or defeating the aggressor is partly a collective good: Everyone desires and will benefit from this outcome, but the costs of producing it are borne separately by each nation. When there are many of them, the collective good may not be obtained as several try to "free ride." This was one reason why four coalitions dissolved before the fifth one finally defeated Napoleon and why throughout the 1930s Great Britain felt that it could put most of the burden of blocking Hitler on France.[69] But superpowers cannot shirk. They must move to contain the

[66] Deutsch and Singer make the opposite and I think less plausible argument: Multipolarity is more stable in part because under this condition each state must divide its attention among the others, thereby reducing the chance that it will see any of them as sufficiently menacing to merit going to war ("Multipolar Power Systems and International Stability"). Deutsch and Singer also endorse Morgenthau's argument that the lack of certainty of alignments in multipolarity makes war less likely (Hans Morgenthau, *Politics Among Nations*, 5th ed., revised [New York: Knopf, 1978], p. 350). It is sometimes argued that Waltz's position turns entirely on his claim that certainty decreases the chances of war: See, for example, Bruce Bueno de Mesquita, "Towards a Scientific Understanding of International Conflict: A Personal View," *International Studies Quarterly*, 29 (June 1985), pp. 130–32. But this ignores the third path that Waltz sees as producing wars in multipolar systems, discussed below.

[67] Quoted in Joseph Jones, *The Fifteen Weeks* (New York: Viking, 1955), p. 141.

[68] Waltz, *Theory of International Politics*, p. 170.

[69] For a typically stimulating, perverse, and yet disturbingly persuasive argument that the conventional wisdom about the causes of the successes and failures of the coalitions is the opposite of the truth, see Paul Schroeder, "Old Wine in New Bottles: Recent Contributions to

adversary whenever and wherever it seeks to expand. Furthermore, the adversary understands this, thus dimming its hopes for significant conquests.

I want to discuss the third difference between bipolarity and multipolarity in more detail because it brings up important systems dynamics. Under bipolarity, superpowers do not need allies because they have sufficient resources so that they can rely on "internal balancing"—the acquisition of arms through domestic building programs.[70] Under multipolarity, by contrast, states are militarily dependent on one another because none can defend itself alone. The need for allies in turn creates dangerous obligations: Great powers may have to fight not because they have direct conflicts of interest but because the alternative is to endanger their security by losing a necessary partner to defeat or defection.

STRUCTURAL VERSUS BEHAVIORAL POLARITY

Waltz's argument is best appreciated against the background of what had been previously believed about polarity and its links to war. Most theorists had defined polarity behaviorally; that is, the number of poles was determined by the number of groupings of states.[71] A system characterized by two tight alliances was seen as bipolar because there were two groups of states, each of which could be considered to be an actor because the states within it acted together. Thus the pre–World War I period was bipolar because the major states were in either the Triple Alliance or the Triple Entente.[72] When scholars who conceived of bipolarity in this way asked whether the Cold War era was stable (and for many this was the main point of looking at earlier periods), they projected onto it the dynamics of the pre–World War I system. "The balance of forces is still approximate, equivocal,

British Foreign Policy and European International Politics, 1789–1848," *Journal of British Studies* 26 (January 1987), pp. 1–25. For an explanation of the circumstances under which states try to pass the buck under multipolarity and when they feel they must support allies, see Christensen and Snyder, "Passed Bucks and Chain Gangs." Randall Schweller has argued that in the 1930s Britain did not pass the buck, but instead operated on the belief that even an Anglo-French coalition lacked the power to defeat Hitler: "Tripolarity and the Second World War," *International Studies Quarterly* 37 (March 1993), pp. 73–104.

[70] Waltz, *Theory of International Politics*, p. 168. Morgenthau noted this characteristic of bipolarity but failed to develop its significance: *Power Among Nations*, p. 351. This argument raises the question of why superpowers sometimes intervene on behalf of their smaller allies and, indeed, why there are any alliances at all. For discussion, see below, pp. 118–22.

[71] See, for example, Aron, *Peace and War*; Hoffmann, "International Law and International Systems"; Deutsch and Singer, "Multipolar Power Systems and International Stability"; Rosecrance, *Action and Reaction in World Politics*; Bruce Bueno de Mesquita, "Measuring Systemic Polarity," *Journal of Conflict Resolution* 19 (June 1975), pp. 187–216. Scholars working with quantitative data often label as polarization what I call behavioral polarity.

[72] The position of Italy, formally a member of the Triple Alliance but actually opportunistically nonaligned, will be put aside here.

[and] continually threatened . . . by a secondary unit changing camp," argued Raymond Aron.[73] John Herz agreed:

> The more rigid the alignments, the greater the sensitivity regarding any changes or threats of changes of the existing line-up. Such sensitivity endangers world peace over the most minute of issues or incidents. . . . [The] more rigid the balance is, the greater the danger that, in the absence of countershifts and realignments, such events may sooner or later lead to that imbalance in which the more powerful can either destroy the opponent or blackmail him into submission.[74]

For Hoffmann, the members of NATO and the Warsaw Pact were like members of a chain gang walking along a ridge—if one slipped off (i.e., followed an aggressive policy or went to war), the others would be forced to follow.[75]

By conceiving of polarity in structural terms, Waltz showed that this view of the Cold War was badly misleading: What is crucial is the number of the great powers, and the system is bipolar if there are only two of them, multipolar if there are more. Indeed, this explains why the kind of instability that characterized the pre-1914 world did not operate during the Cold War. Before World War I, the system was multipolar because there were five or six (if one counts Italy) great powers. The fact that the states formed two alliances did not make it bipolar because the alliances would act as unified entities only as long as the members so chose. Furthermore, since the two camps were of roughly equal power, the defection of any state to the other side, or even to a position of neutrality, would undermine the security of its former partners.

While the common analysis of instability does not apply to structural bipolarity, it does describe the configuration before World War I. The reason is not that the division of the world into two camps created dangerously rigid alignments,[76] but that each state had to fear that its allies might defect if it did not support them. As Waltz puts it, "Flexibility of alignment made for rigidity of strategy."[77] To take a small example, the British government even

---

[73] Aron, *Peace and War*, p. 159; ten pages earlier Aron asserted that the superpowers could not be dragged into war because the system "covers the planet" in contrast to what was the case when Athens and Sparta were rivals, but he did not explain his reasoning: Aron, *Peace and War*, p. 149.

[74] John Herz, *International Politics in the Atomic Age* (New York: Columbia University Press, 1959), pp. 155–56; also see pp. 240–41. Also see Robert Tucker, *The Purposes of American Power* (New York: Praeger, 1981), p. 144.

[75] The image comes from Hoffmann, *Gulliver's Troubles*, chapter 3.

[76] Morgenthau, *Power among Nations*, pp. 213–14, 349–50; A. J. P. Taylor, *The Struggle for Mastery in Europe, 1848–1918* (London: Oxford University Press, 1954), chapter 22; Henry Kissinger, *Diplomacy* (New York: Simon and Schuster, 1994), pp. 182, 194 (his discussion on p. 199 is closer to the truth).

[77] Waltz, *Theory of International Politics*, p. 169. Dependence on allies also helps explain

rejected the German invitation to a military band for fear of offending France.[78]

The influence of allies was clear in July 1914.[79] As the crisis deepened, many British and French decision-makers lost interest in the merits of the issue and even in German motives and intentions. For Britain, Serbia was not worth a war—indeed, it wasn't for France—but because it was for Russia, Britain had to fight or lose a vital ally (Britain would lose two if France stood by Russia and Britain did not). The British ambassador to Russia feared that "we shall have to choose between giving Russia our active support or renouncing her friendship. If we fail her now we cannot hope to maintain that friendly co-operation with her in Asia that is of such vital importance to us."[80] Earlier in the crisis, the permanent under secretary of the Foreign Office put a restrained yet ominous annotation on a cable describing the Russian position: "Russia is a formidable Power and will become increasingly strong. Let us hope our relations with her continue to be friendly."[81] Similarly, on August 2, when Germany and Russia were at war

---

the failure to end the war through a negotiated peace: see, for example, L. L. Farrar, Jr., *Divide and Conquer: German Efforts to Conclude a Separate Peace, 1914–1918* (Boulder, Colo.: East European Quarterly, 1978); David Stevenson, *The First World War and International Politics* (New York: Oxford University Press, 1988); Z. A. B. Zeman, *The Gentlemen Negotiators: A Diplomatic History of World War I* (New York: Macmillan, 1971). Similarly, Winston Churchill and others argued for a military strategy based on defeating Germany by knocking its allies out of the war. But note that states will not be tied to allies if the defense has the advantage: Christensen and Snyder, "Chain Gangs and Passed Bucks."

[78] George Monger, *The End of Isolation* (London: Nelson and Sons, 1963), pp. 328–29. For discussion of similar German deference to Austria, see R. J. Crampton, *The Hollow Detente: Anglo-German Relations in the Balkans, 1911–1914* (Atlantic Highlands, N.J.: Humanities Press, 1980) and Snyder, *Alliance Politics*, chapter 8.

[79] The course of the crisis was also influenced by the fact that while statesmen understood that they were dependent on their allies, they did not realize that their adversaries were as well. Thus each hoped—and sometimes expected—that it could split the opposing alliance. For why some allies had more bargaining leverage than others, see chapter 5 below, pp. 197–204.

[80] G. P. Gooch and Harold Temperley, eds., *British Documents on the Origins of the War, 1898–1914*, vol. 11, *The Outbreak of War* (London: Her Majesty's Stationery Office, 1926), p. 94. For a similar remark by the permanent under secretary, see ibid., p. 157.

In a memorandum to the foreign secretary, Eyre Crowe reached the same conclusion on somewhat different grounds: "It is clear that France and Russia are decided to accept the challenge thrown out to them. Whatever we may think of the merits of the Austrian charges against Serbia, France, and Russia consider that these are the pretexts, and that the bigger cause of Triple Alliance versus Triple *Entente* is definitely engaged" (ibid., p. 81). Later in the crisis he wrote the foreign secretary: "The whole policy of the *entente* can have no meaning if it does not signify that in a just quarrel England would stand by her friends. This honourable expectation has been raised. We cannot repudiate it without exposing our good name to grave criticism" (ibid., p. 229). Honor both personal and national was a concern of many British statesmen, but they thought that British interest also required intervention. I suspect that the latter belief drove the former, but reverse or mutual causation is possible as well.

[81] Ibid., p. 53.

and the czar asked the British ambassador to transmit an official message asking that Britain join, the ambassador added his own views: "I would venture to submit with all respect that if we do not respond to [the czar's] appeal for our support, we shall at end of the war, whatever be its issue, find ourselves without a friend in Europe, while our Indian Empire will no longer be secure from attack by Russia."[82]

As the ambassador's comment indicates, Britain's perceived dependence on its allies meant that if it stayed out of the war any outcome would be menacing. If Germany won, it would dominate the continent and control the Belgian and French coasts; if there were a negotiated settlement, it would probably be at Britain's expense; if Britain's former allies won, Crowe asked, "What would then be their attitude towards England? What about India and the Mediterranean?"[83]

The situation is very different under bipolarity. Because the distribution of power cannot be much changed by their actions, the superpowers' allies lose their ability to influence their larger partners. One of the most striking features of the Cold War was that allies could come and go without major disturbance. Although the U.S. opposed the Chinese revolution and consequent change of alignment, it devoted few resources to the effort.[84] In part the reason was that Truman and his colleagues realized that China could be a bottomless pit and hoped that the new regime would remain friendly. But they also understood that even a hostile China would not endanger American security. While in later years Soviet statesmen exaggerated the threat posed by China and some American leaders entertained excessive hopes for the benefits of better Sino-American relations, the second shift in China's alignment disturbed the international system no more than did the first. France's defection from the military arrangements in NATO had an even smaller impact on anything other than French pride, and France's covert return to coordinated nuclear targeting with the U.S.[85] similarly had no discernable impact on international politics. Even more striking was the Soviet willingness to free East Europe in 1989. What is less important here

[82] Ibid., p. 277. Note, however, that these were the views of statesmen and Foreign Office officials. Many politicians and large segments of the public were not persuaded that these considerations required joining the war; indeed, Britain might not have fought had Germany not invaded Belgium.

[83] Ibid., p. 82. As Zara Steiner points out, "No one considered that a war without British participation might have weakened both sides, thereby preserving Britain's world position at little cost to the mother country": "Foreign Office Views of Germany and the Great War," in R. J. Bullen, H. Pogge von Strandmann, and A. B. Polonsky, eds., *Ideas Into Policy: Aspects of European History, 1880–1950* (London: Croom Helm, 1984), p. 40.

[84] The best analytic survey is Ernest May, *The Truman Administration and China, 1945–1949* (Philadelphia: Lippincott, 1975).

[85] Richard Ullman, "The Covert French Connection," *Foreign Policy*, no. 75 (Summer 1989), pp. 3–33.

than the fact that Gorbachev failed to foresee the consequences of his pressure on his allies to liberalize was his willingness to accept the loss of the USSR's protective glacis. Bipolarity (and nuclear weapons) meant that allies were not required for the USSR to protect itself, at least from foreign attack.

Because it hardly matters if allies defect under bipolarity, they gain little by threatening to do so. The Soviets let the Sino-Soviet dispute widen rather than give China ideological satisfaction, continue to assist her nuclear program, or make symbolic concessions along the Sino-Soviet border; the U.S. refused de Gaulle's demand for a greater say in NATO policy, even though the French position was not unreasonable. Unlike the leading states before 1914, the superpowers refused to allow their partners to draw them into unwanted conflicts. The U.S. bullied its closest allies during the Suez crisis, considered making concessions over Berlin that would have infuriated West Germany, and might well have agreed to promise publicly to remove the missiles from Turkey in October 1962 if this had been needed to end the crisis.[86] Only luck—whether good or bad can still be debated—and Soviet errors prevented Reagan and Gorbachev from striking a revolutionary arms control agreement at Reykjavik without consulting their allies. America's European allies feared both that they could not restrain American recklessness and that the U.S. might form a condominium with the Soviet Union at their expense.[87] Although neither of these nightmares came true, the Europeans were not paranoid: They had little bargaining leverage with which to safeguard their interests.

[86] The explanation for why the U.S. opposed its allies at Suez lies in part in the desire to gain influence in the Third World, an impulse that Waltzian theory finds puzzling: See below, pp. 120–22. For Berlin, see McGeorge Bundy, *Danger and Survival* (New York: Random House, 1988), pp. 427–39; Kissinger, *Diplomacy*, chapter 23; Marc Trachtenberg, *History and Strategy* (Princeton, N.J.: Princeton University Press, 1990), chapter 5; William Burr, "Avoiding the Slippery Slope: The Eisenhower Administration and the Berlin Crisis, November 1958–January 1959," *Diplomatic History* 18 (Spring 1994), pp. 177–207. For Cuba, see McGeorge Bundy, transcriber, and James Blight, editor, "October 27, 1962: Transcripts of the Meeting of the ExComm," *International Security* 12 (Winter 1987/88), pp. 30–92; James Blight, Joseph Nye, Jr., and David Welch, "The Cuban Missile Crisis Revisited," *Foreign Affairs* 66 (Fall 1987), p. 179; also see Mark White, "Dean Rusk's Revelation: New British Evidence on the Cordier Ploy," *The SHAFR Newsletter* 25 (September 1994), pp. 1–9. For the argument that neither the extent of the European allies' influence nor the processes involved are consistent with Waltz, see Thomas Risse-Kappen, *Cooperation Among Democracies: The European Influence on U.S. Foreign Policy* (Princeton, N.J.: Princeton University Press, 1995). For the less-studied cases in which the allies lacked influence, see Frank Costigliola, "Kennedy, the European Allies, and the Failure to Consult," *Political Science Quarterly* 110 (Spring 1995), pp. 103–23, and Arthur Combs, "The Path Not Taken: The British Alternative to U.S. Policy in Vietnam, 1954–1956," *Diplomatic History* 19 (Winter 1995), pp. 33–57.

[87] Michael Mandelbaum, *The Nuclear Revolution: International Politics Before and After Hiroshima* (New York: Cambridge University Press, 1981), pp. 151–52; Snyder, "The Security Dilemma in Alliance Politics"; Snyder, "Alliance Theory."

There is another side to this coin, however: Bipolarity permits small states the freedom to be irresponsible and exploit their superpower patrons because the common defense against the other side is, to a significant extent, a collective good. Since the small partners cannot contribute much to the alliance's military strength, they can enjoy the advantages of saving money by "free riding" on the efforts of their larger partner.[88] The same argument applies to the use of nuclear threats during the Cold War. The decision to fire nuclear weapons rested in American hands, and there was little the West Europeans could do to increase the credibility of the NATO nuclear threat.[89] So it is not surprising that the U.S. took tougher positions than did its allies, who could gain from the American posture and reap a larger portion of the benefits of détente without endangering their security.[90] France could similarly safely pursue a policy of status and pride which called for demonstrating its independence from the U.S.

In summary, once we follow Waltz and Snyder in defining bipolarity structurally rather than behaviorally, we can see that the apparent similarity between the pre–World War I era and the Cold War is only superficial and we can trace the way structure influences both national behavior and systemic stability. Polarity affects the bargaining power that states have, the restraints that bind them, and the opportunities that they enjoy. Under bipolarity each superpower knows that only the other can menace it, realizes that it cannot pass the buck to third parties, and, because it can balance accretions to the other's power by mobilizing its own resources, needs not fear the consequences of one of its allies defecting. This eliminates three

---

[88] Mancur Olson and Richard Zeckhauser, "An Economic Theory of Alliances," *Review of Economics and Statistics* 48 (August 1966), pp. 266–79; Snyder and Diesing, *Conflict Among Nations*, pp. 442–45; Snyder, "Alliance Theory," pp. 120–22. The theory is relatively clear; the empirical evidence is much less so: for summaries of the more recent arguments and findings, see John Oneal and Mark Elrod, "NATO Burden Sharing and the Forces of Change," *International Studies Quarterly* 33 (December 1989), pp. 435–56, and Todd Sandler, "The Economic Theory of Alliances: A Survey," *Journal of Conflict Resolution* 37 (September 1993), pp. 446–83. The growth of what he perceived as allied exploitation of the U.S. was one of the phenomena that led Adam Ulam to state, in one of his typically provocative and undocumented assertions, that "1950 marked the beginning of the end of the bipolar world which had emerged from the war": *The Rivals* (New York: Viking, 1971), p. 155. Superpower alliances can also produce public goods in areas other than security: see Mark Boyer, *International Cooperation and Public Goods: Opportunities for the Western Alliance* (Baltimore, Md.: Johns Hopkins University Press, 1993).

[89] I am putting aside the chance that Britain or France might use their own nuclear weapons. In point of fact, these independent nuclear forces cannot be disposed of so easily, although almost all American analysis during the Cold War ignored them: see Jervis, *The Illogic of American Nuclear Strategy* (Ithaca, N.Y.: Cornell University Press, 1984), pp. 101–2.

[90] A good discussion for the 1977–1982 period can be found in Jay Speakman, "Continuity of Discord: Responses of the Western Allies to the Soviet Invasion of Afghanistan" (unpublished dissertation, Department of Political Science, Columbia University, 1994).

common paths to major war: the first two operated in the 1930s and the third was in part responsible for World War I.[91]

Bipolarity and Stability: Ignoring the Peripheries and Overreacting to Them

These arguments are powerful, but they contain an important contradiction. One strand of Waltz's theory explains that bipolar worlds are peaceful because the superpowers rely on internal balancing and so can ignore allied quarrels that could drag them into war. But a second strand attributes stability to each superpower's knowledge that because there are only two of them, each must seek to block the other throughout the world.[92] Either argument is plausible, but they do not fit well together. If the superpowers cannot be manipulated by allies because they can safeguard their security without assistance, then they do not have to meet all attempts by the adversary to expand.

Furthermore, even as the first logic explains why allies had relatively little influence during the Cold War, it raises the question of why the bipolar world has alliances at all. If the dominant powers could afford to see China and France slip away, why did they develop ties to them in the first place?[93] If the logic of bipolarity was vindicated by Gorbachev's liberation of East Europe, why did his predecessors need to dominate those countries for more than forty years? If we accept Waltz's argument that the superpowers are self-reliant, then the American propensity to intervene in the Third World no longer can be seen as the natural consequence of bipolarity and instead needs to be explained.[94] Here Waltz faces a problem that is generic to Realism. In arguing that the international environment compels certain lines of behavior, these theories are both descriptive and prescriptive, which means that actions that do not conform embarrass the theory as well as harm the country. Thus while Hans Morgenthau's states must follow the dictates

[91] For a slightly different argument about the dangers of multipolarity, see Mearsheimer, "Back to the Future," pp. 14–15.

[92] Although the second strand is most fully developed in an earlier article (Waltz, "The Stability of a Bipolar World," *Daedalus* 93 [Summer 1964], pp. 881–909), it appears in *Theory of International Politics* as well (pp. 170–71).

[93] For a similar line of inquiry, see R. Harrison Wagner, "What Was Bipolarity?" *International Organization* 47 (Winter 1993), pp. 88–96. James McAllister points to the need for and efficacy of external balancing in the early Cold War years: "Alternative Worlds: America, the German Question, and the Origins of Bipolarity" (unpublished Ph.D. dissertation, Department of Political Science, Columbia University, 1997).

[94] Earlier writers also noted that while an abstract analysis of bipolarity and nuclear weapons indicated that superpowers did not need to intervene, "the fact remains that political realities do not conform to, and show no real prospect of conforming to, the results suggested by this analysis" (Robert Osgood and Robert Tucker, *Force, Order, and Justice* [Baltimore: Johns Hopkins University Press, 1967], p. 279).

of their national interests, his theories were developed in part out of his frustration that his adoptive country was not doing so.[95]

Morgenthau did not try to reconcile aberrant behavior with his theory; Waltz does. Ignoring the strand of his argument that sees intervention as natural and stabilizing, he declares it to be an "over-reaction," which he explains reductionistically by domestic politics and failures of statesmanship.[96] But there are alternative accounts that are more consistent with the rest of his analysis. One argues that until the mid-1960s the world was not fully bipolar because the U.S. in fact depended on its allies for military support. Before the deployment of B-52s and ICBMs, overseas bases were necessities; without them, American bombers simply could not reach the Soviet Union.[97] Furthermore, in this period the outcome of World War III was seen as turning not only on nuclear strikes, but also on large-scale conventional warfare in which armies and factories would be crucial. While the U.S. was by far the strongest state in the alliance, only hard-core isolationists doubted that American security required keeping Europe out of Soviet hands.[98] As the Eisenhower administration's initial security policy review put it:

> The U.S. now depends on its overseas alliances for an important, perhaps critical, part of its military capability. Hypothetical gains of freedom of action [produced by isolationism] would become meaningless.
>
> No line was found which would exclude any large areas as not absolutely vital to U.S. security, while not discarding the overseas military bases which are so very important for the present, and without handing large industrial resources to the Soviet Union.[99]

A year later John Foster Dulles replied to NSC members who thought that the U.S. was paying excessive deference to its allies by pointing out that

> No single country, not even the United States, could, out of its own resources, adequately match the strength of a powerful totalitarian state. We were in no

[95] Perhaps the change in emphasis in Waltz's thinking from his article "The Stability of a Bipolar World" to his book also needs to be explained prescriptively. By the time he started *Theory of International Politics*, Waltz had come to be a strong opponent of the war in Vietnam: Waltz, "The Politics of Peace," *International Studies Quarterly* 11 (September 1967), pp. 199–211. He could reconcile this position with his theoretical stance only by declaring that such wars were unnecessary under bipolarity. Or, to reverse the causation, the insight that structural bipolarity rendered the fate of Vietnam irrelevant to American security may have led Waltz to oppose the war.

[96] *Theory of International Politics*, pp. 172–73.

[97] I am indebted to James McAllister for reminding me that the American bomber bases were in Great Britain and North Africa, not Continental Europe, however.

[98] The best general account is Melvyn Leffler, *A Preponderance of Power* (Stanford, Calif.: Stanford University Press, 1992).

[99] U.S. Department of State, *Foreign Relations of the United States, 1952–1954*, vol. 2, *National Security Affairs* (Washington, D.C.: Government Printing Office, 1984), part 1, pp. 413–14.

position to extract from our people what tyrannical rulers could extract from their people. The attempt to do so would "bust us." Accordingly, the only way the free world could hope to maintain sufficient strength so that each of its members did not "go broke," was the pooling of resources.[100]

But these calculations cannot explain either the American commitment to Europe in later periods or the American (and Soviet) attention to the Third World at any point. Here a second argument makes more sense: While neither superpower needed to intervene in third areas in order to maintain its security, there were other reasons to do so. Indeed, the very fact that a superpower can protect itself means that it is free not only to abstain from conflicts throughout the world, but also to pursue them if it believes that important *nonsecurity* values are at stake. Bipolarity gave the superpowers a measure of independence and extra power that they could use as they saw fit. Seen in this light, interventions embarrass Waltz's theory only if they seriously undermined the superpower's security, an outcome that does not seem compatible with the theory.

Because the structure of the system renders systemic imperatives irrelevant, any number of impulses can lead to intervention. In some cases, domestic politics or bureaucratic links may lead the superpower to protect a smaller ally.[101] In other cases, intervention could bring economic rewards far greater than the costs. A parallel, and I think more powerful, argument sees the forces behind intervention as ideological. Either side could support a desired domestic system in a third country even if the security implications were negligible. A related motivation—really saying the same thing differently—is altruism: Each side could believe that its way of life was superior and want others to enjoy it. As Osgood and Tucker point out, "Nations—and particularly great nations—have never equated their survival with physical survival and show little inclination to do so today. . . . [The roots of interventionism] must be found largely in the expansiveness with which men continue to view the collective self and the 'necessities' of this self."[102] Indeed, Waltz notes that "great power gives its possessors a big

[100] Ibid., p. 452. There is an element of circularity here: the war that would require allied support would only occur if the USSR attacked countries the U.S. was committed to protect. But since American leaders believed—quite possibly incorrectly—that its long-term survival depended on keeping West Europe out of Soviet control, the cooperation of these states was required. By 1958 Dulles had changed his position about the importance of Europe, but Eisenhower had not: Burr, "Avoiding the Slippery Slope," pp. 180–81. For a good discussion of the Eisenhower administration's fears, especially of developments in the Third World, see Robert McMahon, "The Illusion of Vulnerability: American Reassessments of the Soviet Threat, 1955–1956," *International History Review* 18 (August 1996), pp. 591–619.

[101] Robert Keohane, "The Big Influence of Small Allies," *Foreign Policy*, no. 2 (Spring 1971), pp. 161–82.

[102] Osgood and Tucker, *Force, Order, and Justice*, p. 280. Also see Jervis, *The Logic of Images in International Relations*, 2d ed. (New York: Columbia University Press, 1989),

stake in [the] system and the ability to act for its sake" and "for the good of other people."[103]

A third line of argument links intervention more closely to the structure of the system in a way that is partly, but only partly, consistent with Waltz. While it is true that what happens in third countries cannot directly menace either superpower, one cannot neglect the indirect and delayed effects which indeed constituted the main rationale—or rationalization—for many American interventions, most notably in Vietnam: Defeat would lead other dominoes to fall, endangering the American position in Europe as well as Asia. The Soviet Union may have had its version of the domino theory, rooted primarily in ideology and domestic politics. For any Communist state to "go capitalist" would have been to cast doubt on the premise that Communism was the wave of the future; for any ally to liberalize or move toward the West would have been to set a precedent for others; for any ruling Communist Party to have lost control would have been to undermine the others, and perhaps to have called into question the legitimacy of the CPSU, as in fact happened after 1989.

Waltz denies the validity of the domino theory and argues that negative rather than positive feedback, balancing rather than bandwagoning, is the dominant dynamic in international politics.[104] What is relevant here is that two mechanisms make domino dynamics more powerful in bipolar than in multipolar systems. First, the relative weakness of third states makes them less likely to balance against the threatening superpower. While for Waltz and his followers this cannot explain superpower intervention because domino effects could sweep the Third World without much impact on American security,[105] a second argument cannot be rebutted in this way. During the Cold War what was at stake in conflicts on the periphery was not physical or material power, but each superpower's image of the other, and particularly

---

pp. 248–49, and George Quester, *American Foreign Policy: The Lost Consensus* (New York: Praeger, 1982).

[103] Waltz, *Theory of International Politics*, pp. 195, 200.

[104] Waltz, *Theory of International Politics*; Stephen Walt, *The Origins of Alliances* (Ithaca, N.Y.: Cornell University Press, 1987); Robert Jervis and Jack Snyder, eds., *Dominoes and Bandwagons: Strategic Beliefs and Great Power Competition in the Eurasian Rimland* (New York: Oxford University Press, 1991). Feedbacks in general and balancing and bandwagoning in particular are the subjects of the next chapter. As I will discuss there, much evidence indicates that balancing is the norm. But the superpowers did not believe this, with the result that small states gained greater leverage than the treatment in Waltz (and here) would suggest.

[105] Waltz, *Theory of International Politics*, pp. 170–76; also see Jervis, *Logic of Images*, pp. 244–50; Stephen Van Evera, "Why Europe Matters, Why the Third World Doesn't," *Journal of Strategic Studies* 13 (June 1990), pp. 1–51; Eric Nordlinger, "America's Strategic Immunity: The Basis of a National Security Strategy," in Robert Jervis and Seweryn Bialer, eds., *Soviet-American Relations After the Cold War* (Durham, N.C.: Duke University Press, 1991), pp. 239–61; Nordlinger, *Isolationism Reconfigured: American Foreign Policy for a New Century* (Princeton, N.J.: Princeton University Press, 1995).

of its resolve. Under bipolarity any dispute becomes a test of wills as the superpowers fear that a failure to prevail will lead others to draw far-reaching inferences about their future behavior. The very fact that so little of intrinsic value is at stake means that each side's behavior reveals its general willingness to pay costs and run risks. In multipolarity, by contrast, there are many axes of conflict and states intervene in local disputes primarily because of the intrinsic interests at stake. Reputational considerations then are secondary as attention is diffused and audiences are multiple.[106]

But even if reputation is more important under bipolarity, intervention remains troublesome for Waltz's theory, highlighting as it does the contradiction between the two strands of his argument about why bipolar systems are stable. It also leads us to look for other variables that could be as important as structure or could interact with it, a topic to which we will now turn.

Structure and Nuclear Weapons

Nuclear weapons are the other new element in post-1945 international politics, and their role provides the obvious alternative to Waltz's argument for bipolarity as the reason why the superpowers remained at peace.[107] They not only made war so clearly destructive that the superpowers knew that their survival depended on avoiding it, but also rendered allies unnecessary for their security—if not detrimental to it—thus mimicking one of the main advantages of bipolarity. The relevant questions can be raised, although not fully answered, by imagining four worlds produced by the two variables of

[106] I have discussed the implications of the reduced role of reputation in a multipolar system for post–Cold War American foreign policy in "What Does the U.S. Want to Deter and How Can It Deter It?" in L. Benjamin Ederington and Michael Mazarr, eds., *Turning Point: The Gulf War and U.S. Military Strategy* (Boulder, Colo.: Westview Press, 1994), pp. 128–31.

[107] For discussions of the role of nuclear weapons in keeping the peace after 1945, see Gaddis, *The Long Peace*, chapter 1; John Mueller, "The Essential Irrelevence of Nuclear Weapons: Stability in the Postwar World," *International Security* 13 (Fall 1988), pp. 55–79; Robert Jervis, "The Political Effects of Nuclear Weapons," ibid., pp. 80–90; Jervis, *Meaning of the Nuclear Revolution*, chapter 1; Glenn Snyder, "The Balance of Power and the Balance of Terror," in Paul Seabury, ed., *The Balance of Power* (San Francisco: Chandler, 1965), pp. 184–201; Benjamin Miller, *When Opponents Cooperate: Great Power Conflict and Collaboration in World Politics* (Ann Arbor: University of Michigan Press, 1995), chapter 3. Waltz's more recent writings place greater stress on the importance of nuclear weapons: "The Origins of War in Neorealist Theory," pp. 624–27, and "Nuclear Myths and Political Realities," *American Political Science Review* 84 (September 1990), pp. 731–46. One of the first to point out that nuclear weapons made allies dispensable and rendered much of geopolitics obsolete was William Borden, *There Will Be No Time* (New York: Macmillan, 1946), especially pp. 160–64. This is noteworthy especially because the thrust of Borden's argument was that in other respects nuclear weapons were like large conventional explosives, a view that underpinned American military strategy during most of the Cold War.

System Structure

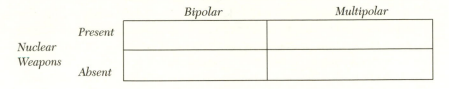

		Bipolar	Multipolar
Nuclear Weapons	Present		
	Absent		

polarity and the presence and absence of nuclear weapons, as shown in the accompanying table.

A bipolar but non-nuclear world would display the stabilizing characteristic of independence from allies discussed in the previous section.[108] Furthermore, because the two protagonists would be large and relatively evenly matched, a war between them probably would be long and bloody. With the costs of fighting so high, a deterrent relationship very much like that produced by nuclear weapons might hold. But this would not be automatic because offense-dominant technology could permit a quick victory, as statesmen believed in 1914, in which case the system could be war prone.[109]

Most American scholars and statesmen doubt that nuclear weapons would stabilize a multipolar system (assuming that without them multipolarity is destabilizing). The most persuasive case to the contrary is made by Waltz, who argues that because second-strike capability makes wars prohibitively costly, pairs of regional rivals would have to stay at peace once they acquired significant nuclear stockpiles.[110] But this would seem to contradict Waltz's thesis that polarity, not nuclear weapons, is central.[111] Although one could reconcile the two positions by arguing that by acquiring nuclear weapons local rivals would recapitulate Soviet-American bipolarity, this applies the concept of structure to parts of the system rather than to its entirety. Furthermore, stressing the role of weapons in determining polarity

[108] It is not clear that such a world has ever existed. We often talk about Athens and Sparta as bipolar rivals, but in fact they could not dominate the other Greek city-states, which was one reason why they fought, and their war was ended by the intervention of Persia.

[109] This possibility is neglected in Mueller, "Essential Irrelevance."

[110] Kenneth Waltz, *The Spread of Nuclear Weapons: More May Be Better*, Adelphi Papers no. 171 (London: International Institute for Strategic Studies, 1981); also see Waltz, "Emerging Structure," pp. 73–74. For recent arguments see, for example, Scott Sagan and Kenneth Waltz, *The Spread of Nuclear Weapons: A Debate* (New York: Norton, 1995); the articles in *Security Studies* 4 and 5 (Summer and Autumn 1995); and Barry Schneider, "Nuclear Proliferation and Counter-Proliferation: Policy Issues and Debates," *Mershon International Studies Review* 38, Supplement 2 (October 1994), pp. 209–34.

[111] Waltz notes that while proliferation would keep the peace between rival states, it would not replicate bipolarity because it would not deal with the other problems that states have: Waltz, "A Reply," *Security Studies* 4 (Summer 1994), p. 803.

would not fit well with Waltz's argument that power is a composite measure from which various elements cannot readily be separated.[112]

From the perspective of this book, what is most interesting is that the impacts of structure and of nuclear capabilities combine in ways that show the difficulties of concentrating on either alone. In a bipolar system, mutual first-strike capability is dangerous but rare because it is relatively easy for superpowers to gain secure retaliatory forces. But unless rivals are totally isolated from one another, neither of these statements is likely to hold in a world of many nuclear powers. Countries A and B might have first-strike capability vis-à-vis each other but could be deterred by the fear that if they attacked they would be vulnerable to destruction by nuclear powers C or D. Indeed, even if C and D did not attack, any retaliation by B, even if much less than totally destructive, would reduce A's relative power when compared with C and D. Even without retaliation, A's attack might leave it exposed by depleting its arsenal. Thus the fact that countries in a multipolar system must consider many rivals makes first-strike capability much less destabilizing than it would be if the system were bipolar. But multipolarity also makes second-strike capability harder to obtain: *Each* state must have a force sufficiently large and protected to be able to withstand an attack from *all* the others. These interactions both remind us that we are dealing with a system and render judgments about stability more complex than had been believed on the basis of examining polarity and weaponry separately.

I have discussed Waltz's theory at some length not only because it has proved so productive, but also because it is the most truly systemic of our theories of international politics. While this does not mean it is correct, many of its problems arise out of its virtues—lucidity, parsimony, and broad reach. By seeking to describe selected dynamics I hope to avoid some of the problems that Waltz's theory cannot. But it also means that the results will not be a full-blown theory.

[112] *Theory of International Politics*, pp. 130–31.

Four

Feedback

Types of Feedback

Feedbacks are central to the ways systems behave.[1] A change in an element or relationship often alters others, which in turn affect the original one. We then are dealing with cycles in which causation is mutual or circular rather than one-way, as it is in most of our theories. As with the interaction processes discussed earlier, it is difficult for observers to assign responsibility and for actors to break out of reinforcing patterns that seem to come from everywhere and nowhere. The actors' behavior collectively causes and explains itself.

Feedback is positive or self-amplifying (and destabilizing) when a change in one direction sets in motion reinforcing pressures that produce further change in the same direction; negative or dampening (and stabilizing) when the change triggers forces that counteract the initial change and return the system to something like its original position. Were it not for negative feedback, there would be no stability as patterns would not last long enough to permit organized society. Without positive feedback, there could be no change and growth.

[1] The literature on feedbacks in social science is enormous. Important treatments are George Richardson, *Feedback Thought in Social Science and Systems Theory* (College Station: University of Pennsylvania Press, 1991); David Easton, *A Systems Analysis of Political Life* (New York: Wiley, 1965), chapters 23–26; Karl Deutsch, *Nerves of Government* (New York: Free Press, 1962); Arthur Stinchombe, *Constructing Social Theories* (New York: Harcourt, Brace, and World, 1968). For discussions of the concept of stability in ecology, see Stuart Pimm, *The Balance of Nature? Ecolological Issues in the Conservation of Species and Communities* (Chicago: University of Chicago Press, 1991); R. J. Putman and S. D. Wratten, *Principles of Ecology* (Berkeley: University of California Press, 1984), chapter 13. In biology, scholars sometimes use the concept of evolutionary stable strategies (ESS), which are arrangements of organisms or strategies that will successfully resist "invasion" by alternatives: John Maynard Smith, *Evolution and the Theory of Games* (Cambridge: Cambridge University Press, 1982); for an application of interest to political scientists, see Robert Axelrod, *The Evolution of Cooperation* (New York: Basic Books, 1984), chapter 5. Note, however, that a configuration could be stable (either in the sense of constituting an ESS or of exhibiting negative feedback) if it came into existence and yet be a theoretical possibility only because it could not be established. For a discussion of this phenomenon in biology, see Karl Sigmund, *Games of Life: Explorations in Ecology, Evolution, and Behaviour* (New York: Oxford University Press, 1993), pp. 194–95.

Within these categories there are many different processes. This is especially true with positive feedback. Most obviously, when two actors are involved, they may move in either symmetrical or complementary directions.[2] To take cases discussed below, symmetrical change is exemplified by a conflict spiral in which both sides become more heavily armed and more hostile to each other. Complementary change occurs during appeasement as one side grows increasingly strong and assertive while the other becomes weak and subservient at an accelerating pace. Although usually at least two actors are involved, feedback can also occur within an individual. Thus the expression or even the feeling of an emotion can lead to its magnification ("The more I think about it, the angrier I become").

To complicate the basic classification, sometimes positive and negative feedbacks operate simultaneously depending on the perspective from which the situation is examined. For example, arms races exemplify positive feedback, but politically the results may be negative feedback if the competition substitutes for war and prevents either side from dominating. Moves can also set off positive feedback in one geographical area and negative feedback in another. Thus if a regional power coerces its neighbor, other states in the area may follow its lead but an outsider may balance against it.

In other systems, positive feedback can prevail for a period of time only to be replaced by negative feedback, or the sequence can occur in reverse. Indeed, positive feedback must eventually be halted by approaching an asymptote, but in most cases countervailing forces are called up before then. For example, the war in Vietnam undermined the American consensus that had supported not only the initial intervention but also a wide range of containment policies. This crippled the American attempt to prevent other Soviet adventures, with the resulting increase of Soviet activism in the Third World. The new Soviet behavior rebuilt much of the American consensus, however, with the result that negative feedback was apparent but only over a decade. Alternatively, for a time two states can successfully block each other's attempt to gain an upper hand until one of them feels that the heightened competition can no longer be sustained, at which point it will make concessions, which may generate pressures for further retreats. This sequence describes the rise and fall of the Cold War, just as a generalized form of the Vietnam dynamic describes the growth and decline of appeasement.

This means that stimuli that set off positive feedback at one point in time can set off negative feedback at another as the state of the system changes. Ecologists find such patterns as animals change their behavior in response to changes in the proportion of those who follow different strategies and also

[2] For a psychological analysis in these terms, see Paul Watzlawick, Janet Beavin, and Don Jackson, *Pragmatics of Human Communication: A Study of Interactional Patterns, Pathologies, and Paradoxes* (New York: Norton, 1967), pp. 67–72.

see cycles in the rise and fall of predators and prey. As the latter increase, so do the former. But this positive feedback ends as predators grow so numerous that the population of prey crashes, which in turn induces a radical decline in the number of predators.[3]

Related reasons explain the rough cycles in world politics which exhibit positive and negative feedback at different points in their trajectories. The basic point was made by an anonymous commentator in the late sixteenth century:

> Peace makes plentie, plentie makes pride, pride breeds quarrel, and quarrel breeds warre: Warre brings spoile, and spoile povertie, povertie pacience, and pacience peace: So peace brings warre and warre brings peace.[4]

More recently, it has been argued that as states become strong, they expand; that expansion initially increases state strength; but after a certain point the empire becomes inefficient and gains enemies and burdens at a faster rate than resources and so declines if not collapses. Thus expansion initially leads to more expansion (positive feedback); it then generates counterbalancing forces that retard or reverse expansion (negative feedback); in the final stages, retreats undermine the state's power, leading to its collapse and accelerating the growth of another state (positive feedback).

Systems may also exhibit negative feedback when confronted by certain kinds of stimuli, or stimuli that fall within certain bounds, and show positive

---

[3] See, for example, Maynard Smith, *Evolution and the Theory of Games*; Richard Dawkins, *The Selfish Gene* (New York: Oxford University Press, 1976); Sigmund, *Games of Life*. As noted in chapter 1, the cycles are rarely smooth and completely regular, partly because of time lags in the operations of the feedbacks. For a general discussion of dynamics of this type, see Thomas Schelling, *Micromotives and Macrobehavior* (New York: Norton, 1978), chapters 3 and 7; pp. 83–87 provide an insightful discussion of the general role of lags in cycles.

[4] Quoted in Russell Buhite and William Hamel, "War for Peace: The Question of an American Preventive War against the Soviet Union, 1945–1955," *Diplomatic History* 14 (Summer 1990), p. 367. The more recent literature is enormous: See, for example, Paul Kennedy, *The Rise and Fall of the Great Powers: Economic Change and Military Conflict from 1500 to 2000* (New York: Random House, 1987); Robert Gilpin, *War and Change in International Politics* (New York: Cambridge University Press, 1981); Joshua Goldstein, *Long Cycles* (New Haven, Conn.: Yale University Press, 1988). Less dramatic but also important is the product cycle common in the production and export of manufactured goods: Raymond Vernon, "International Investment and International Trade in the Product Cycle," *Quarterly Journal of Economics* 80 (May 1966), pp. 190–207; James Kurth, "The Political Consequences of the Product Cycle," *International Organization* 33 (Winter 1978), pp. 1–34. For cycles in the relations between humans and parasites, see William McNeill, *Plagues and Peoples* (Garden City, N.Y.: Doubleday, 1976), pp. 23–25; for a summary of the literature on cycles of ecology and war in primitive societies, see Andrew Vayda and Roy Rappaport, "Ecology: Cultural and Non-Cultural," in James Clifton, ed., *Introduction to Cultural Anthropology* (Boston: Houghton Mifflin, 1968), pp. 494–97; an earlier account is Elman Service, "The Law of Evolutionary Potential," in Marshall Sahlins and Elman Service, eds., *Evolution and Culture* (Ann Arbor: University of Michigan Press, 1960), pp. 93–122.

feedback for different stimuli or stimuli of a greater magnitude. Richard Rosecrance argues that while the balance of power usually contains the accretion of power by major states, if one of them succeeds in becoming dominant, others will seek to work with rather than against it.[5] Systems may also be stable against some disturbances but not others. For example, under some conditions even small wars could lead to far-reaching changes while steps toward peaceful integration would call up countervailing responses; under other conditions the opposite could be the case. Most "primitive" societies appeared to Westerners to be quite fragile because they disintegrated on contact with the modern world, but they had maintained themselves against the disturbances posed by nature and neighboring tribes.[6] Perhaps the Cold War system was stable against the threat of nuclear war (i.e., a crisis that increased the danger of war called up policies that kept the states at peace) but was unstable in terms of the internal changes generated within the superpowers. Current world politics might exhibit negative feedback against the growth of a hegemon but positive feedback in response to cooperation.

In many cases one change leads to others, but these neither reinforce nor dampen the initial one. They may move the system sideways, so to speak.[7] Weather systems are unstable in this sense; long-run forecasts are impossible because unnoticeable events in one area influence what will happen weeks later halfway around the globe. The dynamics of this "butterfly effect," as it is called, the seemingly directed process of evolution through natural selection, and the operation of most dialectic processes, are alike in displaying feedbacks that are difficult to characterize as positive or negative. In many cases there is a drift in a definite direction as one step leads to the next with the original variable being later influenced by its effects, but no simple labeling is possible. Take, for example, Winston Churchill's description of the changes in British naval technology before World War I:

[5] Richard Rosecrance, "A New Concert of Powers," *Foreign Affairs* 71 (Spring 1991), pp. 64–82. The Germans hoped that a proposed treaty with Russia in 1905 would have been so attractive that not only the smaller European states but even major powers in the opposing alliance would join: Eugene Anderson, *The First Moroccan Crisis* (Hamden, Conn.: Archon Books, 1966), pp. 285–86. For more on this general kind of dynamic, see the discussion of tipping, pp. 150–52 below.

[6] A recent discussion of both the operation and the limits of these processes is Katherine Milton, "Civilization and its Discontents: Amazonian Indians Experience the Thin Wedge of Materialism," *Natural History* 101 (March 1992), pp. 37–42. For a related discussion in ecology, see Putman and Wratten, *Principles of Ecology*, pp. 349–50.

[7] This is true for many of the third level of interactions discussed in chapter 2. Some feedback theorists exclude such processes: see Richardson, *Feedback Thought*. For examples of such feedbacks in ecology, see James Brown, "Complex Ecological Systems," in George Cowan, David Pines, and David Meltzer, eds., *Complexity* (Reading, Mass.: Addison-Wesley, 1994), pp. 426–31.

From the original desire to enlarge the gun we were led on step by step to the Fast Division, and in order to get the Fast Division we were forced to rely for vital units of the Fleet upon oil fuel. This led to the general adoption of oil fuel and to all the provisions which were needed to build up a great oil reserve. This led to enormous expense and to tremendous opposition on the Naval Estimates. . . . Finally we found our way to the Anglo-Persian Oil agreement and contract which . . . has led to the acquisition by the Government of a controlling share in oil properties and interests.[8]

Similarly, the well-known phenomenon by which "policy creates politics"[9] illustrates feedback of a sideways nature. Almost any policy affects the incentives facing actors and often alters the institutions and instruments at their disposal. New groups are also likely to form in response to the changed political environment and the new politics will in turn influence later policies. Although some of these feedbacks are amplifying or dampening, in many other cases they force the policy in a different direction.

Diplomatic interactions can also generate feedbacks that are not simply stabilizing or destabilizing. For example, Paul Schroeder argues that when Japan softened its position in the negotiations with the U.S. in the months before Pearl Harbor, the U.S., rather than reciprocating, stiffened its position and increased its objectives. When the problem that originally preoccupied the U.S.—Japan's alliance with Germany—receded in importance as it became clear that Japan would not stand by its partner, new concerns that were harder for Japan to meet were pressed. The result was to leave the two parties as far apart as they had been when negotiations started.[10] In a sense, the American reaction constituted negative feedback since it maintained the unbridgeable gap between the two countries. But it did not maintain either the international system or Japanese-American relations.

To put this differently, some systems may display negative feedback but find a new equilibrium if certain variables change. Thus Anthony Downs argues that while both political parties will move toward the middle of the ideological spectrum in a competitive system, if the voters' preferences shift, the parties will not maintain their original position but will move to a new center of the spectrum.[11] Brian Barry calls this "a stable equilibrium"—one that "does not entail a move back to the *status quo ante* if the system is disturbed by a change in the exogenous variables," as contrasted with a

[8] Winston Churchill, *The World Crisis*, abridged ed. (New York: Scribner's, 1931), p. 81.

[9] The classic study is E. E. Schattschneider, *Politics, Pressures and the Tariff* (New York: Prentice-Hall, 1935).

[10] Paul Schroeder, *The Axis Alliance and Japanese-American Relations* (Ithaca, N.Y.: Cornell University Press, 1958). The Reagan administration's objectives in Nicaragua in the early 1980s similarly grew more ambitious as the Sandinista regime made concessions in the face of increased pressure.

[11] Anthony Downs, *An Economic Theory of Democracy* (New York: Harper and Row, 1957).

"homeostatic system [in which] the equilibrium position is supposed to be maintained in the face of changes in the environment."[12] Ashby and Kaplan similarly talk of ultrastable systems in which disturbances alter the pattern, which then "settles down" to a new equilibrium.[13] In another manifestation of the third kind of interaction discussed in chapter 2, the system and its environment together produce both change and a new equilibrium.

Debates about Feedbacks

At the heart of many arguments lie differing beliefs—or intuitions—about the feedbacks that are operating. For example, little of the scientific disagreement about the "greenhouse effect" has to do with estimates about the direct consequences of increased levels of carbon dioxide and other greenhouse gases; rather, people dispute the magnitude and direction of the feedbacks. Some scientists expect increases in temperature to set off processes that will magnify the change, for example by reducing the size of glaciers and ice sheets and so increasing the sunlight that is absorbed rather than reflected back into space. Others believe that negative feedback will operate through such paths as increased cloud cover and vegetation.[14]

In politics as well, differences in expectations and policy preferences are often rooted in different beliefs about feedbacks. To take a small-scale example, many of the disputes about the likely outcome of a conventional war in Europe during the Cold War turned on whether the analyst built positive or negative feedback into the model. For some, initial victories would serve as "force multipliers" by disorganizing the other side, thereby bringing further victories. Others believed that the more important effect would have been to stretch the supply lines of the side that won the initial battles, thus slowing its subsequent advance.[15] More central to international politics is

[12] Brian Barry, *Sociologists, Economists and Democracy* (Chicago: University of Chicago Press, 1978), p. 170.

[13] W. Ross Ashby, *Design for a Brain*, 2d ed. (London: Chapman & Hall, 1960), pp. 80–137; Morton Kaplan, *System and Process in International Politics* (New York: Wiley, 1957), p. 20.

[14] See Richard Kerr, "Greenhouse Skeptic Out in the Cold," *Science* 246 (December 1, 1989), pp. 1118–19; Kerr, "Greenhouse Science Survives Skeptics," ibid. 256 (May 1992), pp. 1138–40; D. Raynaud et al., "The Ice Record of Greenhouse Gases," ibid. 259 (February 12, 1993), pp. 926–34; George Woodwell and Fred Mackenzie, eds., *Biotic Feedbacks in the Global Climatic System* (New York: Oxford University Press, 1995). These analyses do not yield clear answers, but if positive feedbacks were set off by small perturbations, the temperature on earth would have been sent to extremes by the changes in solar flux in the past. For arguments about the role of feedbacks in forest fires, see Nancy Langston, *Forest Dreams, Forest Nightmares: The Paradox of Old Growth in the Inland West* (Seattle: University of Washington Press, 1995), pp. 30–33.

[15] Stephen Biddle, "The European Conventional Balance: A Reinterpretation of the Debate," *Survival* 30 (March/April 1988), pp. 99–121.

the dispute between balance of power and the domino theory: whether (or under what conditions) states balance against a threat rather than climbing on the bandwagon of the stronger and growing side. These contrasting dynamics will be the subject of much of this chapter. Positive feedback also is central to the spiral model of international politics, which I will treat more briefly because I have discussed it at length elsewhere.[16]

Balance of Power

Balance of power is the best known, and perhaps the best, theory in international politics, although there is no agreement as to exactly what the theory holds, let alone whether it is valid.[17] What is crucial here is that the theory—or one variant of it known as the "automatic" model—illustrates general principles of systems dynamics, especially negative feedback.

Once we make a few simple and undemanding assumptions, the balance of power explains a number of outcomes that, while familiar, cannot otherwise be readily explained: No state has come to dominate the international system; few wars are total; losers rarely are divided up at the end of the war and indeed are reintegrated into the international system; small states, which do not have the resources to protect themselves, usually survive. There is then a deep form of stability in international politics. Although the fates of individual units rise and fall, states and much of the pattern of their interaction remain. The system is never transformed from an anarchical into a hierarchical one.

These patterns will follow if four assumptions hold. First, there must be several independent units. Second, the units must want to survive. They can seek to expand and indeed many usually will, but at minimum they must want to maintain their independence. Third, any unit must be willing to ally with any other on the basis of calculations of interest, which means that

---

[16] Robert Jervis, *Perception and Misperception in International Politics* (Princeton, N.J.: Princeton University Press, 1976), pp. 62–84.

[17] Still the best comprehensive treatment is Inis Claude, *Power and International Relations* (New York: Random House, 1962). The two views of the balance that I will discuss—one seeing restraint arising from interactions within the system and the other seeing a much greater role for self-restraint—correspond to Claude's "automatic" and "manual" versions of the balance: ibid., pp. 43–45. Most British writers endorse varieties of the "manual" version: See the special issue of the *Review of International Studies* 15 (April, 1989); Carsten Holbraad, *The Concert of Europe: A Study in German and British International Theory, 1815–1914* (London: Longman, 1970). Morgenthau starts his discussion of the balance of power by adopting the automatic model but then incorporates many elements of the manual model: Hans Morgenthau, *Politics Among Nations*, 5th ed., revised (New York: Knopf, 1978), chapters 11–12. Waltz, *Theory of International Politics* (Reading, Mass: Addison-Wesley, 1979), espouses the automatic version, a position that I adopt here. Because I am concerned here only with those aspects of the theory that deal with feedbacks, many issues about the balance will be put aside.

ideology and hatreds must not be so strong that they prevent actors from working together when strategic calculations indicate that they should. Fourth, war must be a viable tool of statecraft. This does not mean that states must be anxious to fight, but only that they are willing to do so.[18] Under these conditions, the system will be preserved even as states press every advantage, pay no attention to the common good, adopt ruthless tactics, and expect others to behave the same way. Put differently, states do not strive for balance; the restraints are not internal in the sense of each state's believing that it should be restrained. Rather, restraint and stability arise as ambition checks ambition and self-interest counteracts self-interest.

The basic argument is well known, if contested. For any state to survive, none of the others must be permitted to amass so much power that they can dominate.[19] Although states do not invariably join the weaker side,[20] they must balance against any actor that becomes excessively menacing if they are to safeguard their own independence and security. In a way analogous to the operation of Adam Smith's invisible hand, the maintenance of the system is an unintended consequence of states seeking to advance themselves, not the product of their desire to protect the international community or a preference for balance.[21]

---

[18] Waltz sees fewer conditions as necessary: "That [politics be] anarchic and that it be populated by units wishing to survive": ibid., p. 121. The importance of the ability of states to change alliances on the basis of short-run interest is stressed by George Liska, *Nations in Alliance* (Baltimore, Md.: Johns Hopkins University Press, 1962); A. F. K. Organski, *World Politics*, 2d ed. (New York: Knopf, 1968), pp. 290–92; Morgenthau, *Politics Among Nations*, pp. 196–204; and Martin Wight, "The Balance of Power and International Order," in Alan James, ed., *The Bases of International Order: Essays in Honour of C. A. W. Manning* (London: Oxford University Press, 1973), pp. 104–5. For a further discussion of the conditions necessary for balancing, see Jack Levy, "The Causes of War: A Review of Theories and Evidence," in Philip Tetlock et al., eds., *Behavior, Society, and Nuclear War*, vol. 1 (New York: Oxford University Press, 1989), pp. 228–31.

[19] Note that the theory does not address the question of what leads a state to try to become a hegemon. While it is possible that a system-level argument could be developed here, it seems hard to avoid looking at the nature of the state and its decision makers. It is not likely to be an accident that the main disturbers of the twentieth-century international system oppressed their domestic populations as well.

[20] They often do: Thomas Cusack and Richard Stoll, "Balance Behavior in the International System, 1816–1976," *International Interactions* 16, no. 4 (1991), pp. 255–70; Stephen Walt, *The Origins of Alliances* (Ithaca, N.Y.: Cornell University Press, 1987). In domestic politics, those who are losing often seek to redress the balance by mobilizing previously uninvolved actors: E. E. Schattschneider, *The Semisovereign People* (New York: Holt, Rinehart, and Winston, 1960).

[21] I think that Talcott Parsons is correct to note that we can group together Realists like Hobbes with Liberals like Locke and Smith because both groups see social order arising out of the interaction of individuals who are calculating on the basis of their self-interest as contrasted with theorists like Durkheim who stress the importance of internalized norms: Parsons, *The Structure of Social Action* (New York: McGraw-Hill, 1937).

This is not to say that forming a coalition to block a hegemon is easy: By the time statesmen are sure that a state is gaining dominance, defeating it will be at least in part a collective good, which means that states are likely to minimize their own contributions, passing the buck to others if they can. Despite the use of private incentives like status, influence, and territory, coalition management is difficult and the alliances that defeated Napoleon, the kaiser, and Hitler experienced serious strain. Indeed, they might not have succeeded had the potential hegemon been more cautious.

Nevertheless, the theory passes one important test: No state has been able to dominate the international system. But this is not definitive: Few have tried—Napoleon, Hitler, perhaps the kaiser and Louis XIV. Although others may not have made the effort because they anticipated that they would be blocked, the small number of challenges must undermine our confidence that the system could have been maintained had there been more of them. Furthermore, although the overall balance of power system has never failed, local ones have. Not only have some countries come to dominate their regions (this can perhaps be accommodated within the theory), but isolated systems have fallen under the sway of one actor. While we consider it natural for China to be unified, in fact for centuries it consisted of independent states.[22] Rome's neighbors did not unite to check its power, and the British conquest of India also was made possible by the failure of a local balance.[23] But these cases were geographically limited and did not produce a world empire and put an end to international politics.

The other restraints and puzzles mentioned earlier—the fact that few wars become total and that losers and small states are not divided up—also follow from the dictates of self-interest within the constraints imposed by the anarchical system, although a bit less obviously. Since any state can ally with any other, states do not have permanent friends and enemies. Because today's adversary may be tomorrow's ally, crippling it would be foolish. Furthermore, while the state would gain territory and wealth from dividing up the loser, others might gain even more, thus putting the state at a disadvantage in subsequent conflicts. Of the Ottoman Empire, a Russian diplomat said: "If the cake could not be saved, it must be fairly divided."[24] It may be

[22] Richard Walker, *The Multi-State System of Ancient China* (Hamden, Conn.: Shoestring Press, 1953).

[23] Robert Errington, *The Dawn of Empire: Rome's Rise to World Power* (Ithaca, N.Y.: Cornell University Press, 1972). The most obvious explanation for the latter case—the superiority of British military technology—is not correct: Stephen Peter Rosen, *Social Structures and Strategies: India and its Armies* (Ithaca, N.Y.: Cornell University Press, 1996).

[24] Quoted in Edward Gulick, *Europe's Classical Balance of Power* (New York: Norton, 1955), p. 72. For a discussion of relative and absolute gains in international politics, see David Baldwin, ed., *Neorealism and Neoliberalism in International Politics* (New York: Columbia University Press, 1993). This balance of power logic explains why relative gains matter less in a multipolar system: When adversaries and allies cannot be identified, statesmen cannot tell

presumptuous to correct someone who presumably understood the balance of power very well, but I think he got it backwards: The cake had to be saved because it could *not* be divided evenly. The fear of being disadvantaged by an apportionment led states to keep the empire whole.

The knowledge that allies and enemies are not permanent and the expectation that losers will be treated relatively generously reinforce each other. Because the members of the winning coalition know that they are not likely to remain together after the war, each has to fear accretions to the power of its allies. Because winners know that they are not likely to be able to dismember the loser, why should they prolong the war? That each state knows its allies have reason to contemplate a separate peace provides it with further incentives to move quickly. The result, then, is a relatively moderate outcome not despite but because of the fear and greed of the individual states. This is one reason why international wars are much more likely to end in negotiated settlements than are civil wars.[25]

There is something wrong with this picture, however.[26] Wars against hegemons can become total, losers sometimes are divided up, and postwar relations among states often are very different from those prevailing previously. The reason is that a long and bitter war against the hegemon undermines the assumptions necessary for the operation of the balance. States are likely to come to believe that wars are so destructive that they cannot be a normal instrument of statecraft and to see the hegemon as inherently evil and aggressive, which means that it is not a fit alliance partner and the winning coalition must stay together. As a result, allies are not regarded as being as much of a potential threat as balance of power reasoning would lead us to expect. Postwar politics may then be unusually moderate and a concert system may evolve in which the states positively value the system, develop longer-run conceptions of their self-interests, and forgo competitive gains in the expectation that others will reciprocate. Ironically, then, a war against a would-be hegemon that epitomizes the operation of the balance of power is likely to produce a system in which the actors consciously moderate their behavior and restrain themselves. The negative feedback that acts in the balance of power is not complete; fighting a potential hegemon sets in motion forces that prevent the system from immediately returning to its

---

whether the growth of another's power will help or threaten them. For a formal treatment, see Duncan Snidal, "Relative Gains and the Pattern of International Cooperation," ibid., chapter 7.

[25] For the data, but different explanations, see Roy Licklider, ed., *Stopping the Killing: How Civil Wars End* (New York: New York University Press, 1993), and Barbara Walter, "The Resolution of Civil Wars: Why Negotiations Fail" (unpubished dissertation, Department of Political Science, University of Chicago, 1994).

[26] This discussion is drawn from Robert Jervis, "From Balance to Concert," *World Politics* 38 (October 1985), pp. 58–79, and Jervis, "Security Regimes," *International Organization* 36 (Spring 1982), pp. 362–68.

original position.[27] Hitler was right to believe that balance of power logic would dictate the breakup of the coalition against him once success was in sight; his error was in failing to see that his behavior had altered balance thinking.

An Alternative View—Is It Systemic?

The model of the balance of power presented here is clearly systemic in that it sees a radical separation between intentions and outcomes, as Waltz has so clearly explained.[28] An alternative view of the balance of power that sees more congruence is summarized by Edward Gulick when he says that "balance-of-power theory demanded restraint, abnegation, and the denial of immediate self-interest."[29] Morton Kaplan's conception of the balance of power similarly posits internalized moderation as two of his six rules call for self-restraint: "Stop fighting rather than eliminate an essential national actor," and "permit defeated or constrained essential national actors to reenter the system as acceptable role partners."[30] For Kaplan, these rules not only describe how states behave, they consciously guide statesmen's actions. Furthermore, these restraints are distinct from the rules that stress self-interest and the maximization of resources. In contrast to the automatic version discussed earlier, Kaplan points out that in his computer model, "if actors do not take system stability requirements into account, a 'balance of power' system will be stable only if some extra systemic factor. . . . prevents a roll-up of the system."[31] In other words, stability and restraint are not likely unless the actors seek stability.[32] Statesmen sometimes agree: In 1908 the

[27] The concert system is prone to decay back into balance of power: Jervis, "From Balance to Concert," pp. 61–62.

[28] Waltz, *Theory of International Politics*, 107–11, 120–21.

[29] Gulick, *Europe's Classical Balance of Power*, p. 33; also see pp. 30–32, 304–6. Gulick's historical analysis is quite sound; although his statements are couched in the abstract, they come from a study of the Congress of Vienna, which was a concert system.

[30] Morton Kaplan, *System and Process in International Politics* (New York: Wiley, 1957), p. 23. Kaplan expresses a different view—one much closer to Waltz's—in "Balance of Power, Bipolarity and other Models of International Systems," *American Political Science Review* 51 (September 1957), p. 690.

[31] Morton Kaplan, *Towards Professionalism in International Theory* (New York: Free Press, 1979), p. 136; also see Kaplan, "A Poor Boy's Journey," in Joseph Kruzel and James Rosenau, eds., *Journeys Through World Politics* (Lexington, Mass.: Lexington Books, 1989), pp. 45–47.

[32] Kaplan, *Towards Professionalism*, pp. 39, 73, 86. Also see Kaplan, "The Hard Facts of International Theory," *Journal of International Affairs* 44 (Spring/Summer 1990), p. 19, and Organski, *World Politics*, chapter 12. Some computer simulations of the balance of power support this view: Arnold Reinken, "Computer Explorations of the 'Balance of Power,'" in Morton Kaplan, ed., *New Approaches to International Relations* (New York: St. Martin's, 1968), pp. 469–72; Stuart Bremmer and Michael Mihalka, "Machiavelli in Machina: Or Politics

British foreign secretary rejected the suggestion of his ambassador in Vienna that Britain should seek to induce Austria-Hungary to desert the Triple Alliance, declaring this plan "fraught with considerable danger. The Balance of Power in Europe would be completely upset and Germany would be left without even her nominal allies . . . [and this] may precipitate a conflict."[33]

This formulation is not systemic in the sense that I have used it because the restraints are purposeful rather than being an unintended consequence of the states' struggles. The system is preserved because states want to preserve it and there is little conflict between a state's short-run and long-run interest.[34] But seen differently, this conception of the balance is systemic in that the norms have been internalized through socialization as the actors watch and interact with their peers. Indeed, Paul Schroeder's important study of the transformation of European international politics caused by the Napoleonic Wars stresses that stable peace and the concert were produced not only by the defeat of the aggressor, but also by the painful learning that led the victors to understand that others' interests had to be respected, that smaller states could play a valuable role, and that the eighteenth-century practice of compensation and indemnities led to endless cycles of warfare.[35]

It can be further argued that stability requires that the states form a community, with the terms of membership including acceptance of norms of restraint which may be transnational ideas of the type alluded to by Bull and Hoffmann.[36] In this view, the balance of power is a system in part because

---

Among Hexagons," in Karl Deutsch et al., eds., *Problems of World Modeling: Political and Social Implications* (Cambridge: Ballinger, 1977), chapter 20; Thomas Cusack and Richard Stoll, *Exploring Realpolitik: Probing International Relations Theory With Computer Simulation* (Boulder, Colo.: Lynne Rienner, 1990). In the mathematical model developed by Emerson Niou and Peter Ordeshook ("Stability in Anarchic International Systems," *American Political Science Review* 84 [December 1990], pp. 1207–34), however, anarchy is compatible with stability. Also see Lars-Erik Cederman, "Emergent Polarity: Analyzing State-Formation and Power Politics," *International Studies Quarterly* 38 (December 1994), pp. 501–33.

[33] Quoted in F. R. Bridge, "Relations with Austria-Hungary and the Balkan States, 1905–1908," in F. H. Hinsley, ed., *British Foreign Policy Under Sir Edward Grey* (Cambridge: Cambridge University Press, 1977), p. 176. French statesmen in this period often reasoned similarly: see John Kreiger, *France and the Origins of the First World War* (London: Macmillan, 1983).

[34] Kaplan, *Towards Professionalism*, p. 139; also see pp. 76, 135.

[35] Paul Schroeder, *The Transformation of European Politics, 1787–1848* (New York: Oxford University Press, 1994). John Vasquez also stresses the role of images and learning in maintaining balance of power politics: *The War Puzzle* (New York: Cambridge University Press, 1993), pp. 86–87 and chapter 5. For a discussion of the differences between Schroeder's views and more traditional Realist analysis, see Schroeder, "Did the Vienna Settlement Rest on a Balance of Power?" *American Historical Review* 97 (June 1992), pp. 683–706, and Jervis, "A Political Science Perspective on the Balance of Power and the Concert," ibid., pp. 716–24.

[36] Hedley Bull, *The Anarchical Society* (New York: Columbia University Press, 1977); Stanley Hoffmann, "International Systems and International Law," in Klaus Knorr and Sidney

statesmen conceive of it as one, which does not have to be true in the automatic conception of the balance. Indeed, it is clear that statesmen often do think in systemic terms, not only in seeking to anticipate how others will respond to their moves, but also in seeing their countries as part of a larger whole.[37] But here the central question is whether or how feedbacks operate. To put this another way, it is not easy to explain how the system can be maintained in the face of actors who have interests in exploiting others' moderation.

Nevertheless, it is certainly possible that states feel internal restraints and that, if they do not, the system will be torn apart by high levels of warfare. If the proponents of the automatic balance draw on the analogy to Smith's invisible hand, critics can respond that unalloyed capitalism, like an engine out of control, will produce so much unconstrained energy that it will soon destroy itself. Just as economic liberalism must be embedded in broader societal norms if capitalism is to be compatible with a well-functioning society,[38] perhaps the pursuit of narrow self-interest in the balance of power can yield stability and a modicum of productive peace only if it is bounded by normative conceptions that limit predatory behavior.

Anticipation of the Operation of Balance of Power

States may be restrained by the expectation that if they are not, they will be faced by intense opposition. These cases fall in between the two models discussed above. Indeed, if the view of the balance as automatic is correct, it would be surprising if decision makers heedlessly sought to expand; awareness of the likely feedback would lead them to be restrained. Much has been written about self-defeating expansion,[39] but we should not neglect the fact that leaders may be inhibited by the anticipation of these processes. These cases are literally countless—that is, they cannot be counted because they

Verba, eds., *The International System* (Princeton, N.J.: Princeton University Press, 1961), pp. 207, 211–13. Morgenthau also stresses the importance of a moral consensus in producing a framework of restraints which makes a balance of power possible: Morgenthau, *Politics Among Nations*, pp. 221–28.

[37] See Paul Schroeder, "The Transformation of Political Thinking, 1787–1848," in Jack Snyder and Robert Jervis, eds., *Coping with Complexity in the International System* (Boulder, Colo.: Westview, 1993), pp. 47–70.

[38] The concept of embedded liberalism was developed by Karl Polanyi, *The Great Transformation* (Boston: Beacon Press, 1944) and has been fruitfully applied by John Ruggie in "International Regimes, Transactions, and Change: Embedded Liberalism in the Postwar Economic Order," *International Organization* 36 (Spring 1982), pp. 379–415.

[39] See, for examples, Kennedy, *Rise and Fall of the Great Powers*; Jack Snyder, *Myths of Empire* (Ithaca, N.Y.: Cornell University Press, 1991); Charles Kupchan, *The Vulnerability of Empire* (Ithaca, N.Y.: Cornell University Press, 1994).

do not leave traces in the historical record. While this means that we cannot always determine whether the anticipation of the balance of power explains a state's moderate policy, on some occasions statesmen do consider various moves only to reject them on the grounds that they would incite undue opposition. Thus during the Russo-Turkish war of 1828, many of the czar's advisors "recommended that Russia make peace as quickly as possible and henceforth observe a policy of restraint in the Near East. Any further Russian advance risked the danger of foreign intervention and war with one or more of the European great powers, or the participation of these powers in the partition of the Ottoman Empire with the result that Russia would have powerful and dangerous rivals along its frontiers instead of the hapless Turks."[40] Similarly, although the Soviet Union supported the Loyalist regime during the Spanish Civil War, "nothing was further from the Soviet government's intentions than a satellite Spain. The conquest of a backward nation would have been more than offset by the almost inevitable consequent hostility of France and Britain."[41]

In the same way, decision makers who believe in the action-reaction model of arms races are likely to be deterred from increasing their defense budgets by the expectation that their adversaries would do so as well, and when considering whether to send additional troops to Vietnam, American decision-makers thought a great deal about the likelihood of a matching North Vietnamese response, although in the end this consideration did not prevail. More generally, it is easier for actors to cooperate despite the security dilemma if they understand that others are likely to reciprocate their menacing moves. Thus many of those who opposed the extension of the American alliance system in the 1950s argued that for every ally the U.S. recruited, the Soviet Union would enlist the ally's regional rival; before Norway joined NATO, both it and the U.S. gave considerable thought to whether the Soviet Union would respond by consolidating its hold on Finland; in 1873 Argentina hesitated before signing a treaty with Peru and

[40] Norman Rich, *Why the Crimean War?* (Hanover, N.H.: University Press of New England, 1985), p. 16.

[41] Adam Ulam, *Expansion and Coexistence: The History of Soviet Foreign Policy, 1916–67* (New York: Praeger, 1968), p. 245. Soviet restraint toward Finland after World War II may have the same roots and understanding this, the U.S. also pursued moderate goals: See Jussi Hanhimäki, "'Containment' in a Borderland: The United States and Finland, 1948–49," *Diplomatic History* 18 (Summer 1994), pp. 353–74. Similarly, a state may refrain from defeating an adversary too completely for fear that if it does, it will have to face a stronger or more dangerous rival. For examples, see Melanie Billings-Yun, *Decision Against War: Eisenhower and Dien Bien Phu, 1954* (New York: Columbia University Press, 1988), p. 11; Peter Lowe, *Great Britain and the Origins of the Pacific War* (Oxford: Clarendon Press, 1977), p. 63; and William Simons, "U.S. Coercive Pressure on North Vietnam, Early 1965," in Alexander George and William Simons, eds., *The Limits of Coercive Diplomacy*, 2d ed. (Boulder, Colo.: Westview, 1994), p. 141.

Bolivia out of fear that the result would be a pact between Chile and Brazil.[42]

Finally, even though statesmen generally think very well of their own countries, the more perceptive of them realize that the balance of power makes it dangerous for their countries to be too powerful. Edmund Burke made the point eloquently at the end of the eighteenth century:

> Among precautions against ambition, it may not be amiss to take one precaution against *our* own. I must fairly say, I dread our *own* power and our *own* ambition; I dread our being too much dreaded. It is ridiculous to say we are not men, and that, as men, we shall never wish to aggrandize ourselves in some way or other. Can we say that even at this hour we are not invidiously aggrandized? We are already in possession of almost all the commerce of the world. Our empire in India is an awful thing. If we should come to be in a condition not only to have all this ascendant in commerce, but to be absolutely able, without the least control, to hold the commerce of all other nations totally dependent upon our good pleasure, we may say that we shall not abuse this astonishing and hitherto unheard-of power. But every other nation will think we shall abuse it. It is impossible but that, sooner or later, this stage of things must produce a combination against us which may end in our ruin.[43]

Negative Feedback That Resembles Balance of Power

Turning back from anticipations to responses, we should note that social systems, especially in international politics, exhibit other forms of negative feedback that resemble balance of power in making ambitious behavior self-limiting if not self-defeating and turning strength into weakness. An actor who increases its resources may not be better able to reach its goals—in a system, one can never do "just one thing."[44] If others see the actor's increased strength as menacing them, they may move to block it, thereby decreasing the actor's power and security. As Norman Rich explains in discussing the background to the Crimean War: "Russia's . . . appearance of

[42] U.S. Department of State, *Foreign Relations of the United States, 1949*, vol. 4, *Western Europe* (Washington, D.C.: Government Printing Office, 1975), pp. 65–68; Robert Burr, *By Reason or Force: Chile and the Balance of Power in South America, 1830–1905* (Berkeley: University of California Press, 1965), p. 126. For a parallel discussion, see Glenn Snyder, *Alliance Politics* (Ithaca, N.Y.: Cornell University Press, forthcoming), chapter 2.

[43] Quoted in Morgenthau, *Politics Among Nations*, pp. 169–70, emphasis in the original. Also see the similar analysis of François Fénélon cited in Kenneth Waltz, "America as a Model for the World? A Foreign Policy Perspective," *PS: Political Science and Politics* 24 (December 1991), p. 669, and Waltz, "The Emerging Structure of International Politics," *International Security* 18 (Fall 1993), pp. 74–76, 79.

[44] Garret Hardin, "The Cybernetics of Competition: A Biologist's View of Society," *Perspectives in Biology and Medicine* 7 (Autumn 1963), pp. 58–84.

strength proved to be a serious political liability, for it tended to make other countries even more fearful of Russia and anxious to prevent any further increase in its strength and influence."[45] Most likely to excite are actions that simultaneously reveal menace and improve the actor's power were there to be no response. Thus in the late 1830s and early 1840s, Great Britain hoped that Texas would remain independent of the U.S. and form a counterweight to it. But the greater its efforts, the more the U.S. saw that an independent Texas could be a threat and the greater the pro-annexation sentiment in the U.S. Soviet behavior in Turkey, Iran, and Eastern Europe at the start of the Cold War similarly backfired because it both seemed unreasonable and increased the Soviets' ability to carry out any malign plans they might have.[46]

Many arms races display the same dynamic.[47] Although a country will seek an advantage only if it thinks that its adversary will remain passive because of weakness, overconfidence, or the fear that a matching response will lead to conflict and insecurity, an attempt to exercise the leverage that the advantage in arms is designed to bring is likely to convince the adversary to respond, as the Soviet Union discovered in the late 1970s and 1980s.

[45] Rich, *Why the Crimean War?* p. 3. For a general discussion of dynamics of this kind, see Zeev Maoz, "Power, Capability, and Paradoxical Conflict Outcomes," *World Politics* 41 (January 1989), pp. 239–66. For a general discussion of the ways in which a policy can undermine the preconditions for its success, see chapter 2, pp. 54–58.

[46] Lenin worried about this kind of effect: "The more victorious we are, the more the capitalist exploiters learn to unite and the more determined their onslaught" (quoted in V. S. Semyonov, *Nations and Nationalism* [Moscow: Progress Publishers, 1979], p. 239). He was right: as Eisenhower explained in a speech in April 1953:

> The result [of Soviet policy] has been tragic for the world and, for the Soviet Union, it has been ironic. The amassing of Soviet power alerted free nations to a new danger of aggression. . . . It instilled in [them] . . . the unshakable conviction that, as long as there persists a threat to freedom, they must, at any cost, remain armed, strong, and ready for the risk of war. It inspired them . . . to attain a unity of purpose and will beyond the power of propaganda or pressure to break.

U.S. Department of State, *Foreign Relations of the United States, 1952–1954*, vol. 8, *Eastern Europe, Soviet Union, Eastern Mediterranean* (Washington, D.C.: Government Printing Office, 1988), p. 1149.

[47] Since interacting plants and animals form a system, we should not be surprised to learn that even without calculation, natural selection produces arms races in nature: As predators develop sharper claws and stronger teeth, prey evolve better forms of protection, such as armor, horns, and the propensity to form herds. The classic article is R. Dawkins and J. R. Krebs, "Arms Races Between and Within Species," *Proceedings of the Royal Society, London* B 205 (September 1979), pp. 489–511; also see Leigh Van Valen, "A New Evolutionary Law," *Evolutionary Theory* 1 (July 1973), pp. 1–30; Geerat Vermeij, *Evolution and Escalation: An Ecological History of Life* (Princeton, N.J.: Princeton University Press, 1987). This view contrasts with the argument for the prevalence of evolutionary stable strategies: Nils Stenseth and John Maynard Smith, "Coevolution in Ecosystems: Red Queen Evolution or Stasis?" *Evolution* 38 (July 1984), pp. 870–80.

Processes of escalation display similar negative feedbacks in that the actions of one state call up counterbalancing responses from the adversary, although the feedback is positive in the sense that the level of conflict feeds on itself.

Of course overwhelming power or especially propitious circumstances can allow one state to make great gains at another's expense. But when countries are large and agile, such opportunities will be limited.[48] Indeed, the very fact that a move will bring the state great gains if it is successful will impel the adversary to try to thwart it. For example, in the spring of 1950, if Stalin believed that conquering South Korea would have made a great difference to world politics, he should have given more weight to the likelihood of a forceful American response; to the extent that U.S. leaders believed that conquering North Korea would produce gains beyond the peninsula, they too should have seen that their adversaries had powerful incentives to step in.[49] These processes are not unique to the Cold War: In the 1870s and 1880s, Britain's attempts to solidify its influence in Africa often increased French and German activity, leaving Britain worse off than it had been at the start.[50]

It is not only great powers that overreach themselves. In the summer of 1981, the Palestine Liberation Organization (PLO) enjoyed great military success as artillery and rocket fire against northern Israel produced local civilian flight and worry throughout the country. Israel responded, however, by an invasion that at least temporarily disabled the PLO. But by pushing on to Beruit, this move also carried the seeds of its own destruction by antagonizing much of the world, radicalizing southern Lebanon, and reducing opposition to Syrian domination of the rest of the country.[51] Violence is not necessary for the processes. During the Cold War, the more local powers like India and Egypt sought to decrease superpower influence in their regions and to assert strong leadership, if not hegemony, over their neighbors,

[48] For further discussion, see Jervis, *The Meaning of the Nuclear Revolution* (Ithaca, N.Y.: Cornell University Press, 1989), pp. 230–37 and chapter 7 below, pp. 279–82.

[49] For a brief summary of the benefits the American military expected to flow from Korean unification, see Shu Guang Zhang, *Deterrence and Strategic Culture: Chinese-American Confrontation, 1949–1958* (Ithaca, N.Y.: Cornell University Press, 1992), p. 80. Stalin may have expected the U.S. to intervene in the Chinese civil war because he thought a communist victory would deeply wound the West: David Holloway, *Stalin and the Bomb* (New Haven, Conn.: Yale University Press, 1994), p. 274. A collection of the most recent documents and analyses can be found in *Cold War International History Project Bulletin*, nos. 6–7 (Winter 1995/1996), pp. 30–125.

[50] G. N. Sanderson, "The European Partition of Africa: Coincidence or Conjuncture?" *Journal of Imperial and Commonwealth History* 3 (October 1974), pp. 20–25.

[51] Ben-Gurion understood better in 1948 when he refrained from taking all of Jerusalem in the belief that doing so would have led to irresistable pressures to internationalize the city: Yossi Katz and Shmuel Sandler, "The Origins of the Conception of Israel's State Borders and Its Impact on the Strategy of War in 1948–49," *Journal of Strategic Studies* 18 (June 1995), pp. 164–66.

the more likely were the latter to turn to outsiders for support.[52] It was also difficult for any country to gain the backing of one of the superpowers without enabling its regional rival to enlist the other.

On a smaller scale, negative feedback is similarly set off when a country tries to exact excessive concessions from another, although of course what constitutes excessive often can be determined only after the fact. High demands, especially if increased over time, are likely to persuade others that the state is unreasonable if not aggressive and therefore to lead them to conclude that even limited retreats will be costly because they will be followed by pressure for additional ones. Germany could have won a significant if partial victory over France in the First Moroccan Crisis if it had been content with forcing the resignation of Delcassé, France's belligerent foreign minister. But by demanding more, it stoked French enmity and convinced Britain that German goals were threateningly grandiose. The result was a defeat in the conference at Algeciras and the beginnings of self-encirclement.

Emulation also can restore equilibrium. Thus if a particular technique like negative advertising seems to be successful, it is likely to be widely copied, giving the innovators only a short-term advantage.[53] Robert McNamara and his successors witnessed the operation of this kind of process within the government. On becoming secretary of defense, McNamara introduced cost-benefit analysis in order to change the "rules of the game" within the Pentagon and give him greater power. For several years, the armed services were befuddled. But then they learned the techniques and were able to produce excellent analyses to support their preferences. While the reforms at least slightly increased the power of the secretary and the rationality of procedures, the effects were smaller than foreseen by both advocates and opponents.

Finally, I should note that balance of power dynamics are built into the basic forms of domestic politics. The American Constitution was built on the concept of checks and balances because the Founders believed that potentially dangerous power could best be tamed by countervailing power, to use the term that Galbraith later applied to many aspects of American political

[52] See Walt, *Origins of Alliances*, pp. 66–67, and Howard Wriggins, ed., *Dynamics of Regional Politics: Four Systems on the Indian Ocean Rim* (New York: Columbia University Press, 1992). To take the process back a step, Egypt sought outside assistance in order to overcome an unfavorable local balance, and India sought to counterbalance American support for its regional rival.

[53] The Whigs won the 1840 American presidential elections by copying their opponents' approaches and tactics: The Democrats cried that "we have taught them how to conquer us!" (quoted in Charles Sellers, *The Market Revolution* [New York: Oxford University Press, 1991], p. 363). For a discussion of emulation in military behavior, see Colin Elman, "The Logic of Emulation: The Diffusion of Military Practices in the International System" (Ph.D. dissertation in progress, Department of Political Science, Columbia University).

and economic life.[54] Other aspects of domestic politics illustrate negative feedback as the unintended consequences of the pursuit of narrower self-interest in a way even more analogous to the automatic balance. Most obviously, it is hard for any political party to gain a monopoly of power because the competition can mount matching or competing claims. If the political pendulum swings in one direction, those losing influence usually will increase their unity and activity. Thus when Clinton became president, environmental groups lost members and contributions because "some people believed that there was less need to support environmental causes" and the American Civil Liberties Union told its members that "we now face an anti-rights movement even *more* dangerous and powerful than we had to fight under Reagan and Bush . . . [because] our support and resources have diminished with the misguided complacency that set in with the election."[55] In the aftermath of the Democratic rout in November 1994, the director of an institute that trains liberal interest groups noted that "the silver lining in this disaster is that the ability to alarm and motivate contributors has grown enormously."[56]

Other Forms of Negative Feedback

Stability can be produced even if the disturbing behavior of one actor does not lead to the direct opposition of others. Systems exhibit a very wide range of negative feedbacks, from thermoregulation in animals,[57] to functional mechanisms in societies,[58] to the explicit strategies and tactics adopted by actors to cope with undesired actions of others. Because the field is too large to cover here and my central concern is with international politics, I will focus on processes that share with balance of power the characteristic of limiting an actor's ability to reach its goals.

[54] John Kenneth Galbraith, *American Capitalism: The Concept of Countervailing Power* (Boston: Houghton Mifflin, 1952). Pluralists stress the prevalence of balancing mechanisms; populists see positive feedback as power begets power and wealth begets wealth, leading to an increasingly stratified society. For an analysis of American thinking about equilibrating processes in terms of both physical and biological analogies, see Cynthia Russett, *The Concept of Equilibrium in American Social Thought* (New Haven, Conn.: Yale University Press, 1966).

[55] Quoted in Keith Schneider, "Big Environment Hits a Recession," *New York Times*, January 1, 1995; ACLU memo from Laura Murphy Lee to Ira Glasser, April 19, 1994, p. 1.

[56] Quoted in Neil Lewis, "Liberal Groups Banking on Republicans for Renewal," *New York Times*, November 28, 1994.

[57] Nicholas Mrosovsky, *Rheostasis: The Physiology of Change* (New York: Oxford University Press, 1990).

[58] Michael Faia, *Dynamic Functionalism: Strategy and Tactics* (New York: Cambridge University Press, 1986), especially chapter 5; Kyriakos Kontopoulos, *The Logics of Social Structure* (Cambridge: Cambridge University Press, 1993); Stinchcombe, *Constructing Social Theories*.

Self-Limiting Success

Most obviously, success often brings internal weakness and dissension. Political parties tend to be troubled by factions if not to break apart when they dominate; protest movements often splinter when they grow; wars fought for less-than-vital interests (a luxury only the powerful can afford) are likely to be unpopular.

Only a bit less obviously, while the balance of power relies on the analogy to the free market, in some cases the market is the actual mechanism by which the negative feedback operates. For example, the laws of economics imply that demonstration projects may not survive imitation. Thus an official in the Ivory Coast complained that his country's economic problems were attributable in part to its well-publicized success in the preceding decade: "The World Bank and other international aid agencies, seeing how well we were doing with cocoa and coffee, encouraged other third-world countries to do the same thing and ended up flooding the market."[59] The operation of the market is also likely to reduce the impact of an initially successful boycott because it will lead to price increases that will tempt outsiders to circumvent it and give people in the country great incentives to develop substitutes. Similarly, the greater the success of the American effort to interdict the flow of drugs into the country, the more the price of these drugs will rise, leading users to shift to other illegal substances and drawing new sources and entrepreneurs into the market.

Negative feedback can also operate as success alters an actor's values, outlook, and character. Once a state has enjoyed the perquisites of a great power, it will find it difficult to adjust to a smaller and less privileged role. Senator Fulbright's "arrogance of power" is not limited to the U.S.:[60] The habits and skills of compromise, persuasion, conciliation, and coalition-building atrophy when the state gains sufficient power to rely on the cruder instruments of bribes and threats. As the state and its citizens become accustomed to influence, wealth, and deference they develop a sense of entitlement and great ability. Few tasks are seen as beyond reach; retrenchment is felt to be an abdication of responsibility. If the most vivid portraits of the corruption and decadence brought on by success are to be found in novels, they are not mere literary devices. The cycle of hubris and nemesis is driven by the profound changes in human psychology that success generates.[61]

A more benign form of negative feedback in human psychology is the

[59] Quoted in Kenneth Noble, "Low Export Prices Hurt Ivory Coast," *New York Times*, November 19, 1989.

[60] William Fulbright, *The Arrogance of Power* (New York: Random House, 1966).

[61] A good discussion is Albert Hirschman, *Rival Views of Market Society and Other Recent Essays* (New York: Viking, 1986), chapter 5.

adaptation-level phenomenon that produces psychological homeostasis. Although a new pleasure or pain induces a sharp increase or decrease in the person's sense of well-being, after a time the person adjusts and her level of satisfaction returns to something like its original level: People adapt to the fortunes or misfortunes of their lives in a way that produces greater stability than would otherwise be the case.[62]

Information, Inferences, and Psychology

It is sometimes by the transmission of information rather than by the mobilization of power that actions set in motion equilibrating processes. A physical change that, all things being equal, will further the actor's goal may convey information that has the contrary effect. Indeed, few social acts fail to alter the informational as well as the physical environment. This consideration was overlooked by a security-minded housemate who thought that putting a lock on his bedroom door secured extra protection for his possessions. In fact he was increasing his risk: Any burglar would assume that the one room with a lock contained items of greatest value.[63] More seriously, Great Britain did not anticipate the effects of its attempt to build a coalition to restrain Germany in the spring of 1939. According to German diplomatic records, Hitler told the Hungarian prime minister that "Britain was in no position to render help, but was running around everywhere looking for help. . . . Britain did not impress the Führer."[64]

In other cases, people may act with the primary objective of sending a signal[65] and changing the expectations that others have of them. But the

[62] See, for example, M. H. Appley, ed., *Adaptation-Level Theory: A Symposium* (New York: Academic Press, 1971); for a discussion of the broad implications of this phenomenon, see Robert Lane, *The Market Experience* (New York: Cambridge University Press, 1991), pp. 120, 149–52, 463–65, 511–12, 537–41, 604–5; for an intriguing application of this kind of thought to consumption and human behavior, see Tibor Scitovsky, *The Joyless Economy: An Enquiry into Human Satisfaction and Consumer Dissatisfaction* (New York: Oxford University Press, 1976). For recent findings that people are born with a "set point" for happiness to which they return after events depress or elate them only temporarily, see David Lykken and Auke Tellegen, "Happiness is a Stochastic Phenomenon," *Psychological Science* 7 (May 1996), pp. 186–89.

[63] We never had a robbery, and my friend went on to become a distinguished political scientist. An Italian mafia leader knew better and took no measures to protect his hideout. As the police official noted, "When you are a fugitive, you can't have high fences and bodyguards: they only draw attention" (Alan Cowell, "Busting the Mafia: Italy Advances in War on Crime," *New York Times*, June 27, 1993).

[64] *Documents on German Foreign Policy*, series D, vol. 6 (Washington, D.C.: U.S. Government Printing Office, 1956), p. 378.

[65] For a discussion of signaling and a distinction between types of communications, see Robert Jervis, *The Logic of Images in International Relations*, 2d. ed. (New York: Columbia

very desire to create a certain impression—or rather others' inference that this is the actor's desire—can undercut it. A husband may believe that he can please his wife by being more sensitive to her feelings. But she may find this new behavior suspicious. The person who claims to be speaking "in all honesty" may increase her listener's suspicions; the person who says "I really mean this" is likely to discredit other statements not so prefaced if not to lead the listener to doubt the truth of the current statement.[66]

Turning to politics, signals designed to reassure or frighten others will backfire if they believe that strong messages are being used to cover up a weak position. For example, while it is generally argued that pledging its reputation on standing firm will increase an actor's chance of prevailing by increasing the price it will pay if it backs down, the adversary may reason that if the actor was sufficiently powerful and the issue really was vital, it would not have gone to such artificial lengths to try to show resolve.[67]

The use of information can also be self-limiting if it reveals things that can be turned against the actor. In polite society, to utilize what you have inappropriately overheard is to indicate that you are not fit to travel in those circles. At the other end of the social spectrum, a pool hustler must be careful lest his phrases, mannerisms, or excessive skill reveal that he is an expert. When a state gains valuable information from tapping one of its adversary's communication channels it often faces a dilemma: To use the information (which of course is why it went to the trouble of acquiring it) may be to reveal the source, which will lead the adversary either to cut the channel or exploit it for deception.[68]

Positive Feedback

When interconnections generate positive feedback and a change in one direction calls up forces that continue or magnify this change, relationships will display nonlinearities. As discussed in chapter 2, there will be a disproportion between the magnitude of the cause and the results, which will depend on the state of the system as a whole. The most important ways in which international politics exhibits such feedback are captured by the dom-

University Press, 1989). Interest in this subject has increased recently, especially among economists.

[66] For a parallel discussion of the art of declining unwanted invitations, see Judith Martin, *Miss Manners' Guide for the Turn-of-the-Millennium* (New York: Pharos Books, 1989), pp. 426–29.

[67] For further discussion, see chapter 2, pp. 82–83, and chapter 7, pp. 255–58.

[68] The literature on espionage is filled with discussions of these problems. I drew heavily on it in *Logic of Images*, but unfortunately most scholars seem to regard the field as popular, sensationalist, and peripheral. This is changing with the appearance of strong scholarship in this area.

ino theory and the spiral model, which, although quite different from each other in that the movement is complementary in the former and is symmetrical in the latter, both posit self-reinforcing dynamics. But before discussing them I want to canvass other forms of positive feedback.[69]

Processes and Areas of Positive Feedback

Positive feedback works through changes in the actor, the environment, or the interaction between the two. I will start by focusing on individuals' beliefs, competencies, and values. I will then examine changes located more in the environment, looking at Schelling's "tipping" processes, as well as at the more familiar effects of competition and consensus. After outlining these processes, I will show the ways they can operate in a variety of contexts.

Many activities, such as riding a bicycle, flirting, or writing, can be done better and with less effort the more the person engages in them. Furthermore, as she learns to do them easily and well, her desire to do them is also likely to increase. It is often said of tyrants and expansionists that the appetite grows with the eating. While this is not correct for the most frequently cited example—Hitler's appetite was enormous from the beginning—it may be true for many people and for many kinds of appetites. A minor example is that Ronald Reagan's success in working with the major allies to lower the value of the dollar in 1985 led him "to make policy coordination a major objective of the United States for the first time."[70]

People may be able to manipulate these processes, as in figurative or literal seduction. Each step is designed to entice the partner to do something that she had previously resolved not to do but that now seems overwhelmingly attractive. Here temporary preferences or values are altered, permitting or calling up more extreme behavior by the seducer which pulls the partner toward further activity. Of course the process can be mutual, take place over a longer period of time, and bring deeper changes—in falling in love, each person's attraction and adjustment to the other deepens in response to reinforcing changes in the partner. In general, actors' characters are shaped by their behaviors, how others react to them, and their understandings of the interaction.[71] For example, attributes such as integrity or

[69] For a somewhat idiosyncratic collection of essays, see John Milsum, ed., *Positive Feedback* (Oxford: Pergamon Press, 1968); also see D. A. DeAngelis, W. M. Post, and C. Z. Travis, *Positive Feedback in Natural Systems* (Berlin: Springer, 1980).

[70] Robert Gilpin, *The Political Economy of International Relations* (Princeton, N.J.: Princeton University Press, 1987), p. 156. For a similar case with President Bush, see Philip Zelikow and Condoleezza Rice, *Germany Reunited and Europe Transformed* (Cambridge, Mass.: Harvard University Press, 1995), p. 30.

[71] See Daryl Bem, "Self-Perception Theory," in Leonard Berkowitz, ed., *Advances in Exper-*

corruption may develop as the actor behaves corruptly or with integrity on one occasion and then comes to be seen by others and by himself as a corrupt or an honest person. Such processes may also be at work with nations. The Scandinavian countries are now seen—by themselves as well as by others—as good "world citizens" who are deeply concerned with humanitarian and supranational interests. Perhaps this is derived from either Scandinavian values or the place of these countries in the international structure. But I suspect that the pattern of behavior was more malleable, being created through a self-reinforcing cycle of behavior and expectations.

There is then a large class of what can be called "preference-changing activities." For good and for ill, what we do influences who we are: Many of our desires, aspirations, and tastes come from our experiences, some of which are self-reinforcing. Most people come to like beer and modern art only through long exposure; it is frequently argued that advertising and television have corrupted people not only by appealing to their baser instincts, but also by developing them. To take a dramatic case, Aldrich Ames explains how what he had intended as a single incident of passing harmless information to the Soviets led him to become a permanent spy: After the first transaction "it came home to me. . . . that I had crossed a line which I had not clearly considered before. . . . [and] I could never step back."[72]

INFORMATION AND EXPECTATIONS

Positive feedback can also operate through information and changed interpretations. The well-known cases of self-fulfilling prophecies and the transformation of individuals to fit the expectations of those with whom they are interacting fit this model. Descriptions of a situation can change it when what is being described depends in part on actors' behavior. If people are told they are living in an earthquake zone, this information will lower their property values, an effect that will be magnified if many of them seek to leave, but the chance of an earthquake will not be affected. By contrast, descriptions of the economic and social health of a neighborhood can be

---

imental Social Psychology (New York: Academic Press, 1972), pp. 1–61. For an application to foreign policy, see Deborah Larson, *Origins of Containment: A Psychological Explanation* (Princeton, N.J.: Princeton University Press, 1985). Also see the discussion in chapter 2, pp. 50–54.

[72] Quoted in U.S. Senate Select Committee on Intelligence, "An Assessment of the Aldrich H. Ames Espionage Case and Its Implications for U.S. Intelligence," November 1, 1994, p. 21. For the argument that people choose behavior in part because it will change their tastes, see the essays in Gary Becker, *Accounting for Tastes* (Cambridge, Mass.: Harvard University Press, 1996), part 1. Also see George Ainslie, *Picoeconomics: The Strategic Interaction of Successive Motivational States Within the Person* (New York: Cambridge University Press, 1992), and Henry Aaron, "Public Policy, Values, and Consciousness," *Journal of Economic Perspectives* 8 (Spring 1994), pp. 4–8.

self-confirming because they depend in large measure on the characteristics, attitudes, and behavior of people who live there, which in turn are influenced by the descriptions people believe (and think others believe). Thus media spokespersons are incorrect to claim that they merely report what is happening, as banks that are described as being weak and people who live in neighborhoods reported as deteriorating are quick to point out. Indeed, descriptive information alters actors' incentives in two ways. First, it can change their views of the object being described. If I hear that my bank may be insolvent, I will want to withdraw my funds even if I am the only person to receive this information. Second, if the information is shared more widely, the knowledge that others are likely to change their behavior will affect mine: Since others will try to withdraw their money from the bank or leave the neighborhood, I not only should do so, but also must move more quickly than they do. The development and collapse of speculative schemes may be a product more of the second than the first process as each person seeks to maximize his investment by anticipating what others will do.[73] Both impulses are tapped when movies are advertised as drawing large audiences. If I think that my taste is like most other people's, the fact that the movie is popular tells me that I am likely to enjoy it. Since people often talk about movies they have seen, it also tells me that seeing it will enable me to join in what is likely to be a frequent topic of conversation. The more people who see the movie, the more it will be discussed, giving others still increased incentives to see it. In politics both forces combine to provide a powerful role for reports that a certain position can prevail when many people are willing to act on their preference for that position only if they think it can be sustained.[74]

As people respond to what they believe is a new situation, they may generate confirming information, as the chief scientific advisor to the RAF explained in the fall of 1943:

> The present German [air defense] system is unstable in that once the controller has formed a picture of the situation it becomes increasingly easy for him to convince himself he is right. Having made his guess at the target from the early track of bombers, he sends his fighters to a convenient beacon. These fighters are then

[73] Most of John Kenneth Galbraith's amusing *A Short History of Financial Euphoria* (New York: Viking, 1993) assumes that people are shortsighted and foolish, although pp. 76 and 83 are more perceptive.

[74] For a good study of this dynamic in the Senate vote against confirming Judge Carswell for the Supreme Court, see Richard Harris, *Decision* (New York: Dutton, 1971). During Watergate, President Nixon believed that "the main danger of being impeached would come precisely from the public's being conditioned to the idea that I was going to be impeached": *RN: Memoirs of Richard Nixon* (New York: Grosset & Dunlap, 1978), p. 972. For a general discussion of feedbacks of this type, see Bryan Jones, *Reconceiving Decision-Making in Democratic Politics* (Chicago: University of Chicago Press, 1994), pp. 191–204.

reported by sound observations and, unless the observers are extremely skilled, they may easily be misidentified. The controller then interprets the observations as referring to British aircraft, and is thus confirmed in his initial misjudgment, and so may order up more fighters which may again be misidentified.[75]

Similarly, when an intelligence service tells its agents that it thinks the adversary may be developing a certain weapon, it is almost certain to receive many confirming reports, which in turn will lead it to seek additional information which will have the same self-reinforcing effect.

Indeed, this effect can occur entirely through changes in information processing without any shift in the external environment. Because people assimilate incoming information to their preexisting beliefs, tentative ideas and expectations will grow firmer as the person is exposed to a stream of ambiguous or even arguably disconfirming information.[76] Thus warning systems can self-excite when they go on alert: When a decision maker thinks that an attack is likely, he will place more credence in reports indicating that a war is imminent than he would if the same information were received in a period of calm, and actions of the other side that usually would be missed or seen as innocent will be perceived as evincing hostile intentions. And the more such "information" is received, the greater the fear of attack.

TIPPING

When several actors are involved, a small change can have large effects even if power, beliefs, and preferences remain constant. In a typically lucid and stimulating treatment, Schelling shows how neighborhoods can "tip" even if most people favor a significant degree of integration. Imagine one hundred white families living in an area. One is so racist that it will move out if any blacks enter; another will tolerate one black family but not two; a third does not mind (and may even welcome) one or two blacks but will leave if three move in, and so on. If any blacks enter, the whole neighborhood will unravel as each consecutive change pushes another white family beyond its tolerance point.[77] Some revolutions and mass protests gain strength in this way.

[75] R. V. Jones, *Most Secret War: British Scientific Intelligence, 1939–1945* (London: Hamish Hamilton, 1978), p. 381.

[76] Jervis, *Perception and Misperception*, pp. 181–87.

[77] Schelling, *Micromotives*, chapter 4. A Serbian woman who reluctantly moved out when a Sarajavo suburb was turned over to the Bosian Muslims provides a contemporary example: "The federation police are O.K. . . . And in a way I look forward to seeing them because some will be old friends. But I can't stay here anymore, because nothing is left. . . . I am moving because everyone else is gone and my child will have no one else to play with" (quoted in Kit Roane, "As Sarajevo Declares Siege Over, Serbs Still Pack," *New York Times*, March 1, 1996). For applications and extensions, see Bernard Grofman, "Rational Choice Models and Self-Fulfilling and Self-Defeating Prophesies," in Werner Leinfellner and Eckehart Kohler, eds.,

As long as most people are inactive, only a few will risk their livelihoods and lives for the slight chance of success. Others will be willing to join when the risk is a bit lower and the chance of success a bit greater; if they join, others who are even less willing to accept risks will follow, especially if they conclude that opposition to the regime is widespread. More generally, when actors prefer to deal with others who resemble them or when a strategy does best when it interacts with a like strategy, then positive feedback can lead to the rapid growth of a type of actor or behavior.[78]

In the simplest cases, tipping occurs as actors respond to their new environments without behaving strategically or drawing inferences about how others will behave. Greater complexity can be introduced by considering how actors estimate how others are likely to respond to changes and how they can seek to manipulate these responses. For example, I may be willing to remain in the neighborhood if it remains 15 percent black, but may leave sooner because I anticipate that once the percentage climbs into the double digits, many whites will flee. A third layer of feedback can operate if the changes alter people's preferences. Thus protests may grow if the original and limited movement leads many bystanders to alter their views not only about the chances of success, but also about the legitimacy of the cause.

The same process works in reverse. As those who are more active and concerned leave an enterprise, some others, who would have been willing to stay under previous circumstances, will follow suit. Just as withdrawals of cash both weaken a bank and deepen the perception that it is likely to fail, so an organization can rapidly disintegrate as its members expect it to fail and

---

Developments in the Methodology of Social Science (Boston: D. Reidel, 1974), pp. 381–83; Becker, *Accounting for Tastes,* chapter 9; Courtney Brown, *Serpents in the Sand: Essays on the Nonlinear Nature of Politics and Human Destiny* (Ann Arbor: University of Michigan Press, 1995), pp. 36–54. For a related model, see George Akerlof, "The Market for 'Lemons': Quality Uncertainty and the Market Mechanism," *The Quarterly Journal of Economics* 84 (August 1970), pp. 599–617; also see Randolph Siverson and Harvey Starr, *The Diffusion of War* (Ann Arbor: University of Michigan Press, 1991). For an accessible discussion of tipping models and epidemiological approaches to urban disorders, see Malcolm Gladwell, "The Tipping Point," *The New Yorker,* June 3, 1996, pp. 32–38. In some revolutions, such as those in Eastern Europe in 1989, the process looks the same but actually is a bit different because people are judging not how their fellow citizens will react but whether the authorities will use force: for variants of the more conventional view, see Timur Kuran, "Now out of Never: The Element of Surprise in the East European Revolution of 1989," *World Politics* 44 (October 1991), pp. 7–48, Susanne Lohmann, "The Dynamics of Informational Cascades: The Monday Demonstrations in Liepzig, East Germany, 1989–91," ibid. 47 (October 1994), pp. 42–101.

[78] See, for example, Hendrik Spruyt, *The Sovereign State and Its Competitors* (Princeton, N.J.: Princeton University Press, 1994); Robert Axelrod, *The Evolution of Cooperation* (New York: Basic Books, 1984); W. Richard Scott, John Meyer, and Associates, *Institutional Environment and Organizations: Structural Complexity and Individualism* (Thousand Oaks, Calif.: Sage, 1994). For similar findings in ecology, see Timothy Allen and Thomas Hoekstra, *Toward a Unified Ecology* (New York: Columbia University Press, 1992), pp. 148–50, 306–7. For a related discussion, see chapter 2, pp. 51–53.

withdraw their support from it.[79] In the same way, whether a person cooperates in a multiperson prisoner's dilemma depends in part on his estimates of how many others will cooperate; the behavior of each affects the others' incentives.[80] For example, if a few people drop out of the collective efforts to maintain irrigation ditches, the cost to those who remain will rise, perhaps leading some who had previously felt that participation was barely worthwhile to cease their efforts, which in turn may push others over the edge.[81]

CONSENSUS EFFECTS

Dynamics similar to the tipping process operate when actors want to do what others are doing, what they think others will do, or, even more, when they want to take a position that is slightly more extreme than others. These systems can be very sensitive to initial disturbances, and the collectivity will behave very differently than each individual would if she were not concerned about the reactions of others. Many people want to believe what their friends and neighbors do; people often seek to vote for the political candidate they think will win even when they will not be rewarded for doing so.[82]

This is how fads and fashions gain momentum. They rarely settle into a stable equilibrium when each actor wants to be slightly more extreme than the others. Thus, up to a point, skirts keep getting longer and longer or shorter and shorter, ties grow and shrink in width, and tail fins on automobiles take on outrageous shapes.[83] Academics should not laugh: Scholarly disciplines develop in this manner. Although rare originality gathers the greatest rewards, most scholarship is based on conforming rather closely to the questions others have asked, the techniques they have used, and the

[79] Albert Hirschman, *Exit, Voice, and Loyalty* (Cambridge, Mass.: Harvard University Press, 1970); for a nice example, see Steven Solnick, "The Breakdown of Hierarchies in the Soviet Union and China: A Neoinstitutional Perspective," *World Politics* 48 (January 1996), pp. 209–38.

[80] The seminal work is again by Schelling: *Micromotives*, chapter 7; also see Howard Margolis, "Free Riding Versus Cooperation," in Richard Zeckhauser, ed., *Strategy and Choice* (Cambridge, Mass.: MIT Press, 1991), chapter 4.

[81] See Eleanor Ostrom, *Governing the Commons: The Evolution of Institutions for Collective Action* (New York: Cambridge University Press, 1990); Marc Reisner, *Cadillac Desert: The American West and Its Disappearing Water* (New York: Penguin, 1987), pp. 93–94.

[82] The literature here is very large. The earlier work talked of the "breakage effect"—the classic study is Bernard Berelson, Paul Lazarsfeld, and William McPhee, *Voting* (Chicago: University of Chicago Press, 1954); a more recent treatment is Elizabeth Noelle-Newmann, *The Spiral of Silence: Public Opinion—Our Social Skin* (Chicago: University of Chicago Press, 1984). See Stephen Jones, *The Economics of Conformism* (New York: Basil Blackwell, 1984) for an analysis of this general phenomenon from the perspective of economics.

[83] There is, of course, more to the full story than this: Georg Simmel's classic "Fashion," originally published in 1904, is reprinted in *American Journal of Sociology* 62 (May 1957), pp. 541–58.

perspectives they have adopted while trying to push prevailing trends a bit further. Hence professors of English move further from literature and closer to incomprehensibility and political scientists become more mathematical. Sometimes the result is the growth of knowledge, but perhaps more often it resembles Winnie the Pooh and his colleagues in their pursuit of Woozles.[84]

Of greater importance, a similar process can drive evolution. Less well known than natural selection is the process of sexual selection: The reproductive success of any individual is related to his or her ability not only to survive, but also to attract mates. When mate selection is influenced by judgments of the partner's traits that are not linked to fitness, there can be self-reinforcement that produces "runaway" evolution. To take the best-known example, if peahens have a choice among suitors and, for any reason, prefer males with longer or more colorful tails, then positive feedback can be set in motion and peacocks will evolve ever larger and more gaudy tails even at some cost to their own chances of survival. At every point in time peacocks with the largest tails will leave the most descendants; the sons produced by any females who preferred short-tailed males would find fewer mates and leave fewer offspring. Although this process is limited by the search costs of females and the extent to which the sexually selected trait is too disabling, the results are very different from the stability that occurs when negative feedback in the form of natural selection produces animals that are well adapted to their physical environments.[85]

COMPETITION

Earlier I noted that arms races and related phenomena demonstrate positive feedback as each actor seeks to stay even with if not get ahead of others. Positive feedback can be revealed even more sharply when two rivals compete for the favor of a third party. Thus in electoral politics, parties can quickly move toward what they perceive to be a popular stance in anticipation that, if they fail to do so, the other party will take advantage of their

[84] The classic study is Robert Jervis, "Cumulation, Correlations, and Woozles" in James Rosenau, ed., *In Search of Global Patterns* (New York: Free Press, 1976), pp. 181–85; also see Schelling, *Micromotives*, p. 118.

[85] Runaway selection is only one part of the larger category of sexual selection, and the subject remains contested: see, for example, Maynard Smith, *Evolution and the Theory of Games*, pp. 131–37; Niles Eldredge and Marjorie Grene, *Interactions: The Biological Context of Social Systems* (New York: Columbia University Press, 1992), and Malte Andersson, *Sexual Selection* (Princeton, N.J.: Princeton University Press, 1994) (chapter 10 discusses the constraints on the positive feedback). A summary of the logic can be found in Sigmund, *Games of Life*, pp. 128–31; also see ibid., pp. 189–90 for a discussion of the way in which certain strategies can encourage the evolution of more of their own kind, a subject touched on above, chapter 2, pp. 46–47.

restraint.[86] Similar is the famed "race to the bottom" among states seeking to reduce regulation in order to attract corporate headquarters or to cut welfare benefits to lower taxes and court mobile businesses. Today's newspaper carries New York Governor Pataki's explanation for why he supports gambling casinos. Pointing to Atlantic City and the Indian casinos in Connecticut, he said: "I think the most important thing is to be able to stop losing billions of dollars to surrounding states. . . . I think we want to see [New York's] historic tourism areas able to successfully compete."[87]

Related dynamics operate in the international arena. Thus even though— or perhaps because—many NATO countries distrusted West Germany's opening to the Soviet Union in the early 1970s, "each of [German Prime Minister] Brandt's colleagues—including Nixon—sought to preempt Germany by conducting an active détente policy of his own. In this sense *Ostpolitik* had effects far beyond those intended. It contributed to a race to Moscow."[88] One of the rationales for the U.S. selling arms to Iran in the mid-1980s was to take advantage of the potential for positive feedback in the competition with the USSR. As one official put it, both the U.S. and the USSR "lack . . . preferred access to Iran. Whoever gets there first is in a strong position to work towards the exclusion of the other."[89] This analysis was incorrect, but in situations in which loyalties are unformed and alignments are fluid, the actor who first establishes good relations with another may be able to gain an increasing advantage over competitors.

POWER

In many political areas, power is central to the operation of positive feedback as actors use their positions to maintain themselves. For example, in many countries the ruling party gains great advantages from the government control of television coverage.[90] But behavior does not have to aim at increasing

[86] See, for example, the case presented in David Beam, Timothy Conlan, and Margaret Wrightson, "Solving the Riddle of Tax Reform: Party Competition and the Politics of Ideas," *Political Science Quarterly* 105 (Summer 1990), pp. 193–218. As the authors note, this effect does not require that the legislation actually be popular but only that members of each party fear "that a skillful political opponent might turn the issue against them at some later date" (ibid., p. 201).

[87] Quoted in Raymond Hernandez, "Pataki Panel Says Casinos Could Bring in $2.6 Billion," *New York Times*, August 31, 1996.

[88] Henry Kissinger, *Years of Upheaval* (Boston: Little, Brown, 1982), p. 146; also see p. 176. But note the negative feedback in the form of the reduced value of Brandt's policy to Germany because the Soviets needed him less as the supply of suitors increased.

[89] Quoted in John Tower, Edmund Muskie, and Brent Scowcroft, *President's Special Review Board* (known as the Tower Commission Report) (Washington, D.C.: Government Printing Office, 1989), p. B-6.

[90] For some nice illustrations, see Tim Golden, "Mexican TV Picks Its Political Shots," *New York Times*, July 22, 1994, and Alexander Stille, "Italy: The Convulsions of Normalcy," *New York Review of Books* 43 (June 6, 1996), pp. 42–46.

the actor's power in order for it to have this effect. New laws and government agencies become the focus of concerned parties, often in a way that increases the power of both interest groups and the bureaucracies that affect them, and the adoption of a policy that requires a large role for a part of the state will usually increase that organization's influence.[91] The classic example is Schumpeter's argument about the role of armies in imperialism: "Created by the wars that required it, the machine now created the wars it required."[92] The same process occurs on a smaller scale. Once troops are committed, the role of the military in setting relevant policy is likely to increase; once an issue is subject to formal negotiations, the diplomats not only gain increased influence, they are also likely to press for expanded negotiations to deal with any problems that arise in the course of the discussions. The reasons why a nuclear weapons program is hard to reverse apply more generally: "Once a nuclear program becomes established, it will act as a magnet for new justifications and motives [and new bureaucracies and interests], and soon no nonproliferation policy may be able to eliminate the program."[93]

Positive Feedback and Path Dependence—The Big Impact of Small Advantages

The idea that power, wealth, and advantage can build on themselves is enshrined in the familiar saying "Nothing succeeds like success."[94] How well an actor does at time t may be determined less by its skills and virtues than by how it was positioned at time t-1; small and often accidental differences between two actors at an early stage can lead to enormous divergences later on; many aspects of politics and society are to be explained not by the inherent suitability of the actors and patterns but rather by quirks and small perturbations that occurred much earlier.[95] In what is known as path depen-

[91] For a review, see Paul Pierson, "When Effect Becomes Cause: Policy Feedback and Political Change," *World Politics* 45 (July 1993), pp. 595–628.

[92] Joseph Schumpeter, *Imperialism, Social Classes* (Cleveland: World Publishing, 1955), p. 25.

[93] Michael Mazarr, "Going Just a Little Nuclear: Nonproliferation Lessons from North Korea," *International Security* 20 (Fall 1995), p. 101.

[94] Robert Merton has pointed to the operation of what he refers to as "the Matthew Principle"—"to him that hath shall be given": Merton, *The Sociology of Science* (Chicago: University of Chicago Press, 1973), pp. 99–136.

[95] Thus a study that helped start this line of argument in economic development found that "marked divergences between ultimate outcomes may flow from seemingly negligible differences in remote beginnings": Paul David, *Technical Choice, Innovation, and Economic Growth* (New York: Cambridge University Press, 1975), p. 16. This pattern contrasts with ones in which initial conditions are unimportant because the system can reach the same end point by multiple paths—what is known as equifinality. Arguments for the importance of the "legacies of the past" see a form of lock-in operating and are opposed by claims for the power of factors that are either deeply rooted or current but transient.

dence, the result is instability in the sense that many alternatives are possible at the early stages, but stability in that once the process starts, the path will be "locked in" even if it becomes inefficient or disadvantageous. Looking back after the pattern is established, we may overestimate the degree of determinism involved. To take a physical analogy, a river may run through a deep gorge not because the gorge was always much lower than its surroundings, but because eons ago a slight indentation channeled a bit more water there than elsewhere, with the result that the water's erosion slowly created a deep canyon.[96] Indeed, many cities developed where and how they did not because of the "natural advantages" we are so quick to detect after the fact, but because their establishment set off self-reinforcing expectations and behaviors.[97]

In its emphasis on the importance of contingency, this perspective fits comfortably with the outlook of historians who argue that only rarely is the flow of events completely determined. Because they study details, are fascinated by them, and believe they are crucial (which of these beliefs determines the others is an interesting question), they often find "Cleopatra's noses"—instances in which the flow of events is strongly influenced by some unpredictable aspect of the situation, such as the size of Cleopatra's nose which, had it been different, would have made her less attractive to Marc Antony and changed the course of history. But historians are less prone to accept the other half of the argument that positive feedback creates great stability after it has been operating for a time. Most economists are even more offended by this aspect of the process because they believe that market forces will induce efficient equilibria during every period. In this view, history does not—indeed cannot—constrain current choices; products and forms of organization that win out in the competition with others do so because they best fit their environments, not because they have shaped their environments; innovators and new competitors can readily arise and inefficiencies cannot prevail for long. But if contingency and positive feedback play a large role, then many possible worlds are compatible with the basic laws of physics, chemistry, biology, and economics.

In much the same way, Stephen Jay Gould argues that the general laws of

[96] For computer simulations showing that a similar process can produce the familiar characteristic of evenly spaced cusps on an ocean beach, see B. T. Werner and T. M. Fink, "Beach Cusps as Self-Organizing Patterns," *Science* 260 (May 14, 1993), pp. 968–71; also see Michael Shermer, "The Chaos of History: On a Chaotic Model that Represents the Role of Contingency and Necessity in Historical Sequences," *Nonlinear Science Today* 2 (April 1993), p. 8. An early sociological analysis in this vein was Herbert Spencer, *The Study of Sociology* (Ann Arbor: University of Michigan Press, 1961) (first published in 1880), pp. 56–67.

[97] William Cronon, *Nature's Metropolis: Chicago and the Great West* (New York: Norton, 1991); Mark Lytle, "An Environmental Approach to American Diplomatic History," *Diplomatic History* 20 (Spring 1996), pp. 294–95.

biology and natural selection have not entirely determined the forms of life that dominate the earth. In the earliest times, a great many kinds of creatures existed and those who survived to be the ancestors of what we see around us were no better adapted and more fit than those who did not. We may then be the product of "massive historical contingency."[98] Dramatic events rather than competition and reinforcing initial advantages may have been at work here, but the latter are seen by some as explaining the development of the international hierarchy. According to Immanuel Wallerstein, the enormous current gap between the developed and underdeveloped states is to be explained by the small and almost accidental disparity in the early modern period that allowed Western Europe to grow increasingly strong and powerful while making it increasingly difficult for states in the periphery of the international system to do so.[99] The same argument was made more narrowly by E. J. Hobsbawn when he showed that by being the first country to build a textile industry, Great Britain was able to dominate the world market, thereby both fueling Britain's industrial revolution and inhibiting development in other states.[100] History could have come out very differently; the states that are now in the first rank are not necessarily inherently superior to the others.

This kind of argument has been applied to specific aspects of economic development. Contrary to the standard view that economic activity is char-

---

[98] Stephen Jay Gould, *Wonderful Life* (New York: Norton, 1989), p. 233. Gould also stresses the extent to which biological structures constrain and enable evolution: See, for example, "Common Pathways of Illumination," *Natural History* 103 (December 1994), pp. 10–20; also see Gould, "Fungal Forgery," *Natural History* 102 (September 1993), pp. 12–21. For a good discussion of how contingency at an early stage can set in motion forces that establish necessity at later stages, see Shermer, "Chaos of History," pp. 1–13. For the related argument that many biological processes and relationships, being the product of evolution, cannot be derived from parsimonious laws, contrary to the pattern in physics, see Francis Crick, *What Mad Pursuit* (New York: Basic Books, 1988), pp. 109–11, 138–41. For good discussions of positive feedback in biological and ecological communities, see Stuart Kauffman, *The Origins of Order: Self-Organization and Selection in Evolution* (New York: Oxford University Press, 1993), especially pp. 13–14; Allen and Hoekstra, *Toward a Unified Ecology*, pp. 68–72, 92; James Brown, *Macroevolution* (Chicago: University of Chicago Press, 1995), pp. 33–35; Daniel Botkin, *Discordant Harmonies: A New Ecology for the Twenty-first Century* (New York: Oxford University Press, 1990), pp. 61–63. These ideas were not foreign to Darwin: Charles Darwin, *The Origin of Species* (New York: Modern Library, 1936), pp. 310–12, 364–65.

[99] Wallerstein's first and best statement is "The Rise and Demise of the World Capitalist System: Concepts for Comparative Analysis," *Comparative Studies in Society and History* 16 (September 1974), pp. 387–415.

[100] E. J. Hobsbawm, *Industry and Empire: The Making of Modern English Society, 1750 to the Present Day* (New York: Pantheon, 1968). For a general rebuttal, see Paul Bairoch, *Economics and World History: Myths and Paradoxes* (Chicago: University of Chicago Press, 1993), chapters 5–8. Other theorists argue that there are at least as many advantages as disadvantages to developing relatively late. Still the best discussion is Alexander Gerschenkron, *Economic Backwardness in Historical Perspective* (Cambridge: Harvard University Press, 1962).

acterized by diminishing returns on the margin (a form of negative feedback), development of many technologies and economic activities invokes returns to scale and positive feedback. Perhaps the best-known example is Paul David's discussion of the typewriter keyboard. Once QWERTY was established as the industry standard, it became in each manufacturer's interest to adopt it and in each typist's interest to learn it. Although technological changes have made other arrangements much more efficient, they cannot get a foothold because they would require great coordination and the abandonment of much mechanical and human capital.[101]

Brian Arthur finds similar patterns when a number of not uncommon conditions are met: At the start, multiple patterns, outcomes, or equilibria are possible; there are high incentives for each actor to behave in ways that are compatible with the actions of others (e.g., one cannot have a railroad network if each railroad and equipment manufacturer builds for a different gauge); the successful entrepreneur needs to anticipate the behavior of others, who must similarly estimate what others will do; there is a steep learning curve and high initial fixed costs, which give a sizeable advantage to any technology or pattern that gets a head start and restricts change even if alternative arrangements would be more efficient if they could be established.[102] As Arthur explains:

> The parts of the economy that are resource-based (agriculture, bulk-goods production, mining) are still for the most part subject to diminishing returns. Here

[101] Paul David, "Clio and the Economics of QWERTY," *American Economic Review* 75 (May 1985), pp. 332–37. It is perhaps illustrative of path dependence that the rebuttal is less frequently cited: S. J. Liebowitz and Stephen Margolis, "The Fable of the Keys," *Journal of Law and Economics* 33 (April 1990), pp. 1–25. A summary of David's general analysis which also provides a good guide to the literature is Paul David, "Path-Dependence in Economic Processes: Implications for Policy Analysis in Dynamical System Contexts" (Stanford, Calif.: Center for Economic Policy Research, April 1992). For a related discussion of positive feedbacks in economic systems, see Paul Krugman, *The Self-Organizing Economy* (Cambridge, Mass.: Blackwell, 1996).

[102] W. Brian Arthur, "Self-Reinforcing Mechanisms in Economics," in Philip Anderson, Kenneth Arrow, and David Pines, eds., *The Economy as an Evolving Complex System* (Redwood City, Calif.: Addison-Wesley, 1988), pp. 9–32; Arthur, "Competing Technologies, Increasing Returns, and Lock-In by Historical Events," *Economic Journal* 99 (March 1989), pp. 116–31; Arthur, "Positive Feedbacks in the Economy," *Scientific American*, February 1990, pp. 92–99 (these essays are reprinted in Arthur, *Increasing Returns and Path Dependence in the Economy* [Ann Arbor: University of Michigan Press, 1994]). Also see Amihai Glazer, "The Advantages of Being First," *American Economic Review* 75 (June 1985), pp. 473–80; Paul Krugman, "History Versus Expectations," *Quarterly Journal of Economics* 103 (May 1991), pp. 651–67; Geoffrey Hodgson, *Economics and Evolution: Bringing Life Back into Economics* (Ann Arbor: University of Michigan Press, 1993), pp. 203–7; Schelling, *Micromotives*, p. 15. For similar processes in ecology, see Allen and Hoekstra, *Toward a Unified Ecology*, chapter 6. An early statement of general applicability is Magoroh Maruyama, "The Second Cybernetics: Deviation-Amplifying Mutual Causal Processes," *American Scientist* 51 (June 1963), pp. 161–79.

conventional economics rightly holds sway. The parts of the economy that are knowledge-based, on the other hand, are largely subject to increasing returns. Products such as computers, pharmaceuticals, missiles, aircraft, automobiles, software, telecommunications equipment or fiber optics are complicated to design and to manufacture. . . . Increased production brings additional benefits: producing more units means gaining more experience in the manufacturing process and achieving greater understanding of how to produce additional units even more cheaply. Moreover, experience gained with one product or technology can make it easier to produce new products incorporating similar or related technologies. . . . Not only do the costs of producing high-technology products fall as a company makes more of them, but the benefits of using them increase. Many items such as computers or telecommunications equipment work in networks that require compatibility; when one brand gains a significant market share, people have a strong incentive to buy more of the same product so as to be able to exchange information with those using it already.[103]

As Arthur indicates, these processes can be found in many areas, both large and small. For example, they explain how the videotape market became dominated by VHS machines rather than Betamax and may account for the spread of the AC electrical system.[104] Similarly, a technologically advanced Power PC chip has been developed but will be adopted only if software companies can be induced to write software for it.

> That is a tricky, chicken-and-egg issue that will depend on whether the Power PC chips look like winners. If it appears that the chip architecture will be used on millions of computers, then the software companies that produce applications like spread-sheets and word-processing programs will make sure their software runs on the Power PC. And computer makers will be reluctant to use the chip in their machines unless it appears to have the backing of the software community.
>
> "This isn't about technology," said Mr. Shaffer of Technologic Partners. "It's about momentum and market share."[105]

In these cases, people need to be on the winning side and the concept of momentum is more useful than it is in athletic contests. (This is also true in the selection of candidates for political office, especially when the process involves a series of events, each of which establishes the context for the

[103] Arthur, "Positive Feedbacks in the Economy," p. 93.

[104] Thomas Hughes, *Networks of Power: Electrification in Western Society, 1880–1930* (Baltimore, Md.: Johns Hopkins University Press, 1983).

[105] Steven Lohr, "In Pursuit of Computing's Holy Grail," *New York Times*, May 23, 1993; for general analyses of effects of this kind, see Michael Katz and Carl Shapiro, "Network Externalities, Competition, and Compatibility," *American Economic Review* 75 (June 1985), pp. 424–40, and Katz and Shapiro, "Systems Competition and Network Effects," *Journal of Economic Perspectives* 8 (Spring 1994), pp. 93–115; for a rebuttal see S. J. Liebowitz and Stephen Margolis, "Network Externalities: An Uncommon Tragedy," ibid., pp. 133–50.

subsequent ones, as happens with the current American system for selecting presidential nominees.[106])

Douglass North has come to see similar forces as shaping the course of economic development. His initial work saw economic growth as the product of political arrangements that protected property rights and allowed the free market to function at its most efficient.[107] But further study led him to see a much greater role for path dependence and positive feedback and to argue that once institutions and arrangements are in place, they can be maintained by actors behaving rationally despite the outcomes being suboptimal.[108]

Arguments for the importance of initial advantages have recently been applied to national economic policies and international trade. The standard view holds that protectionism and export subsidies harm the state as well as others. But proponents of strategic trade theory argue that when there is a steep learning curve and major returns to scale, actors who gain a head start can prevent rivals from establishing themselves and that states therefore may be well advised to shelter and support certain industries.[109] More is at

[106] See Larry Bartels, *Presidential Primaries and the Dynamics of Public Choice* (Princeton, N.J.: Princeton University Press, 1988). For related dynamics in a different context, see James Lebovic, "Before the Storm: Momentum and the Onset of the Gulf War," *International Studies Quarterly* 38 (September 1994), pp. 447–74.

[107] Douglass North and Robert Thomas, *The Rise of the Western World: A New Economic History* (Cambridge: Cambridge University Press, 1973).

[108] North, *Institutions, Institutional Change and Economic Performance* (New York: Norton, 1990); North, "Economic Performance Through Time," *American Economic Review* 84 (June 1994), pp. 359–68.

[109] This theory is fiercely disputed, in part because of its challenge to the dominant paradigm of free trade: see, for example, Paul Krugman, ed., *Strategic Trade Policy and the New International Economics* (Cambridge, Mass.: MIT Press, 1986); Krugman, *Rethinking International Trade* (Cambridge, Mass.: MIT Press, 1991); Krugman, *Peddling Prosperity: Economic Sense and Nonsense in the Age of Diminished Expectations* (New York: Norton, 1994); Klaus Stegemann, "Policy Rivalry Among Industrial States: What Can We Learn from Models of Strategic Trade Policy?" *International Organization* 43 (Winter 1989), pp. 73–100; Helen Milner and David Yoffie, "Between Free Trade and Protectionism: Strategic Trade Policy and the Theory of Corporate Trade Demand," *International Organization* 43 (Spring 1989), pp. 239–72; Chalmers Johnson, Laura D'Andrea Tyson, and John Zysman, eds., *Politics and Productivity, How Japan's Development Strategy Works* (Boston: Ballinger, 1989); Tyson, *Who's Bashing Whom? Trade Conflict in High Technology Industries* (Washington, D.C.: Institute for International Economics, 1993); J. David Richardson, "'New' Trade Theory and Policy a Decade Old: Assessment in a Pacific Context," in Richard Higgott, Richard Leaver, and John Ravenhill, eds., *Pacific Economic Relations in the 1990s* (Boston: Allen & Unwin, 1993), pp. 83–105. There is a family resemblance between these arguments and the old "infant industry" rationale for protectionism in the early stages, an argument that is accepted even by many neoclassical economists. But the new theory is more far-reaching and represents a greater alteration of the free-trade doctrine. Important modifications of the argument are presented by Marc Busch, "The Strategic Trade Calculus of States: Cooperation and Conflict in Emerging Industries" (unpublished dissertation, Department of Political Science, Columbia University, 1994).

stake here than "only" market shares. The relations among wealth, domination of leading economic sectors, and political power are mutually supportive: A country that pushes ahead in "cutting edge" technologies gains greater wealth and political influence as a strong economy gives it instruments to further economic development and exploit others on unrelated issues. For example, a Japan that dominated the advanced computer chip industry could not only refuse to export the most advanced models until its own manufacturers had put them into place, thereby increasing their leads over rival firms, but might also try to use foreign dependence on their products to reinforce economic dominance (for example, by demanding that foreign firms cease certain lines of advanced research) or even to gain unrelated political ends, as sketched in the infamous *Japan That Can Say No*.[110]

It is then not surprising that people's stance toward trade disputes with Japan are strongly influenced by beliefs about whether far-reaching feedbacks are at work. Those who stress the need to be concerned with relative as opposed to absolute gains believe that if Japan grows more rapidly than the U.S. and is able to move ahead of it in high technology, future American growth will be slowed and American power will be weakened. Those who are guided by neoclassical economic principles can focus on absolute gains because they do not see such amplifying processes at work, and so they doubt both the need for and the efficacy of many interventionist trade practices.

Other Areas of Positive Feedback

To try to describe all other instances in which positive feedback plays a significant role in politics would take more space than I have. Since the previous discussion has been quite lengthy, here I will be telegraphic.

Peace and Prosperity

It is possible that there are both vicious and virtuous circles linking economic growth, democracy, and a peaceful foreign policy. Any one of these elements supports and is supported by the other two; it is hard for any of them to thrive for long without the others.

Communication Systems

For messages to carry meaning, both the signaler and the receiver must understand them the same way; trying to establish a language that only you can use makes no sense. Thus in both ordinary and diplomatic languages actors need to adopt the same rules that others do, regardless of what these

---

[110] Shitaro Ishihara, *The Japan That Can Say No* (New York: Simon and Schuster, 1991).

rules are, and as more people abide by any given rules, the more reason others will have to follow them.[111]

Mutualism

As two species coevolve in close interaction with each other, they may develop a mutualistic or symbiotic relationship in which the health of each depends on the fate of the other. As a result, natural selection will make them increasingly interdependent and the success of each will feed the success of the partner.

Expansion

Throughout the nineteenth century, small colonial settlements generated local resistance, the quelling of which required the European power to push its control farther into the hinterland. But the new frontier itself was likely to become "turbulent," thereby calling for still more expansion.[112] Some scholars have seen the carving up of Africa as having the same dynamic through the acquisition of one colony creating the need to maintain its security in the face of the conflict it generated.[113] A small-scale parallel is provided by an aspect of the Aldrich Ames case mentioned earlier. One reason why Ames continued to provide the Soviets with names of American agents, contrary to his original intentions, was that he needed to remove anyone who might be in a position to expose his treason.[114]

Regional Integration

Following World War II, European statesmen began limited economic cooperation only to find that they could not readily stop there because their actions created both problems and opportunities that required further integration. Furthermore, as the power of supranational institutions grew, interest groups turned to them, thereby giving them greater importance, which

[111] Jervis, *Logic of Images*; David Lewis, *Convention: A Philosophical Study* (Cambridge, Mass.: Harvard University Press, 1969).

[112] John Galbraith, *Reluctant Empire: British Policy on the South African Frontier, 1834–1854* (Berkeley: University of California Press, 1963); Galbraith, "The 'Turbulent Frontier' as a Factor in British Expansion," *Comparative Studies in Society and History* 2 (October 1968), pp. 150–68. Similar processes can entrap statesmen and produce more deep involvement in ventures than they had originally intended, although the once-popular belief that American policy in Vietnam is to be explained in this way is largely incorrect. For some Israeli decisionmakers, this was at work during the invasion of Lebanon in 1982: Avner Yaniv, *Dilemmas of Security: Politics, Strategy, and the Israeli Experience in Lebanon* (New York: Oxford University Press, 1987), pp. 110–27.

[113] Ronald Robinson and John Gallagher with Alice Denny, *Africa and the Victorians: The Official Mind of Imperialism* (New York: St. Martin's, 1967).

[114] Senate Select Committee on Intelligence, "Assessment of the Aldrich H. Ames Espionage Case," p. 22; also see appendix 3, pp. 20–21.

in turn increased the pressures and resources for new measures.[115] Even if the course of integration is in part controlled by intergovernmental bargaining,[116] the incentives, pressures, and opportunities that affect governments are influenced by the consequences of the previous steps toward integration.

The Transformation of Reform into Revolution

It is a commonplace that radical reform from above is one of the hardest political processes to control.[117] Supporters of the old arrangements may be able to successfully resist change (negative feedback), but if they cannot, there is a good chance that once the old structures start to crumble, the entire regime will be swept away. For this reason, those who are aware of the dynamics may avoid taking the first steps even if they favor moderate reform.[118]

[115] The literature is enormous. See, for example, Karl Deutsch, *Political Community at the International Level* (Garden City, N.Y.: Doubleday, 1954); Ernst Haas, *The Uniting of Europe* (Stanford, Calif.: Stanford University Press, 1958); the special issue of *International Organization* 24 (Autumn 1970), *Regional Integration*, edited by Leon Lindberg and Stuart Scheingold; Ernst Haas, *The Obsolescence of Regional Integration Theory* (Berkeley: Institute of International Studies, University of California, 1975); Steven Genco, "Integration Theory and System Change in Western Europe: The Neglected Role of Systems Transformation Episodes," in Ole Holsti, Randolph Siverson, and Alexander George, eds., *Change in the International System* (Boulder, Colo.: Westview, 1980), chapter 3; Kathleen McNamara, "Common Markets, Common Currencies: Systems Effects and the European Community," in Snyder and Jervis, eds., *Coping With Complexity*, chapter 12; Robert Keohane and Stanley Hoffmann, eds., *The New European Community: Decisionmaking and Institutional Change* (Boulder, Colo.: Westview 1991); Loukas Tsoukalis, *The European Economy: The Politics and Economics of Integration* (New York: Oxford University Press, 1991). The process is not automatic: See Stanley Hoffmann, "Obstinent or Obsolete? The Fate of the Nation-State and the Case of Western Europe," *Daedalus*, Summer 1966, pp. 862–915. The strongest rebuttals to Haas's analysis of the early stages of European integration are Alan Milward, *The European Rescue of the Nation-State* (London: Routledge, 1992), and Milward et al., *The Frontier of National Sovereignty: History and Theory, 1945–1992* (London: Routledge, 1993).

[116] Andrew Moravcsik, "Negotiating the Single European Act," *International Organization* 45 (Winter 1991), pp. 19–56; Michael Baun, "The Maastricht Treaty as High Politics: Germany, France, and European Integration," *Political Science Quarterly* 110 (Winter 1995–96), pp. 605–24. For a defense of the role of spillovers, see Wayne Sandholtz, "Institutions and Collective Action: The New Telecommunications in Western Europe," *World Politics* 45 (January 1993), pp. 242–70. For a discussion that draws on both approaches and that also stresses the dynamics of competition, see Dorette Corbey, "Dialectical Functionalism: Stagnation as a Booster of European Integration," *International Organization* 49 (Spring 1995), pp. 253–84.

[117] For a discussion of this process in terms of spillover, see Joseph Rothschild, *Return to Diversity: A Political History of East Central Europe Since World War II*, 2d ed. (New York: Oxford University Press, 1993), pp. 169–71.

[118] Fidel Castro may have learned this lesson from the events in Eastern Europe and the USSR: Jorge Dominguez, "The Secrets of Castro's Staying Power," *Foreign Affairs* 72 (Spring 1993), p. 99. For another case where decision makers acted on their anticipation that small concessions would have undesirable positive feedback, see John Offner, *An Unwanted War:*

Politics, Publicity, and the Media

An issue is considered newsworthy to the extent that it is being treated by the media, and they and politicians take their cues from each other. Subjects like Clinton's sexual affairs are then likely to receive either no attention or a great deal of it; new media forms like talk shows often have great influence by triggering other coverage; politicians may devote major efforts to getting a few reporters interested in a story knowing that once it appears, it will be repeated; reporters often urge politicians to speak about an issue so that they can cover it.

Alignments and Alliances

Bonds between countries can intensify through positive feedback, as I will discuss in detail in chapter 6. States that work together on one issue tend to acquire each other's friends and adversaries and to be drawn together by the reactions of others. Indeed, these dynamics give alliances much of their force.

Battles

When an army is uncertain of its own strength and morale, a defeat can turn into a rout. As Clausewitz put it,

> if a victory has primarily shaken the opponent's confidence . . . then the lost engagement turns into defeat on a scale not produced by every victory. Since in this type of débacle the morale of the defeated is affected to a far higher degree, the total inability to offer resistance is frequently the result. . . . The scale of a victory does not increase simply at a rate commensurate with the increase in size of the defeated armies, but progressively. The outcome of a major battle has a greater psychological effect on the loser than the winner. This, in turn, gives rise to additional loss of material strength [through abandonment of weapons in retreat or desertions from the army], which is echoed in loss of morale; the two become mutually interactive as each enhances and intensifies the other.[119]

This effect is especially pronounced when the loser cannot retreat to prepared defensive positions, which explains why desert warfare and engagements between fleets are particularly likely to be decisive. Armies are vulnerable to positive feedback at particular points: The elder Moltke "said that mistakes made during the initial concentration of armies could scarcely ever be rectified during the course of a war"[120] and for reasons of both morale

---

The Diplomacy of the United States and Spain Over Cuba, 1895–1898 (Chapel Hill: University of North Carolina Press, 1992), p. 28.

[119] Carl von Clausewitz, *On War*, edited and translated by Michael Howard and Peter Paret (Princeton, N.J.: Princeton University Press, 1976) pp. 235, 253.

[120] Arden Bucholz, *Moltke, Schlieffen, and Prussian War Planning* (New York: Berg, 1991), p. 55.

and material strength, victory or defeat in one theater is likely to increase the chances of victory or defeat elsewhere.[121]

In closing this section, I should note that a failure to anticipate positive feedback is one reason why consequences are often unintended. In many cases, actors take a limited move that turns out to set in motion forces that call for further moves in the same direction; they often begin a small-scale endeavor in the belief that it is worth a minor effort only to find that their actions have changed them and their environments in a way that requires greater involvement; desired flexibility is lost as commitments grow as others respond to them; temporary expedients develop into longer-term arrangements as interests prove to be more malleable and the course of events more difficult to control than people believe. Looking back, actors and observers may see the results as inevitable, just as we assume that a river running through a deep canyon had to be located there. While this is indeed sometimes the case, when conditions are unsettled and the initial move changes the actors and their environment, the final outcome, which at the end is bolstered by many supporting elements, may have been only one among many that were initially possible.

Domino Dynamics

In international politics the best-known kind of positive feedback is summarized by the metaphor of falling dominoes. Strength attracts rather than repels; states seek to cooperate with those who are most powerful. As Stalin is reported to have said in 1938, "We must come to terms with the superior power like Nazi Germany."[122] At the heart of many national security debates are competing beliefs about the prevalence of balancing and domino dynamics. Those who call for intervention in far-off disputes usually claim that the consequences of even a small defeat will be very great because others will flock to the winning side.[123] Those who see no need for intervention argue either that the effects will be quite limited (i.e., that the world is not tightly interconnected enough to generate strong feedbacks) or that local forces will rally against the disturber (i.e., that negative feedback in the form of the balance of power will prevail).[124]

[121] Winston Churchill claimed such an interaction between the Balkan and Western fronts in World War I: *World Crisis*, pp. 583–84.

[122] Quoted in W. G. Krivitsky, *I Was Stalin's Agent* (London: Right Book Club, 1940), pp. 39.

[123] Ironically, the expectation of domino dynamics can trigger a quick operation of balancing against the perceived growth of the adversary's power. See below, chapter 7, pp. 266–71 for a discussion of this and other self-denying prophecies operating with domino beliefs.

[124] For a more complete discussion of why statesmen expect dominoes to fall and the condi-

Domino dynamics can act through several mechanisms. Most obviously and directly, conquest can increase a country's economic and military strength, which in turn facilitates further expansion.[125] The victories of Napoleon and Hitler had this characteristic. But conquest may not be necessary to gain increased support. What an advisor to the French high commissioner for Indochina said in the spring of 1950 applies more widely: "Eighty percent [of the people in Southeast Asia] are less interested in ideology than in being on [the] winning side."[126] When this is the case, the outcome can be strongly influenced by small perturbations and self-fulfilling prophecies since actors are not only reading the same information but are judging each other's reactions to it. Those who are courting others' support will pay a high price to secure victories of little intrinsic significance if this will set off a bandwagon and will be as concerned with influencing interpretations of events as with affecting events themselves. All these processes can work through a tipping dynamic. The first state to join an expansionist coalition may be the most vulnerable or the easiest to coerce. This accretion of power can make the coalition strong enough to conquer or coerce a state that previously resisted. This new expansion in turn can recruit stronger states, now weaker than the disturbing force.

REPUTATION

Since 1945, the main transmitter of domino dynamics has been believed to be reputation. If a state retreats in one instance, allies and adversaries will see it as weak in capability or resolve and so expect it to back down in the future. Prestige and credibility must be protected; small defeats can damage them, and so will have amplified consequences far removed in time and space. For example, Zbigniew Brzezinski believed that the Soviets invaded

tions under which they are likely to do so, see Robert Jervis, "Domino Beliefs and Strategic Behavior," in Robert Jervis and Jack Snyder, eds., *Dominoes and Bandwagons: Strategic Beliefs and Great Power Competition in the Eurasian Rimland* (New York: Oxford University Press, 1991), pp. 20–50. As Paul Schroeder has persuasively argued, states have alternatives other than balancing and bandwagoning, which means that much of the political science debate is conceptually impoverished: Paul Schroeder, "Historical Reality vs. Neo-realist Theory," *International Security* 19 (Summer 1994), pp. 72–107. For the argument that during the Cold War events in one Third World country had little impact on others, see Max Singer and Aaron Wildavsky, "A Third World Averaging Strategy," in Paul Seabury, ed., *U.S. Foreign Policy: Perspectives and Proposals for the 1970's* (New York: McGraw-Hill, 1969), pp. 13–35. For Waltz's discussion of balancing versus bandwagoning, see *Theory of International Politics*, pp. 125–28.

[125] For a good recent discussion, see Peter Liberman, "The Spoils of Conquest," *International Security* 18 (Fall 1993), pp. 125–53, and Liberman, *Does Conquest Pay? The Exploitation of Occupied Industrial Societies* (Princeton, N.J.: Princeton University Press, 1996).

[126] U.S. Department of State, *Foreign Relations of the United States, 1950*, vol. 3, *Western Europe* (Washington, D.C.: Government Printing Office, 1977), p. 938.

Afghanistan because they were "emboldened by our lack of response over Ethiopia."[127]

American policy in Southeast Asia was justified largely in these terms. As Dean Rusk put it in a rare memorandum to President Johnson (Rusk only wrote Johnson when he felt the issue was very important), "The integrity of the U.S. commitment is the principal pillar of peace throughout the world. If that commitment becomes unreliable, the communist world would draw conclusions that would lead to our ruin and almost certainly to a catastrophic war."[128] Richard Nixon's views were similar: It is "our will and character that is being tested. . . . If we fail to meet this challenge, all other nations will be on notice that despite its overwhelming power the United States, when a real crisis comes, will be found wanting."[129] As the conflict drew to a close in the spring of 1975, Kissinger said that if the U.S. discontinued military aid to South Vietnam and Cambodia, "then we are likely to find a massive shift in the foreign policies of many countries, and a fundamental threat over a period of time to [our] security."[130] Four years earlier, Kissinger argued that the U.S. had to "tilt" toward Pakistan when India attacked what was then East Pakistan because "the treaty with Pakistan was identical to several other bilateral and multilateral agreements" and so to ignore it would be to cast doubt on the American pledges to other countries.[131]

While these beliefs may be especially prominent in the U.S., examples can be found from other countries and other eras.[132] The German foreign minister explained why his country had to stand firm in the second Moroccan crisis by arguing that if it did not, "our credit in the world, not only for

---

[127] Zbigniew Brzezinski, *Power and Principle* (New York: Farrar, Straus & Giroux, 1983), p. 429.

[128] Quoted in Herbert Schandler, *The Unmaking of a President: Lyndon Johnson and Vietnam* (Princeton, N.J.: Princeton University Press, 1977), p. 29. Johnson agreed: See Lyndon Johnson, *The Vantage Point* (New York: Holt, Rinehart, and Winston, 1971), pp. 148–52.

[129] *New York Times*, May 1, 1970.

[130] Quoted in Leslie Gelb, "A Weakened America Is Not What Other Nations See," ibid., March 30, 1975. Also see Bernard Gwertzman, "Gloom on World Situation Grips Kissinger and Aides," ibid., March 20, 1975. As the title of Gelb's story indicates, leaders in and experts on most other countries denied that such far-reaching inferences were being drawn from American behavior. On this point, see Ted Hopf, *Peripheral Visions: Deterrence Theory and Soviet Foreign Policy in the Third World, 1965–1990* (Ann Arbor: University of Michigan Press, 1994).

[131] Kissinger, *White House Years*, p. 895. Indeed, the expectation of positive feedback generated by reputation made extended deterrence both necessary and possible during the Cold War: see chapter 1, pp. 23–24 above.

[132] Patrick Morgan, "Saving Face for the Sake of Deterrence," in Robert Jervis, Richard Ned Lebow, and Janice Stein, *Psychology and Deterrence* (Baltimore, Md.: Johns Hopkins University Press, 1985), pp. 125–52, argues that these beliefs particularly characterized postwar American decision-makers.

the moment, but also for all future international actions, suffers an intolerable blow."[133] As is so often the case, the basic point can be found in Thucydides. Pericles argued against acceding to the demand to withdraw the Megarian decree in terms that probably were familiar even then: "If you give in, you will immediately be confronted with some greater demand, since they will think that you only gave way on this point through fear."[134]

GENERAL VALIDITY OF THE DOMINO THEORY

The central question, of course, is whether—or under what circumstances —politics is characterized by positive feedback rather than by balancing. Given the importance of this topic for both theory and policy, it is surprising that it has been the subject of so few empirical studies.[135] Partly for this reason, my own conclusions must remain tentative. I will first analyze the general validity of the domino theory and then turn to the conditions under which these dynamics are most likely to operate.

Obviously, the most extreme form of positive feedback has not ruled international politics: One state has never been able to parlay increased strength into complete domination. It is also clear that during the Cold War the more extreme domino predictions were not fulfilled. The establishment

[133] Quoted in Ima Barlow, *The Agadir Crisis* (Chapel Hill: University of North Carolina Press, 1940), p. 266.

[134] Thucydides, *History of the Peloponnesian War*, translated by Rex Warner (Harmondsworth, England: Penguin, 1954), p. 92.

[135] See Walt, *Origins of Alliances*; Jervis and Snyder, eds., *Dominoes and Bandwagons*; Jerome Slater, "Dominoes in Central America: Where They Fall? Does It Matter?" *International Security* 12 (Fall 1987), pp. 105–34; Betty Glad and Charles Taber, "The Domino Theory," in Betty Glad, ed., *War: The Psychological Dimension* (Newbury Park, Calif.: Sage, 1990), pp. 56–81; Ross Gregory, "The Domino Theory," in Alexander de Conde, ed., *Encyclopedia of American Foreign Policy*, vol. 1 (New York: Scribner's, 1978), pp. 275–80; Robert Mandel, "The Effectiveness of Gunboat Diplomacy," *International Studies Quarterly* 30 (March 1986), pp. 68–69; Paul Huth and Bruce Russett, "After Deterrence Fails: Escalation to War?" paper presented to the Conference on the Risk of Accidental Nuclear War, University of British Columbia, Vancouver, British Columbia, May 1986; Huth, *Extended Deterrence and the Prevention of War* (New Haven, Conn.: Yale University Press, 1988), pp. 80–82; Snyder and Diesing, *Conflict Among Nations*, pp. 187–89; Eric J. Labs, "Do Weak States Bandwagon?" *Security Studies* 1 (Spring 1992), pp. 383–416; Robert Kaufman, "To Balance or to Bandwagon? Alignment Decisions in 1930s Europe," ibid., pp. 417–47; Stephen Walt, "Alliance, Threats, and U.S. Grand Strategy: A Reply to Kaufman and Labs," ibid., pp. 448–82; Robert Kaufman, "The Lessons of the 1930s, Alliance Theory, and U.S. Grand Strategy: A Reply to Stephen Walt," ibid. 1 (Summer 1992), pp. 690–96; Joao Resende-Santos, "System and Agent: Comments on Labs and Kaufman," ibid., pp. 697–702; Jerome Slater, "The Domino Theory and International Politics: The Case of Vietnam," ibid. 3 (Winter 1993/94), pp. 186–224; Douglas Macdonald, "Falling Dominoes and System Dynamics: A Risk Aversion Perspective," ibid., pp. 225–58; Macdonald, "Communist Bloc Expansion in the Early Cold War," *International Security* 20 (Winter 1995/96), pp. 152–88.

of Castro's regime did not lead to the communization of Latin America; although Cambodia and Laos followed South Vietnam into communism in 1975, other countries in the region did not and the Europeans' faith in the American promises of extended deterrence were not affected. The American defeat may have encouraged Soviet and Cuban intervention in Angola and—more arguably—in Ethiopia, but the crucial factor here was the perception of American domestic reaction to the war (driven more by its costs than by its outcome), not the reputational effect of having lost.[136]

Furthermore, it is hard to argue that if the U.S. had prevailed in Vietnam or taken a stronger stand in the African disputes, the USSR would have behaved differently in Afghanistan.[137] To take a more recent case, the American defeats in Lebanon in the 1980s did not reduce the extent to which others in the Mideast looked to it for support and assistance, a result consistent with Walt's finding that almost 90 percent of those alliances in the Middle East that were traceable to external threats were aimed at blocking, not accommodating, the menacing power.[138] A survey of a longer period of time and a broader geographical area similarly finds that "the historical facts of the period 1689–1815 tend to favor the self-adjustment [or balance of power] theory over the domino theory."[139]

The other side of this coin is that strongly motivated challengers will continue to seek changes in the status quo even if previous attempts have failed. In examining a series of cases in which the U.S. sought to provide extended deterrence in the Middle East, Janice Stein finds that "the demonstration [of resolve] in one case had no appreciable impact on the outcome of the next."[140] This is not so surprising: Even disinterested observers are likely to be able to find many reasons why a state that stood firm in one confrontation will not do so subsequently. Those who find the status quo very unsatisfactory, furthermore, will feel psychological pressures to believe that it can be changed.

The domino theory also presents an oversimplified and misleading view of the role of reputation. Judgments about others' general willingness to pay costs and run risks rarely dominate decision makers' thoughts; usually more

---

[136] Hopf, *Peripheral Visions*. This fact is obliquely recognized by Henry Kissinger, although he does not draw the obvious implication for American policy: *Diplomacy* (New York: Simon and Schuster, 1994), p. 699.

[137] For an offhand claim to the contrary, see ibid., p. 701.

[138] Walt, *Origins of Alliances*, p. 149. Such alliances also lasted longer than did those reflecting bandwagoning: ibid., p. 152.

[139] Daniel Baugh, "Great Britain's 'Blue-Water' Policy, 1689–1815," *International History Review* 10 (February 1988), p. 48; also see Cusack and Stoll, "Balance Behavior in the International System."

[140] Janice Stein, "Extended Deterrence in the Middle East: American Strategy Reconsidered," *World Politics* 39 (April 1987), p. 351.

attention is given to the specific situation the other side is believed to face.[141] In a careful examination of the crises in the decade preceding World War I, Jonathan Mercer found that a state which forced an adversary to back down rarely perceived the latter as weak and prone to retreat again, as the domino theory and most of the writings on reputation would lead us to expect. Instead, the state usually attributed the adversary's behavior to the situation in which it found itself, which might not recur in the future.[142] Just before he invaded Poland, Hitler rebutted his resisting military advisors by saying, "Our enemies are little worms. I saw them at Munich."[143] But this was the only such remark Snyder and Diesing could find when they examined a large number of confrontations from the early twentieth century to 1962. I have located a few others: Eisenhower told congressional leaders that he could take a strong stand in Berlin because he knew that the Soviets had bluffed in other cases; Stalin may have permitted Kim Il Sung to attack South Korea because the U.S. acquiesced in Mao's victory in China; the Hungarian rebels pushed further in October 1956 because the initial Soviet response was weak.[144] But in general while statesmen do care a great deal about their reputations because they think that others are strongly influenced by them, when they have to estimate how others are likely to behave, their focus is likely to be elsewhere. Thus, contrary to American expectations about the inferences others would draw from the American defeat in Vietnam, they themselves did not see further retreats as likely to follow the

[141] For further discussions, see Stephen Maxwell, *Rationality in Deterrence* (London: Institute for Strategic Studies, 1968), Adelphi Papers no. 50; Bruce Russett, "The Calculus of Deterrence," *Journal of Conflict Resolution* 7 (June 1963), pp. 97–109; George and Smoke, *Deterrence in American Foreign Policy*, pp. 552–61; Jervis, "Deterrence Theory Revisited," *World Politics* 31 (January 1979), pp. 317–22; Janice Stein, "Extended Deterrence in the Middle East"; James McConnell, "The 'Rules of the Game': A Theory on the Practice of Superpower Naval Diplomacy," in Bradford Dismukes and James McConnell, eds., *Soviet Naval Diplomacy* (New York: Pergamon, 1979), pp. 240–80. For a parallel argument that states estimate their own and their adversary's resolve on different bases, see Snyder and Diesing, *Conflict Among Nations*, pp. 496–97. Although there is some evidence that the outcome of one interaction between two states is likely to influence the course of future interactions, the role of reputation is not clear and domino effects do not seem to dominate: Paul Huth and Bruce Russett, "What Makes Deterrence Work? Cases From 1900 to 1980," *World Politics* 36 (July 1894), pp. 496–526; Huth, *Extended Deterrence*, chapter 4. Also see Russell Leng, "When Will They Ever Learn? Coercive Bargaining in Recurrent Crises," *Journal of Conflict Resolution* 27 (September 1983), pp. 379–419, and Leng, *Interstate Crisis Behavior, 1816–1980: Realism versus Reciprocity* (Cambridge: Cambridge University Press, 1993).

[142] Jonathan Mercer, *Reputation and International Politics* (Ithaca, N.Y.: Cornell University Press, 1996).

[143] Quoted in Snyder and Diesing, *Conflict Among Nations*, p. 187.

[144] Marc Trachtenberg, "Berlin Crisis," unpublished manuscript, p. 30; Macdonald, "Communist Bloc Expansion," pp. 174, 177–78; Rothschild, *Return to Diversity*, p. 159. Lincoln may have thought the South was bluffing in 1860–61 because he remembered past Southern threats to dissolve the Union: David Donald, *Lincoln* (New York: Simon and Schuster, 1995), p. 260.

Soviet withdrawal from Afghanistan (even though in retrospect such an inference would have been warranted).

In stressing the importance of international interactions, the domino theory, like balance of power, slights domestic politics, which in fact often determines how states react to menace. Thus the famous Belgian bandwagoning of the 1930s cannot be explained by the growth of Hitler's power, instead being the product of the "Belgian desires to be independent of France [which] resulted from domestic constraints on the governments in Brussels."[145] Similarly, Steven David has shown that many Third World leaders during the Cold War bandwagoned with a foreign power in order to defeat internal rivals.[146]

CONDITIONS UNDER WHICH DOMINO EFFECTS ARE LIKELY

If the frequency of positive feedback in the form of domino effects often has been exaggerated, the effect does occur and is more likely under some conditions than others. Three categories of conditions can be isolated, each with several subcomponents: the state of the international system, the nature of the specific situation, and statesmen's beliefs and goals.

Three aspects of the international system play a role. The first is whether military technology and political strategy give offense or defense the advantage. Positive feedback will operate most strongly when attacking is easier than defending, initial gains multiply, and it is hard for states to protect themselves unless they are members of a strong coalition.[147] There is more room for argument about the impact of nuclear weapons. On the one hand,

[145] Martin Alexander, "The Fall of France, 1940," *Journal of Strategic Studies* 13 (March 1990), p. 15. In addition to the literature cited there, see David Kieft, *Belgium's Return to Neutrality* (New York: Oxford University Press, 1972), especially pp. 96–97. For the general argument that domestic politics makes democracies slow to balance, see Kaufman, "To Balance or to Bandwagon," pp. 423, 436–38, and Kaufman, *Arms Control During the Pre-Nuclear Era: The United States and Naval Limitation Between the Two World Wars* (New York: Columbia University Press, 1990).

[146] Steven David, "Explaining Third World Alignment," *World Politics* 43 (January 1991), pp. 233–56; David, *Choosing Sides: Alignment and Realignment in the Third World* (Baltimore, Md.: Johns Hopkins University Press, 1991). Also see Wriggins, ed., *Dynamics of Regional Politics*; Deborah Larson, "Bandwagon Images in American Foreign Policy: Myth or Reality?" in Jervis and Snyder, eds., *Dominoes and Bandwagons*, chapter 4; Jack Levy and Michael Barnett, "Alliance Formation, Domestic Political Economy, and Third World Security," *International Organization* 45 (Summer 1991), pp. 369–95.

[147] For a nuanced treatment, see Ted Hopf, "Polarity, the Offense-Defense Balance, and War," *American Political Science Review* 85 (June 1991), pp. 475–93. Causality can run the other way as well—a strong desire to avoid a commitment to a third party can produce the perception either that its independence is not necessary to the security of the state or that defense dominance permits it to defend itself without assistance from the state: Thomas Christensen and Jack Snyder, "Chain Gangs and Passed Bucks: Predicting Alliance Patterns in Multipolarity," *International Organization* 44 (Spring 1990), pp. 161–62.

their existence—or, to be more precise, mutual second strike capability— may increase domino effects by making credibility central. On the other hand, the physical importance of potential dominoes is decreased as the superpowers can fight without assistance. It is hard to say what this predicts about the behavior of potential dominoes, however.

The familiar question of whether a bipolar world is more stable than a multipolar one in the face of small losses is similarly hard to answer.[148] The fact that under bipolarity power is concentrated in the hands of two super- powers means that positive feedback will not be troublesome, but the fact that all issues are linked to superpower rivalry means that what each side does anywhere is likely to be seen as predicting its behavior in other cases. In multipolar eras, by contrast, retreating in the face of one adversary might not affect the image held by other ones.[149] Again, however, there is little systematic research on the behavior of potential dominoes under the two structures.

The presence and direction of feedback is also influenced by specific as- pects of the situation. Most obviously, domino effects are likely if states are weak: One reason why a number of small European countries (and Italy) sided with Germany in the late 1930s was the belief that resistance would not succeed.[150] Similarly, in the spring of 1920 the British Foreign Office worried about withdrawing from the Caucasus:

> Once the Allied troops leave Batum, Georgia will be deprived of any further moral or material support, and there is little doubt that she will, in the course of a few weeks, throw in her lot with the Bolsheviks. . . . As for Armenia, with the Bol- sheviks in Azerbaijan, the Turks in the southwest and the Georgians in a hesitating frame of mind, there is little doubt that [it] . . . will in the end become Bolshevik.[151]

---

[148] Waltz, *Theory of International Politics*; Karl Deutsch and J. David Singer, "Multipolar Power Systems and International Stability," *World Politics* 16 (April 1964), pp. 390–406; Rich- ard Rosecrance, "Bipolarity, Multipolarity, and the Future," *Journal of Conflict Resolution* 10 (September 1966), pp. 314–27. For an early claim for the stability of a bipolar world, William Liscum Borden, *There Will Be No Time* (New York: Macmillan, 1946), pp. 160–65.

[149] For the problems that arise for American deterrence policy, see Robert Jervis, "What Do We Want to Deter and How Do We Deter It?" in L. Benjamin Ederington and Michael Mazarr, eds., *Turning Point: The Gulf War and U.S. Military Strategy* (Boulder, Colo.: West- view, 1994), pp. 128–31.

[150] On Italy, see Donald Cameron Watt, *How War Came: The Immediate Origins of the Second World War, 1938–1939* (New York: Pantheon, 1989), pp. 199–200; also see Kaufman, "To Balance or to Bandwagon?" For a treatment of the interwar period in this context, see Randall Schweller, "Tripolarity and the Second World War," *International Studies Quarterly* 37 (March 1993), pp. 73–103. For general discussions of weakness leading to bandwagoning, see Walt, *Origins of Alliances*, pp. 29–30, and Snyder, *Alliance Politics*, chapter 6.

[151] Quoted in John Rose, "Batum as Domino, 1919–1920," *International History Review* 2 (January 1980), p. 283.

Unlike many domino prophecies, this one proved correct; given the weakness of the states involved, it could hardly have been otherwise. The other side of this coin is that a state that is trying to encourage balancing needs to convince third parties that resistance can succeed. This was one of the main tasks of American diplomacy in the late 1940s.[152] Similarly, British propaganda during World War II aimed at showing neutrals not that Hitler was evil, but that he could be defeated.[153]

Decision makers' goals and beliefs also are important. As Randall Schweller has shown, revisionists are more likely to bandwagon than are defenders of the status quo. The former will see large-scale change as an opportunity to realize their ambitions. Protecting the status quo, on the other hand, more often calls for balancing against a disturber.[154] The prevalence of revisionist goals helps explain the bandwagoning behavior of some of the European states in the 1930s. To combat this dynamic, status quo powers seek to minimize the grievances others feel not only toward them but also toward each other.

Finally, when patterns of behavior and conceptions of interest are in flux, small events can have a large influence on the path that will be followed. Thus Secretary of State Baker's argument about the importance of the reaction to Iraq's invasion of Kuwait was not entirely self-serving:

> The current crisis is the first opportunity [in the post–Cold War era] to limit [the] dangers [of aggression], to reinforce the standards for civilized behavior found in the United Nations Charter, and to help shape a more peaceful international order built on the promise of recent trends in Europe and elsewhere. So it's our view, Mr. Chairman, that we must seize this opportunity to solidify the ground rules of the new order.[155]

The aftermath of most large wars may similarly bring uncertainty which permits several kinds of positive feedback, including the possibility of falling dominoes. The balance can be delicately poised at other times as well. One reason why the U.S. intervened in South Vietnam was the disturbing developments in nearby countries, and while most attention has been focused on the decision to commit forces in 1964–65, one can ask why policy was not reexamined in the wake of the Indonesian revolution in the fall of 1965 that greatly reduced Communist power in the region and made domino dynamics less likely.

---

[152] Larson, "Bandwagon Images in American Foreign Policy," pp. 95–101.

[153] Robert Cole, *Britain and the War of Words in Neutral Europe, 1939–45* (London: Macmillan, 1990).

[154] Schweller, "Tripolarity and the Second World War," and "Bandwagoning for Profit: Bringing the Revisionist State Back In," *International Security* 19 (Summer 1994), pp. 72–107.

[155] "Excerpts From Baker Testimony on U.S. and Gulf," *New York Times*, September 5, 1990.

Spirals as Positive Feedback

Domino dynamics are not the only form of positive feedback in international politics. The spiral model of conflict argues that states can be caught in a cycle of reinforcing hostility, arms, and conflict driven by the security dilemma and ancillary psychological dynamics, including the failure of decision makers to understand the dilemma.[156] While the result is negative feedback in that attempts to increase security are self-defeating, it is positive feedback because an arms buildup leads to still more increases. Indeed, conflict itself grows out of the interaction process and develops much further than can be explained by the initial dispute. In a process that resembles a malign version of regional integration, conflict can alter beliefs, needs, and goals in a way that makes the world more hostile and calls for more aggressive efforts to cope with it. A state that has made enemies of many others will find its security requirements greatly increased: It will seek to suppress internal dissent, gain military superiority, and "Finlandize" its neighbors lest they ally with the state's enemies. Nkrumah's Ghana found itself in a version of this trap when it allowed refugees from neighboring countries to carry on propaganda campaigns against their home regimes without intending to poison the relations between the states. But as others responded with hostility, relations with them "became so bad . . . that overthrow of their regimes became a compelling means for Ghana to end its growing isolation."[157]

These processes can also operate more quickly. The most virulent example is what Schelling has described as "the reciprocal fear of surprise attack."[158] Each side prefers peace to war but also believes that if war comes it will fare better if it lands the first blow. Rumors of war may then become

[156] Jervis, *Perception and Misperception*, pp. 62–113; for a discussion of spiral versus deterrence in a variety of settings, see Paul Stern et al., eds., *Perspectives on Deterrence* (New York: Oxford University Press, 1989); for the role of domestic politics in this process, see Richard Ned Lebow, *Between Peace and War* (Baltimore, Md.: Johns Hopkins University Press, 1981); for the original presentations of the security dilemma, see Herbert Butterfield, *History and Human Relations* (London: Collins, 1951), pp. 19–20; John Herz, "Idealist Internationalism and the Security Dilemma," *World Politics* 2 (January 1950), pp. 157–80. For the tendency for the perceived stakes to increase as conflict does, see Joel Brockner and Jeffrey Rubin, *Entrapment in Escalating Conflict* (New York: Springer, 1985). Arnold Wolfers divides wars into those springing from evil and those that constitute tragedy and credits Harold Lasswell as distinguishing between "mad Caesars" who are driven to expand by their aggressiveness and "hysterical Caesars" who are driven by fear and the elusive desire for absolute security: *Discord and Collaboration* (Baltimore, Md.: Johns Hopkins University Press, 1962), p. 84.

[157] W. Scott Thompson, *Ghana's Foreign Policy, 1957–1966* (Princeton, N.J.: Princeton University Press, 1969), p. 336.

[158] Schelling, *The Strategy of Conflict* (Cambridge, Mass.: Harvard University Press, 1960), pp. 207–29. This has led to an enormous literature on "crisis stability" which I believe can fruitfully be seen as a theory of the causes of war: Robert Jervis, "Arms Control, Stability, and Causes of War," *Political Science Quarterly* 108 (Summer 1993), pp. 239–54.

self-fulfilling. As each side fears that war is becoming more likely, it moves to put itself in a better position to fight; the other side sees this and becomes increasingly convinced that war cannot be avoided and so takes parallel measures; the first side observes this and responds accordingly.

These theories are clear, but do they explain much about international politics? Obviously, the Cold War did not produce preemptive strikes—perhaps because decision makers understood the danger and moved to control it. For an actual case, some scholars point to the "crisis slide" of July 1914 during which the fear of war produced actions that made war more likely. Other analysts dispute this interpretation, however, arguing that the states fought not because of the incentives generated by the mobilization races, but because their initial positions were incompatible.[159] In fact, it is hard to find a clear case of a war produced entirely by mutual fear of preemption.[160]

Just as July 1914 used to be held up as the prime exemplar of short-run spiral dynamics, so the more general origins of World War I have served as the model for the way in which spirals of arms and tension could generate unnecessary conflict. Here too historical revisionism has done its work and the pendulum has swung back toward explaining the war by irreconcilable differences, domestic sources of expansionism, and German culpability.[161] But there is still room to argue that the conflict was exacerbated by the interaction between the two sides in that preferences for hostile policies were in part the product of the difficulty of gaining mutual security. For many other conflicts as well, an element of positive feedback may be present even if it is not dominant—e.g., the Cold War, the India-Pakistan war of 1965, the Arab-Israeli war two years later, many cases in which limited wars escalate, as well as the classic case of the Peloponnesian Wars as explained by Thucydides.[162]

[159] See, for example, Paul Schroeder, "World War I as Galloping Gertie," *Journal of Modern History* 44 (September 1972), pp. 319–44; Marc Trachtenberg, "The Meaning of Mobilization in 1914," *International Security* 15 (Winter 1990/91), pp. 120–50; Jack Levy, "Preferences, Constraints, and Choices in July 1914," ibid., pp. 151–86; and the letters by Christensen, Levy, and Trachtenberg in ibid. 16 (Summer 1991), pp. 189–203.

[160] Dan Reiter, "Exploding the Powder Keg Myth: Preemptive Wars Almost Never Happen," *International Security* 20 (Fall 1995), pp. 5–34; also see Randall Schweller, "Domestic Structure and Preventive War: Are Democracies More Pacific?" *World Politics* 44 (January 1992), pp. 235–69. Stephen Van Evera, *Causes of War*, vol. 1, *The Structure of Power and the Roots of War* (Ithaca, N.Y.: Cornell University Press, forthcoming), convincingly argues both that the reciprocal fear of surprise attack has not been responsible for any war but that the perception of offensive advantage has operated through other pathways to make war more likely in a large number of cases, including 1914.

[161] The key book is Fritz Fischer, *War of Illusions: German Policies From 1911 to 1914* (New York: Norton, 1975).

[162] Sumit Ganguly, "Deterrence Failure Revisited: The Indo-Pakistan War of 1965," *Journal of Strategic Studies* 13 (December 1990), pp. 77–93; Janice Stein, "The Arab-Israeli War of

Balance of Power, Dominoes, and Spirals:
Feedback and Force

Balance of power theory, the domino theory, and the spiral model make different arguments about the feedback set off by the threat or use of force. Under the balance of power, past a certain point the state's success in expanding will sufficiently menace others so that they will block it, thereby producing a form of stability. When the domino theory is correct, states feel unable to balance against a successful aggressor and, by choosing to join with it, augment its power and enhance its prospects for further victories. The spiral model shares with balance of power the claim that the exercise of power is self-defeating. But, with the domino theory, it foresees positive feedback, although here it is conflict rather than the state's power that feeds on itself. For balance of power theorists, wars, although regrettable, check aggressors and preserve the system. In the spiral model, wars are tragedies that could have been avoided were it not for the security dilemma and misperception.[163] The other side of the coin is that the spiral model, the domino theory, and, to some extent, balance of power see rewards and conciliation as producing positive feedback, although to quite different ends. While the spiral model holds that these tactics will steadily reduce conflict and increase cooperation, the domino and balance arguments see conciliation as leading aggressors to increase their demands.

I very much doubt whether balance of power theory, deterrence, or the spiral model is correct all the time; rather each generalization applies under certain conditions. Together these processes show the variety of feedbacks that characterize international politics and underscore the central roles that they play. It is hard to imagine a sustained analysis of political or social life that does not discuss the sources and operation of dynamics like these. How they and other system effects play out in bargaining and alliance relations are the subjects of the next two chapters.

1967: Inadvertent War through Miscalculated Escalation," in Alexander George, ed., *Avoiding War* (Boulder, Colo.: Westview Press, 1991), chapter 8; Richard Smoke, *War: Controlling Escalation* (Cambridge: Harvard University Press, 1977).

[163] But even an unnecessary war may preserve the essential elements of the system. One can then argue that the process was one of negative feedback when looked at over a longer period of time and from a broader perspective. Seen in this light, the balance of power and the spiral model are only superficially in conflict. But this position is too Olympian.

Five

Relations, Alternatives, and Bargaining

A SYSTEMS perspective helps us understand how actors' bargaining power and strategies are affected by the opportunities and dangers that *others* face. I will start by focusing on the simplified situations in which there are only three actors. In international politics this may not be a grave distortion. While there are always more than three states in the system, in many cases three are most central.[1]

Triangular Relations

The most obvious and yet important statement follows from the basic conception of a system as composed of elements that are interconnected: The relations—existing, potential, and desired—between any pair of countries influence and are influenced by the relations between each of those countries and a third actor. If relations between A and B change, so will relations between A and C and between B and C, often producing subsequent changes in the relations between A and B. Furthermore, A is likely to set its policy toward B with at least one eye on how this will affect relations with C.

This is not to say that every small perturbation will seriously affect all the relations in the triangle. As Bülow, the German chancellor, told the Reichstag in 1897 when Italy (Germany's ally) reached an agreement over spheres of influence in North Africa with France (Germany's adversary): "In a happy marriage, the husband does not get excited if his wife has an innocent *tour de valse* with another man."[2] But in politics as in marriages a dance can lead to something more lasting, and in fact Bülow was more worried than he let on, and with good reason: To the extent that Italy patched up its quarrels with France, it would have less need for German support.

An improvement in relations between two adversaries is almost certain to affect third parties. Sometimes the latter will benefit—e.g., they may have been caught in the conflict between the two or may seek good relations with

---

[1] For a discussion of tripolar systems, see Randolph Schweller, *Deadly Imbalances: Tripolarity and Hitler's Strategy for World Conquest* (New York: Columbia University, forthcoming). The path-breaking study of coalition formation among triads is Theodore Caplow, *Two Against One: Coalitions in Triads* (Englewood Cliffs, N.J.: Prentice Hall, 1968).

[2] Quoted in Christopher Andrew, *Théophile Delcassé and the Making of the Entente Cordiale* (London: Macmillan, 1968), p. 146.

them both. More often, third parties will suffer by losing bargaining power. For example, as tensions between Germany and Great Britain eased in 1912, the latter gained "a freer hand in dealing with Russian pressures in Persia."[3] Understanding this dynamic, in 1794 the U.S. reacted to the menace of an alliance between Spain and Britain, the two European powers with North American possessions, by signing Jay's Treaty with England which made an anti-American coalition less likely and eased the way for Pickney's Treaty with Spain.[4] In extreme cases, a third state will lose not its influence but its independence when its enemies patch up their quarrels. This was Poland's fate in 1939. Looser agreements can have the effect, even without the intention, of menacing third parties or limiting their freedom. Thus Israel might not have moved into Lebanon in 1982 in the absence of the Camp David agreement with Egypt that freed her from the threat of attack on her southern border, and improved relations with the U.S. may have facilitated the Chinese incursion into Vietnam.[5]

The other side of this coin is that when relations between two countries deteriorate, a third party is likely to benefit, as Germany did from the Anglo-French enmity created by the former's occupation of Egypt in 1882, and, to a lesser extent, from U.S.-Japanese friction in 1907.[6] A century later, Vietnam's invasion of Cambodia heightened China's enmity toward its southern neighbor and so led it to adopt a more conciliatory stance toward the noncommunist countries of Southeast Asia.[7] In one of the most important cases in this century, Hitler was the main beneficiary—other than Franco—of

[3] L. L. Farrar, Jr., *Arrogance and Anxiety: The Ambivalence of German Power, 1848–1914* (Iowa City: University of Iowa Press, 1981), p. 43.

[4] See the discussion in Robert Tucker and David Hendrickson, *Empire of Liberty: The Statecraft of Thomas Jefferson* (New York: Oxford University Press, 1990), pp. 64–71.

[5] William Quandt, *Camp David: Peacemaking and Politics* (Washington, D.C.: the Brookings Institution, 1986), p. 321; the Chinese "were in effect freeing one front by a tacit nonaggression treaty with us": Henry Kissinger, *White House Years* (Boston: Little, Brown, 1979), p. 1063. For the plausible argument that China might not have been able to break with the USSR in the 1960s had not the American threat declined, thereby reducing Chinese "dependence on the military power of the Soviet Union," see Herbert Dinerstein, "The Soviet Outlook: America, Europe, and China," in Robert Osgood et al., eds., *Retreat from Empire?* (Baltimore, Md.: Johns Hopkins University Press, 1973), p. 125.

[6] Charles Neu, *An Uncertain Friendship: Theodore Roosevelt and Japan, 1906–1909* (Cambridge, Mass.: Harvard University Press, 1967), pp. 163–67; two years earlier Germany had lost bargaining leverage over the U.S. when the Japanese victory over Russia reduced American "fear of German mischief-making in the Far East": Raymond Esthus, *Theodore Roosevelt and the International Rivalries* (Waltham, Mass.: Ginn-Blaisdell, 1970), pp. 53–54; also see Ute Mehnert, "German *Weltpolitik* and the American Two-Front Dilemma: The 'Japanese Peril' in German-American Relations, 1904–1917," *Journal of American History* 82 (March 1996), pp. 1452–77.

[7] Henry Kamm, "China Plays Down Support of Asian Rebels," *New York Times*, February 2, 1981. For another case, see Steven Erlanger, "Ukraine's Opportunity: Western Suspicions of Russia," ibid., April 17, 1994.

Mussolini's intervention in the Spanish Civil War. By erecting a new barrier between Italy and the Western powers, Mussolini's stance made it harder for him to resist German blandishments and lowered the price Germany had to pay for Italian support. At the end of World War II, Stalin similarly hoped that Anglo-American frictions would permit Soviet gains, but he also realized that conflict with the U.S. could produce Anglo-American cooperation.[8] Turning to the future, trade frictions between the U.S. and Japan are likely to decline if an increasingly assertive PRC threatens them both.

Unless the state is strong enough to combat two united adversaries, it will have to conciliate one as relations with the other worsen. Thus in the early 1880s Bismarck realized that to quarrel with Britain would only benefit France and Russia, who could then demand that Germany pay a higher price for their support.[9] Around the same time, Argentina had to make concessions to Chile when friction with Brazil increased, and the later rapprochement between Argentina and Brazil led Chile to bribe Peru in order to gain that country's support as a counterweight. Peru in turn had to make major boundary concessions to Ecuador in order "to allow it single-mindedly to deal with [the dispute with Chile over the provinces of] Tacna and Arica, free of the threat of possible Chilean-Ecuadoran cooperation." Fifteen years later, Chile was able to turn the tables on its northern rival by settling its disputes with Argentina and Bolivia.[10]

A state gains security as well as bargaining power when its main adversaries are themselves divided by important rivalries. Not only will it be freed from the nightmare of their uniting against it, but each of the rivals will have an interest in seeing that the other does not conquer the state, for in that eventuality the victor would be in a position to dominate. This helps explain why military planners rarely engage in the truly "worst case" analysis of imagining a situation in which everyone unites against their state. To put this another way, the need for each state to look to possible future threats provides others with a degree of protection against some coalitions. Thus the interesting dialogue between Britain's leading admiral and his civilian superior at the end of the nineteenth century in which the former argued that Britain could not be content with a fleet that could defeat its leading adver-

---

[8] Vladimir Pechatnov, "The Big Three After World War II," Cold War International History Project, Woodrow Wilson International Center for Scholars, Working Paper no. 13, July 1995, pp. 4–5, 11–13, 17–19; Fraser Harbutt, *The Iron Curtain: Churchill, America, and the Origins of the Cold War* (New York: Oxford University Press, 1986).

[9] Paul Kennedy, *The Rise of the Anglo-German Antagonism, 1860–1914* (London: Allen & Unwin, 1980), chapter 9.

[10] Robert Burr, *By Reason or Force: Chile and the Balancing of Power in South America, 1830–1905* (Berkeley: University of California Press, 1965), pp. 112–13, 187, 200, 259 (the quotation is from p. 200). For another example, see Kurt Rosenbaum, *Community of Fate: German-Soviet Diplomatic Relations, 1922–1928* (Syracuse, N.Y.: Syracuse University Press, 1965), p. 241.

saries, France and Russia, who were then allied. Absent an even larger navy, in the event of war

> we should have to trust to the forbearance of Germany, perhaps the greediest and most determined of our commercial rivals, not to take us at a disadvantage when so circumstanced. This is not a satisfactory position for the Power which lives by the sea, and claims to be supreme upon it. The only true policy lies in unquestioned superiority.

The First Lord of the Admiralty replied that this

> passage states that in a certain eventuality, we should have to trust to the "forbearance" of Germany. I should say, not to her forbearance, but to her strong political interest. The triumph of Russia and France over England would be of supreme danger to Germany, and she will not promote it.[11]

Indeed, the longevity of the British Empire owed much to the existence of conflicts among its potential adversaries that were so severe that even the temptation of dividing the empire could not overcome them and that led each to see that it could not permit a rival to defeat England and thereby grow dangerously strong.[12] In the same way, although a reduction of Russian power in the late nineteenth and early twentieth centuries would have removed the threat to Britain at Constantinople and India, for this to occur as a result of a Russian defeat at German hands would have been unaccept-

[11] Quoted in Arthur Marder, *The Anatomy of British Seapower* (New York: Octagon, 1976), p. 299. Similarly, two years later the Director of Naval Intelligence argued that:

> I consider a combination of France and Russia and Germany against us as absolutely incredible. Whether they like it or not our existence as a naval power is essential to the tranquillity of Germany and France. What would be the security of Germany if France and Russia had crushed us and annexed the remains of our navy. . . ? (ibid., pp. 463–64)

Interestingly enough, Eyre Crow's influential "balance of power memorandum" argued that while Germany was a serious threat, British "interests would not be served by Germany being reduced to the rank of a weak Power as this might easily lead to a Franco-Russian predominance equally, if not more, formidable to the British Empire": "Memorandum on the Present State of British Relations with France and Germany," January 1, 1907, in G. P. Gooch and Harold Temperley, eds., *British Documents on the Origins of the War, 1898–1914*, vol. 3, *The Testing of the Entente, 1904–6* (London: His Majesty's Stationery Office, 1928), p. 417. Put differently, a state may often have no choice but to provide another with extended deterrence: according to an 1889 diplomatic report, when the German minister threatened force against a Mexican bond default, the foreign minister replied that "even before the appearance of his fleet in the Gulf of Mexico, ten thousand soldiers of the American army would occupy Mexico": quoted in Friedrich Katz, *The Secret War in Mexico: Europe, the United States, and the Mexican Revolution* (Chicago: University of Chicago Press, 1981), p. 53. For a theoretical discussion of this phenomenon, see Schweller, *Deadly Imbalances*.

[12] Paul Kennedy, "Why Did the British Empire Last So Long?" in Kennedy, *Strategy and Diplomacy, 1870–1945* (London: Allen & Unwin, 1983), pp. 212–14.

able because of the even greater threat that Germany would pose. Later in the century, the Soviet Union owed its birth, early existence, and survival in World War II to the fact that while both Germany and Britain wanted to see the regime perish, neither could afford to see it come under the sway of the other.

Henry Kissinger used similar reasoning to refute those who believed that the PRC would exploit the American opening to China in order to harm the U.S. As he explained in a memorandum to Nixon, "We have assumed that [the Chinese] are acting in part in response to the Soviet military threat along their borders, and it would not help them to humiliate us if they want to use us in some way as a counterpart to the Soviets."[13] The same incentives translated the worsening of Soviet-American relations caused by the war in Vietnam into a reduction of Soviet pressure on the PRC. Indeed, Adam Ulam offers the intriguing speculation that it was this security that permitted Mao to launch the Cultural Revolution; under other circumstances, Russia might have sought to take advantage of China's disorder.[14]

In summary, when three states constitute a system, ramifications are likely to dominate the immediate and direct effects of behavior. Power often comes not from military or economic strength, but from being in or creating a configuration in which one's potential enemies are in conflict with each other. Whether a state needs to conciliate another is often determined by the degree to which each of them needs support against others. As noted in chapter 2, only rarely can the bilateral relations be understood in isolation.

The Pivot

In some triangles, one state is able to gain a pivotal position, i.e., the ability to align with either of the other two who lack this flexibility.[15] While there are systemic pressures against this configuration,[16] special circumstances— which occur with some frequency—permit it. In some ways, the pivot resembles that so-called holder of the balance. Contrary to what is sometimes

---

[13] Kissinger, *White House Years*, p. 735. In comparing North Vietnamese and Chinese interests, he argued: "Hanoi was engaged in a ceaseless assault on the authority of our government; China's stake had to be in a Washington with the authority and determination to maintain the global balance of power" (ibid., p. 711).

[14] Adam Ulam, *The Rivals* (New York: Viking, 1971), pp. 363–64.

[15] A similar configuration is possible with more than three actors: See, for example, Josef Joffe's discussion of the "hub and spokes" alliances in "'Bismarck' or 'Britain'? Toward an American Grand Strategy after Bipolarity," *International Security* 19 (Spring 1995), pp. 94–117.

[16] See chapter 6.

argued, however,[17] this role is not required for the operation of the balance of power. As I discussed in the previous chapter, self-interest can prevent hegemony and limit national power even if no state remains above the fray. Nevertheless, a state whose interests do not dictate remaining closely tied to any other can benefit by being able to sell its support at a high price.[18] Thus Kissinger's rebuttal to those who urged the U.S. to reach an agreement with the Soviet Union without first establishing relations with China: "These people don't recognize that without a China trip we wouldn't have had a Moscow trip."[19]

A state in the pivot can make gains that are out of proportion to its economic and military resources. Before World War I, Italy could bargain effectively with both sides, not only because its military effectiveness was overestimated, but also because it had the freedom to choose its alignment. Similarly, in 1910 the Russian foreign minister felt he was in a strong position.

> Sazonov knew Russia was still too weak for great adventures, but he felt that the antagonism which existed between England and Germany might permit Russia to extort a little blackmail from both sides. He knew England feared that Russia might make an alliance with Germany: England would, therefore, hesitate to op-

[17] The classic statement is Hans Morgenthau, *Politics Among Nations*, 5th ed., rev. (New York: Knopf, 1978), pp. 200–204.

[18] See Schweller's discussion of the *tertius gaudens* (enjoying third) in *Deadly Imbalances*; Geoffrey Blainey's analysis of "fighting waterbirds" in *The Causes of War* (New York: Free Press, 1973), chapter 4; Glenn Snyder's discussion of incitement in *Alliance Politics*, (Ithaca, N.Y.: Cornell University Press, forthcoming), chapter 10. Also see Caplow, *Two Against One*, p. 20; Georg Simmel, *The Sociology of Georg Simmel*, translated by Kurt Wolff (New York: Free Press, 1964), pp. 154–69; Ronald Burt, *Structural Holes: The Social Structure of Competition* (Cambridge, Mass.: Harvard University Press, 1992), pp. 30–49; David Knoke, *Political Networks: The Structural Perspective* (Cambridge: Cambridge University Press, 1990), pp. 144–47. When two actors need the support of a third, each should make bids up to the point where it is indifferent as to whether its offer is accepted or not. That is, it should be willing to pay a price in terms of concessions to the third actor that equal the perceived advantages that will accrue to it by gaining that actor's support, although bargaining skill or the inability of its rival to make a good offer may enable it to win over the third actor at a lower price. This, in addition to the psychological process of rationalization, may explain why actors who lose in severe bidding competitions may feel little regret. In fact, if there is a great deal of uncertainty about how much the third state's support is worth, the winner is likely to pay more than it gains: see Richard Thaler, *The Winner's Curse: Paradoxes and Anomalies of Economic Life* (New York: Free Press, 1992), chapter 5.

[19] Kissinger, *White House Years*, p. 886. He made this remark in connection with the claim that a failure to support Pakistan in the 1971 war would have led Peking to perceive a "U.S.-Soviet condominium [which] . . . almost surely would have undone our China initiative" (ibid.). I find this implausible. Not only is there little evidence that China would have drawn this inference, but the possibility of closer Soviet-American cooperation might have acted as an incentive for the Chinese to be more conciliatory toward the U.S.

pose Russian plans. Cautiously but confidently, Russian policy became more active in Asia. When the British protested against the subjugation of northern Persia, Sazonov paid no heed; England needed Russia too much to risk a break. Britain, fearing Germany, must make concessions to Russia; Germany, fearing Britain, must also make concessions.[20]

Most recently, Croatia was able to make great gains in part because it could switch its alignment from Bosnia to Serbia and back again.

A state that is in the pivot may be able to influence the behavior of others for broad interests as well as for its own good. This is Kissinger's argument for why it was important for the U.S. to avoid siding unequivocally with either the USSR or the PRC: "If we appeared irresolute or leaning toward Moscow, Peking would be driven to accommodation with the Soviet Union. If we adopted the Chinese attitude, however, we might not even help Peking; we might, in fact, tempt a Soviet preemptive attack on China".[21]

The fact that this analysis is self-serving does not mean that it is incorrect. States that have freedom of action can use it to generate or at least reward moderation. During the Cold War many Third World states claimed to be willing to assist either the U.S. or the USSR, depending on which was doing more to defuse tensions, and it is not unusual for a state to tell each of two rivals that it will support the most reasonable side, or at least that it will not support the side that is aggressive.

So it is not surprising that the state's main reason for patching up a quarrel with another will often be to free it from dependence on a third party. In the 1880s, the Russian foreign minister wanted to control his country's expansion in Central Asia because by threatening British India it limited Russia's diplomatic flexibility. As long as war with England was a real possibility, Russia not only could not threaten others with a Russo-British common front, but also had to court them as potential allies, thus reducing its ability to exact concessions from them.[22] The other side of this coin is equally obvious: States that seek the pivot must hope that others cannot patch up their quarrels.

What determines whether a state can choose between two possible part-

[20] Raymond Sontag, *European Diplomatic History, 1871–1932* (New York: Appleton-Century-Crofts, 1933), pp. 141–42. Although throughout the Cold War the U.S. sought to bring its allies together, its leaders also realized that quarrels among them would "offer certain advantages to the United States": Thomas Hughes, quoted in Frank Costigliola, "Kennedy, the European Allies, and the Failure to Consult," *Political Science Quarterly* 110 (Spring 1995), p. 110. In an election with three candidates or parties and a runoff system, it may be better to come in third than second—in that event, the actor can sell its support to either of the others.

[21] Kissinger, *White House Years*, p. 1076.

[22] W. N. Medlicott, "Bismarck and the Three Emperors' Alliance, 1881–87," *Transactions of the Royal Historical Society*, 4th series, vol. 27, 1945, pp. 67–68.

ners rather than being forced to rely on one of them? Geography plays a role. Two states with a common border are likely to have more conflicts than either will have with third states farther away.[23] In eras when isolation gave some states great freedom of choice, those on the peripheries could be pivotal because they were likely neither to be locked into conflicts with any particular state nor to be menaced by the results of anything other than a large and decisive war. It was easier for Palmerston than for a Continental statesman to announce that his country had no permanent enemies or permanent friends, only permanent interests, and it is geography more than character that made British behavior "perfidious." When geography changes as states disappear or are created, others are likely to gain or lose freedom. Thus the reestablishment of Poland after World War I, although costing the new Soviet Union territory, gave it a bargaining tool because it could join with Germany to wipe Poland out and, before this happened, gained a buffer that allowed it to avoid a firm alignment with France.[24]

Short of shifts of boundaries, geography is fixed (although its implications can be altered by technology). Goals and policies are subject to choice, however. Status quo states often have diplomatic advantages because by not seeking to menace others, they are likely to have a wide range of alliance partners. This was one of the keys to Bismarck's diplomatic success after 1871. By contrast, a country bent on overturning the existing system is likely to make enemies of several states at once. Similarly, states that have frequently fought in the past are likely to find that a third state can play the role of a pivot. Conversely, advantage will accrue to an actor who controls an asset that both of the others seek. Donald Zagoria argues that this was true for the U.S. in the early 1980s: "Both Russia and China want something from the United States that they cannot get from each other. Both want trade and technology."[25] A nonideological state in a system riven by ideological disputes may be similarly advantaged by being an acceptable alliance partner to others who cannot join a coalition with each other.

[23] The importance of common borders is stressed in Gary Goertz and Paul Diehl, *Territorial Changes and International Conflict* (London: Routledge, 1992); K. J. Holsti, *Peace and War: Armed Conflicts and International Order, 1648–1989* (Cambridge: Cambridge University Press, 1991); John Vasquez, *The War Puzzle* (Cambridge: Cambridge University Press, 1993); and Paul Huth, *Standing Your Ground: Territorial Disputes and International Conflict* (Ann Arbor: University of Michigan Press, 1996).

[24] See Lenin, quoted in Herbert Mason, Jr., *The Rise and Fall of the Luftwaffe, 1918–1940* (New York: Dial Press, 1973), p. 99, and Arthur Balfour, the British foreign secretary, quoted in Henry Kissinger, *Diplomacy* (New York: Simon and Schuster, 1994), p. 243. For a similar African case, see Saadia Touval, *The Boundary Politics of Independent Africa* (Cambridge, Mass.: Harvard University Press, 1972), pp. 131–33.

[25] Donald Zagoria, "The Moscow-Beijing Détente," *Foreign Affairs* 61 (Spring 1983), p. 871. For a related formulation, see Henry Kissinger, *Years of Upheaval* (Boston: Little, Brown, 1982), p. 70. Also see below, chapter 6, pp. 235–36.

What is important is the relative conflict of interest and antagonism among the states. That is, a state that has sharp conflicts with two others may still be well positioned if the other two are divided by differences even less bridgeable.[26] Thus although the Anglo-French clash at Fashoda increased the British fear that France would respond to German feelers for joint cooperation against England, the British did not panic because they understood what an official made explicit several years later: "So long as Alsace-Lorraine remains part of the German Empire there cannot . . . be any real political understanding between France and Germany."[27] In the 1970s and 1980s the PRC hoped that relations between the U.S. and USSR would deteriorate (although not lead to war) because this would strengthen its bargaining position,[28] while the American policy of improving relations with China in order to exert pressure on the Soviet Union was premised on the assumption that the Sino-Soviet dispute was so serious that the USSR could not respond to the American moves by ending it.

Because judgments of the relative magnitude of disagreements are difficult, statesmen are prone to make errors, especially when others' reactions to their policies constitute one of the elements in the equation. Thus in 1886 Friedrich von Holstein, an influential member of the German Foreign Office, reacted to discussions between France and Russia by voicing the conviction that "our best safeguard now lies in the hatred and contempt felt by the Tsar for the French Republic."[29] This perception was not inaccurate, but Holstein and his colleagues failed to see that this barrier might be lower than that which German policy was erecting between it and Russia. Similarly, in 1898 when the kaiser wrote "Impossible!" in the margin of a telegram beside the passage in which his envoy reported that British statesmen were saying that if Germany and England could not reach an agreement, they could turn to Russia, he neglected the fact that German behavior could make an Anglo-Russian entente the least unattractive alternative.[30]

[26] For an otherwise good discussion that is marred by missing this point, see Martin Wright, *Systems of States* (Leicester: Leicester University Press, 1977), pp. 174–76.

[27] Eugene Anderson, *The First Moroccan Crisis, 1904–1906* (Hamden, Conn.: Archon Books, 1966), p. 44; Bertie quoted in K. A. Hamilton, "Great Britain and France, 1905–1911," in F. H. Hinsley, ed., *British Foreign Policy Under Sir Edward Grey* (Cambridge: Cambridge University Press, 1977), p. 124. Similarly, in 1969 "when Lin Piao described the Soviet Union as an equal threat [compared to the U.S.], the fundamental precondition of triangular diplomacy had been fulfilled" (quoted in Kissinger, *Diplomacy*, p. 725).

[28] See, for example, ibid., p. 1076.

[29] Quoted in George Kennan, *The Decline of Bismarck's European Order* (Princeton, N.J.: Princeton University Press, 1979), p. 187.

[30] Quoted in J. L. Garvin, *The Life of Joseph Chamberlain*, vol. 3, *Empire and World Policy* (London: Macmillan, 1934), p. 275. For a similar German misjudgment of the possibilities of taking advantage of frictions between the U.S. and Japan in the decade before World War I, see Mehnert, "German *Weltpolitik* and the American Two-Front Dilemma." For Soviet analyses of how closely the U.S. and PRC could work together, see Morris Rothenberg, *Whither China:*

A state may then move into a pivotal position not because of anything it has done, but because of the increased conflict between others. Throughout the 1980s, the Western powers, taken as a unit, were pivotal in the Iran-Iraq-West triangle because while they had serious conflicts with both countries, the Iran-Iraq war was a still more serious divide. This changed, however, with the Iraqi invasion of Kuwait. Since both sides needed Iranian support, that country collected concessions from them: Iraq freed Iranian prisoners of war, withdrew from Iranian territory, and abandoned its claim to control of the Shatt-al-Arab, while the West approved a World Bank loan.[31] Conversely, when adversaries are able to cooperate, actors can be displaced from the pivot, as many states found at the end of the Cold War.

Related dynamics explain why it was others, rather than Great Britain, who gained bargaining leverage from the fact that Britain was able to withstand the German assault in 1940. "Owing to our unexpected resistance," Churchill trenchantly remarked, the Vichy authorities "have been able to market their treachery at a slightly higher rate than would otherwise have been possible."[32] Similarly, although he wanted to improve relations with Russia, Churchill rejected Foreign Secretary Eden's suggestion that he fly to Moscow: "A mere visit would do no good. They might simply trade it to Germany."[33] In much the same way, during the Napoleonic Wars British statesmen were right to complain that under the American conception of neutral rights the British success in sweeping enemy shipping from the seas would result, not in depriving France of trade, but in giving the Americans the profit from carrying it.[34] Indeed, triangular relations are often destabilized if one side believes that the other is gaining most of the benefit of tensions with a third party, which explains why both the U.S. and the PRC sought to reassure the other that the tie would not be dropped if and when the Soviet Union made major concessions.[35]

The View from the Kremlin (Coral Gables, Fla.: Center for Advanced International Studies, University of Miami, 1977), pp. 271–73.

[31] Elaine Sciolino, "Iran Frees U.S. Prisoner Amid Conciliation Signs," *New York Times*, September 15, 1990; Youssef Ibrahim, "Iran and Iraq Agree on a Half-Mile Border Zone," ibid., January 9, 1991.

[32] Quoted in John Colville, *The Fringes of Power: 10 Downing Street Diaries, 1939–1955* (New York: Norton, 1985), p. 283.

[33] Quoted in Harbutt, *Iron Curtain*, p. 33.

[34] Furthermore, they would be carrying it in ships manned in considerable proportion by British sailors, for whom the vast increase in American shipping created a great demand: Tucker and Hendrickson, *Empire of Liberty*, pp. 190–95; 202–3.

[35] Kissinger reports that "Mao warned us against 'standing on China's shoulders to reach Moscow.'" (*White House Years*, p. 763; also see Kissinger, *Years of Upheaval*, p. 54); Zbigniew Brzezinski, *Power and Principle* (New York: Farrar, Straus & Giroux, 1983), p. 207; Harvey Nelsen, *Power and Insecurity: Beijing, Moscow, and Washington, 1944–1988* (Boulder, Colo.: Lynne Rienner, 1989), pp. 101–2.

The very freedom of action that being in the pivot confers can be a handicap, however. As Schelling showed so well, the absence of alternatives can strengthen an actor's hand.[36] The application here is that a state's attempt to recruit an ally in its endeavor may be defeated by the latter's fear that the state will abandon it if it becomes convenient to do so. In order to overcome this inability to commit itself, the state may move out of the pivot and demonstrate that it has a deeply rooted quarrel with the prospective ally's adversary. A. J. P. Taylor argues that Bismarck's seemingly foolish policy of colonial conflict with Britain in 1884 was aimed at showing France that it could align with Germany without fear that Bismarck would drop this connection whenever he wanted to because he now needed French support against Britain.[37] That the interpretation is incorrect in this case[38] does not detract from the logic involved. Thus in the first few years of the twentieth century, growing Anglo-German hostility led French statesmen to look with favor on working with England, a policy they had previously rejected on the grounds that Britain could not be relied upon because it could always come to an agreement with Germany.[39] Fidel Castro's policy in the years immediately following his revolution may provide another example. It appears that he sought close ties with the Soviet Union from the beginning but that the Soviets could not be sure of Castro's bona fides. To convince them, he increased tensions with the U.S.[40] When Mao came to power he may have similarly decided to recognize Ho Chi Minh's regime and seize U.S. consular compounds in Beijing in order to show the USSR he was commited to

[36] Thomas Schelling, *The Strategy of Conflict* (Cambridge, Mass.: Harvard University Press, 1960).

[37] A. J. P. Taylor, *Germany's First Bid for Colonies, 1884–1885* (Hamden, Conn.: Archon Books, 1967).

[38] Henry Ashby Turner, "Bismarck's Imperialist Venture: Anti-British in Origin?" in Prosser Gifford and Wm. Roger Louis, eds., *Britain and Germany in Africa* (New Haven, Conn.: Yale University Press, 1967), pp. 47–82.

[39] John Krieger, *France and the Origins of the First World War* (London: Macmillan, 1983), pp. 18–19.

[40] Edward Gonzalez, "Castro's Revolution, Cuban Communist Appeals, and the Soviet Response," *World Politics* 21 (October 1968), pp. 39–68. Although this does not seem to have been part of Mao's calculations, a similar effect was produced by the PRC's entrance into the Korean war: Stalin's confidence in China as an ally increased because the PRC had demonstrated its commitment to the socialist cause and erected a high barrier to Sino-American cooperation. See Sergi Goncharov, John Lewis, and Xue Litai, *Uncertain Partners: Stalin, Mao, and the Korean War* (Stanford, Calif.: Stanford University Press, 1993); "Minutes, Mao's Conversations with a Yugoslavian Communist Union Delegation, Beijing, September 1956," translated by Zhang Shu Guang and Chen Jian, *Cold War International History Project Bulletin*, nos. 6–7 (Winter 1995/1996), pp. 148–49. On a lighter note, a scholar may write a critical book review in order to show the author's rival that he is—and has little choice but to remain—a loyal member of the latter's camp.

their cause; twenty years later he may have provoked fighting on the Sino-Soviet border to show that it was safe for the U.S. to approach him.[41]

States may shun the pivot for more obvious reasons as well. As we will discuss in the next chapter, Bismarck's critics and successors believed that his policy of maintaining ties to antagonists was excessively complex and duplicitous and that a simpler alignment would better protect German security. More commonly, states that believe that another is deeply menacing will usually try to construct a coalition to confront it rather than seeking a bargaining advantage by straddling the two sides. Ideology and domestic politics can similarly call for unequivocal opposition, and these factors also played a role in leading the new PRC regime to support the USSR from the start of the Cold War.

SEEKING AND MAINTAINING THE PIVOT: DIVIDE AND INFLUENCE

In most circumstances, however, being in the pivot is advantageous. Because statesmen understand this, they may not be content to let nature take its course but often will encourage frictions among their rivals, and indeed sometimes among their allies. One student of early-twentieth-century European international politics notes that "German statesmen often seemed to believe that Germany could find security only in a world in which the other powers were prevented by their mutual hostility from combining against her."[42] Germany's policies in fact brought others together, but the basic impulse was not peculiarly German or misguided: It is a recurring tactic of states that have conflicts with other states that have potential conflicts with

[41] William Steuck, *The Korean War: An International History* (Princeton, N.J.: Princeton University Press, 1995), p. 38; Richard Solomon, *Chinese Political Negotiating Behavior, 1967–1984* (Santa Monica, Calif.: RAND, 1995), pp. 76–77. Kissinger says that these "clashes had first alerted us to the desirability of restoring contact with Beijing" (*Years of Upheaval*, p. 46) and that the U.S. replied with a section of Nixon's foreign policy report to Congress signaling that the U.S. both viewed the USSR as more of a threat than China and realized that the two communist countries were unlikely to cooperate with each other, thus giving "the Chinese . . . an option to move toward us" (Kissinger, *White House Years*, p. 222). When trying to soldify their relationship with the U.S. in 1980, the Chinese recounted how the Soviets had mismanaged their security assistance to the PRC in order to communicate that "the break with Moscow was irreparable and therefore that the United States could trust China as a reliable security partner who would not double-cross it by turning back to the Soviets": Solomon, *Chinese Political Negotiating Behavior*, pp. 72–73.

[42] Andrew, *Delcassé*, p. 204. As this case shows, the tactic can backfire if it is practiced heavy-handedly or in inauspicious situations. If the other states detect moves to sow discord among them, they may infer that the state is especially aggressive and decide that they must make special efforts to overcome their differences in order to contain the common threat. For British perceptions of German policy at the turn of the century, see Kenneth Bourne, *The Foreign Policy of Victorian England 1830–1902* (Oxford: Clarendon Press, 1970), p. 465; for parallel American perceptions, see Mehnert, "German *Weltpolitik* and the American Two-Front Dilemma," pp. 1457, 1465.

each other. Thus in 1837, Chile supported the Bolivian attempt to acquire Peruvian territory in the expectation that this would not only weaken Peru but also be "a source of controversy which would keep these two nations at each other's throats."[43] Similarly, it appears that one reason why Stalin authorized the North Korean attack on the South was that he foresaw that the U.S. was likely to respond by protecting Formosa, which would increase Sino-American conflict and so keep the PRC dependent on the Soviet Union.[44]

It is plausible that this was Stalin's thinking: The PRC hoped to see the National Liberation Front established as the government of South Vietnam in 1975 rather than see Vietnam united,[45] and for a short time in the late stages of the Chinese civil war Stalin may have sought to partition China into Nationalist and Communist territories, which would have made Soviet support indispensable for the latter (and perhaps for the former).[46] In the aftermath of the revolution it also appears "that Stalin intentionally prevented China from developing wider international contacts. . . . [When] the UN secretary general . . . told Soviet Foreign Minister Vyacheslav Molotov that the [Soviet boycott of the Security Council in protest against the exclusion of the PRC] was counterproductive and that there was a good chance that the PRC would be admitted to the UN at a very early date if the boycott were dropped, Molotov 'merely smiled.'"[47] Similarly, the Bosnian Muslims might have increased their power early in their conflict had they been able to reignite the fighting between Serbs and Croatians in the Krajina region of Croatia. But actual fighting may not be necessary to produce bargaining leverage: perhaps trying to make the best of the situation, in the wake of the Gulf War "some American policymakers argued that Saddam's survival pro-

[43] Burr, *By Reason or Force*, p. 50.

[44] Adam Ulam, *The Communists: The Story of Power and Lost Illusions, 1948–1991* (New York: Scribner's, 1992), pp. 81–82; Goncharov, Lewis, and Litai, *Uncertain Partners*. In 1972, two Soviet scholars published an analysis of Sino-Soviet relations which hinted at this logic: see Rothenberg, *Whither China*, p. 159. The Soviets similarly may have aided Israel in 1948 because the success of that country would make the Arabs need Soviet support: Michael Cohen, "The Superpowers in the Middle East," *International History Review* 17 (May 1995), pp. 341–42. A related tactic is to encourage a crisis in an area in which two potential rivals will find it hardest to cooperate: Coral Bell, *The Conventions of Crisis* (London: Oxford University Press, 1971), pp. 65–67.

[45] Nelsen, *Power and Insecurity*, p. 103.

[46] This matter is in dispute: See Brian Murray, "Stalin, the Cold War, and the Division of China: A Multi-Archival Mystery," Cold War International History Project, Woodrow Wilson International Center for Scholars, Working Paper no. 12, June 1995; Douglas Macdonald, "Communist Bloc Expansion in the Early Cold War: Challenging Realism, Refuting Revisionism," *International Security* 20 (Winter 1995/96), p. 175.

[47] Nelsen, *Power and Insecurity*, pp. 7–8; the internal quote is from Robert Simmons, *The Strained Alliance: Peking, Moscow, and the Politics of the Korean War* (New York: Free Press, 1979), p. 92.

vided a strategic benefit by keeping Saudi Arabia dependent on the United States for protection."[48] The PRC similarly may have urged the U.S. to adopt a firmer policy toward the USSR in the late 1970s in order to increase Soviet-American conflict, and therefore China's value to the U.S., just as twenty years earlier it may have urged the USSR to stand up to the U.S. in order to preclude a Soviet-American understanding at China's expense.[49]

After a war the winner may change borders to create conflict among those who might otherwise come together to seek revenge. Philip of Macedon made Thebes cede territory to Athens so that the latter could not afford to alienate him;[50] in 1945 Russia moved Poland's border to the west not only to gain land but also to increase Poland's need for Soviet support against Germany; in 1990–91 the U.S. strongly opposed permitting Iraq to retain control of the two islands off the Kuwaiti coast not only because of an abstract commitment to combating aggression but also because without those islands Iraq's need for control of the Shatt-al-Arab would be much greater, thereby increasing the conflict between Iraq and Iran. It is ironic that one of the terms of alliance between Spain and France when they were fighting England at the end of the nineteenth century was that France would support Spain's effort to regain Gibraltar. As a French diplomat pointed out, "It is in England's interest to return Gibraltar. It is ours to see that she keeps it in order that France will always be necessary to Spain."[51] Conversely, states that seek to maintain good relations with each other may avoid being put in a situation in which third parties can play one off against the other. It was for this reason that Tallyrand argued that the 1805 peace treaty between Austria and France should be drawn so that they did not have a common border.[52]

In addition to or instead of actually increasing the divisions between its adversaries, a state can claim to believe that it has more diplomatic flexibility than they have because of their great conflicts with each other. Thus in the summer of 1977 when the PRC declared its dissatisfaction with Carter's policy toward Taiwan, it also stressed that China had other diplomatic options. As a spokesman put it: "If you compare . . . Europe and China in terms of which part is of the greater interest to the Soviet Union, I think it is Europe. . . . If one poses the question as to which will be the first to be

---

[48] Rick Atkinson, *Crusade* (Boston: Houghton Mifflin, 1993), p. 497. For an example from late eighteenth-century European history, see Paul Schroeder, *The Transformation of European History, 1763–1848* (New York: Oxford University Press, 1994), p. 63. One of Schroeder's central arguments is that British policy usually aimed at making Austria dependent in order to make it "fight for British interests fundamentally contrary to [Austria's] own" (ibid., p. 132).

[49] Solomon, *Chinese Political Negotiating Behavior*, pp. 106–7.

[50] Andrew Burn, *Alexander The Great* (London: Hodder and Stoughton, 1947), p. 45.

[51] Quoted in Richard Morris, *The Peacemakers* (New York: Harper and Row, 1965), p. 394.

[52] Duff Cooper, *Tallyrand* (London: Jonathan Cape, 1932), p. 149.

bitten by the polar bear, it is not necessarily China. Perhaps it will be Europe."[53]

President Nixon used the same tactic when he met Mao and said: "We must ask ourselves . . . why the Soviets have more forces on the border facing you than they do on the border facing Western Europe?"[54] Soviet leaders similarly may have hoped either to restrain the U.S. or receive concessions from it in the spring of 1972 when they said that the American bombing of Haiphong might foster increased Sino-Soviet cooperation.[55]

Alternatives and Bargaining Leverage

States gain and lose bargaining leverage over an actual or potential alliance partner in rough proportion to the alternatives available to them both.[56] In a

[53] Quoted in Harrison Salisbury, "China 'Quite Unhappy' with Carter Over Taiwan, a Top Leader Says," *New York Times*, August 30, 1977. Richard Solomon employs a cultural and psychological framework to analyze the Chinese propensity to lead others to believe that they need China more than China needs them: *Chinese Political Negotiating Behavior*, pp. 20–24, 78–79, 83–87. For an earlier Soviet claim that the Soviet Union was less menaced by the PRC than was the U.S. and so was better positioned to bargain with both of them, see Richard Wich, *Sino-Soviet Crisis Politics* (Cambridge, Mass.: Harvard University Press, 1980), pp. 229–30. For the kaiser's attempt to use this tactic against Russia in 1898 and the czar's quick reply, see René Albrecht-Carrié, *Britain and France* (Garden City, N.Y.: Doubleday, 1970), pp. 303–4.

[54] Richard Nixon, *RN: The Memoirs of Richard Nixon* (New York: Grosset & Dunlap, 1978), p. 563.

[55] Hedrick Smith, "Soviet Hints Mining Fosters Cooperation with China to Aid Hanoi," *New York Times*, May 18, 1972. In the mid-1920s, Germany played up the possibilities of ties with Russia in order to try to extract concessions from the West: Rosenbaum, *Community of Fate*, pp. 129, 145, 241. For ideological reasons, however, states may wish to exaggerate the extent to which their adversaries are jointly working against them. Thus throughout the 1960s both the USSR and the PRC accused the other of colluding with the U.S. While these claims reduced their bargaining power by indicating that the U.S. was not a threat to the other communist state, this loss was worth paying in order to undermine the other's revolutionary credentials abroad and ideological legitimacy at home.

[56] Glenn Snyder has used these concepts to explain intra-alliance bargaining, and my treatment draws on his: see Glenn Snyder and Paul Diesing, *Conflict Among Nations* (Princeton, N.J.: Princeton University Press, 1977), pp. 430–40; Snyder, "The Security Dilemma in Alliance Politics," *World Politics* 36 (July 1984), pp. 461–95; Snyder, "Alliance Theory: A Neorealist First Cut," *Journal of International Affairs* 44 (Spring/Summer 1990), pp. 103–24; Snyder, *Alliance Politics*. For a good study, see Howard Wriggins, "Up for Auction: Malta Bargains with Great Britain, 1971," in I. William Zartman, ed., *The 50% Solution* (Garden City, N.Y.: Doubleday, 1976), pp. 208–34. For discussions of bargaining power in terms of the opportunity costs of the courses of action available to the actor, see John Harsanyi, "Measurement of Social Power: Opportunity Costs and the Theory of Two-Person Bargaining Games," *Behavioral Science* 7 (January 1962), pp. 67–80; John Thibaut and Harold Kelley, *The Social Psychology of Groups* (New York: Wiley, 1959); and Harold Kelley and John Thibaut, *Interpersonal Relations* (New York: Wiley, 1978). The importance of alternatives was perhaps first stressed by Albert Hirschman in his classic *National Power and the Structure of International Trade* (Berkeley: Univer-

"natural alliance" the partners share many common interests that can be reached only by working together. This means that each can have some faith that the other will continue to cooperate with it and that special inducements are not needed to gain the others' support. But when connections are less tight than this, the option to break with the partner generates influence; the ability to leave a relationship generates power within it.[57] It also raises a danger that if the partner's fear of being abandoned becomes excessive, it may see little point in investing in the alliance at all.[58] Because statesmen understand these connections, they often pick alliance partners "with an eye to the post-formation balance of dependence and influence."[59]

Many cases show how the availability of alternatives can allow a state to

---

sity of California Press, 1945) (also see his *Exit, Voice, and Loyalty* [Cambridge, Mass.: Harvard University Press, 1970]), and has received attention from students of interdependence: See, for example, Robert Keohane and Joseph Nye, Jr., *Power and Interdependence* (Boston: Little, Brown, 1977). For a general treatment, see David Baldwin, *Paradoxes of Power* (New York: Basil Blackwell, 1989), especially chapter 8. Also see Samuel Bacharach and Edward Lawler, *Bargaining* (San Francisco: Jossey-Bass, 1981), pp. 59–79; Jon Elster, *The Cement of Society* (New York: Cambridge University Press, 1989), pp. 76–81; Burt, *Structural Holes*; Helen Milner, *Bargaining and Cooperation: Domestic Politics and International Relations* (Princeton, N.J.: Princeton University Press, forthcoming). Recent work on the importance of "asset specificity" is consistent with these insights: Oliver Williamson, *The Economic Institutions of Capitalism* (New York: Free Press, 1985). For discussions of the freedom that Third World countries can gain by having choice among financial partners, see Sylvia Maxfield, *Governing Capital: International Finance and Mexican Politics* (Ithaca, N.Y.: Cornell University Press, 1990), and Jung-en Woo, *Race to the Swift: State and Finance in Korean Industrialization* (New York: Columbia University Press, 1991).

[57] "Our relationships to possible opponents should be such . . . that our options toward both of them are always greater than their options toward each other": Kissinger, *White House Years*, p. 165. As Luce and Raiffa point out, some of the normative implications of this source of influence are disturbing: If a rich person and a poor person bargain over dividing a sum of money, the former is advantaged because she can more easily tolerate no agreement: Duncan Luce and Howard Raiffa, *Games and Decisions* (New York: Wiley, 1957), pp. 129–32.

[58] For the twin anxieties of "abandonment" and "entrapment" that are central to alliance politics, see Michael Mandelbaum, *The Nuclear Revolution: International Politics Before and After Hiroshima* (New York: Cambridge University Press, 1981), pp. 151–52; Snyder, "Security Dilemma in Alliance Politics"; Snyder, *Alliance Politics*.

[59] Snyder, "Alliance Theory," p. 114; for a general discussion of alliances as a means of control, see Paul Schroeder, "Alliances, 1815–1945: Weapons of Power and Tools of Management," in Klaus Knorr, ed., *Historical Dimensions of National Security Problems* (Lawrence: University of Kansas Press, 1976), pp. 227–62. One reason why Bismarck chose Austria as a partner when a choice was forced on him was that he believed that in an alliance with Austria, Germany would be the "rider," but with Russia, would be the "horse." He reached this conclusion through his analysis of the others' alternatives: "If Germany was allied with Russia, and if on any occasion Germany refused to support Russian policy, the Tsar could enforce submission by threatening to join forces with France. Francis Joseph could not . . . use the threat of a union with France; Germany could reply by going over to the side of Russia" (Sontag, *European Diplomatic History*, pp. 19–20). For an eighteenth-century example, see Steven Ross, *European Diplomatic History, 1789–1815* (Garden City, N.Y.: Doubleday, 1969), pp. 34–35.

bargain effectively. During the Napoleonic wars Britain and Russia bene-fited from recruiting Prussia to the coalition largely because this "would compel Austria to fight an all-out war, because Prussia would also be in the coalition competing for gains at Austria's expense in Germany, while Russia and Britain, as leaders and arbiters of the coalition, decided which rewards each of the subordinate partners would get."[60] Somewhat more benignly, after World War II the U.S. may have had greater influence over its Eu-ropean allies than over Japan because while it had no choice but to rely on the latter, it could play the Europeans off against one another.[61] The U.S. also found that concessions to Third World states were often necessary when those actors could credibly claim to be able to turn to the USSR if the U.S. was not forthcoming.[62]

This perspective makes clear that power is a function not only of the relative strengths of the actors and the relationships between them, but also of the existing and possible relations between each of them and third par-ties. A state that has many resources but that needs the support of a smaller and weaker partner may have to pay it a high price, especially if the other state has a viable alternative. Conversely, a state will be in a strong bargain-ing position vis-à-vis a potential ally if it can turn elsewhere with little diffi-culty. A German diplomat's retrospective analysis of the relationship be-tween his country and Austria-Hungary before World War I seems like common sense but ignores this point: "Germany is the *stronger* of the Al-lies. . . . The stronger partner is in a position to propose a *conference* and the weaker is *compelled* to accept."[63] It may be correct that Germany could have exercised greater influence over Austria, but this conclusion does not follow from the relative strengths of the two countries if Germany needed Austrian support. During the first years of World War I the reason the Brit-ish foreign secretary felt that he had a weak hand in bargaining with his allies was not that they had more resources than his country but that "Ger-many has taken care to make it known to our Allies that each one of them

---

[60] Schroeder, *Tranformation of European Politics*, p. 203.

[61] Robert Gilpin, *U.S. Power and the Multinational Corporation* (New York: Basic Books, 1975), pp. 109–11.

[62] See, for example, Michael Handel, *Weak States in the International System* (London: Cass, 1981), pp. 87–90; Robert McMahon, *Cold War on the Periphery: The United States, India, and Pakistan* (New York: Columbia University Press, 1994), pp. 71–72.

[63] Philipp Eulenburg-Hertefeld, quoted in John Röhl, ed., *1914: Delusion or Design?* (New York: St. Martin's, 1973), p. 135, emphasis in the original. As Morgenthau noted, this is one reason why strength does not equal power: "A weak nation may well possess an asset which is of such great value for its strong ally as to be irreplaceable" (*Power Among Nations*, p. 192). Machiavelli's oft-cited enjunction to princes not to make alliance with stronger states lest they be exploited actually is qualified and seems to apply mainly to offensive alliances: Niccolo Machiavelli, *The Prince and The Discources*, translated by Luigi Ricci, revised by E. R. P. Vincent (New York: Modern Library, 1950), p. 84.

individually, or at any rate France and Russia, could have peace tomorrow on comparatively favorable terms, if they would separate themselves from us. Our Allies have, therefore, an alternative to continuing the war which is not open to us."[64]

The distribution of bargaining power changes as events and choices alter states' needs for alliance partners in general and for specific other countries. When the British occupation of Egypt in 1882 alienated France, Germany was doubly advantaged: Britain could not afford to antagonize Germany, and Germany did not have to fear an Anglo-French combination. According to one scholar, this configuration "is probably the main reason why Bismarck was soon quarrelling with England over colonial rivalry in Africa."[65] Similarly, when Bismarck restored the ties between his country and Russia, he became "freed . . . from the fear of a Franco-Russian alliance and thus he had less need to court Paris."[66] Metternich, too, moved most confidently when relations between Britain and France were bad.[67] Leverage will also change if a potential partner becomes firmly committed to the alliance. Hence Winston Churchill's reply when a colleague noted that his message to Roosevelt shortly after Pearl Harbor had a different tone than previous ones: "Oh! that is the way we talked to her while we were wooing her; now that the she is in the harem, we talk to her quite differently!"[68] Of course need for others can increase as well: a state that has suffered the loss of a partner will be in a worse position vis-à-vis other members of the coalition because it will not be able to tolerate further defections.[69] Similarly, in domestic politics if one faction resigns from a government and a replacement is not readily at hand, the remaining members of the regime who are least committed to its continuance will be able to exact additional concessions.

Statesmen must judge the alternatives others have in order to determine the bargaining leverage that others have over them; they need to gauge their

[64] Quoted in David French, *British Strategy and War Aims, 1914–1916* (Boston: Allen & Unwin, 1986), pp. 168–69.

[65] Bourne, *Foreign Policy of Victorian England*, p. 140.

[66] Paul Kennedy, *Rise of the Anglo-German Antagonism*, p. 160. A few years earlier, Bismarck was spurred to act in the crisis over Rumania by the news that France was about to strike a bargain with England, a move that would diminish its need for German support: Bruce Waller, *Bismarck at the Crossroads* (London: Athlone Press, 1974), p. 166. For another case, see Akira Iriye, "Japan's Policies Toward the United States," in James Morley, ed., *Japan's Foreign Policy, 1868–1941: A Research Guide* (New York: Columbia University Press, 1974), p. 422.

[67] Roger Bullen, *Palmerston, Guizot and the Collapse of the Entente Cordiale* (London: Athlone Press, 1974), p. 181.

[68] Quoted in Arthur Bryant, *The Turn of the Tide: 1940–1945*, (London: Collins, 1957), p. 282. He put it more elegantly to the prime minister of Australia: "We have no longer any need to strike attitudes to win United States' sympathy": quoted in Martin Gilbert, *Winston S. Churchill*, vol. 7, *Road to Victory, 1941–1945* (Boston: Houghton Mifflin, 1986), p. 4.

[69] For an example, see Schroeder, *Transformation of European Politics*, p. 43.

own alternatives in order to compare what others are offering (or threatening) with what they can get elsewhere. Both kinds of estimates were at play during the Camp David negotiations, one working for and the other against Israel. According to one official, President Carter decided that if the negotiations broke down, he would side with the Egyptians not only because he thought they had been more reasonable, but also because "the Israelis would have nowhere else to go" while the Egyptians could reestablish their close ties with the USSR.[70] But in another respect Isreal's position was more advantageous: Its leaders believed that the alternative to an agreement— the breakdown of negotiations—was preferable to making concessions on the West Bank. For Egypt, the end of negotiations would sacrifice Sinai, an outcome that was seen by Sadat as worse than abandoning the Palestinians.

Pushes and Pulls

A state may gain alternatives by either pushes or pulls. Most obviously, a state that can choose from an array of partners can drive a hard bargain for its support, and a state that has nowhere else to turn will have to be a supplicant or *demandeur*. But a state also gains bargaining leverage if its situation is so grim that it will have to desert its ally—or collapse—unless the latter provides greater assistance.[71] Vulnerability then can be a bargaining asset, but only if the other needs the state.

Weakness was one of the main sources of French leverage over Britain in the decade before World War I and the nine months before World War II. Until the Munich crisis, Chamberlain and his colleagues believed that with the strongest army in Europe, France could withstand a German attack with little help from Great Britain. This allowed Britain to engage in buck-passing by maintaining only a small army and refusing to guarantee France's vital interests. But when British leaders came to believe that France might not be willing and able to resist, they were forced to alter their policy.[72]

---

[70] Quandt, *Camp David*, p. 285.

[71] The classic treatment of strength through weakness is Schelling, *Strategy of Conflict*. For a good application to bargaining between a superpower and its clients, see Douglas Macdonald, *Adventures in Chaos* (Cambridge, Mass.: Harvard University Press, 1992). On the advantages of relative invulnerability, see Schroeder's analysis of Russian and British policies in *Tranformation of European Politics* and Eric Nordlinger's arguments about the U.S. in *Isolationism Reconfigured* (Princeton, N.J.: Princeton University Press, 1995). For discussions of how the different kinds of national vulnerability affect behavior, see Steven David, *Choosing Sides: Alignment and Realignment in the Third World* (Baltimore, Md.: Johns Hopkins University Press, 1991), and Gregory Gause III, "Gulf Regional Politics: Revolution, War, and Rivalry," in Howard Wriggins, ed., *Dynamics of Regional Politics* (New York: Columbia University Press, 1992), pp. 23–88.

[72] For a good summary, see Michael Howard, *The Continental Commitment* (Har-

Indeed, earlier France may have exacerbated its own weakness by failing to extend the Maginot Line to the sea, leaving open the invasion routes through Belgium and thereby making it harder for Britain to avoid a commitment to send troops to fight on the French left flank.[73] Similarly, Bismarck's efforts to pressure Britain into joining his alliance came closest to succeeding when the weakness of Germany's diplomatic position made credible his threat to join with Russia unless Britain supported him.[74]

Ironically, then, the state may not be able to divide an opposing coalition by weakening one of its members. If another member depends on the coalition, it will have no choice but to bolster its troubled partner. Thus the successful German coercion of France in the initial stages of the first Moroccan Crisis did not sever the new bonds between France and England, as Germany had expected, but rather tightened them. Britain not only saw German behavior as evidence of aggressive intentions but also feared that France could not or would not resist unless it were certain of British support. Similarly, in late 1917 and early 1918 the Germans hoped that driving Russia from the war would induce Britain to abandon its French ally. In fact, British dependence on France increased.[75]

In politics (as perhaps in love[76]), to admit your need for the other may be to place yourself at a disadvantage. We just saw how a state's need for support could work in its favor. But this is true only if two conditions are met: Without support the state would collapse or have to change its policy, and the other's security rests on that policy continuing. But lacking this connection between the fates of the two states, a state that badly needs the support of another can be forced to pay a high price for it. Thus in 1905 the British

---

mondsworth, England: Penguin, 1974), chapters 5–6. For an alternative argument, see Schweller, *Deadly Imbalances.* Ironically, the destruction of Czechoslovakia, first as a significant power and then as a state, permitted by Britain in preference to being drawn into deep Continental commitments, resulted in much greater French leverage because it made that country clearly incapable of resisting Germany without full British assistance.

[73] See Barry Posen, *The Sources of Military Doctrine: France, Britain, and Germany Between the World Wars* (Ithaca, N.Y.: Cornell University Press, 1984), pp. 113–15. It has been argued that some British leaders understood this and urged Britain to declare that under no circumstances would it send an army to the Continent, thereby forcing France to extend its defenses: Anthony Adamthwaite, *France and the Coming of the Second World War, 1936–1939* (London: Frank Cass, 1977), p. 71; R. J. Minney, *The Private Papers of Hore-Belisha* (London: Collins, 1960), p. 59.

[74] Fritz Fischer, *War of Illusions* (New York: Norton, 1975), p. 46. Similarly, having suffered grave defeats in early 1942 and seeing little active support from his Western allies, Stalin gave a speech that opened the door to peace talks with Germany. British alarm contributed to putting on the Dieppe raid, but Hitler had also read the speech and so anticipated such a move: Brian Loring Villa, *Unauthorized Action: Mountbatten and the Dieppe Raid* (New York: Oxford University Press, 1989), pp. 8–9.

[75] See the discussion in L. L. Farrar, *Divide and Conquer* (Boulder, Colo.: East European Quarterly [distributed by Columbia University Press], 1978), pp. 100–101.

[76] Harold Kelley, "Common-Sense Psychology and Scientific Psychology," *Annual Review of Psychology* 43 (1992), pp. 2–3.

permanent undersecretary at the Foreign Office wrote to the ambassador in Berlin: "I wish we could make the lunatics here who denounce Germany in such unmeasured terms and howl for an agreement with Russia understand that the natural effect is to . . . encourage the Russians to believe that they can get all they want at our expense and without coming to any agreement with us."[77] Chamberlain and his colleagues felt the same way in the spring and summer of 1939, believing that people like Churchill who called for greater British efforts to ally with the Soviet Union not only exaggerated the virtues of such a pact but also strengthened Stalin's hand by stressing how much England needed him.

The Influence of Structure

We have seen that states' needs and alignment alternatives influence their bargaining leverage but have not explained how these needs and alternatives arise. In part they come from the structure of the international system. As noted in chapter 3, under bipolarity the superpowers need not fear the defection of an ally and so are free to pay little heed to their preferences. The situation is very different in multipolarity when even the strongest state needs allies. The bargaining relationships are particularly interesting and important when the system is structurally multipolar but behaviorally bipolar—that is, when the states are of relatively equal power and are divided into two hostile camps, as they were before 1914.[78]

What determines the distribution of bargaining power among states in this configuration? Why were the weaker members of the Triple Alliance and Triple Entente able to drag their partners into war in 1914 rather than the stronger restraining the weaker by using their own threats to defect? Critical here is the credibility of threats to leave the coalition, which depend on the value of the coalition to each state and the attractiveness of the alternatives available to it. A state that reaps great benefits from maintaining bonds with its partners is not likely to be able to exert much influence over them or to resist their demands. Conversely, a state that is not well served by its alignment may be able to better its position by threatening to defect.[79] Of course the value of the alliance only has meaning in comparison with the utility of the best available alternative policy. If adopting the role of a neutral

[77] Quoted in George Monger, *The End of Isolation* (London: Nelson, 1963), pp. 177–78.

[78] Kenneth Waltz, *Theory of International Politics* (Reading, Mass.: Addison Wesley, 1979), pp. 163–70; Snyder and Diesing, *Conflict Among Nations*, chapter 6; Robert Jervis, "Systems Theories and Diplomatic History," in Paul Lauren, ed., *Diplomacy* (New York: Free Press, 1979), pp. 224–26.

[79] In the aftermath of the Second Balkan War, Austria's foreign minister complained to the German ambassador that Austria might as well have belonged "to the other grouping" for all the good Berlin had been: Samuel Williamson, Jr., *Austria-Hungary and the Origins of the First World War* (New York: St. Martin's, 1991), p. 149.

would leave the state dangerously exposed, then the threat to move into this position will carry little weight even if the state is gaining little from its coalition; if joining the other side is out of the question, then the state's bargaining power with its partners will be low. But if there are incentives for it to defect to the other side, then it should be able to exercise more influence.

The history of the decade preceding World War I is consistent with this picture. Austro-Hungarian leverage over Germany was due to the dual facts of its weakness and its value to Germany. If we could rely on the version of history that was believed thirty years ago, we could argue that Germany reluctantly went to war in 1914 only because it was compelled to follow its partner's lead in punishing Serbia. But thanks to the studies of Fritz Fischer and those who have followed him, it is clear (although much else remains in dispute) that Germany was at least as belligerent as Austria.[80] The general alliance dynamic described here was still at work, however: One reason for German belligerence was the feeling that time was not on its side, and one reason for this was the belief that Austrian power would decline unless bold measures were taken.[81] Thus in the absence of German willingness or ability to befriend at least one member of the Entente (and I am putting aside the question of why this was so), Germany was tied to Austria and so could not settle international disputes at its expense.

Foreseeing this problem, Bismarck had diligently sought good relations with Russia as well as with Austria, which allowed Germany a check over Austria due to the latter's knowledge that Germany did not have to support it.[82] When Bismarck's successors dropped the Reinsurance Treaty with Russia, the latter's foreign minister immediately grasped the implications: "Vienna has been liberated from the wise and well-meaning, but also stern control of Prince Bismarck."[83] (Another indirect effect was to enable Britain

[80] Fischer, *War of Illusions*; a good synthesis is James Joll, *The Origins of the First World War* (London: Longman, 1984). For Austria's policy, see Williamson, *Austria-Hungary*.

[81] A. J. P. Taylor and others argue that in fact time was on Germany's side because its economy was growing rapidly and that if it had avoided war would naturally have come to dominate Europe: A. J. P. Taylor, *The Struggle for Mastery in Europe* (New York: Oxford University Press, 1954), p. 528. But this kind of analysis is misleading because it omits the fate of Germany's partner. For an argument that German power in fact was not increasing relative to that of its adversaries, see Charles Doran, *Systems in Crisis* (New York: Cambridge University Press, 1991), pp. 70–89.

[82] This is not to exaggerate the strength of Bismarck's hand. The Balkan Crisis of 1877–78 forced a choice, and he signed an alliance with Austria which temporarily left Germany without a tie to Russia.

[83] Quoted in Kissinger, *Diplomacy*, p. 179. Germany sometimes tried to reestablish this control by leading Austria to believe that it was on good terms with Russia, but the effect was not powerful: Oswald Wedel, *Austro-Germany Diplomatic Relations, 1908–1914* (Stanford, Calif.: Stanford University Press, 1932), pp. 37–38. After the first Moroccan Crisis, Bulow gave the kaiser the not very helpful advice that "we must let our relative isolation be noticed by the

to resist German pressure to join it in preserving the status quo in the Mediterranean because Germany now had no choice but to support Italy and Austria in these endeavors, which had not been the case under Bismarck.[84])

Within the Entente as well, bargaining power depended less on physical strength than on perceived alternatives. Thus despite the fact that Great Britain had a larger and more modern economy than its partners, its influence was limited by the fear that its allies would defect. In the first Moroccan Crisis the permanent undersecretary of the Foreign Office spoke for many when he predicted that "if France is left in the lurch an agreement of alliance between France, Germany and Russia in the near future is certain."[85] France then needed to be assured that Britain would stand by it. As the foreign minister, Sir Edward Grey, put it: "The weak point is that [France] might some day have a scare that we intend to change [our policy]. . . . and will have to make her own terms with Germany."[86] But to the extent that France understood British fears, it could control the alliance's policy. To use Mandelbaum's and Snyder's terminology, the British fear that France feared abandonment allowed Britain to be entrapped.[87] Indeed, France soon felt more confident of British support than of Russian support despite the fact that it had an alliance with the latter. "The explanation of this paradox lies in the French estimate of the relative dependence of Russia and England on France. Russian military strength was growing; Russia might feel strong enough to stand alone."[88]

While Britain made a number of overtures to Germany, its freedom of maneuver was inhibited by the fear that if France could not count on British loyalty, it would make its own arrangement with Germany before Britain's doing so diminished its bargaining power. As noted earlier, the British even refrained from sending a military band to Berlin for fear that this would

---

Austrians as little as possible": quoted in Eugene Anderson, *The First Moroccan Crisis* (Hamden, Conn.: Archon Books, 1966), p. 399.

[84] Norman Rich, *Friedrich von Holstein: Politics and Diplomacy in the Era of Bismarck and Wilhlem II*, vol. 1 (Cambridge: Cambridge University Press, 1965), p. 323.

[85] Quoted in Gooch and Temperley, eds., *Documents on the Origins of the War*, p. 268; also see Zara Steiner, *Britain and the Origins of the First World War* (London: St. Martin's, 1977), p. 43.

[86] Quoted in C. J. Lowe and M. L. Dockrill, *The Mirage of Power*, vol. I, *British Foreign Policy, 1902–14* (London: Routledge & Kegan Paul, 1972), p. 25.

[87] Mandelbaum, *Nuclear Revolution*, pp. 151–52; Snyder, "Security Dilemma in Alliance Politics"; Snyder, *Alliance Politics*. Grey understood that this relationship not only tied Britain to France, but, for this reason, allowed Germany to put pressure on Britain through France: Keith Wilson, *The Policy of the Entente* (Cambridge: Cambridge University Press, 1985), pp. 46–47, 93.

[88] Sontag, *European Diplomatic History*, pp. 174–75; also see Snyder and Diesing, *Conflict Among Nations*, p. 433, and Snyder, *Alliance Politics*, chapter 7. British statesmen believed that Russia had reason to lack confidence in British support because the relationship was not formalized in an alliance, however: Wilson, *Policy of the Entente*, pp. 88, 93.

upset France.[89] Britain similarly not only failed to restrain Russia in 1914 but also allowed that country to take advantage of it by expanding the Russian sphere of influence in Persia. British leaders felt that they had no alternative: Russia could do Britain great harm unless the alliance was maintained, and without Entente assistance in the Balkans, Russia might be better off joining Germany and moving against Britain in Asia.[90]

It was more than accidental but less than strictly determined that the states that were weaker and less satisfied than their partners—Austria and Russia—had the greater bargaining power. Situations in which Britain and Germany were better able to control their allies would not have violated any laws of international systems. If Germany had not developed conflicts with each member of the Entente—e.g., if Bismarck's policy of maintaining at least the possibility of good relations with Russia had been continued—it would have had more alternatives and therefore more influence over Austria (and also would have been less pessimistic about how a peaceful world would evolve). If the British domestic opposition to alliance commitments had been so strong that its leaders could have argued that Britain could fight only in response to the most blatant German aggression, it might have been able to curb its allies. These kinds of influences were understood at the time: In 1909 a British diplomat wanted to see Italy remain in the Triple Alliance because, being "dependent on the goodwill of France and England in the event of a continental war," it would restrain Austria and Germany.[91]

Indeed, in the 1930s preferences and the distribution of intra-alliance bargaining power did produced peace, albeit one that altered the status quo.[92] Because France was directly threatened by Germany, lacked alternative allies or the possibility of conciliating Germany, and was thought to have a strong army, Britain would have had the bargaining advantage even without weakness in French leadership and Chamberlain's great self-confidence.

[89] Monger, *End of Isolation*, pp. 328–29; also see Wilson, *Policy of the Entente*, p. 35.

[90] Steiner, *Britain and the Origins of the First World War*, pp. 114–17, 182–83; Michael Ekstein, "Great Britain and the Triple Entente on the Eve of the Sarajevo Crisis," in Hinsley, ed., *British Foreign Policy Under Sir Edward Grey*, chapter 18. Russian statesmen understood this: In October 1910 the foreign minister said that "we may rest assured that the English, engaged in the pursuit of political aims of vital importance in Europe, may, in case of necessity, be prepared to sacrifice certain interests in Asia in order to keep [the Anglo-Russian] Convention alive which is of such importance to them. This is a circumstance which we can, of course, exploit for ourselves, as, for instance, in Persian affairs" (quoted in Wilson, *Policy of the Entente*, p. 83).

[91] Quoted in M. B. Cooper, "British Policy in the Balkans, 1908–9," *The Historical Journal* 7 (June 1964), p. 279.

[92] For a related argument, see Thomas Christensen and Jack Snyder, "Chain Gangs and Passed Bucks: Predicting Alliance Patterns in Multipolarity," *International Organization* 44 (Spring 1990), pp. 137–68. At one point in the rivalry between Athens and Sparta, the latter was restrained by Corinth: Donald Kagan, *On the Origins of War and the Preservation of Peace* (New York: Doubleday, 1995), pp. 36–37.

The fact that Britain used it to restrain what little belligerence France displayed is partly attributable to the views of British leaders (with Churchill in power, British policy would have been different) but largely stems from the fact that Britain, not being literally on the front line, could maintain its tradition of appeasement.[93]

But the 1914 pattern would seem to be the more common: Both weakness and dissatisfaction are likely to contribute to power within an alliance. States that are getting relatively little out of the alliance, or will get little out of it unless their preferences are controlling, can credibly claim to be ready to defect; the warning that the government or even the state will collapse unless it receives support is available only to the weak. Dissatisfied states by definition and weak states by elective affinity are also likely to want to change the status quo, which means that a state that seeks to drag its partner into war is likely to have more bargaining power than the state that favors restraint.[94]

An earlier chapter discussed the argument that small allies have less bargaining leverage under bipolarity than under multipolarity because superpowers can protect themselves.[95] What is relevant here is that the smaller states should be less disadvantaged when the superpower thinks that it needs them. The U.S. certainly believed that it needed West Europe during the first fifteen years of the Cold War; indeed it could not have successfully fought a war without European industrial strength and military bases. Although precise comparisons are difficult, it does appear that, as our argument suggests, the Europeans had more influence over the U.S. before the early 1960s than they did later. Even though the Europeans could not credibly threaten to join with the USSR—domestic politics, the repulsive nature of the Soviet regime, and incompatible foreign policy goals prohibited this—they might have retreated into neutralism or, in the immediate postwar years, collapsed. The result was the Marshall Plan, NATO, and a significant place for Britain and France in postwar diplomacy. Summits, for example, were meetings of the "Big Four"; Soviet and American leaders met together alone for the first time only when Khrushchev visited the U.S. in 1959. The deference was more than symbolic as the U.S. shaped its policy with at least one eye on allied reaction. For example, in 1948 the U.S. dropped consideration of proposals for German unification because of

[93] Paul Kennedy, "The Tradition of Appeasement in British Foreign Policy, 1865–1939," in *Strategy and Diplomacy*, chapter 1; Paul Schroeder, "Munich and the British Tradition," *Historical Journal* 19 (March 1976), pp. 223–43. An outstanding analysis of the difference between British and French policy remains Arnold Wolfers, *Britain and France Between Two Wars* (New York: Harcourt Brace, 1940).

[94] Gathering empirical evidence would not be easy because cases of restraint do not lead to war and so are hard to detect.

[95] For further discussion, see above, chapter 3, pp. 112–18.

strong British and French opposition, and American policy during the Korean War was significantly influenced by allied, and even neutral, opinion.[96]

Much of the general influence of the Third World over the U.S. and the variation of it over individual statesmen can be similarly explained. Some American decision-makers believed in the domino theory. For them, the loss of one country was highly consequential because other countries in the region would be lost, European allies frightened, and the Soviets and Chinese emboldened. These leaders felt they had no choice but to support Third World regimes against subversion and left-wing opposition. As a Buddhist leaflet distributed in Vietnam in 1965 put it, "We can insult the Americans as much as we please and they must still do our bidding and grant us aid."[97] When American leaders thought the effects of a defeat in the Third World would be much less, the U.S. was harder to manipulate. To some (slight) extent, Democrats tended to be more skeptical of the domino theory than Republicans, an effect usually offset by the fact that for them even a limited international defeat would have major domestic effects: Having "lost" China and being seen as "soft on communism," they could ill afford further setbacks of this kind. In general, though, Americans who were good Waltzians were less susceptible to Third World influence than were those who did not understand the freedom granted them by the bipolar structure.[98]

On the Soviet side, our approach leads us to expect that allies' influence would increase in proportion to three factors: the likelihood that they would

[96] Wilson Miscamble, *George F. Kennan and the Making of American Foreign Policy, 1947–1950* (Princeton, N.J.: Princeton University Press, 1992), pp. 169–73; U.S. Department of State, *Foreign Relations of the United States, 1952–1954*, vol. 15, *Korea* (Washington, D.C.: Government Printing Office, 1984). For a general discussion of European influence over American foreign policy, see Thomas Risse-Kappen, *Cooperation Among Democracies: The European Influence on U.S. Foreign Policy* (Princeton, N.J.: Princeton University Press, 1995). (Risse-Kappen sees bargaining power as a less important source of influence than alliance norms.) Here again, there is a methodological problem: We tend not to notice cases in which allies fail to exert influence. For a discussion of lack of consultation, see Costigliola, "Kennedy, the European Allies, and the Failure to Consult"; for a case in which Britain sought influence, but to no avail, see Arthur Combs, "The Path Not Taken: The British Alternative to U.S. Policy in Vietnam, 1954–1956," *Diplomatic History* 19 (Winter 1995), pp. 33–58.

[97] Quoted in Brian VanDeMark, *Into the Quagmire: Lyndon Johnson and the Escalation of the Vietnam War* (New York: Oxford University Press, 1991), p. 212. For a general discussion of this dynamic, see Macdonald, *Adventures in Chaos*. American policy-makers were often aware of the problem and tried to assert their freedom to withdraw aid, generally without success: See, for example, President Kennedy's instructions on what Ambassador Lodge should tell Diem in the fall of 1963 and McNamara's recommendation shortly thereafter: Department of State, *Foreign Relations of the United States, 1961–1963*, vol. 4, *Vietnam, August-December 1963* (Washington, D.C.: Government Printing Office, 1991), pp. 252–53, 338–39.

[98] Thus among Realists, the debate about American policy in Vietnam turned largely on expectations of domino dynamics.

collapse unless their preferences were adopted, the alternatives they had, and the USSR's need for them. What sketchy evidence is available fits this picture. Weakness gave East Germany considerable leverage over the Soviet Union, and the East German regime got more of what it wanted when it was weaker.[99] The possibility of collapse rather than defection usually was at work because both Soviet troops and the self-interests of local Communist leaders precluded the option of joining the West, or even becoming neutral. (When it became attractive in other cases, as it did to Hungary's Nagy and Afghanistan's Amin, the Soviet Union intervened.) With ties to the West ruled out, the main, although still limited, source of alternatives for the USSR's allies was the PRC. We would expect that the Sino-Soviet split would have increased the leverage of local Communist parties, whether in power or not. This seems to have been the case.[100] Finally, our approach leads us to believe that in 1989 the East Europeans would lose all leverage when the Soviet regime concluded that it had little need for them. For reasons that partly lie beyond the international system, Gorbachev came to believe that the U.S. was not a threat, that dominating East Europe increased rather than decreased Soviet-American tension, and that the collapse of hard-line regimes would not damage, and probably would further, his domestic objectives. The East European regimes then had little with which to threaten him.

In summary, the bargaining leverage that a state has over its allies is largely determined by their respective needs for support, the alternatives that are available to them, and their vulnerabilities which both increase the price they will pay for assistance and lend credibility to their threats to defect from the alliance if support is not forthcoming. In a multipolar world, a state that is well served by the alliance and will suffer if it breaks up can be exploited by allies who have more choices or who are so weak that they can only support the alliance if it adopts their preferred policy. Before 1914, the states that were well positioned were more belligerent and weaker than their partners, an outcome that is made likely but not determined by the structure. Under bipolarity, superpowers have less need of small allies and cannot be pulled into unwanted conflicts by them, as Waltz and Snyder have

[99] Hope Harrison, "The Bargaining Power of Weaker Allies in Bipolarity and Crisis: The Dynamics of Soviet–East German Relations, 1953–1961" (unpublished dissertation, Department of Political Science, Columbia University, 1994).

[100] Ibid.; earlier studies of the Sino-Soviet split concentrated on the relations between those countries but provide some evidence for this proposition: Donald Zagoria, *The Sino-Soviet Conflict, 1956–1961* (Princeton, N.J.: Princeton University Press, 1962); Alfred Low, *The Sino-Soviet Dispute* (Rutherford, N.J.: Fairleigh Dickinson University Press, 1976); only a slight effect is found by Edwina Moreton, "The Triangle in Eastern Europe," in Gerald Segal, ed., *The China Factor: Peking and the Superpowers* (New York: Holmes and Meier, 1982), pp. 126–49.

explained. But the same factors of need, vulnerability, and alternatives continue to determine much of the variation in the allies' influence.

Structure Does Not Determine—Room for Judgments

The previous analysis has demonstrated the importance of the system's structure, which here includes the pattern of interests and alignment possibilities as well as the distribution of capabilities. But the external environment is rarely so compelling as to obviate the need for difficult judgments and choices. As a result, it will not be possible to develop a full picture of behavior in a system without expanding our focus. The history of relations among the U.S., PRC, and USSR so well reveals the limits of structure, the possibility of errors, and the role of idiosyncratic events and decision making that I will use episodes from it for an extended example to close this chapter.[101] The importance of perceptions and choice does not mean that the less subjective factors discussed earlier play no role. Thus the PRC increased its support for the U.S. when it believed that American policy was dangerously "soft" on the USSR in the mid- and late 1970s and felt free to take a more belligerent stance on the Taiwan issue when Reagan's "hard line" increased American need for the PRC and removed the danger of a Soviet-American détente. Indeed, it is far from clear that the PRC would have been interested in a rapprochement with the U.S. had it not been for the the Soviet invasion of Czechoslovakia which carried an implicit threat and the coming American withdrawal from Vietnam which had the potential for reducing Soviet-American conflict.[102] But calculations and beliefs often need to be considered.

In the wake of the Chinese revolution there was a debate in the U.S.

[101] The literature is enormous: See, for example, Lowell Dittmer, "The Strategic Triangle: An Elementary Game-Theoretic Analysis," *World Politics* 31 (July 1981), pp. 485–515; Dittmer, *Sino-Soviet Normalization and Its International Implications* (Seattle: University of Washington Press, 1992), part 3; Michael Tatu, *The Great Power Triangle Washington-Moscow-Peking* (Paris: The Atlantic Institute, Atlantic Papers, #3, 1970); Nelsen, *Power and Insecurity*; Robert Ross, "International Bargaining and Domestic Politics: U.S.-China Relations since 1972," *World Politics* 38 (January 1986), pp. 255–87; Ross, ed., *China, the United States, and the Soviet Union: Tripolarity and Policymaking in the Cold War* (New York: Sharpe, 1993); Ross, *Negotiating Cooperation: The United States and China, 1969–1989* (Stanford, Calif.: Stanford University Press, 1995); Banning Garrett, "The United States and the Great Power Triangle," in Segal, ed., *The China Factor, pp. 76–102;* Raju Thomas, ed., *The Great-Power Triangle and Asian Security* (Lexington, Mass.: Lexington Books, 1983).

[102] For the argument that the Sino-American rapprochement was caused by a change in Chinese policy, but one that was largely rooted in domestic politics, see Arthur Waldron, "From Nonexistent to Almost Normal: U.S.-China Relations in the 1960s," in Diane Kunz, ed., *The Diplomacy of the Crucial Decade* (New York: Columbia University Press, 1994), pp. 219–50.

about whether the two Communist powers would inevitably act together, requiring the U.S. to treat China as as much of an enemy as the Soviet Union. Although many people believed this to be the case, Secretary of State Acheson and some associates believed that Chinese nationalism would eventually turn the PRC against the Soviet Union and argued that the U.S. should encourage this possibility by keeping the door open to good relations.[103] That Acheson and his opponents could disagree shows that the objective situation may not be compelling enough to produce agreement on the fundamental point of whether adversaries can be divided.

When North Korea attacked its neighbor—an event not to be explained by structure—the administration became deeply hostile toward the PRC, an attitude that was solidified by the Chinese entry into the war. What is important here is that both the causes and the effects of the intervention were driven by interpretations of behavior. We now know that Chinese relations with the USSR were uneasy and that China fought in part because it feared that American troops along the Yalu, and even north of the 38th parallel, would menace its security.[104] While in retrospect this fear appears natural, American statesmen at the time did not anticipate it. Instead, knowing that they did not intend to harm China, they assumed that China would realize this. China's intervention then led them to infer that the PRC either was a puppet of the Soviet Union or that it was deeply and irrationally hostile to the U.S. In either case, the U.S. faced joint foes. The Truman administration then concluded that there was no way to play these states off against each other and gain the role of pivot.

While Eisenhower and Dulles agreed with this interpretation, they did not think that the "Sino-Soviet" bloc would necessarily last long. In this, their view was closer to Acheson's than was appreciated at the time. Their tactics were very different, however: They thought that the best way to divide the two countries was to treat them as a unit and show each that close

[103] But even Acheson felt that it was up to the Chinese regime to demonstrate its independence from Moscow; America might be prepared to respond but it would not take the initiative. Although the latter position found very few advocates (and probably would not have produced the desired Chinese reaction), it too was not foreclosed by the structure of the international system. For a good discussion, see Miscamble, *Kennan and the Making of American Foreign Policy*, pp. 234–46.

[104] Until recently it was believed that the PRC would not have intervened in Korea had American troops stopped at the narrow neck of the Korean peninsula. Thomas Christensen's analysis of newly discovered documents shows that this is not the case: "Threats, Assurances, and the Last Chance for Peace: The Lessons of Mao's Korean War Telegrams," *International Security* 17 (Summer 1992), pp. 122–54. Much about the Chinese policy remains unclear, however: For a recent treatment see Chen Jian, *China's Road to the Korean War* (New York: Columbia University Press, 1994), and the articles and documents in *Cold War International Project Bulletin*, nos. 6–7 (Winter 1995/96), pp. 30–125.

ties would increase the chance that it would be drawn into conflict on the other's behalf.[105] (Interestingly enough, at about this time the PRC held the parallel belief that "maintaining the campaign against Taiwan would 'enlarge the contradiction between England and the United States.'"[106]) Thus in December 1953 Dulles explained that U.S. support for the Chinese Nationalists was built "on the theory of exerting maximum strain causing the Chinese Communists to demand more from Russia and thereby placing additional stress on Russian-Chinese relations."[107] Domestic critics and leaders of allied countries such as Great Britain dissented, arguing that the U.S. was driving its adversaries together.[108] Without access to Soviet and Chinese archives we cannot know the full impact of the American strategy,[109] but what matters here is not who was right, but the very fact that the situation permitted sharply divergent analyses of how the opposing camp could be broken up.

The importance and limits of structure are also revealed by American policy in Vietnam. Again, both proponents and opponents of the war argued that their favored policy would separate the USSR from China and that the alternative would unite them. The administration claimed that resisting the

[105] John Lewis Gaddis, *The Long Peace* (New York: Oxford University Press, 1987), chapter 6. This argument was advanced earlier, but with less evidence, in Gaddis, *Strategies of Containment* (New York: Oxford University Press, 1982), pp. 193–96, and David Mayers, *Cracking the Monolith* (Baton Rouge: Louisiana State University, 1986).

[106] Gordon Chang and He Di, "The Absence of War in the U.S.—China Confrontation over Quemoy: Contingency, Luck, Deterrence?" *American Historical Review* 98 (December 1993), p. 1516 (the internal quote is from an official Chinese document).

[107] Quoted in Gaddis, *Strategies of Containment*, p. 194. Also see Meyers, *Cracking the Monolith*, pp. 119–20. The same logic guided American policy during the crises over Quemoy and Matsu. As Dulles put it,

> [T]he best hope for intensifying the strain and difficulties between Communist China and Russia would be to keep the Chinese under maximum pressure rather than by relieving such pressure. . . . [P]ressure and strain would compel them to make more demands on the USSR which the latter would be unable to meet and the strain would consequently increase. . . . [T]his was the course to be followed rather than to seek to divide the Chinese and the Soviets by a sort of competition with Russia as to who would treat China best.

Quoted in Gaddis, *Long Peace*, p. 148; also see p. 180.

[108] The Russians claimed to agree: Foreign Minister Molotov told John Foster Dulles in 1954 that America's "bankrupt" China policy "merely forced China closer to [the] Soviet Union." U.S. Department of State, *Foreign Relations of the United States, 1952–1954*, vol. 14, *China and Japan* (Washington, D.C.: Government Printing Office, 1985), p. 354.

[109] For recent discussions, see John Lewis and Litai Xue, *China Builds the Bomb* (Stanford, Calif.: Stanford University Press, 1988), pp. 160–63; Shu Guang Zhang, *Deterrence and Strategic Culture: Chinese-American Confrontations, 1949–1958* (Ithaca, N.Y.: Cornell University Press, 1992), chapters 6–8; Vladislav Zubok and Constantine Pleshakov, *Inside the Kremlin's Cold War* (Cambridge, Mass.: Harvard University Press, 1996), chapter 7; and the articles and documents in *Cold War International History Project Bulletin*, nos. 6–7, (Winter 1995/1996), pp. 208–31.

Communists would magnify Sino-Soviet differences by demonstrating that expansion was impossible and drawing China and the USSR into conflicts over strategy, burden sharing, and influence over Vietnam. Opponents of the war claimed that these states would pull closer because they were confronting a common enemy and that by seeking to contain both of them the U.S. relieved each of the necessity of containing the other.

As American decision-makers first considered and then implemented an opening to China in the final two decades of the Cold War, they confronted the argument of Soviet experts who warned that better relations with China could worsen, rather than improve, Soviet-American relations. According to a State Department paper quoted by Kissinger, these analysts argued that American

> overtures [to China] will . . . introduce irritants into the U.S.-Soviet relationship. Furthermore, if a significant improvement in the Sino-American relationship should come about, the Soviets might well adopt a harder line both at home and in international affairs. . . . The fact that . . . [this could occur] argues for caution in making moves toward better relations with China.[110]

Kissinger ridicules this view as hidebound and insensitive to the subtlety of the policy he and Nixon were planning. It clearly was timid and unimaginative: While the Soviet experts were correct to argue that relations with the Soviet Union were more important to the U.S. than relations with China, it did not follow that the latter could not be used to American advantage.[111] Kissinger reports that even before his secret trip to Peking Ambassador Dobrynin told him that China "was a 'neuralgic' point with Moscow" and recounts that in subsequent years "no occasion was too unpromising for [Brezhnev] to pursue his obsession with China" in conversations with American leaders.[112] Indeed, by showing great concern and implying that they would not or could not outbid the U.S. for China's support, Soviet leaders increased the American bargaining leverage. But the State Department memorandum was not foolish: The Soviet Union could have responded by becoming more rather than less intransigent. Although definitive judgments are still not possible, there is much plausibility to the argument of William Hyland, a Soviet expert and close associate of Kissinger's, that the deteriora-

---

[110] Quoted in Kissinger, *White House Years*, p. 189.

[111] Missing this point, the Soviets kept telling the Americans that the U.S. had to give priority to U.S.-Soviet relations because the USSR was more important to the U.S. than was the PRC.

[112] Ibid., p. 524; Kissinger, *Years of Upheaval*, p. 1173. Also see Nixon, *RN*, p. 878. Raymond Garthoff's point should not be forgotten, however: "Kissinger's judgment neglects the possibility that the Soviet leaders truly believed the Chinese *were* a potential menace both to the United States and to the Soviet Union, and that the Americans might come to see that fact": Garthoff, *Détente and Confrontation* (Washington, D.C.: the Brookings Institution, 1985), p. 242.

tion of Soviet-American relations in 1973–76 was in part caused by improved Sino-American relations as "the Soviets gradually came to make a U.S. willingness to drop the China option and take up a semi-alliance with Moscow a critical test of détente."[113]

The later disagreement between Vance and Brzezinski on policy toward China was similarly conditioned, but not determined, by structure. The secretary of state believed that if the U.S. were to move too close to China, Soviet-American relations would suffer: "If we abandoned or relaxed our policy of evenhandedness, we would jeopardize . . . more stable and predictable relationships with both Moscow and Peking."[114] Brzezinski, by contrast, argued that greater and more overt Sino-American cooperation would enhance leverage over the Soviet Union, which would react by making concessions: "I believed that a strategic response [in the form of closer ties to China] was necessary" because of "Moscow's misuse of détente."[115] Both statesmen were aware of and tried to utilize triangular dynamics, but their strategies were very different. To take a specific case which epitomizes the dispute, Vance wanted to delay the announcement of normalization of Sino-American relations until the crucial meeting with Gromyko that was expected to put the finishing touches on SALT II, but Brzezinski convinced Carter to move ahead on the grounds that normalization certainly would not harm relations with the Soviet Union and might well improve them, as the Soviets viewed the American hand as having been strengthened. In reality, Brzezinski's confidence was misplaced, the Soviets hardened their position, and the SALT treaty was delayed several months (which was one cause of its eventual demise). The Soviet reaction, in turn, was not completely determined by the objective situation but was influenced by beliefs about American goals.[116] As the State Department noted, "At some undefined point, Soviet perceptions of the threat of U.S.-Chinese military collaboration would stiffen Soviet positions on even the major issues of U.S.-Soviet relations."[117] Clearly there was room for disagreement in the USSR on where this point was, which created at least as much room for disagreement in the U.S. as to which Soviet analysis would control policy.

In many cases in addition to the Sino-American-Soviet triangle, statesmen disagree as to who is the main threat and whether carrots or sticks will be more likely to divide their adversaries. The policy that is followed depends on the beliefs of those who are in power, and miscalculations are common.

[113] William Hyland, *Soviet-American Relations: A New Cold War?* (Santa Monica, Calif.: RAND Corp., May 1981), p. 25.

[114] Cyrus Vance, *Hard Choices* (New York: Simon and Schuster, 1983), p. 114.

[115] Zbigniew Brzezinski, *Power and Principle* (New York: Farrar, Straus & Giroux, 1983), pp. 203–4.

[116] Dittmer, "Strategic Triangle," p. 511.

[117] Quoted in Garrett, "United States and the Great Power Triangle," p. 88.

As we saw earlier, at the turn of the century German leaders failed to correctly gauge the alternatives available to Great Britain, the concessions Britain would be willing to make to improve relations with France and Russia, and the impact that their own actions would have on British perceptions of Germany. Structure should be the starting place for analysis of strategies and bargaining, but it can rarely yield definitive answers.

In summary, many of the interaction effects discussed in chapter 2 can be seen in the potential and actual alignments among states. The relations between two states are strongly influenced by the existing and desired relations between each of them and a third actor. The interconnections in the system produce ramifications as changes in relations between two states have widespread and often unanticipated consequences. As states bargain with each other, they seek to have more alternatives than their partners, and as both a cause and an effect of this, to gain the pivotal position in triangular relations. Structure strongly influences the state's needs and alternatives, which in turn establish its bargaining power. States weak in physical resources can have great influence when the system is structurally multipolar but behaviorally bipolar because they are likely to be both needed and vulnerable. But even under bipolarity, analysis of perceived needs and alternatives can help tell us when the smaller allies will have most leverage.

These are not the only dynamics at work among potential or actual allies. In the next chapter, we will turn to the forces that tend to polarize systems. Strategic and psychological considerations lead states to develop good relations with the allies of their allies and the enemies of their enemies and, although they often try to avoid it, to share their allies' adversaries. Such consistency becomes complete only in extreme circumstances, but the pressures for it are common and explain a good deal of international politics.

Six

Alignments and Consistency

THE ELEMENTS in a social system often form a configuration that is consistent or balanced (using these terms as synonyms). The pure case, in which the system is divided into two camps, is characterized by three conditions: Each actor has friendly relations with every other actor in its camp, each actor has hostile relations with every actor in the other camp, and there are no actors outside either camp—i.e., no neutrals.[1] Although these cases are uncommon, the forces driving a system toward consistency are strong and widespread. Indeed, the phenomenon has been found in many different realms and has been described by psychologists, sociologists, and political scientists. The pattern also appears in animal behavior—alliances among chimpanzees are likely to be balanced.[2] Consistency, then, can be thought of as the "natural order"[3] of a system. That is, a system will become consistent if nothing stops it. Because many other forces can intervene, imbalance is not surprising in a statistical sense, but it does need to be explained. As we will see, much of the explanation comes from the preferences and strategies of the actors. Al-

[1] For measurements of balance, see Bruce Bueno de Mesquita, "Measuring Systemic Polarity," *Journal of Conflict Resolution* 19 (June 1975), pp. 187–216; Michael Wallace, "Alliance Polarization, Cross-Cutting, and International War, 1815–1964: A Measurement and Some Preliminary Evidence," ibid. 17 (December 1973), pp. 575–604; David Rapkin, William Thompson, and Jon Christopherson, "Bipolarity and Bipolarization in the Cold War Era: Conceptualization, Measurement, and Validity," ibid. 23 (June 1979), pp. 261–95; James Lee Ray, "The Measurement of System Structure," in J. David Singer and Paul Diehl, eds., *Measuring the Correlates of War* (Ann Arbor: University of Michigan Press, 1990), pp. 106–12; Frank Wayman and T. Clifton Morgan, "Measuring Polarity in the International System," in ibid., pp. 139–56; Paul Huth, D. Scott Bennett, and Christopher Gelpi, "System Uncertainty, Risk Propensity, and International Conflict," *Journal of Conflict Resolution* 36 (September 1992), p. 496. Parallel issues of the measurement of consistency in small groups are treated in Robert Abelson, "Mathematical Models in Social Psychology," in Leonard Berkowitz, ed., *Advances in Experimental Social Psychology*, vol. 3 (New York: Academic Press, 1967), pp. 15–19. Note that balanced configurations can arise nonsystemically because all the actors in one camp could have something important in common that both unites them and divides them from those in the other camp. This would be the case, for example, if religion or ideology dominated international politics and each state adhered to one of two hostile creeds.

[2] See Jane Goodall, *The Chimpanzees of Gombe* (Cambridge, Mass.: Harvard University Press, 1986), pp. 418–35; 573–76; also see Alexander Harcourt and Frans de Waal, eds., *Coalitions and Alliances in Humans and Other Animals* (Oxford: Oxford University Press, 1992).

[3] Stephen Toulmin, *Foresight and Understanding* (New York: Harper and Row, 1963), chapters 3 and 4.

though it is their behavior that drives some configurations to balance, actors often seek imbalance and under some conditions can achieve it.

How and Why Systems Become Consistent

Systems become balanced through processes summarized by the old Arab proverbs: "The friend of my friend is my friend; the enemy of my friend is my enemy; the enemy of my enemy is my friend."[4] Because systems are interconnected, the relations between two actors are often determined less by their common and conflicting bilateral interests than by their relations with other actors, which means that a shift in stance sets off a chain of consequences. As an actor becomes the friend of an enemy's enemy or the adversary of an adversary's ally, its strategic situation will change, producing new dangers and new opportunities, which in turn will affect subsequent alignments and alliances.[5] George Kennan's summary of the effects of the Balkan crisis of 1887–88 brings out some of the dynamics:

[4] International politics has been discussed in these terms by Frank Harary, "A Structural Analysis of the Situation in the Middle East in 1956," *Journal of Conflict Resolution* 5 (June 1961), pp. 167–78; Brian Healy and Arthur Stein, "The Balance of Power in International History," ibid. 17 (March 1973), pp. 33–62; H. Brooke McDonald and Richard Rosecrance, "Alliance and Structural Balance in the International System," ibid. 29 (March 1985), pp. 57–82; Michael Sullivan, *International Relations: Theories and Evidence* (Englewood Cliffs, N.J.: Prentice Hall, 1976), pp. 226–51; also see Robert Axelrod and D. Scott Bennett, "A Landscape Theory of Aggregation," *British Journal of Political Science* 23 (April 1993), pp. 211–33. The discussion here borrows from my earlier treatment in "Systems Theories and Diplomatic History," in Paul Lauren, ed., *Diplomacy: New Approaches* (New York: Free Press, 1979), pp. 226–39. An American official provided a modern formulation in explaining the Western arms sales to Iraq during and after the Iran-Iraq war: "The enemy of my enemy is my customer" (quoted in David Albright and Mark Hibbs, "Iraq's Shop-Till-You-Drop Nuclear Program," *Bulletin of the Atomic Scientists*, April 1992, p. 30). For sociological formulations, see George Homans, *The Human Group* (New York: Harcourt, Brace & World, 1950); Lewis Coser, *The Functions of Social Conflict* (Glencoe, Ill.: Free Press, 1955), chapter 8; James Davis and Samuel Leinhardt, "The Structure of Positive Interpersonal Relations in Small Groups," in Joseph Berger et al., eds., *Sociological Theories in Progress* (Boston: Houghton Mifflin, 1972), pp. 218–51; Mark Granovetter, "The Strength of Weak Ties," *American Journal of Sociology* 78 (May 1973), pp. 1360–80; Howard Taylor, *Balance in Small Groups* (New York: Van Nostrand Reinhold, 1970). A parallel dynamic often increases national unity—and even creates national identity—in response to foreign attack, a process that can be experimentally replicating among small groups: Kurt Lewin's classic papers on this subject are collected in *Resolving Social Conflicts* (New York: Harper and Row, 1948). The application of balance to intergroup relations is summarized in Donald Campbell and Robert LeVine, "Ethnocentrism and Intergroup Relations," in Robert Abelson et al., eds., *Theories of Cognitive Consistency: A Sourcebook* (Chicago: Rand McNally, 1968), pp. 555–59.

[5] Alliances are formal commitments to support the other under specified circumstances (and often in specified ways); alignments are patterns of similar diplomatic behavior. Because most of the dynamics under consideration here apply to both, I will usually treat them as similar.

The deterioration of Russo-German relations . . . served to destroy whatever lingering hopes might have existed in Petersburg that there could be a war against the Austrians from which Germany could in some way be brought to remain aloof. From this time on the Russian general staff was compelled to proceed . . . on the assumption that any war it might initiate against Austria would also mean a war against Germany. And from this it was only a step to the recognition that in a war against Germany it would be the behavior of the French that would probably make the decisive difference between success or failure of the Russian effort.[6]

More simply, in the 1920s changes in Yugoslavia's relations with Italy led to changes in its relations with France—and with France's allies.[7]

States not only enact the Arab proverbs, they proclaim them. The longest-lasting treaty in international history (the Anglo-Portugese treaty of 1373) declared that "as true and faithful friends they shall henceforth reciprocally be friends to friends, and enemies to enemies. . . . Also, neither party shall form friendships with the enemies, rivals, or persecutors of the other party."[8] In the same vein, before China entered the Korean War it explained: "North Korea's friends are our friends, North Korea's enemy is our enemy, North Korea's defense is our defense, North Korea's victory is our victory."[9] The opponents of Jay's Treaty in 1795 cried: "Damn John Jay! Damn everyone who won't damn John Jay!" God's promise to Abraham was similar: "I will bless them that bless thee, and curse him that curseth thee" (Genesis 12:2–3). Furthermore, statesmen are prone to believe that their enemies will be friends with each other. Although the language seems almost a parody of communist paranoia and rhetoric, the substance of the Soviet analysis in the wake of the Sino-Soviet border clashes in March 1969 is not unusual:

The new dangerous provocations of the Maoists reveal Beijing's intention to activate the opportunistic political flirtation with the imperialist countries—above all

[6] George Kennan, *The Decline of Bismarck's European Order* (Princeton, N.J.: Princeton University Press, 1979), p. 371.

[7] Alan Cassels, *Mussolini's Early Diplomacy* (Princeton, N.J.: Princeton University Press, 1970), pp. 139–41, 335–36.

[8] *Treaties Containing Guarantees or Engagements by Great Britain*, vol. 59 (London: Her Majesty's Stationary Office, 1898), p. 67; for an unsuccessful atttempt to utilize this clause almost six hundred years later see George Kennan, *Measures Short of War: Lectures at the National War College, 1946–47*, eds. Giles Harlow and George Maerz (Washington, D.C.: National Defense University Press, 1990), pp. 140–41. During the Bosnian crisis of 1908–9 the British foreign secretary explained that had he not taken a Russian suggestion on one issue, "we should have had the support of only Germany and Austria. . . . I should [then] not have been comfortable . . . , for I should have felt that they were all the time enjoying the invidious position in which their support placed us in opposition to France and Russia" (quoted in M. B. Cooper, "British Policy in the Balkans, 1908–9," *The Historical Journal* 7 [June 1964], p. 273).

[9] Quoted in Shu Guang Zhang, *Deterrence and Strategic Culture: Chinese-American Confrontations, 1949–1958* (Ithaca, N.Y.: Cornell University Press, 1992), p. 94.

with the United States and West Germany. It is no accident that the ambush on the Soviet border unit was staged by the Chinese agencies at a time when Bonn started its provocation of holding the election of the Federal President in West Berlin.[10]

The most general and important effect is that the international system can polarize as alliances spread consistency throughout it: For example, in the war of the Austrian Succession, Piedmont-Sardinia fought beside Austria because they shared an enemy in Spain and an ally in Great Britain.[11] Alignments during and before World War II illustrate several aspects of this process. Most obviously, Germany and Japan supported each other only because they had common enemies. Earlier, Britain was unable to conciliate Japan because such a policy would have separated it from the U.S.[12] (some British officials also opposed coming to terms with Japan on the grounds that doing so would "surely bring nearer the day when [Japan] will attack Russia," which would strengthen Germany[13]). As conflict increased, the 1940 Japanese alliance with Germany, signed in the expectation of discouraging the U.S. from opposing Japan's efforts to dominate China, had the opposite effect as Americans saw Japan as linked to the state that was such a menace in Europe. Ironically, as we noted in chapter 1, the failure of Britain's earlier attempt to defy consistency by courting the U.S. while conciliating Japan ultimately worked to Britain's advantage: One reason the U.S. could not reach an understanding with Japan in 1941 was that the American public would not tolerate appeasing an aggressor in Asia while opposing one in Europe, and Japan attacked Pearl Harbor rather than only moving against Dutch and British territory in Southeast Asia in the belief that the U.S. was so closely tied to Great Britain that it would treat such an attack as aggression against itself. Finally, American participation in Europe was eased by Hitler's declaring war in response to the fighting between the U.S. and Japan.

[10] "Soviet Report to GDR Leadership on 2 March 1969 Sino-Soviet Border Clashes," translated by Christian Ostermann, *Cold War International History Project Bulletin*, nos. 6–7 (Winter 1995/1996), pp. 189–90.

[11] Reed Browning, *The War of the Austrian Succession* (New York: St. Martin's, 1993), pp. 81–82. In the course of the war, balance generally increased and inconsistencies developed only on the peripheries of the system: Timothy Crawford, "Consistency in the War of the Austrian Succession" (unpublished paper, Department of Political Science, Columbia University).

[12] A typical conclusion reached by the Defence Requirements Sub-Committee in 1934 was: "There is much to be said for the view that our subservience to the United States has been one of the principal factors in the deterioration of our former good relations with Japan . . ." (quoted in B. J. C. McKercher, "'Our Most Dangerous Enemy': Great Britain Pre-eminent in the 1930s," *International History Review* 13 [November 1991], pp. 775–76).

[13] Charles Orde quoted in Wm. Roger Louis, "The Road to Singapore: British Imperialism in the Far East, 1932–42," in Wolfgang Mommsen and Lothar Kettenacker, eds., *The Fascist Challenge and the Policy of Appeasement* (London: Allen & Unwin, 1983), p. 364.

In addition to increasing consistency by spreading ties to previously uninvolved actors, changes in alignment patterns can reinforce nascent bonds within the original group. In some cases, countries that have worked together—or even worked along parallel lines—on one issue will come to work together on unrelated issues as the members of the group seek to support it and each other. Especially likely are symmetrical changes in the intensity of relations among states that are already tentatively arrayed in a balanced pattern. Thus when India and the Soviet Union solidified their ties in 1971, Pakistan and China, already friendly because of the shared enmity toward India and the Soviet Union, pulled even closer together.[14] This positive feedback means that the degree of mutual support among the countries in one camp and the hostility between states in different camps may become much greater than what would have been produced by the original conflicts. When this process operates, systems are unstable in the sense that the initial stimulus sets in motion reinforcing changes but are stable in their creation of later structures that can be altered only with great difficulty.

It is this dynamic that gives alliances much of their force.[15] At first glance, a Realist would have to argue that alliances merely affirm state interests rather than change them. At most, a commitment can give a state additional reasons for coming to another's aid by trying its reputation to doing so. But in fact when a state aligns or works with another, its interests are likely to change in a way that will bring it closer to the other as it attracts the friends of its new friend and earns the enmity of the latter's enemies. A state that opposes another will usually develop bad relations with any third party that supports the other because the state and the third party will now seek to weaken if not harm each other; the opposite side of this coin is that the state will gain if its allies' allies are strengthened. Because of the expectations and reactions of others, the state will face a different world than it did before its alignment, and, as we will see when we examine pre–World War I diplomacy, may find that what was supposed to be a limited commitment has become much more entangling.

Because the elements in a system are interconnected, a change of the identity of a country's enemy will affect many other alignments as well. Thus

[14] Yaacov Vertzberger, *The Enduring Entente: Sino-Pakistan Relations, 1960–1980* (New York: Praeger, 1983: CSIS, The Washington Papers no. 95). For another example, see Cassels, *Mussolini's Early Diplomacy*, p. 353.

[15] For a similar argument, see Glenn Snyder and Paul Diesing, *Conflict Among Nations* (Princeton, N.J.: Princeton University Press, 1977), pp. 426–27, and Snyder, *Alliance Politics* (Ithaca, N.Y.: Cornell University Press, forthcoming). Of course if these processes were entirely predictable, statesmen would undertake only those alignments that moved them toward desired goals, in which case one could argue that the alignments merely reflected preferences. But, as much of this chapter will demonstrate, decision makers do not fully anticipate the consequences of their acts in this regard and there is sufficient freedom of choice so that complete predictability is not likely.

the rise of the German menace in Europe twice influenced relations among countries in the Americas. As British statesmen became increasingly fearful of German power around the turn of the twentieth century, they placed greater value on maintaining sufficiently good relations with the U.S. so that in the event of a European war America would stay neutral if not support Great Britain. The price was to cede dominance of the Western Hemisphere to the U.S. But America's neighbors benefited from the rise of German power before World War II as the U.S., worried about German inroads in South America, cultivated good relations there. Especially striking was the mild reaction to the Mexican oil expropriation of 1938. Under normal circumstances, the U.S. would have replied with economic sanctions, threats, and even the use of force. But since the menace from Germany (and Japan) was acute, access to oil and relatively smooth relations had to be maintained even at the cost of swallowing outrageous Mexican behavior.[16]

Like most clichés, "Politics makes strange bedfellows" has much validity. In many cases, the warming of relations between two states is best explained by changes in relations between one of them and a third party.[17] For example, India agreed to a visit by Israel's foreign minister not because of newfound affection for that country but because of the increased criticism of India's policy in Kashmir on the part of Muslim states.[18] In the interwar period, the state of Soviet-German relations was largely determined by changes in the level of tensions between Germany and the West.[19] Most strikingly, in almost every war between two coalitions, some countries fight beside those with whom they have many disputes because they share ene-

---

[16] Indeed, the earlier "Good Neighbor" policy toward South America owed something to Roosevelt's European concerns: Robert Dallek, *Franklin D. Roosevelt and American Foreign Policy, 1932–1945* (New York: Oxford University Press, 1979), pp. 174–75.

[17] From this perspective, the conversation between the British foreign secretary and the Japanese ambassador four days after the signing of the Nazi-Soviet Pact, while unusual in tone, was to be expected. According to the foreign secretary,

> I informed the Ambassador that I have been much entertained by a report which our Ambassador in Berlin had brought home with him to the effect that Herr Hitler had been furious at the action of the Japanese in protesting against the new German-Soviet pact. The Ambassador laughed, and said there was a strong feeling against the pact in his country. This new fact must have considerable bearing on the attitude of the new Japanese Government, and the Ambassador agreed that the double-crossing of Japan by Germany and of ourselves by Russia must cause both the Japanese and British Governments to reconsider the positions in which they found themselves and to consider a possible improvement in their mutual relations.

Quoted in Peter Lowe, *Great Britain and the Origins of the Pacific War* (Oxford: Clarendon Press, 1977), p. 100.

[18] Sanjoy Hazarika, "Israeli Leads Delegation to India Seeking Economic and Arms Ties," *New York Times*, May 18, 1993.

[19] See, for example, Gerhard Weinberg, *The Foreign Policy of Hitler's Germany*, vol. 1, *Diplomatic Revolution in Europe, 1933–36* (Chicago: University of Chicago Press, 1970), p. 74.

mies. Furthermore, because conflict between one pair of nations can erupt suddenly, so can reconciliation between another pair, as was the case between Britain and the Soviet Union on June 21, 1941.

States are also likely to develop good relations with each other if they share allies. It will be difficult for both A and C to maintain their close ties with B if they are adversaries. If the alliance with B is highly valued, A and C will have to mute their quarrels, and the desire to increase the coalition's strength will give both A and C incentives to bring the other into the fold. There will be a cost, however, if the main target of the alliance between A and B is not the same as that of C and B. In this case, if A and C join together they will not only bolster each other, which they will resist doing if they have bilateral conflicts, but also will pay the price of taking on the other's adversaries. For these reasons, the impact of having a common friend is less than that of having a common adversary; systems are more likely to be unbalanced by not having those with common allies be themselves allies than they are by having states fail to unite in the face of a common adversary.

States can also manipulate the dynamics that produce consistency in order to produce a desired alignment: If a state wants to make or solidify an alliance with another, it may pick a quarrel with the other's adversary. In the previous chapter, I noted A. J. P. Taylor's argument that in order to draw France into his orbit, Bismarck created a colonial conflict with France's adversary, Great Britain.[20] Greater evidence supports the view that one reason why Anwar Sadat distanced himself from the USSR in late 1972 was his belief that this would bring financial assistance from the conservative and anticommunist Arab oil kingdoms.[21] While Nixon and Kissinger did not create the crisis between India and Pakistan in 1971, they did realize that the resulting friction between the U.S. and India would increase the common interest between the U.S. and China. The same reasoning explains why British leaders foresaw some gain in the Ottoman Empire's siding with Germany in 1914: "The best method of persuading the Balkan States to join the Allies would be alliance against their common and traditional enemy, the Turk."[22]

[20] A. J. P. Taylor, *Germany's First Bid for Colonies, 1884–1885* (Hamden, Conn.: Archon Books, 1967). But a more careful investigation shows that the traditional interpretation of the incident is probably correct: Henry Ashby Turner, "Bismarck's Imperialist Venture: Anti-British in Origin?" in Prosser Gifford and Wm. Roger Louis, eds., *Britain and Germany in Africa* (New Haven, Conn.: Yale University Press, 1967), pp. 47–82. For other examples, see above, chapter 5, pp. 187–88.

[21] Alvin Rubinstein, *Red Star on the Nile* (Princeton, N.J.: Princeton University Press, 1977), pp. 195–97.

[22] Martin Gilbert, *Winston Churchill*, vol. 3, *1914–1916, The Challenge of War* (Boston: Houghton Mifflin, 1971), p. 200. The problem, however, was that the Balkans were rife with local conflicts and so, as I will discuss below, it was unlikely that all these states would fight on the same side. One historian argues that the Allies would have benefited if Turkey had joined

Although systems may not become completely polarized, it is rare to find extreme inconsistencies. I cannot think of any case in which a country fought two countries which in turn were fighting each other, although during World War II factions in China and Yugoslavia fought both each other and the foreign invader. Even here, the intensity of the conflict between one actor and each of its adversaries varied inversely with the degree of feuding with the other. Turning to international politics, Britain's conflict with Egypt in 1956 brought it into alignment with Israel while it maintained ties to Jordan, its traditional client in the area.[23] So less than two weeks before Britain met with France and Israel to plan the attack on Suez, an Israeli raid on Jordan led Britain to remind its future ally that it was pledged to defend Jordan against an Israeli attack. As Moshe Dayan put it in his diary,

> save for the Almighty, only the British are capable of complicating affairs to such a degree. At the very moment when they are preparing to topple Nasser, who is a common enemy of theirs and Israel's, they insist on getting the Iraqi Army into Jordan, even if such action leads to war between Israel and Jordan in which they, the British, will take part against Israel.[24]

Dayan was unfair to the British on two counts. First, it was the odd situation rather than anything particularly British that led to this strange state of affairs. Second, the British were aware of the anomaly and sought to contain it by maintaining the peace between Israel and Jordan, as our argument leads us to expect.[25] The Middle East was the site of another case that approached striking inconsistency. During the 1991 Gulf War, the Arab countries found it deeply uncomfortable to be on the same side with Israel. Indeed, they could participate in the coalition only because Israel was not formally a member. Once the fighting started, the coalition feared that Israel would retaliate against the Iraqi Scud attacks, and the hope of such a response largely explains why Iraq launched the missiles.[26]

If three-way fights are rare if not nonexistent, three-way hostilities are more common. But most of these cases are unstable and unusual conditions

---

with Germany in 1939: the Balkan states would have been "active partners of the West" rather than being "neutral suppliers of Germany": Lynn Curtright, "Great Britain, the Balkans, and Turkey in the Autumn of 1939," *International History Review* 10 (August 1988), p. 434.

[23] Stuart Cohen, "A Still Stranger Aspect of Suez: British Operational Plans to Attack Israel, 1955–1956," ibid. 10 (May 1988), pp. 261–81.

[24] Moshe Dayan, *Diary of the Sinai Campaign, 1956* (London: Weidenfeld and Nicolson, 1966), p. 61.

[25] Cohen, "A Still Stranger Aspect of Suez," p. 278.

[26] The U.S. apparently gained commitments from the Arab states to remain in the coalition even if Iraq drew Israel into the war, but in the event their reaction would not have been easy to predict: Rick Atkinson, *Crusade: The Untold Story of the Persian Gulf War* (Boston: Houghton Mifflin, 1993), p. 83. The U.S. was similarly uncomfortable to find itself arrayed with Iran in supporting Bosnia: See, for example, Elaine Sciolino, "What's Iran Doing in Bosnia, Anyway?" *New York Times*, December 10, 1995.

are required to produce them. Thus although the era in which the U.S., PRC, and USSR each had high conflicts with the other two violates consistency, it would have been hard to imagine that two of these states would not have eventually reached a rapprochement.[27] From this perspective, two aspects of the conflict in the former Yugoslavia are anomalous. First, Croatia, Bosnia, and Kosovo failed to coordinate their efforts against Serbia, with the fighting in Bosnia starting only after that in Croatia had reached a stalemate.[28] Second and more strikingly, at times Bosnian Muslims, Croats, and Serbs fought one another almost simultaneously. Before an uneasy alliance of the former two emerged, the situation came very close to complete imbalance, with each actor against each of the other two. But in the end a degree of consistency prevailed.

Causes of Consistency

Consistency does not work by teleology: It is driven by actors' calculations of power and interest, sometimes supplemented by emotion. Most obviously, two states that have a quarrel with a third will benefit from working together. Herodotus records that when the Greek city-states fought Persia they promised to "put an end to all their enmities and wars with each other."[29] Iraq's invasion of Kuwait led the U.S. to put aside its conflicts—even strong ones—with Arab states such as Syria; seek better relations with Iran, which it had previously viewed as the greatest menace in the region; invite the USSR to use its diplomatic influence despite the fact that keeping that country out of the region had been America's longstanding objective; and develop bad relations with the Arab state to which it had been closest (Jordan) because that state refused to oppose Iraq. Similarly, a state that needs to cooperate with another is not likely to disrupt relations by developing good relations with a government that the other opposes.[30]

[27] What an anonymous diplomat said about a Sino-Soviet-American squabble at the UN in 1971 could be generalized: "It's like a football game between three teams. It seems to me that one of them would be better off staying out of the game." Quoted in Henry Tanner, "Soviet and China, Feuding Ideologically at U.N., Are Seen as Asking Rest of World to Chooose Sides," ibid., November 28, 1971.

[28] Croatian officials sometimes admitted that peace in Bosnia might lead the Serbs to turn on them with renewed force: John Darnton, "U.N. Forcing Croatia to Acknowledge Its 'Invisible' Army in Bosnia," ibid., February 16, 1994.

[29] Quoted in Donald Kagan, *The Outbreak of the Peloponnesian War* (Ithaca, N.Y.: Cornell University Press, 1969), p. 32.

[30] In 1954 when a British diplomat argued that Great Britain should keep its distance from the regime the American-sponsored coup had just established in Guatemala, Prime Minister Churchill replied that he was not going "to allow Guatemala to jeopardize our relations with the United States" (quoted in Charles Moran, *Churchill: Taken from the Diaries of Lord Moran* [Boston: Houghton Mifflin, 1966], p. 603).

These patterns should be familiar to Americans: One of the main impe-
tuses for the thirteen colonies to form a union was expressed in the flag
picturing a snake cut into thirteen segments with the motto "Join or Die." As
the proponents of the Constitution argued, if some American states were
enemies of others, it would be difficult to prevent a meddling European
power from allying with one and so gaining undue influence. Furthermore,
the disadvantaged American state would have to turn to another European
power for protection, thus drawing America more deeply into European
quarrels.[31]

"We are their second front, and they are ours," Prime Minister Nehru
declared when both India and the Soviet Union developed bad relations
with China.[32] The point is a general one: The fact that a state that could
triumph if it could fight its adversaries one at a time may be defeated if it is
forced to take them on simultaneously gives them an incentive to overcome
any frictions between them and work together. Even when the prospect of
armed conflict is distant, the mutual need for diplomatic support can produce consistency. Thus it is not surprising that the Sino-American rapprochement was followed by the signing of a Soviet-Indian Friendship
Treaty. Because China was now less threatened by the U.S. and so could be
more assertive toward India and the USSR, closer cooperation between
these two countries was likely, especially since the U.S. was an adversary of
both. To forestall this balance Kissinger had assured the Indian ambassador
that "our relations with China, however good they might be, have nothing to
do with India and under no circumstances will we tolerate anti-Indian notions."[33] Indeed, one can argue that the threat to India decreased as the
U.S. gained greater influence over the PRC which, being less isolated,
would take a less paranoid view of its neighbors.[34] But such reasoning and
reassurances usually are outweighed by the perceived increase in the adversary's power and the greater freedom of maneuver it has gained by winning
over a new friend. Kissinger, in fact, had hoped that the opening to China

[31] See Federalist Papers #4, 5, and 41.

[32] Quoted in Martin Wight, "The Balance of Power and International Order," in Alan James,
ed., *The Bases of International Order: Essays in Honour of C. A. W. Manning* (London: Oxford
University Press, 1973), p. 89. For discussion of similar dynamics in Sino-Soviet-American
relations, see Michel Tatu, *The Great Power Triangle: Washington-Moscow-Peking* (Paris: The
Atlantic Institute, 1970), p. 24.

[33] T. N. Kaul, *The Kissinger Years: Indo-American Relations* (New Delhi: Arnold Heinemann, 1980), p. 48, italics omitted.

[34] Perhaps this is why Kissinger reports that the news of the Sino-Indian Treaty "came [as a]
bombshell" to him: *White House Years* (Boston: Little, Brown, 1979), p. 866; also see p. 767.
This is not to argue that the American opening to China was the only cause of India's desire to
reach an agreement with the USSR: See Richard Sisson and Leo Rose, *War and Secession:
Pakistan, India, and the Creation of Bangladesh* (Berkeley: University of California Press,
1990), pp. 196–202. It is also interesting that in order to minimize American hostility, the
Indian government "emphasized that the treaty did not constitute an alliance or even a 'tilt'
toward the U.S.S.R." (ibid., p. 201).

would provide leverage against the Soviet Union; India had every reason to expect that China would foresee a similar advantage if the system were to remain only partially balanced. (Other consequences of Nixon's trip, although not foreseen by American diplomats, also follow from balance theory: Japan, now in an inconsistent position, felt uneasy; Ceylon, weary of India, moved closer to the U.S.; South Korea, fearing decreased American support, exchanged emissaries with the North; and the USSR stepped up its efforts to see that North Vietnam sided with it instead of China.[35])

The system is sometimes nudged toward consistency by an actor who will pay a price if it remains unbalanced. Most clearly, a state that is linked to two others who are on bad terms with each other will have an interest in bringing the latter together if it otherwise will have to choose between them or needs concerted action by all three.[36] States in this position often act as mediators or go-betweens in an attempt to create a solid structure that will provide them with maximum support. Thus in 1904 France diffused the Dogger Bank crisis that threatened to produce war between Russia (its ally) and Britain (with whom it was negotiating an entente) and, three years later, help broker an entente between them. French efforts to ease tensions between Italy and Yugoslavia in order to bring both states into the anti-German coalition in 1934 were less successful. The Yugoslav king was invited to make a state visit to France, which unfortunately resulted in his assassination by a Croatian nationalist (perhaps in Italian pay).[37] A related strategy is to develop close relations with a state in order to gain support from others who also are tied to it, as the king of Prussia did when at the start of the War of the Austrian Succession he tried to win France to his side by "mak[ing] France's friends his friends."[38]

[35] John Lee, "Display of U.S.-China Goodwill Causing Apprehension in Japan," *New York Times*, February 24, 1972; "U.S. Admiral Will Visit a More Friendly Ceylon," ibid., March 5, 1972; John Sterba, "Ceylon Warming Toward The U.S.," ibid., April 10, 1972; Raymond Garthoff, *Détente and Confrontation: American-Soviet Relations from Nixon to Reagan* (Washington, D.C.: the Brookings Institution, 1985), p. 245; Lowell Dittmer, *Sino-Soviet Normalization and Its International Implications, 1945–1990* (Seattle: University of Washington Press, 1992), p. 198; Chong-Sik Lee, "The Détente and Korea," in William Griffith, ed., *The World and The Great Power Triangles* (Cambridge, Mass.: MIT Press, 1975), pp. 332–39, 349–71.

[36] As we saw in the previous chapter, when these conditions do not hold, a state may benefit by being in the pivot and having good relations with others who cannot work together.

[37] Robert Young, *In Command of France* (Cambridge, Mass.: Harvard University Press, 1978), pp. 73–74. The German attempt to mediate the differences between China and Japan during this period also failed, although less dramatically; during World War II Great Britain tried to ease relations between the Polish government in exile and the USSR; and while some communist states gained bargaining leverage from the rivalry between the PRC and the USSR, Vietnam, which was fighting the U.S., sought to get its two patrons to cooperate: Weinberg, *Foreign Policy of Hitler's Germany*, pp. 341–45; Richard Wich, *Sino-Soviet Crisis Politics* (Cambridge, Mass.: Harvard University Press, 1980), pp. 201–13. For discussion of a complex case, see John Garver, "Sino-Indian Rapprochement and the Sino-Pakistan Entente," *Political Science Quarterly* 111 (Summer 1996), pp. 323–47.

[38] Browning, *The War of the Austrian Succesion*, p. 50.

States sometimes seek a balanced configuration even at the cost of increasing the ranks of their enemies. Doing so may not only set a useful precedent by showing others that they cannot maintain ties to both sides but can also serve a strategic purpose. Despite the obvious costs, Britain and France might have been well advised to declare war on Italy at the start of World War II: As long as Italy was not in the war, it could be a conduit for goods going to Germany, thus decreasing the effectiveness of the allied blockade. Furthermore, long seacoasts made Italy vulnerable, and protecting them would have been a significant diversion of German resources.[39] Britain and France seriously contemplated this kind of policy when it made less sense, as they nearly aided Finland in early 1940 at the cost of war with the Soviet Union.[40] In retrospect, this seems ludicrous and the motives may have been at least as much emotional as strategic. But it was argued that the allies would be better off with the USSR as a full enemy than they were with it supporting Germany behind the shield of noncombatancy.

Consistency may also be sought as an end in itself. Although it is often argued that unbalanced systems are more apt to remain at peace because the units have cross-cutting interests, actors may be more impressed by the resulting strains and complexity that can lead to diplomatic tensions and miscalculations. Thus while Bismarck engineered an inconsistent system by maintaining good relations with both Austria and Russia, those who replaced him saw this policy as immoral and too confusing to be a lasting basis for peace and so refused to renew the Reinsurance Treaty with Russia. As one diplomatic historian put it, the German leaders explained that "instead of the complications—'chicanery' was the word hinted at—of Bismarckian diplomacy, German policy was now to be simple, open, straightforward."[41] The results were unfortunate, but the reasoning was not entirely unusual or foolish.

The Enemy of My Enemy Is My Friend

The strongest force for consistency is a common enemy, which can override even the sharpest differences between actors. As George Liska observes, "Alliances are against, and only derivatively for, someone or something."[42]

[39] Williamson Murray, *The Change in the European Balance of Power, 1938–1939* (Princeton, N.J.: Princeton University Press, 1984), pp. 314–21.

[40] The fullest account is Douglas Clark, *Three Days to Catastrophe: Britain and the Russo-Finnish War* (London: Hammond, Hammond, 1966).

[41] Raymond Sontag, *European Diplomatic History, 1871–1932* (New York: Appleton-Century-Crofts, 1933), pp. 50–51.

[42] George Liska, *Nations in Alliance* (Baltimore, Md.: Johns Hopkins University Press, 1962), p. 12. But statesmen often deny that they are brought together by a shared fear or enmity. For example, Indira Gandhi explained the Indo-Soviet treaty not by common opposition to the U.S., China, and Pakistan, but by shared views "on the maintenance of peace and the elimination of colonialism" ("India and the World," *Foreign Affairs* 51 [October 1972], p. 73). It

Thus even though Churchill was deeply hostile to the Soviet Union, as Nazi power increased he argued for putting everything aside and allying with the Soviet Union. When German overreaching allowed him to implement this policy in June 1941 he explained: "I have only one purpose, the destruction of Hitler, and my life is much simplified thereby. If Hitler invaded Hell, I would make at least a favorable reference to the Devil in the House of Commons."[43] It is not surprising that in the Napoleonic Wars, the British foreign secretary announced a similar principle, though less colorfully: "We shall proceed upon the principle that any nation of Europe that starts up with a determination to oppose a power which . . . is the common enemy of all nations [i.e., France], whatever may be the existing political relations of that nation and Great Britain, becomes instantly our essential ally."[44] In the tense atmosphere of 1949, Dwight Eisenhower defined a "friendly" country as any nation that was opposing the Soviet Union.[45] India and the USSR were almost the only countries to maintain good relations with Vietnam after that state conquered Cambodia; they were enemies of Vietnam's main enemy, China. A knowledge only of the outlook, values, and interests of the U.S. and Savimbi's faction in Angola would leave one mystified about their good relations during the Cold War unless one also knew that they were both enemies of the Soviet Union and its allies (indeed, being anti-Soviet was the only way Savimbi could gain American support).[46]

As these cases indicate, there is a rough proportionality between the mag-

---

is almost as though it were believed that having a common enemy was not an honorable reason for an alliance. Gandhi, like many Indians, also portrayed American opposition to her country and its ties to Pakistan as stemming from a rejection of Indian independence and self-assertion rather than from the support that India was perceived to be lending to the USSR and the hope of gaining Pakistani assistance in the Cold War: ibid., pp. 74–75.

[43] Winston Churchill, *The Second World War*, vol. 3, *The Grand Alliance* (Boston: Houghton Mifflin, 1950), p. 370; also see p. 372. When explaining why the Allies had to work with Admiral Darlan, a German sympathizer, in North Africa, Franklin Roosevelt used a Balkan proverb to make the same point: "My children, it is permitted you in time of great danger to walk with the devil until you have crossed the bridge" (Warren Kimball, ed., *Roosevelt and Churchill: The Complete Correspondence*, vol. 2, *The Alliance Forged* [Princeton, N.J.: Princeton University Press, 1984], p. 22).

[44] Quoted in John Sherwig, *Guineas and Gunpowder: British Foreign Aid in the Wars with France, 1793–1815* (Cambridge, Mass.: Harvard University Press, 1969), p. 197.

[45] Charles Maier, "Introduction," in George Kistiakowsky, *A Scientist in the White House* (Cambridge, Mass.: Harvard University Press, 1976), p. xxi. Thus it is not entirely surprising that in the late 1960s Soviet leaders asserted the existence of "secret contacts" between West Germany and the PRC, two of its main enemies: Morris Rothenberg, *Wither China: The View From the Kremlin* (Coral Gables, Fla.: Center for Advanced Studies, University of Miami, 1977), p. 237.

[46] For a similar example earlier in the century, see Clarence Clendenen, *The United States and Pancho Villa* (Ithaca, N.Y.: Cornell University Press, 1961), p. 27. For supporting quantitative data, see D. Scott Bennett, "Security, Bargaining, and the End of Interstate Rivalry," *International Studies Quarterly* 40 (June 1996), pp. 164–65, 176–79.

nitude of the conflict with the enemy and the strength of the unifying force generated. Relatedly, the more deeply two countries are divided from each other, the greater the external threat that will be required to bring them together. Any reader of science fiction knows the story of the quarreling nations of Earth uniting in the face of an invasion from outer space. Ronald Reagan found this idea so appealing that he explained it to Gorbachev when they first met at Geneva in 1985.[47] Perhaps less fancifully, some people believe that the pressures of global environmental degradation may produce worldwide cooperation. These processes work in reverse as well: The diminution of a shared threat is likely to loosen if not dissolve the bonds of an opposing alliance. Even analysts who reject the common argument that the end of the Cold War spells the end of NATO can see the reasons for the prediction. Indeed, although popular accounts of the increased conflict between the U.S. and the PRC stress bilateral disputes and Chinese domestic politics, the key change is the demise of the USSR. A Sino-American war, now possible, was out of the question when the shared Soviet threat required each country to avoid alienating or weakening the other.

These dynamics also mean that unless state A is strong enough to stand alone, for B to make an enemy of it is likely to drive it into the arms of a third state, especially one with conflicts with B. Thus as we noted in chapter 1, it was Jefferson, a bitter foe of Great Britain, who responded to the news that France might gain control of Louisiana by declaring: "The day that France takes possession of New Orleans . . . we must marry ourselves to the British fleet and nation."[48] To treat two states as outcasts is likely to push them together even if they share no other interests, as Britain and France found to their dismay when Germany and the USSR formed a common front at Rapallo in 1922 (and in the 1920s Western statesmen argued that "the more difficult our relations with Russia [become], the more important it [is] that we should attach Germany solidly to the Western Powers"[49]).

---

[47] Don Oberdorfer, *The Turn: From the Cold War to a New Era* (New York: Poseidon Press, 1991), p. 144; also see the testimony of American and Soviet officials in William Wohlforth, ed., *Witnesses to the End of the Cold War* (Baltimore, Md.: Johns Hopkins University Press, 1996), pp. 96–97, and Raymond Garthoff, *The Great Transformation* (Washington, D.C.: the Brookings Institution, 1994), p. 257.

[48] Quoted in Robert Tucker and David Hendrickson, *Empire of Liberty: The Statecraft of Thomas Jefferson* (New York: Oxford University Press, 1990), p. 113. Tucker and Hendrickson go on to argue that Jefferson was not serious, but while this fits with their portrait of the president, their case is not strong: ibid., pp. 114–15. Napoleon's decision to sell the Louisiana Territory was in part based on the desire to bolster the enemy of his enemy: by "affirm[ing] forever the power of the United States, . . . I have just given England a maritime rival that sooner or later will lay low her pride" (quoted in Henry Kissinger, *Diplomacy* [New York: Simon and Schuster, 1994], p. 31).

[49] Austin Chamberlain quoted in Jon Jacobson, *Locarno Diplomacy: Germany and the West, 1925–1929* (Princeton, N.J.: Princeton University Press, 1972), p. 123.

Those who urge the West to treat Iran and Iraq as equally repellent risk a similar result.[50]

Understanding these dynamics, a state that is courting another will seek to reduce or minimize any threats to the latter that might lead it to align against the state. Thus each member of the U.S.-India-Pakistan triangle tried to convince the others that their security was not menaced by the state's friend. The U.S., which sought good relations with both, tried to bring them together and, when that policy failed, sought to convince each of the other's peaceful intent (and of shared danger from Russia and/or China); India tried to persuade the U.S. that the Soviet Union was not a menace to either of them; after 1962 Pakistan, which had drawn close to China, tried to maintain its ties to the U.S. by explaining to the Americans that they did not need to fear the PRC.[51]

Because neither the source and magnitude of the threat nor the extent of the differences with potential allies are objective, we can test the theory by looking at people who make different evaluations as long as we are alert to the possibility that causation can flow in both directions. In the early years of the twentieth century, Delcassé continued to support the Franco-Russian alliance when many others thought it a costly encumbrance because he feared Germany more than they did.[52] In the late 1930s our argument leads us to expect two kinds of people to be most favorable toward an alliance with the Soviet Union: those on the left of the political spectrum who were most comfortable—or least uncomfortable—working with the USSR and those who saw the greatest threat from Germany. This seems to have been the case. In Britain and France the Socialists favored cooperation much more than did the Conservatives. Among the latter, those who were most worried about Hitler were most favorable toward an alliance: While Churchill's ideological antipathy toward Bolshevism was no less than Chamberlain's, his perception of threat was much greater. American policy during the Cold War reveals the same pattern. Conservatives were quicker than liberals to call for the U.S. to work with right-wing regimes. They found less to object to in these governments and tended to be more worried about the Soviet Union.

[50] For divergent views of the wisdom of the American policy, see Anthony Lake, "Confronting Backlash States," *Foreign Affairs* 73 (March/April 1994), pp. 45–55; F. Gregory Gause III, "The Illogic of Dual Containment," ibid., pp. 56–66; Martin Indyk et al., "Symposium on Dual Containment: U.S. Policy Toward Iran and Iraq," *Middle East Policy* 3, no. 1 (1994), pp. 1–26. For discussion of the Chinese movement away from their policy of "dual confrontation" and toward a rapprochement with the United States, see Wich, *Sino-Soviet Crisis Politics*, and Arthur Waldron, "From Nonexistent to Almost Normal: U.S.-China Relations in the 1960s," in Diane Kunze, ed., *The Diplomacy of the Crucial Decade* (New York: Columbia University Press, 1994), chapter 7.

[51] McMahon, *Cold War on the Periphery.*

[52] Christopher Andrew, *Theophile Delcassé and the Making of the Entente Cordiale* (London: Macmillan, 1968), pp. 248–51.

Similarly, because most Europeans saw the Soviet Union as less of a threat than did the Americans, they refused to subordinate all other considerations to building an anti-Soviet coalition.

The career of Robert Vansitart, a leading British diplomat, is illustrative in this regard. Because he was convinced that Germany was the main threat to British security in the pre–World War I era as well as in the 1930s, he always judged policies by whether they maximized the opposition to Germany, which meant supporting countries that were or could be turned into Germany's opponents even if doing so sacrificed other values. In 1911, although Vansitart was distressed by the Italian annexation of Tripoli and Russian adventures in Persia, he "was prepared to acquiesce in them . . . because both powers were essential to counter-balance German continental dominance."[53] When Italy invaded Ethiopia a quarter of a century later, he favored accommodation in order to maintain the Stresa front that Italy, Britain, and France had formed against Germany. Those who urged firmness against Italy argued that Britain should consistently oppose aggression even if this meant making the system inconsistent or even pushing Italy into the German camp. For them, morality, principle, and the need to put international politics on a new footing were crucial; the German threat did not so dominate that everything else had to be subordinated to it.

States may also differ in their estimates of whether others judge a conflict as so severe that they will make it the axis of their alignments. During the Falklands crisis the U.S. thought that if Britain and Argentina came to blows, the latter would seek ties with the Soviet Union and Cuba.[54] The U.S. worried even more that if it openly supported Great Britain, South American countries would turn against it. Both these fears implied that the South Americans would make this dispute the overriding one in setting their policies. The British disagreed, correctly so. The South Americans had so many concerns that they could not afford to let their policy be driven by the American support for Argentina's adversary. Furthermore, the domestic and ideological barriers between Argentina and the communist countries were sufficiently great so that they could not be overcome even by common hostility to Britain and the U.S.[55]

Because countries are likely to develop conflicts with their neighbors, consistency often produces the checkerboard pattern that Kautilya, the an-

[53] Norman Rose, *Vansitart: Study of a Diplomat* (London: Heinemann, 1978), p. 35. For discussion of disagreements within the Reagan administration over whether the magnitude of the Soviet threat required the U.S. to conciliate the PRC by keeping its distance from Taiwan, see Robert Ross, *Negotiating Cooperation: The United States and China, 1969–89* (Stanford, Calif.: Stanford University Press, 1995), pp. 169–70.

[54] Lawrence Freedman and Virginia Gamba-Stonehouse, *Signals of War: The Falklands Conflict of 1982* (Princeton, N.J.: Princeton University Press, 1991), p. 235.

[55] The Argentine government did make an overture toward Cuba, but it was vigorously resisted by the military: ibid., pp. 345–51.

cient Indian student of international politics, may have been the first to observe.[56] States on either side of a country are likely to be natural allies, and the state that is in the middle will seek to join with those located on the far sides of its neighbors. As Donald Kagan notes, "It was a general rule in the world of the Greek city-states that neighbors were at least mutually suspicious and often hostile," and this strongly influenced the formation of alliances.[57] Although geography was not the only consideration at work, it is not surprising that during the interwar period France allied with Germany's eastern neighbors and that Germany eventually leapfrogged them to ally with Russia, recapitulating the standard pattern of eighteenth-century diplomacy.[58] In the 1970s, two of China's neighbors—Vietnam and the Soviet Union—allied; China, in turn, was tied to Vietnam's neighbor, Cambodia.

None of this is to say that sharing a common adversary will induce unvarying or complete cooperation. Even states that are fighting common enemies can be divided by conflicting interests, mistrust, and deficiencies of statecraft. The latter two factors hindered the ability of Germany and Japan to concert their efforts during World War II.[59] More importantly, defeating the enemy is rarely the only goal that states have; coalition management is notoriously difficult because each state looks after its own interests, which are likely to include some that harm its partners. Indeed, as we discussed in chapter 4, since states must anticipate postwar politics, they realize that a coalition victory can endanger them if their partners gain more power than they do. Thus the nature of international politics creates friction within a coalition even if the partners lack specific points of contention. Nevertheless, as long as the conflict with the current enemy is paramount, disputes with those who share this enemy are to be minimized.

WHO IS THE MAIN ENEMY?

Remember the way Churchill prefaced his explanation for aiding his longtime ideological foe, the Soviet Union—"I have only one purpose . . . and my life is much simplified thereby."[60] Facing an overriding threat makes

[56] George Modelski, "Kautilya: Foreign Policy and International System in the Ancient Hindu World," *American Political Science Review* 58 (September 1964), pp. 549–60. Also see Lewis Namier's "system of odd-and-even numbers": *Conflicts* (London: Macmillan, 1942), p. 14, and *Vanished Supremacies* (London: Hamish Hamilton, 1958), p. 170. For a recent discussion, see Karl Mueller, "Alignment Balancing and Stability in Eastern Europe," *Security Studies* 5 (Autumn 1995), pp. 50–53.

[57] Kagan, *Outbreak of the Peloponnesian War*, pp. 88–89.

[58] On the eighteenth century, see David Ogg, *Europe of the Ancien Regime, 1715–1783* (New York: Harper and Row, 1966), and Paul Schroeder, *The Tranformation of European Politics, 1763–1848* (New York: Oxford University Press, 1994), chapter 1.

[59] A good discussion is Johanna Menzel Meskill, *Hitler and Japan: The Hollow Alliance* (New York: Atherton, 1966).

[60] Quoted in Churchill, *The Second World War*, vol. 3, p. 370.

preferences and behavior easy to determine, both for the person and for outside observers. This is implicit in Mao Tse Tung's theory of the united front. In the words of one scholar, Mao believed that

> during each historical era a single chief reactionary enemy was to be identified and targeted as the primary enemy. All other, less evil reactionaries were to be "united with" during this era and won over to opposition to the primary enemy. Contradictions would still exist between these lesser enemies and the truly progressive elements of the united front, but during that particular stage of historical development those conflicts were "secondary" and had to be handled in such a way as to not detract from the common struggle against the primary enemy.[61]

This perspective points to what is often the central question for statesmen: Which state—if any—poses a threat so severe that all other considerations must be subordinated to it? Throughout the 1960s and 1970s this was the first question Mao and his colleagues had to answer. As they came to believe that the answer was the USSR and not the U.S., they came to seek ties to the latter.[62] Similarly, the U.S. was not ready for a rapprochement until it decided that, Vietnam notwithstanding, Chinese-instigated "people's wars" were less of a danger than Soviet power. For obvious reasons, when a state has conflicts with two others and wants to win one of them over, it is likely to try to convince the potential partner that the third party, not the state, is the main enemy. At various times during their triangular relations, the U.S., USSR, and the PRC tried to explain to one of the others that the third state was the most aggressive; after the Iranian revolution the U.S. sought to convince Iran that it was the USSR, not the U.S., that was the real "great Satan."

[61] John Garner, "Sino-Vietnamese Conflict and the Sino-American Rapprochement," *Political Science Quarterly* 96 (Fall 1981), p. 463; also see Ross, *Negotiating Cooperation*, p. 51.

[62] See, for example, Wich, *Sino-Soviet Crisis Politics*; Waldron, "From Nonexistent to Almost Normal"; Harvey Nelsen, *Power and Insecurity: Beijing, Moscow, and Washington, 1944–1988* (Boulder, Colo.: Lynne Rienner, 1989); Linda Dillon, Bruce Burton, and Walter Sonderland, "Who Was the Principal Enemy? Shifts in the Official Chinese Perceptions of the Superpowers, 1968–1969," *Asian Survey* 17 (May 1977), pp. 456–74. For Soviet discussion of Chinese beliefs, see Rothenberg, *Whither China*, p. 259. Of course states differently situated will have different priorities. Thus because its empire was vital to Britain and relations on the Continent were vital to the powers situated there, the latter's "policies towards the outside world depended upon events in Europe, [while] Britain's attitude towards European powers usually depended upon what was happening in the outside world" (Paul Kennedy, "The Continental Commitment and the Special Relationship in Twentieth Century British Foreign Policy," *Journal of the Royal United Services Institute for Defence Studies* 128 [September 1983], p. 9). For similar arguments about American and British concerns over naval arms control in the interwar period, see Gerald Wheeler, *Prelude to Pearl Harbor* (Columbia: University of Missouri Press, 1963), pp. 149–62, and Jon Tetsuro Sumida, "'The Best Laid Plans': The Development of British Battle-Fleet Tactics, 1919–1942," *International History Review* 14 (November 1992), p. 687.

The identification of the main adversary may be easy only in retrospect, if then. Shortly after it won its independence, the U.S. was bitterly divided over whether Britain or France posed the greatest danger and therefore over whose enemies had to be conciliated. Here domestic ideology and politics drove foreign assessments. In other cases, difficulties and differences can be traced to ambiguity in the external environment. One scholar argues that "it seems hardly credible that British statesmen [in the nineteenth century] should have been so slow to recognize Russia as the 'natural enemy'" because Great Britain and Russia "alone confronted each other as acquisitive imperial states in areas outside Europe."[63] But in many periods France and Germany seemed at least as worrisome. Thus Edward Ingram's characterization of British policy in the first part of the nineteenth century:

> While fighting France [in the Napoleonic Wars, British statesmen] had to decide whether their European or imperial interests were more important, whether France could threaten either, and if it was necessary to subordinate the one to the other. During the 1830s after the dramatic change in British attitudes towards France and Russia, the problem was simplified. Fighting in Persia like fighting in the Crimea might help to protect both the balance of power in Europe and the British Empire from the overweening power of Russia. During the Napoleonic Wars the British had to choose. While they needed Russia in the Third Coalition, they could not oppose Russian expansion in the Caucasus.[64]

To extend this example, when the German threat loomed large in the years before World War I, the British were unable to resist Russian encroachments in Persia and, when the war itself dictated a simplification of concerns akin to that noted by Churchill, even agreed that Russia could take Constantinople.[65]

Here the rise of a greater menace made the situation clear. In other cases, states alter their estimates of the situation without a great change in the external world. Thus Zbigniew Brzezinski reports that when he went to Beijing in May 1978, "I went with a secret Presidential instruction. It authorized me to tell the Chinese (and I quote): 'The United States has made up

---

[63] Gerald Graham, *Great Britain in the Indian Ocean, 1810–1850* (London: Oxford University Press, 1967), p. 3.

[64] Edward Ingram, "An Aspiring Buffer State: Anglo-Persian Relations in the Third Coalition, 1804–1807," *Historical Journal* 16 (September 1973), p. 532.

[65] Other conflicts complicated Britain's choices in the Balkan crises of the late nineteenth century: British material interests called for resisting Russian pressure on the Ottoman Empire, but ideology and domestic politics made it impossible to defend the "unspeakable Turk," especially in light of the Ottoman aversion to reform and predilection for massacring Christians. (See, for example, R. T. Shannon, *Gladstone and the Bulgarian Agitation, 1876* [London: Nelson & Sons, 1963].) Britain faced a similar dilemma in the 1820s when the Greek revolution, which Britain favored ideologically, was supported by Russia, whose influence in Western Europe, let alone the Mediterranean, was a menace to Great Britain.

its mind'—because the Chinese had kept saying in their propaganda that we had been half-hearted and had not made up our minds."[66] Over the objections of Secretary of State Vance, Carter had decided that the Soviet Union was so strong and hostile that the U.S. had to work with any powerful state that had serious conflicts with it even if doing so required giving up other values.

If it is difficult for statesmen to identify their main adversary, it is not surprising that they can misjudge whether their actions will lead others to unite against them and so misestimate the degree and form of consistency that will be produced by various moves. Hence while German statesmen initially were disturbed when France and Russia allied in 1893, they soon concluded that the result would be more to their liking, reasoning that because the agreement "brought together London's two most formidable naval and colonial rivals," Britain would soon have to seek better relations with its other adversary, Germany.[67] As it turned out, the first reaction was closer to the truth. But the incorrect German prediction was not unreasonable. Neither was the expectation that the entente between England and France would lead Russia to break with the latter.[68] The fear of a Japanese leader in November 1941 is stranger, but makes some sense from his country's perspective. He told his colleagues:

What we should always keep in mind here is what would happen to relations between Germany and Great Britain and Germany and the United States, all of them being countries whose population belongs to the white race, if Japan should enter the war. Hitler has said that the Japanese are a second-class race, and Germany has not declared war against the United States. . . . [If Japan attacks the United States, then the Americans'] indignation against the Japanese will be stronger than their hatred of Hitler. The Germans in the United States are considering ways of bringing about peace between the United States and Germany. I fear, therefore, that if Japan begins a war against the United States, Germany and Great Britain and Germany and the United States will come to terms, leaving Japan by herself. That is, we must be prepared for the possibility that hatred of the yellow

---

[66] Quoted in George Urban, "A Long Conversation with Dr. Zbigniew Brzezinski: 'The Perils of Foreign Policy,'" *Encounter* 56 (May 1981), p. 28; also see Brzezinski, *Power and Principle* (New York: Farrar, Straus & Giroux, 1983), pp. 197, 207–8.

[67] Paul Kennedy, *The Realities Behind Diplomacy* (London: Fontana, 1981), p. 102. For an unfounded worry that a state's disruptive action might unite previously divided adversaries, see Roger Bullen, *Palmerston, Guizot, and the Collapse of the Entente Cordiale* (London: Athlone, 1974), p. 165.

[68] See the kaiser's colorful remarks quoted in Andrew, *Delcassé*, p. 228. Adolf Hitler made the related misjudgment that the success of the coalition against him in 1945 would lead to its breakup as the Western allies came to fear the USSR more than Germany. Such a dynamic was indeed characteristic of the balance of power but does not operate in a war against a hegemon: See chapter 4, pp. 134–35, above.

race might shift the hatred now being directed against Germany to Japan, thus resulting in the German-British war's being turned against Japan.[69]

Such an alignment indeed would have been consistent—and might have had some appeal to Hitler, who sought peace with Great Britain. The assumption was that the most important dividing line in world politics was racial. This idea offends Realism, but if the premise had been correct the conclusion would have followed.

Balance as a Psychological Dynamic

While strategic calculations can push an international system toward balance, that there is more to it than this is indicated by the fact that systems tend toward balance even when considerations of power and advantage are absent. Thus people's attitude structures tend to be balanced. That is, positively valued elements tend to be associated with each other, negatively valued elements are seen as linked, and the relations between the liked and disliked elements are seen as negative. People tend to think that good things (and bad things) go together and thereby minimize the perceived trade-offs among desired values.[70] Belief systems then usually display overkill: Goals

[69] Hara Yoshimichi, president of the Privy Council, quoted in Nobutaka Ike, ed., *Japan's Decision for War* (Stanford, Calif.: Stanford University Press, 1967), p. 237. Not surprisingly, earlier in this century the Balkans provided examples of actors having to choose between ethnicity and ties of traditional interest as grounds for alignment: see Samuel Williamson, Jr., *Austria-Hungary and the Origins of the First World War* (New York: St. Martin's, 1991), pp. 95–96. Of course ethnic loyalties are neither unambiguous nor are they always sufficient to provide clear guidelines. For example, after the Soviet invasion of Afghanistan, a Kuwaiti spokesman explained his country's refusal to help orient Arab politics toward supporting the embattled Muslims: "The crisis of Afghanistan should not divert our attention from the real problem. Jerusalem is more sacred to us than Kabul" (quoted in "The Doctrine's Acid," *Newsweek*, February 18, 1980, p. 53).

[70] For further discussion of value trade-offs, see Jervis, *Perception and Misperception*, pp. 128–42. The work on consistency in attitudes and social structure derives from Fritz Heider, *The Psychology of Interpersonal Relations* (New York: Wiley, 1958). Research on attitude structures was spurred by Robert Abelson and Milton Rosenberg, "Symbolic Psycho-logic: A Model of Attitudinal Cognition," *Behavioral Science* 3 (January 1958), pp. 1–13. Much of the subsequent research is summarized in Abelson et al., eds., *Theories of Cognitive Consistency*; Robert Zajonc, "Cognitive Theories in Social Psychology," in Gardner Lindzey and Elliot Aronson, eds., *The Handbook of Social Psychology*, 2d. ed. (Reading, Mass.: Addison-Wesley, 1968), vol. 1, pp. 320–411; Robert Abelson, "Whatever Became of Consistency Theory?" *Personality and Social Psychology Bulletin* 9 (March 1983), pp. 37–54. Howard Taylor, *Balance in Small Groups* (New York: Van Nostrand, 1970), is a good summary of the literature in that area. Of course consistency is not an all-or-none characteristic but is a matter of degree. Exactly how to measure the extent of consistency is not simple: See Abelson and Rosenberg, "Symbolic Psycho-logic"; Dorwin Cartwright and Frank Harary, "Structural Balance: A Generalization of Heider's Theory," *Psychological Review* 63 (September 1956), pp. 277–93. One can also try to

that are desirable are likely to be seen as feasible, and one reason why people can say that the ends do not justify the means is that they happily believe that good ends in fact cannot be produced by unacceptable procedures. That beliefs are structured in this way can be explained in part by the relations in the external world. For example, part of the reason why people expect their friends to like each other is that people with mutual friends are likely to have other things in common; one reason why disfavored means are viewed unfavorably is the experience of their having led to undesired outcomes in the past. But logic and experience are insufficient to explain all the consistency we find in people's perceptions and beliefs. The operation of extralogical factors is also indicated by the fact that we often find unbalanced structures uncomfortable even when considerations of power and strategy are absent. We are not only surprised but upset to learn that two of our friends do not like each other. This is true even if we do not have to choose between our two friends. We also find it disconcerting when those we dislike also dislike each other. Politically this advantages us because it divides and weakens those we oppose. But this configuration casts doubt on our judgment; we feel uncomfortable sharing the same evaluation with someone we find disreputable.[71]

In much of the previous discussion, I have used the terms *friends* and *allies* as synonyms. Of course, the two can be distinguished. In social life as well as politics, we may receive support from those who do not wish us well or like us. So what is interesting is our tendency to equate the two, to assume that allies indeed are friends. In a classic experiment, Aronson and Cope showed that even in the absence of strategic or logical reasons to do so, people tended to like those who punished their enemies and rewarded their friends.[72] In other words, people unwarrantedly expanded the realm in which they expected commonalities between themselves and the third party and infused the relationship with affect. This propensity is also present in politics, especially when the alignment is important. Thus most of the American public and many officials changed not only their policy preferences but also their attitudes toward the Soviet Union when that country was attacked by Nazi Germany. Before the signing of the Nazi-Soviet pact, liberal antifascists had sought to believe the best about the USSR and after the war tended to assume the innocence of those who were the target of right-wing

---

measure the intensity of positive or negative relations instead of making a simple dichotomy: See Theodore Newcomb, *The Acquaintance Process* (New York: Holt, Rinehart and Winston, 1961).

[71] For a discussion of the conflict between balance theory and strategic objectives in interpersonal relations, see Philip Brickman and Charles Horn, "Balance Theory and Interpersonal Coping in Triads," *Journal of Personality and Social Psychology* 26 (April 1973), pp. 347–55.

[72] Elliot Aronson and Vernon Cope, "My Enemy's Enemy Is My Friend," ibid. 8 (January 1968), pp. 8–12.

accusations of spying and betrayal. Similarly, although it was Ronald Reagan's international strategy that led him to support Jonas Savimbi in Angola and the Contras in Nicaragua, it cannot explain why he saw the former as a believer in democracy and the latter as "the moral equal of our Founding Fathers." While cynics may have no difficulty in supporting those with whom they have little sympathy or in cooperating with others who have very different interests and values, many people find such arrangements disturbing. They need to construct a more comfortable (i.e., balanced) set of beliefs, which suggests that the pressures for political and social systems to be consistent may be an aspect of deep feeling that pervades human life rather than only being a product of strategy and the pursuit of advantage.

Conditions and Limits

Although the pressures toward balance are powerful, they do not tell the entire story. Indeed they cannot determine the exact configuration of the system because there are many different ways in which a system can be consistent, and dynamics as contradictory as balancing against a major threat and bandwagoning with it can lead to equally consistent systems. Furthermore, states often seek inconsistent arrangements in order to gain leverage over others or to avoid collecting additional enemies. So to analyze which configuration will form, we need to examine the preferences, beliefs, and strategies of the actors. Statesmen are not entirely directed by outside forces: They have some success in building desired configurations and avoiding others.

Avoiding Undesired Balance

Balance may be the "natural order," but some balanced configurations are undesired by powerful actors. Although balance theory does not see any problems with a system in which A, B, C, and D all have good relations with one another and bad relations with E, E will. For this reason, such configurations can develop only under unusual circumstances. Thus Poland was so weak internally and externally that it could be divided among Austria, Prussia, and Russia. At the other extreme, states that are strong enough to menace everyone else and arrogant enough to believe that they can succeed may also find themselves facing a grand coalition. Status quo powers may face a consistent, but undesired, system if they are outnumbered by revisionists, as was true in the 1930s when Great Britain and France were arrayed against

Germany, Japan, and Italy.[73] The British attempt to alter this configuration came to naught for reasons both systemic and nonsystemic. Public opinion prevented the British government from appeasing Italy over Ethiopia, and American opposition prevented it from offering the inducements that could have detached Japan from the hostile coalition.[74] Ironically, British antipathy toward the Soviet Union similarly inhibited the French effort to add that country to the anti-German side.[75]

Britain or France might have tried even harder to break up the Axis had either been completely without allies. The more isolated a state becomes, the more willing it will be to sacrifice other values in order to gain partners. This was the case for Britain around the turn of the twentieth century. While some called the British isolation "splendid," perceptive statesmen felt more menaced, knowing that its far-flung colonial empire made it the actual or potential enemy of most other powers, who might therefore unite against it.[76] When Salisbury became prime minister in the spring of 1885, his comment on the performance of the preceding liberal government led by Gladstone was only slightly unfair: "They have at least achieved their long desired 'Concert of Europe.' They have succeeded in uniting the Continent of Europe—against England."[77] Indeed, in the Balkan crisis of 1887 Bismarck threatened such a coalition unless Great Britain cooperated with Austria

---

[73] For a discussion of aggressors ganging up against status quo states, see Randall Schweller, *Deadly Imbalances: Tripolarity and Hitler's Strategy for World Conquest* (New York: Columbia University Press, forthcoming).

[74] Neville Chamberlain spoke for many of his colleagues: "I have *no* doubt we could easily make an agreement with [the Japanese] if the U.S.A. were out of the picture. It is the Americans who are the difficulty and I don't know how we can get over it" (quoted in N. H. Gibbs, *Grand Strategy*, vol. 1, *Rearmament Policy* [London: Her Majesty's Stationery Office, 1976], pp. 394–95). Some officials, such as Warren Fischer, the permanent undersecretary at the Treasury, and F. O. Lindley, British ambassador to Japan, were willing to resolve this dilemma by sacrificing American friendship (ibid., p. 94). But most officials were not, thus rendering little more than a pious wish the Defence Requirements Sub-Committee's call for returning "at least to our old terms of cordiality and respect with Japan" (ibid., p. 95). Also see the views of officials quoted in Andrew Gordon, "The Admiralty and Imperial Overstretch, 1902–1941," *Journal of Strategic Studies* 17 (March 1994), pp. 68–71.

[75] When France signed a treaty with the latter in 1935, some French officials argued that "the closer association with Russia would injure relations with England and thus put paid to the eternal hope of ensuring closer military cooperation with Great Britain" (Young, *In Command of France*, p. 94). Alliance ties also made it impossible for Britain and France to reach a separate peace with Austria-Hungary toward the end of World War I because that country was the main enemy of Italy: see A. J. P. Taylor, *The Struggle for Mastery in Europe, 1848–1918* (London: Oxford University Press, 1954), p. 548.

[76] See, for example, C. J. Lowe, *Salisbury and the Mediterranean, 1886–1896* (London: Routledge & Kegan Paul, 1965); George Monger, *The End of Isolation: British Foreign Policy, 1900–1907* (London: Nelson and Sons, 1963); J. A. S. Grenville, *Lord Salisbury and Foreign Policy: The Close of the Nineteenth Century* (London: Athlone, 1964).

[77] Quoted in Bourne, *Foreign Policy of Victorian England*, p. 144.

and Italy to contain Russia, a stance that would have relieved Britain's isolation but made it dependent on Germany. So at the turn of the century Britain sought support, finding it first in Japan, then in France, and finally in Russia. Although the long-run consequences were not entirely to Britain's liking, they did show Britain's ability to prevent the formation of a consistent structure in which it was everyone's enemy.

Seeking Imbalance: Trying to Be Friends with Two Adversaries

Just as a state may prefer one balanced structure to another, so two somewhat overlapping interests may lead it to seek imbalance. First, as we saw in the previous chapter, an actor gains bargaining leverage over others if it can stay linked to them while they are unable to get on good terms with each other. This was Bismarck's goal and while the U.S. may not have sought such a configuration, it too benefits from the fact that in most areas of the world it is now the preferred partner of states that cannot readily work together.[78] Second, consistency can be costly because as the state gains allies, balancing dynamics are likely to draw it into quarrels in which it has no direct stake.

For these reasons, state A often will seek support from B and C even though the latter two have conflicts with each other. When this is impossible, it will try to keep ties to one of them without becoming a target of the other's enmity. But while it is readily understandable that states should want to avoid choosing between potential friends since doing so will diminish their support if not create enemies, maintaining good relations with two adversaries is likely to come close to, if it does not flatly entail, contradictory commitments.[79] Under some circumstances, the state may be able to offer support to one without directly menacing the other: State A could promise B that it would come to its assistance if it is attacked by D but not by C, which is both an adversary of B and an ally of A. Even here, however, C has cause for complaint because by relieving B of the fear of attack by D, A has permitted it to concentrate on its conflict with C. It is also possible for the state to make strictly defensive commitments to two adversaries and pledge

[78] Josef Joffe refers to this as the hub and spokes pattern and draws a parallel between Bismarck's alliances and those that he believes the U.S. can and should maintain: "'Bismarck' or 'Britain'? Toward an American Grand Strategy after Bipolarity," *International Security* 19 (Spring 1995), pp. 94–117.

[79] Indeed, when foreign policy commentators refer to a policy as "balanced" they mean "evenhanded"—i.e., maintaining decent relations with two adversaries by treating each fairly. The argument here is that this is a difficult task which can be accomplished only under special circumstances. But the claim by state A that aiding B would violate a state's commitment to C is generally accepted as a legitimate reason for not doing so and will not lead B to increase its hostility: for an example, see Paul Schroeder, "The Lost Intermediaries: The Impact of 1870 on the European System," *International History Review* 6 (February 1984), pp. 17–19; for a discussion of the inference processes involved, see Jervis, *Perception and Misperception*, pp. 37–43.

to come to the other's aid if and only if the other is subject to an unprovoked attack (some of Bismarck's treaties were of this type). But the difficulties of determining whether an attack is unprovoked make this a difficult path to follow.[80]

This is not to say that a state can never succeed in establishing an unbalanced configuration, as the previous chapter's discussion of the pivot shows. Indeed, six considerations may permit inconsistency. First, two adversaries may court the state.[81] Thus the relations among Italy, the Triple Alliance (of which Italy technically was a member), and the Triple Entente were inconsistent in the years before 1914 because both sides thought that they could gain Italian support if they did not press it too hard.

Second, the major actors may permit neutrality. Indeed, as Paul Schroeder notes, in their debate over whether states tend to balance or bandwagon, political scientists have overlooked the fact that many states are able to "hide"—i.e., stay out of the fray all together.[82] During the Cold War, notwithstanding the superpowers' harsh rhetoric, only rarely did they force the neutrals into alignment.[83] Although the experience of the U.S. in the two World Wars indicates that a powerful state often has interests widespread enough to entangle it in any major conflict, it may be able to make itself indispensable to others who cannot afford to demand that it choose between them.[84] At the start of the twentieth century, the importance of French loans to Russia (and to Russia's Balkan clients) allowed the Franco-Russian alliance to survive the stress placed on it by improved Anglo-French relations.[85] A dominant state also can maintain ties to clients who do not have good relations with each other: The conflicts among the countries in South America have not prevented the U.S. from being on good terms with most of them, and even when the Beagle Channel Islands dispute brought Argentina and Chile to the brink of war, neither could press the U.S. to come down on one side or the other. Indeed, during the Cold War—and perhaps after it as well—American calls for allied unity could not disguise

[80] This point is stressed in Snyder, *Alliance Politics*.

[81] This may partially explain the findings reported in Michael Sullivan, *International Relations: Theories and Evidence* (Englewood Cliffs, N.J.: Prentice Hall, 1976), pp. 246–47. Also see Joshua Goldstein and John Freeman, *Three-Way Street* (Chicago: University of Chicago Press, 1990).

[82] Paul Schroeder, "Historical Reality vs. Neo-realist Theory," *International Security* 19 (Summer 1994), pp. 108–48. The classic study of such attempts in warime is Annette Baker Fox, *The Power of Small States: Diplomacy in World War II* (Chicago: University of Chicago Press, 1959); for a prewar case, see Weinberg, *Foreign Policy of Hitler's Germany*, p. 326.

[83] H. W. Brands, *The Specter of Neutralism: The United States and the Emergence of the Third World, 1947–1960* (New York: Columbia University Press, 1989).

[84] For related arguments, see Granovetter, "Strength of Weak Ties," and Ronald Burt, *Structual Holes: The Social Structure of Competition* (Cambridge, Mass.: Harvard University Press, 1992).

[85] Andrew, *Delcassé*, chapter 12; also see chapter 5 above, p. 184.

the fact that it often gained bargaining leverage when such unity proved beyond reach.

Ideology, personal rivalries, and historical animosities can also produce inconsistencies. Ideological incompatibility in part explains why Great Britain was lackadaisical in its pursuit of an alliance with the USSR in 1939 and why for years the U.S. and the PRC remained hostile despite their shared hostility toward the Soviet Union. (It is not surprising that the establishment of good relations was accompanied by acknowledgments of the primacy of interest over domestic political philosophy.[86]) Similarly, to the extent that the considerations that drive consistency are strategic ones to which the general public is relatively insensitive, states in which public opinion is powerful are less likely to follow the dictates of balance. Thus the British public felt that morality and justice required their country to oppose Italy's conquest of Ethiopia even at the cost of alienating a potential enemy of Germany. When monarchs ruled, dynastic ties and family feuds rather than public opinion sometimes produced inconsistencies, as when Kaiser Wilhelm supported Greece after the Second Balkan War because the king of Greece was the kaiser's brother-in-law.[87] Memories of old antagonisms also can lead states who "should" work together to find it difficult to do so, as was the case for Japan and South Korea during the Cold War.[88]

A fourth factor that can be at work is diplomatic skill, exemplified by Bismarck's ability to maintain at least intermittently good relations with Russia while at the same time being allied to Austria. Bismarck assiduously worked to limit Russia's other alignment options, to minimize and disguise the extent to which Germany had to support Austria in the Balkans, and to keep the peace there. It is not clear that the inconsistency could have been maintained indefinitely, but a less surefooted diplomat would not have been able to create it at all.[89] Less benignly, part of the reason for Hitler's diplo-

---

[86] Henry Kissinger, *White House Years*, pp. 192, 1063; Richard Nixon, *RN: The Memoirs of Richard Nixon* (New York: Grosset & Dunlap, 1978), p. 565.

[87] R. J. Crampton, *The Hollow Detente: Anglo-German Relations in the Balkans, 1911–1914* (Atlantic Highlands, N.J.: Humanities Press, 1980), p. 108. For a case in which personal dislikes ruled out a coalition that otherwise would have formed, see Michael Laver and Norman Schofield, *Multiparty Government* (New York: Oxford University Press, 1990), p. 199.

[88] Victor Cha, *Alignment Despite Antagonism: The United States–Korea–Japan Security Triangle* (Stanford, Calif.: Stanford University Press, forthcoming). Even here, however, relations between Korea and Japan improved when the shared threat from North Korea and the PRC increased, as balance theory would lead us to expect. Secretary of War Stimson opposed using the atomic bomb on the historic city of Kyoto because "the bitterness which would be caused by such a wanton act might make it impossible during the long post-war period to reconcile the Japanese to us in that area rather than to the Russians" (quoted in Barton Bernstein, "The Atomic Bombing Reconsidered," *Foreign Affairs* 74 [January/February 1995], p. 147).

[89] Power played a role as well. Note the French foreign minister's reason for rejecting Russia's feeler in the wake of its humiliation at the Congress of Berlin: "Bismarck has his eye on me. If a treaty were on the anvil he might reply with war." As Sontag comments, "Bismarck was vigilant; whenever Franco-Russian relations became too intimate, a new German army bill was

matic and coercive successes lay in his ability to drive along the fault lines between those whom he was seeking to dominate.[90] In domestic if not in international politics, a person who is able to make himself liked by others who have little in common is also in a good position to put together an unbalanced coalition.[91]

Fifth, isolated or pariah states may violate consistency by shunning or being shunned by a diverse set of states.[92] Yemen in the 1920s and l930s and Myanmar in the current era wanted nothing to do with the rest of the world;[93] until its regime changed, Albania was hostile simultaneously to the U.S., the USSR, and China; no country was willing to openly establish good relations with racist South Africa. (But the disputes that divided those who opposed these states meant that they did not have to worry about being assaulted by the entire group.)

Finally, although bipolarity is often taken to imply consistency, the fact that superpower patrons shouldered the responsibility for the security of others enabled the latter to pursue secondary goals, some of which decreased the consistency of the system. Thus the West Europeans often sought to maintain at least tolerable relations with the Soviet Union, even at the cost of friction with their American ally.[94] Indeed, clients were free to assert their independence in ways that had the effect—and often the purpose—of straining their relations with their patron (as France did) and to squabble with each other (as was true for Japan and South Korea), if not engage in violent conflict (as Greece and Turkey did).

DIFFERENCES IN STRATEGIES PRODUCING IMBALANCE

An alternative explanation for European behavior during the Cold War constitutes an additional limit to consistency. The Europeans often claimed that much of the tension in East-West relations was caused by the unnecessarily belligerent American policy and that the danger of war would be decreased

introduced" (Sontag, *European Diplomatic History*, p. 29; for similar cases, see Snyder, *Alliance Politics*, chapter 10). Salisbury's skill helps explain how Britain managed to keep on good terms with both Turkey and Russia during the Bosnian crisis of 1908–9: Cooper, "British Policy in the Balkans."

[90] This is stressed by E. M. Robertson, *Hitler's Pre-War Policy and Military Plans* (London: Longmans, 1963), especially p. 7.

[91] See, for example, Robert Dallek's discussion of Lyndon Johnson: *Lone Star Rising: Lyndon Johnson and his Times, 1908–1960* (New York: Oxford University Press, 1991), pp. 352–56.

[92] Good surveys are Deon Geldenhuys, *Isolated States: A Comparative Analysis* (Cambridge: Cambridge University Press, 1990), and Richard Betts, "Paranoids, Pygmies, Pariahs and Nonproliferation Revisited," *Security Studies* 2 (Spring/Summer 1993), pp. 100–126.

[93] On the former case, see Anthony Clayton, *The British Empire as a Superpower: 1919–39* (Athens: University of Georgia Press, 1986), pp. 482–84.

[94] This I think explains the findings in Ole Holsti, P. Terrence Hopmann, and John Sullivan, *Unity and Disintegration in International Alliances: Comparative Studies* (New York: Wiley, 1973), pp. 118–25.

if they conciliated the Soviet Union. As this example shows, if one alliance member believes in deterrence theory—i.e., thinks that it can prevail and keep the peace by following a "hard line"—and the other partner thinks that the spiral model is more accurate—i.e., worries about the danger of inadvertent war growing out of mutual insecurities and misapplied deterrence policies—then the allies will treat the adversary differently. Indeed, the Europeans thought that war was more likely if the world was divided into two hostile camps and argued—certainly self-servingly, but perhaps sincerely— for a division of labor in which the U.S. concentrated on deterrence and the Europeans maintained somewhat better relations with the USSR. The result was not inconsistency in the sense of cross-cutting alliances, but a milder form in which the degree of hostility between the Soviet Union and members of NATO was not uniform.[95]

A related difference in strategy can cause even more inconsistency. As Samuel Huntington has noted, when faced with a hostile alliance a state can choose either to win over some of its members or to isolate and weaken them.[96] For any number of reasons, states can differ on which approach is preferred. During the Cold War, the Americans tended to believe that treating the "Soviet bloc" as a bloc was the best way to decrease the strength of the USSR and eventually to separate the USSR from its clients,[97] while the Europeans saw greater possibilities for reaching these goals by being more lenient toward the PRC and East Europe. Thus they sought less consistency by treating different adversaries differently and, because the U.S. did not, their stance also produced inconsistency in the form of states that were allied behaving differently toward their common adversaries.

Conditions under Which Balance Is Likely

For two related reasons, systems are more likely to be balanced when conflict is high. First, a cause or an effect (or both) of high conflict is that one

[95] For a discussion of the divergent American and European policies in the late 1970s in these terms, see Jay Speakman, "Continuity of Discord: Responses of the Western Allies to the Soviet Invasion of Afghanistan" (unpublished dissertation, Department of Political Science, Columbia University, 1994), chapter 12. For a Chinese view of parallel differences between the PRC and the USSR over strategy toward the West, see "Report, 'My Observations on the Soviet Union,' Zhou Enlai to Mao Zedong and the Central Leadership, 24 January 1957 (Excerpt)," translated by Zhang Shu Guang and Chen Jian, *Cold War International History Project Bulletin*, nos. 6–7 (Winter 1995/1996), p. 154. For an earlier example, see Browning, *War of the Austrian Succession*, p. 225.

[96] Samuel Huntington, "The Renewal of Strategy," in Huntington, ed., *The Strategic Imperative: New Policies for American Security* (Cambridge, Mass.: Ballinger, 1982), pp. 18–21.

[97] This is most clear for Eisenhower's policy toward the PRC: see David Mayers, *Cracking the Monolith: U.S. Policy Against the Sino-Soviet Alliance, 1949–1955* (Baton Rouge: Louisiana State University Press, 1986), and John Lewis Gaddis, *The Long Peace* (New York: Oxford University Press, 1987), chapter 6.

issue is overriding. As noted earlier, consistency implies that states set their policies on the basis of their relations with a key ally or adversary, which they will resist doing if they have intrinsic interests that pull them in different directions.[98] If state A has important conflicts with both B and C, it may not be willing or able to take advantage of a dispute between them; if A and B are divided by a bilateral dispute, they may not draw together even if A is supporting C, which in turn has good relations with B. On these grounds Henry Kissinger argued that American support for Pakistan in 1971 would not produce lasting enmity between India and the U.S. or strengthened ties between India and the Soviet Union: "Nixon and I . . . . were convinced that India's nonalignment derived . . . from its perception of its national interest; these calculations were likely to reassert themselves as soon as the crisis was over."[99] In other words, India's interests were so deeply embedded that they would not be disturbed by the second-order considerations of other states' stances toward their adversary.

Second, international systems are likely to be consistent when states seek every advantage and try to dominate and destroy others—when the "game of power politics [is] really played hard."[100] Under these circumstances, both the pushes and the pulls toward alignment will be very great: The major powers will hold out inducements for others to join them and will have little patience if others attempt to give the adversary even minor assistance. What the French ambassador to Moscow reported on the eve of World War II about Soviet policy could be said about many other countries when vital issues are at stake: The question was not "whether the USSR will, or will not, be with us, but with *whom* they will be."[101] The British policy throughout much of the 1930s was based on the concept of "limited liability"—the idea that the U.K. would undertake only limited actions for containing German power. In the face of a challenge which enforced consistency, however, neither this impulse nor the related British refusal to join France in guaranteeing the countries on Germany's eastern borders could be maintained. Similarly, Tito ended his resistance to accepting American military aid after the Soviet-supported invasion of South Korea led him to

[98] For an example, see J. Leitch Wright, Jr., *Anglo-Spanish Rivalry in North America* (Athens: University of Georgia Press, 1971), pp. 126–27. The familiar claim that conflict is less likely if a system is characterized by cross-cutting cleavages may have the causal relationship reversed. That is, it is not so much that cross-cutting cleavages reduce conflict by keeping the system from becoming balanced as it is that cleavages can cross-cut effectively only when no single issue is of primary importance.

[99] *White House Years*, p. 898; similar claims were made when the U.S. first formed an alliance with Pakistan and were partially correct: McMahon, *Cold War on the Periphery*, pp. 177–78.

[100] Kenneth Waltz, *Theory of International Politics* (Reading, Mass.: Addison-Wesley, 1979), p. 167.

[101] Quoted in Lewis Namier, *In the Nazi Era* (London: Macmillan, 1952), p. 171.

fear a similar fate, and the crushing of the Prague Spring led Albania's Hoxha to make overtures to Yugoslavia and Rumania.[102]

When the game is played less hard, there will be less consistency as states' policies are guided more by the specific interests at stake.[103] Thus it is not surprising that Albania could return to its isolated position and denounce China when the Soviet threat eased[104] or that the end of the Cold War has meant a relaxation of rigid alignment patterns, sometimes robbing Third World countries of support that previously was automatic. For example, when a Middle East peace conference appeared possible in 1991, the Israelis thought of asking for "some sort of a general commitment from the United States to be sympathetic to Israel . . . because . . . without the backdrop of United States-Soviet competition, America's natural inclination to side with Isreal, just because Moscow was siding with the Arabs, . . . greatly diminished."[105]

When tensions between the great powers are high but the peripheral states have conflicts with their neighbors, there is likely to be balance, but in a form that frustrates the former as the power that wins the support of one local state will find itself opposed by that state's enemies. Hence the British plans for getting all the Balkan states on their side in World War I failed because shared hostility to Austria and Turkey was less important to them than were their conflicts with one another.[106] The belief that the global

---

[102] Joseph Rothschild, *Return to Diversity: A Political History of East Central Europe Since World War II*, 2d. ed. (New York: Oxford University Press, 1993), pp. 142–43, 175–76.

[103] For a related discussion, see Snyder, *Alliance Politics*, chapter 2.

[104] Rothschild, *Return to Diversity*, p. 177.

[105] Thomas Friedman, "A Window on Deep Israel-U.S. Tensions," *New York Times*, September 9, 1991.

[106] One reason why Churchill, then First Lord of the Admiralty, advocated attacking Turkey at the Dardanelles early in the war was the belief that this was "the best way of forcing the Balkan States to resolve their quarrels and join the Allies as a united bloc" (Gilbert, *Churchill*, vol. 3, p. 200). But while Greece was relatively easy to recruit because Turkey had joined the Central Powers, Bulgaria and Greece were rivals, and so the former chose to fight on the opposite side from the latter. Churchill's postwar views are so poignant, parochial, and elegant as to merit quoting at length:

How unteachable, how blinded by their passions are the races of men! The Great War . . . offered to the Christian peoples of the Balkans their supreme opportunity. . . . By a single spontaneous realisation of their common interests the Confederation of the Balkans would have become one of the great Powers of Europe. . . . A concerted armed neutrality followed by decisive intervention . . . against their common enemies, Turkey and Austria, could easily have given each individual State the major part of its legitimate ambitions, and would have given all safety, prosperity and power. They chose instead to drink in company the corrosive cup of internecine warfare. And the cup is not yet drained.

Churchill, *The World Crisis*, abridged ed. (New York: Scribner's, 1931), p. 685; also see p. 386. For similar cases, see Cooper, "British Policy in the Balkans," p. 276; Charles Fedorak, "In Search of a Necessary Ally: Addington, Hawkesbury, and Russia, 1801–1804," *Inter-*

issues of the Cold War should override petty regional rivalries similarly proved false. Neither the U.S. nor the USSR could recruit both India and Pakistan; Reagan's attempt to form a "strategic consensus" in the Middle East against the Soviet Union failed; when a leftist revolution led Ethiopia to switch allegiance from the U.S. to the USSR, the latter lost its close ties with Somalia.

But even the dire circumstances of all-out war may not compel complete consistency if some states see advantage in limiting or avoiding conflict with their allies' enemies. Thus until the last days of World War II the Soviet Union refrained from fighting Japan. Differences in objectives explain why Finland, which followed Germany in attacking the USSR in June 1941, not only did not treat the U.S. and U.K. as enemies (and was not treated as one by them), but also halted its army upon reaching the border that had been in place before the Winter War. The Soviet Union, in turn, treated Finland more leniently than it did Germany's full partners. Bulgaria was at war with the U.S. and Great Britain but, until September 1944, had cordial relations with the Soviet Union; Hungary fought the USSR but until Hitler imposed a new government in March 1944 did not fire on overflying Western bombers (which in turn did not drop their bombs on it).[107] Consistency was not complete during World War I either. After its entry, Italy did not ally with Russia and despite a commitment to fight "against all [the Entente's] enemies" within a month, allowed three months to pass before joining the war against Turkey, and fifteen months to elapse before declaring war on Germany.[108] Because the U.S. sought the flexibility that would enable it to broker a peace settlement, it too kept its distance from those on whose side it was fighting. Rather than becoming one of the Allied powers, the U.S. fought as an "Associated Power," refrained from declaring war on Austria until December 7, 1917, and never did so against Turkey. The situation was even less consistent in Asia: The Chinese desire to join the Entente powers was initially frustrated by the opposition of Japan, a more powerful Entente supporter who did not want to see China gain influence and prestige. Later in the war, Japan dropped its opposition, although by this time many Chinese had developed doubts, as had the U.S., which initially had sought to have China follow its lead and declare war on Germany.[109] It was not an

---

national History Review 13 (May 1991), p. 236; Clayton, British Empire as a Superpower, p. 120.

[107] Rothschild, Return to Diversity, pp. 41–43. For equally odd cases from an earlier era, see Browning, War of the Austrian Succession, pp. 140, 149, 160–61.

[108] Taylor, Struggle for Mastery in Europe, p. 546.

[109] See Stephen Craft, "Angling for an Invitation to Paris: China's Entry into the First World War," International History Review 16 (February 1994), pp. 1–24. When Italy changed sides (and regimes) during World War II, it wanted to be accepted as an ally of Britain and the U.S., but partly because of domestic politics those countries only granted it the status of a co-belligerent.

accident that the states which were able to resist the pressures for consistency even under conditions of high conflict were on the peripheries of the system: They were not bound to the warring parties by as high densities of interaction and had greater freedom of maneuver.

NECESSITY FOR CHOICE

Even though they sometimes can avoid balance, more often than actors would like, they have to choose. While it may be in their interest to be on good terms with others who have conflicts with each other, this is difficult to do because it requires the consent of both sides. On many occasions statesmen realize they need to make an explicit decision on alignment: Much as British statesmen thought the American position in Asia during the interwar period was unreasonable, they saw that if they could not alter it they would have to sacrifice their ties to Japan; after the war Japan could not develop decent relations with the PRC until the U.S. had done so; the U.S. eventually realized that it could not bring both India and Pakistan into its camp.

But, as the last case illustrates, the understanding that consistency cannot be overcome is often slow in coming. It appears that many statesmen overestimate their ability to get others to patch up their quarrels, as the U.S. did, or to keep them isolated from each other and dependent on the state, as Britain did in the interwar years when it opposed Germany and sought to isolate the USSR without foreseeing that this would push the two of them together. When at the start of the Peloponnesian War, the Corcyraean Assembly voted to reaffirm its defensive alliance with Athens and yet "to be friends with [Spartans] as they had in the past,"[110] it was even more naive given that Athens and Sparta were at war. The common dilemma and the way in which people avoid facing it was epitomized in 1905 by a British leader's denial that the recently signed entente with France was aimed at Germany: "Our earnest wish is to be friends with both, and not only with them, but with other countries also."[111] While it would have taken special circumstances or special skill to achieve this objective, the exact ways in which the international interactions defeated British hopes are interesting enough to merit a more detailed examination to close this chapter.

[110] Quoted in Donald Kagan, *The Archidamian War* (Ithaca, N.Y.: Cornell University Press, 1974), p. 176.

[111] Quoted in A. J. Anthony Morris, *Radicalism Against War, 1906–1914* (London: Longman, 1972), p. 46. Similarly, the Japanese foreign minister said that his country could sign a treaty with the PRC which contained an "anti-hegemony" clause without undermining the effort to improve relations with the Soviet Union: Richard Halloran, "Japan to Sign China Pact Despite Soviet Warnings," *New York Times*, January 14, 1976. A study of interpersonal relations similarly finds that the general preference for balanced structures was overcome when the person believed that imbalance would be strategically useful: Brickman and Horn, "Balance Theory and Interpersonal Coping in Triads."

Pre–World War I Diplomacy: The Formation of a Balanced System

The evolution of pre–World War I alignments conformed to the principles of systems dynamics: What was done at one time or on one issue created dangers and opportunities at later times and on other issues; strong feedbacks were in operation; the characteristics of the system could not be inferred from the bilateral relations; outcomes markedly diverged from intentions. Furthermore, initial behavior produced reactions that unanticipatedly altered states' interests, reduced their freedom of maneuver, and generated a balanced system despite statesmen's desires and expectations.[112]

Perhaps the most striking fact about World War I—and the obvious clue that we cannot understand the diplomacy by examining bilateral relations— is that many states are on the wrong side. While an observer who knew only the direct conflicts would not be surprised that France fought Germany or that Russia fought Austria-Hungary, she would have a hard time explaining why Russia and France, who had few common interests, were allies, and why Austria and France fought each other even though they had no quarrels. It made even less sense for Britain and Austria to fight since no issues divided them and they shared an interest in maintaining the European equilibrium and the health—or at least survival—of the Ottoman Empire.[113] Furthermore, Britain had more intrinsic conflicts with those who became its allies than with those it would fight. Britain was divided from France by traditional rivalry as well as by important colonial disputes; it was menaced by Russia in Central Asia and the Balkans.[114]

What is most striking is that Germany and England were natural allies, as many German statesmen and not a few Englishmen noted. Both countries

[112] Consistency was not complete as Italy had commitments to both sides that were contradictory in spirit if not in letter. Italy's weakness was seen as giving it license to avoid a firm alignment, a stance that facilitated its concentration on colonial issues. Furthermore, Germany began the war expecting inconsistency in the form of British neutrality, and it is at least possible that this goal could have been reached if Germany had not invaded Belgium. For an analysis of the European alliances from 1871 to 1914, see Snyder, *Alliance Politics*.

[113] It is often argued that the failure to maintain good relations between Great Britain and Austria constituted a lost opportunity for the latter or the failure of the former to understand the useful role of intermediary states: Williamson, *Austria-Hungary and the Origins of the First World War*, pp. 111–12, and Paul Schroeder, "World War I as Galloping Gertie," *Journal of Modern History* 44 (September 1972), pp. 319–44. In other words, these states (and the world at large) would have been better off if they had resisted the pressures toward consistency.

[114] Paul Kennedy, "The First World War and the International Power System," *International Security* 9 (Summer 1984), pp. 7–40; William Wohlforth, "The Perception of Power: Russia in the pre-1914 Balance," *World Politics* 39 (April 1987), pp. 353–81; Michael Ekstein, "Great Britain and the Triple Entente on the Eve of the Sarajevo Crisis," in F. H. Hinsley, ed., *British Foreign Policy Under Sir Edward Grey* (Cambridge: Cambridge University Press, 1977), pp. 342–44; Keith Wilson, *The Policy of the Entente* (Cambridge: Cambridge University Press, 1985).

were satisfied with the territorial status quo and had much to lose by a major war. Their commercial rivalry was unimportant in comparison and was disturbing in large part because of the fear that the other's economic strength would be turned against it in wartime.[115] Germany's navy was a greater source of friction, but it too appeared to be a menace largely because of the political conflicts that, as we will see, grew more out of alliance commitments than direct disputes.[116]

Three conditions favored consistency. First, although no one could predict when a major war would start, everyone believed it was coming[117] and, as we noted earlier, consistency is particularly likely when the "game is played hard." Second, everyone expected the war to be short, which meant that it was vital for states to secure allies before the fighting started. Statesmen remembered well that during the Austro-Prussian War of 1866 and the Franco-Prussian War the loser's attempts to recruit allies were overtaken by the swift course of military events. Third, Bismarck's successors sought to increase the consistency of the system by seeking a coalition of all the status quo states, including Great Britain.

Balance theory predicts that even without this preference, eventually Germany would have had to bring Austria and Russia together or choose between them. But even if the former proved impossible, the theory cannot tell us how the system would be balanced—which ally Germany would select. Here other systemic forces are relevant, although not completely determining. Germany believed that the danger of a Franco-Austrian treaty was greater than that of a Franco-Russian one because Austria was weak and would have to turn to France if it was abandoned by Germany. Not only was Russia strong enough to stand alone, but conflicts over central Asia and Constantinople would make it difficult for Russia to establish ties to England.[118] When Bismarck's successors did choose by dropping the Reinsurance Treaty with Russia, they also reasoned that reactionary Russia and a France still proud of its revolutionary heritage could not reach an accommodation. But balance theory argues that they would.[119]

[115] As one British traveler put it on his return from Germany, "Every one of these new factory chimneys is a gun pointed at England" (quoted in Paul Kennedy, *The Rise of the Anglo-German Antagonism, 1860–1914* [London: Allen & Unwin, 1980], p. 315).

[116] Although Schroeder does not stress alliance dynamics, he too denies the centrality of the naval race: "World War I as Galloping Gertie," pp. 329–31; for a mixed judgment, see Kennedy, *Rise of Anglo-German Antagonism*, pp. 416–31. It should also be noted that the naval race was not an issue in the last two years of peace, Germany in essence having conceded at least temporary defeat.

[117] James Joll, "1914: The Unspoken Assumptions," in H. W. Koch, ed., *The Origins of the First World War* (London: Macmillan, 1972), pp. 307–28.

[118] For a slightly different explanation, see Sontag, *European Diplomatic History*, pp. 19–20.

[119] The development of the alliance is lucidly discussed by George Kennan, *The Fateful*

Just as Germany believed it could drop the Reinsurance Treaty without sponsoring a Franco-Russian alliance, so Great Britain sought only limited arrangements to solve specific problems.[120] But this too proved impossible, as balance theory suggests. While here as well the theory cannot say with whom Britain would become aligned—and at a number of points Britain was not clear which way to turn—it does say that Britain could not develop good relations with some members of one camp without developing good relations with the others in that coalition and bad relations with the states on the other side.

The Development of the Ententes

One reason why England did not side with the Triple Alliance (Italy was the third member along with Germany and Austria) was that Germany acted on the assumption that Britain had no choice but to do so. Just as German statesmen overestimated the barriers to a Franco-Russian alliance, so they overestimated the immutability of the conflicts dividing England from Russia and France and therefore thought it was safe—indeed wise—to threaten England in order to show it that failing to support Germany would be very costly. The result was that Britain turned elsewhere. Initially it formed a limited partnership with Japan to gain a measure of security against Russian pressure,[121] but the basic problem remained that because the British Empire was worldwide, all the other powers might unite against it. The remedy, then, was to end some of these colonial disputes by an agreement with France. Intended as a substitute for a firm alignment with one side, the Entente of 1904 became a prelude to it; designed to increase British diplomatic flexibility, it had the opposite effect; agreed to with little thought to its implications for relations with Germany, it set in motion forces that greatly increased Anglo-German tensions, which in turn generated

Alliance: France, Russia, and the Coming of the First World War (New York: Pantheon, 1984), who argues that it was in many ways unfortunate. The final impetus to forming it was the early renewal of the Triple Alliance in 1891, accompanied by the rumors that Britain was about to join it: Snyder, *Alliance Politics*, chapter 5. Interestingly enough, the Franco-Russian agreement specified that the alliance was to remain in force as long as the Triple Alliance did.

[120] In the words of one scholar, the British "wished to remain a World Power, not to become a European one": Wilson, *Policy of the Entente*, p. 5.

[121] The history is recounted in Ian Nish, *The Anglo-Japanese Alliance* (London: Athlone, 1966). Britain also sought to remain on good terms with the other significant peripheral power by appeasing the U.S. in the disputes over influence in South America and Canadian territory and fishing rights. Here as elsewhere German leaders misjudged and expected balance to work to her advantage in the form of common enmity toward Japan driving the U.S. toward Germany while neglecting the possibility that fear of Germany would prove stronger: Ute Mehnert, "German *Weltpolitik* and the American Two-Front Dilemma: The 'Japanese Peril' in German-American Relations, 1904–1917," *Journal of American History* 82 (March 1996), pp. 1452–77.

much stronger ties to France. Also unforeseen—although desired—were closer relations with Russia and undesired conflicts with Austria. In other words, the agreement set in motion a process that made the system much more consistent.[122]

The existence of troublesome disputes with France and Russia explains why Britain began the process of alignment. As one Foreign Office official put it: "An unfriendly France and Russia would give us infinite trouble . . . in localities where we should find it extremely difficult to maintain our own."[123] Looking back almost two years after the signing of the Entente, Eyre Crowe made the point well: "with France, with Russia, and with the United States [there were] ancient and real sources of conflict, springing from imperfectly patched-up differences of past centuries, the inelastic stipulations of antiquated treaties, or the troubles incidental to unsettled colonial frontiers."[124]

Conversely, the lack of specific disputes with Germany made it hard to reach a limited agreement rather than the kind of general commitment that Britain always wanted to avoid. As Crowe noted,

> The Anglo-French *entente* has a very material basis and tangible object—namely, the adjustment of a number of actually-existing serious differences. . . . But for an Anglo-German understanding on the same lines there is no room, since none could be built upon the same foundation. It has been shown that there are no questions of any importance now at issue between the two countries. Any understanding must therefore be entirely different in object and scope.[125]

[122] The strongest form of my argument would be that the system was highly path-dependent: i.e., that if Britain and Germany had been able to reach a limited agreement that called up the opposition of other powers in the way described below, the system would have become consistent, but with very different alliances than those that actually formed. I find this counterfactual plausible, but it may downplay the bilateral conflicts of interest more than even I am willing to do.

[123] Quoted in K. A. Hamilton, "Great Britain and France, 1911–1914," in Hinsley, ed., *British Foreign Policy Under Sir Edward Grey*, p. 341.

[124] G. P. Gooch and Harold Temperley, eds., *British Documents on the Origins of the War*, vol. 3, *The Testing of the Entente, 1904–06* (London: His Majesty's Stationery Office, 1928), p. 408.

[125] Ibid., p. 418. Crowe put the point even more sharply six months earlier. The British ambassador to Germany reported that the German prime minister "had expressed his satisfaction at the cordiality of the reception [given by the king of England to a visiting delegation from Germany] which he hoped would now lead to the establishment of a friendly understanding between the two Governments." Crowe minuted:

> All this talking about an "understanding" between the two countries has an air of unreality. [Unlike the case with France and Russia], with Germany we have no differences whatever. An understanding which does not consist in the removal of differences can only mean a plan of cooperation in political transactions. . . . It is difficult to see on what points such cooperation between England and Germany is at this moment appropriate. (Ibid., pp. 357–58)

The analysis of the foreign secretary, Sir Edward Grey, was similar: There was nothing "out of which an *Entente* [with Germany] might be made. At present, there was nothing [of significance] to discuss between the two Governments. . . . In fact, I regarded the relations between England and Germany as being now normal, and I saw no reason for saying anything about them."[126]

The greatest source of tension with France was the British occupation of Egypt, which France felt had been part of its sphere of influence. Although Britain beat back the French challenge at Fashoda in 1898, it still needed relief from the international control of Egyptian finances which left it vulnerable to interference from the other European powers. France, in turn, sought a dominant role in Morocco and hence proposed the most obvious agreement: Neither country would resist the other's moves in North Africa. But British officials in Egypt felt this was inadequate and wanted French help in gaining the approval of the other European powers for the administrative reforms they were planning. At first, the French objected. Faced with British insistence, however, they finally agreed, asking in return for "British support in Morocco as the necessary counterpart. . . . [The British foreign secretary] immediately accepted without realizing how far this clause threatened to lead him. In his view, it was merely a question of 'moral support.'"[127]

Had both sides been prescient, France would have proposed this provision and Britain would have refused. But the feedbacks were hard to anticipate, especially because they depended on a self-defeating German reaction: The agreement itself was not sufficient to trigger the dynamics of alignment. Although the Entente also settled colonial disagreements in Newfoundland, west and central Africa, Siam, Madagascar, and the New Hebrides, these sections of the treaty are now forgotten because they succeeded quietly. With no other countries having claims in these areas, the implemention did not require either side to impinge on other powers and so the effects remained limited, as was intended.[128] Similarly, the 1890 agreement by which Germany gained Helgoland from Great Britain in return for limiting its claims in east Africa had little impact on relations between the two countries because joint efforts were not required to execute it over the op-

---

[126] Ibid., p. 361.

[127] Quoted in Pierre Guillen, "The Entente of 1904 as a Colonial Settlement," in Prosser Gifford and Wm. Roger Louis, eds., *France and Britain in Africa* (New Haven, Conn.: Yale University Press, 1971), p. 365. Also see Monger, *End of Isolation*, pp. 157–59. For a dissent on this and several other points about the British motives for the Entente, see Schroeder, "World War I as Galloping Gertie," pp. 324–25.

[128] C. J. Lowe and M. L. Dockrill, *The Mirage of Power*, vol. 1, *British Foreign Policy, 1902–14* (London: Routledge & Kegan Paul, 1972), p. 8; for a similar case, see Nancy Mitchell, "The Height of the German Challenge: The Venezuela Blockade, 1902–3," *Diplomatic History* 20 (Spring 1996), pp. 185–209.

position of other countries. The Russian ambassador to Berlin feared this agreement would have far-reaching efects: "When one is united by numerous interests and positive engagements on one point of the globe, one is almost certain to proceed in concert in all the great questions that may arise. . . . Virtually the entente with Germany has been accomplished. It cannot help but react upon the relations of England with the other powers of the Triple Alliance."[129] The understandable error was in failing to see that future relations would be determined not so much by the agreement itself as by the feedbacks set off by carrying it out.

In signing the Entente with France, Britain sought to reduce frictions and menaces, not threaten others, let alone align against them. As a British statesman explained to the kaiser, the British had "no notion of forming a tripartite alliance of France, Russia and England against him. . . . As for our *entente* we had some time since difficulties with France over Newfoundland and Egypt, and we had made a good business arrangement about these complicated matters."[130] The British foreign secretary's report of a conversation with the German ambassador during the Moroccan Crisis made the same point:

> Count Metternich said that, if England was to use the French *entente* always to side with France against Germany, of course Germany would come to look on England as her enemy. I said there had been no question of always siding with France against Germany. Since the *entente* was framed there had been one point of difference—the subject of Morocco. . . . I could again assure him that, were the Morocco difficulty to be satisfactorily settled, it was our desire to show that the *entente* was not to be used in a sense hostile to Germany.[131]

But, regardless of British intentions, things were not that simple. Carrying out a pledge to support France in Morocco brought Britain into conflict with Germany, in part because of the German perception that the Entente was laying the foundations for an Anglo-French alliance. Following the "wedge" strategy later practiced by Dulles and Eisenhower, the kaiser and his advisors believed that the way to nip this threat in the bud was to move sharply against France, showing it that British support was of little value and reminding the British that alignment could draw them into unwanted conflicts. These calculations led Germany to trigger the first Moroccan Crisis by refusing to accept French domination of that country. The consequences

[129] Quoted in William Langer, *The Diplomacy of Imperialism*, 2d ed. (New York: Knopf, 1965), p. 7; some British observers agreed: See Jean Stengers, "British and German Imperial Rivalry: A Conclusion," in Gifford and Louis, eds., *Britain and Germany in Africa*, p. 343.

[130] Extract from the diaries of Lord Haldane, in Gooch and Temperley, eds., *British Documents on the Origins of the War*, vol. 3, p. 379.

[131] Grey in ibid., p. 263. Lord Rosebery was more clear-sighted: "My mournful and supreme conviction is that this agreement is much more likely to lead to complications than to peace" (quoted in Churchill, *World Crisis*, p. 12).

were the opposite of what Germany had sought, however, as England not only supported France but also stiffened the latter's resolve at crucial points. Anglo-German tensions then increased and, partly as a result, Anglo-French bonds tightened.[132]

The initial British expectations that the scope of the Entente would be contained were not totally unreasonable, but in an interconnected world a colonial settlement had to have implications for European politics. By obtaining French backing for the reforms in Egypt, Britain was reducing potential German leverage; by promising to give France diplomatic support in Morocco, Britain was demonstrating that, at least on some occasions, France could find itself ranged with Russia and Great Britain. But if Germany had not strongly resisted the Moroccan agreement, the menace would have remained latent. Crowe's judgment in his famous "Balance of Power" memorandum of January 1907 is essentially accurate on this point: because of the Moroccan Crisis,

> the Anglo-French *entente* had acquired a different significance from that which it had at the moment of its inception. Then there had been but a friendly settlement of particular outstanding differences, giving hope for future harmonious relations between two neighboring countries that had got into the habit of looking at one another askance; now there had emerged an element of common resistance to outside dictation and aggression, a unity of special interests tending to develop into active co-operation against a third Power. It is essential to bear in mind that this new feature of the *entente* was the direct effect produced by Germany's effort to break it up, and that, failing the active or threatening hostility of Germany, such anti-German bias as the *entente* must be admitted to have at one time assumed, would certainly not exist at present, nor probably survive in the future.[133]

The German reaction led British statesmen to conclude that France had to be supported lest it give way and allow Germany full sway over the Continent and that England had to oppose Germany directly. Indeed, British leaders came to see that their country's security required not only backing France but also gaining its support. British and German behavior—and each one's interpretations of the other—altered the environment and brought into play the dynamics of consistency that ruled out the flexibility each had sought. The world after the Moroccan Crisis was different from

[132] The British foreign secretary also became concerned with Britain's reputation: if we back down, he said, "we should not only have lost a good freind . . . but we should, by the impression we had created, have deprived ourselves of the power to make new friends" (quoted in Wilson, *Policy of the Entente*, p. 35).

[133] Eyre Crowe, "Memorandum on the Present State of Relations with France and Germany," in Gooch and Temperley, eds., *British Documents on the Origins of the War*, vol. 3, p. 402. While Henry Kissinger notes that the bonds of the Entente proved to be much tighter than foreseen, he incorrectly attributes its power to "moral and pyschological ties": *Diplomacy*, pp. 183, 191.

the world before it; old policies could not be resurrected, as the British had hoped. Several years later, a critic of Britain's policy argued: "as long as we maintain our present close relationship with France, inevitably we are less friendly toward Germany. When is a statesman going to arise who is capable of creating a Triple Federation of Germany, Great Britain and France?"[134] The first observation is acute and was insufficiently recognized by British decision-makers when they signed and implemented the Entente. But the same logic shows why it would have taken more of a miracle than statesmanship could provide to establish an all-embracing coalition.

While the Entente brought an end to colonial disputes with France, this gain in security was more than offset by the increased German hostility. This in turn heightened the British imperative to minimize other conflicts, especially with Russia. Although the second Anglo-Japanese alliance had greatly reduced the menace to India, southwest Asia remained an area of friction. Furthermore, the configuration of the international system made a rapprochement with Russia natural since Russia was the adversary of Germany and the ally of France. Thus it is not surprising that Anglo-Russian cooperation increased, most dramatically when the two countries signed a convention dividing Persia into spheres of influence.[135] France smoothed the way for this agreement between its two allies, as balance theory leads us to expect.[136]

Just as the British had believed that being on good terms with Germany was compatible with an entente with France, so, too, many Russians thought that their agreement would have only limited consequences and would not produce tensions with Germany.[137] As the Russian foreign minister put it

[134] Quoted in Morris, *Radicalism Against War*, p. 359.

[135] One indirect effect on the convention was a reduction of British infuence over Sweden, Russia's adversary, which reacted in accord with consistency theory and moved closer to Germany: David Sweet, "The Baltic in British Diplomacy Before the First World War," *Historical Journal* 13 (September 1970), pp. 480–81.

[136] The British ambassador to France reported that the French prime minister told him that he had explained to the Russian foreign minister that France was "anxious that Russia and England should come to agreements, that France meant to remain the Ally of Russia and the friend of England and would not drop either one or the other." G. P. Gooch and Harold Temperley, eds., *British Documents on the Origins of the War, 1898–1914*, vol. 4, *The Anglo-Russian Rapprochement, 1903–7* (London: His Majesty's Stationery Office, 1929), p. 245. But Keith Wilson goes too far in arguing that Britain's "most powerful reason" for coming to an agreement with France was to recruit that country to the effort to befriend Russia: Wilson, *Policy of the Entente*, p. 71.

[137] Lowe and Dockrill, *Mirage of Power*, pp. 79–80. Despite their experience with the Entente, the British had similar illusions as well. In reply to a question in the House of Commons as to whether the negotiations with Russia involved "general political relationships," Grey replied:

The direct object of the negotiations is to prevent conflict and difficulties between the two Powers . . . in the part of Asia which affects the Indian frontier and the Russian fron-

two years later, it was "imperative that Russia should act with the greatest prudence towards Germany and give the latter no cause for complaint that the improvement of relations between Russia and England had entailed a corresponding deterioration of the relations between Russia and Germany."[138] But this proved difficult, for all the familiar reasons. Germany had to see the agreement as a threat and, being unwilling to drop the alliance with Austria and unable to re-create Bismarck's unbalanced system, responded with hostility. The cost to Germany was not all benefit to Britain, however: When Russia cheated on the Persian agreement by steadily expanding the area and scope of its control, Britain could not afford to retaliate, which would not only have increased the threat from Russia but would have weakened the ties to France as well and so left Britain isolated.[139] Indeed, positive feedback increased the intensity of the consistency as the greater need to block Germany and solidify the Ententes led England to develop naval understandings with Russia in 1913.

This is not to say that consistency was the only force at work: Germany had or created conflicts with France, Russia, and Great Britain. But the alignments cannot be understood only in terms of direct bilateral interests. The countries that formed the Triple Entente had little in common except hostility toward members of the Triple Alliance. Furthermore, much of the conflict between some members of each camp—especially Germany and Great Britain—arose more from alliance dynamics than from preexisting interests. While the polarization of the system occurred because of the acts of individual states, no one sought the configuration that resulted. Even Germany, which moved to simplify the system by dropping the Reinsurance Treaty with Russia, did not seek such a high degree of consistency. British statesmen intended only to limit the number of enemies they faced. The Entente with France was seen as an alternative to firm alignments and lasting antagonisms, but that is just what it produced as each move altered the perceptions, behavior, and interests of those who took them and those who felt they were their targets.

---

tiers. . . . What the indirect result will be as regards general political relationships must depend on how such an agreement works in practice and what effect it has on public opinion in both countries. (Quoted in Morris, *Radicalism Against War*, p. 65)

Largely for reasons of domestic politics, Grey told his subordinates not to use the term *Triple Entente*: Wilson, *Policy of the Entente*, pp. 25–26. But by April 1914 the British ambassador in Berlin saw the situation accurately: "I doubt, no! I am sure we cannot have it both ways: i.e., form a defensive alliance with France and Russia and at the same time be on cordial terms with Germany" (quoted in Ekstein, "Great Britain and the Triple Entente," p. 344).

[138] Quoted in Harold Nicolson, *Sir Arthur Nicolson, First Lord Carnock* (London: Constable, 1930), p. 273.

[139] For a discussion of why Britain's bargaining position was weak, see above, chapter 5, pp. 196–97, 199–201.

While the results of the diplomacy of the pre–World War I years were un-usual, the dynamics were not. As we have seen throughout this chapter, the most important determinant of a state's relations with another often lies in the relations each has with third parties. In other words, underlying or in-trinsic interests do not dictate the course of international history. States alter and establish their orientations toward some actors through the effect of ties made or sought with others. Although cross-cutting conflicts and the inter-ests of states in keeping their enemies to a minimum mean that systems rarely become completely consistent, it is even more rare for pressures in that direction to be absent. Alignments are more than passive reflectors of interests. They set in motion forces that create and ameliorate conflicts, sometimes as statesmen foresee, but often as they do not.

Seven

Acting in a System

SYSTEM effects can occur with inanimate objects, but greater complexities are introduced with human beings whose behavior is influenced by their expectations of what others will do, who realize that others are influenced by their expectations of the actor's likely behavior, and who have their own ideas about system effects.[1] This is an area filled with paradoxes and self-reflective phenomena, and any discussion must be tentative and incomplete.

Information, Beliefs, and Action

In some cases actors benefit from being at the same level of understanding and sophistication as their adversary-partners; in other cases, being a step ahead—or behind—is desirable. Not only a little, but also extensive, knowledge can be dangerous. This means that system effects change as actors learn about them and about others' beliefs about them. When I worked at Herman Kahn's Hudson Institute in the early 1960s, a common topic of lunchtime discussion was: Would the U.S. be more secure or less secure if the Soviet Union had institutes like ours? If America's adversaries believed all the writings of Kahn and Schelling? Some of their writings? If they knew we believed them even if they rejected them? Was it better for us to act as

---

[1] Keynes's important observation fits many situations:

Professional investment may be likened to those newspaper competitions in which the competitors have to pick out the six prettiest faces from a hundred photographs, the prize being awarded to the competitor whose choice most nearly corresponds to the average preferences of the competitors as a whole; so that each competitor has to pick, not those faces which he himself finds prettiest, but those which he thinks likeliest to catch the fancy of the competitors, all of whom are looking at the problem from the same point of view. (John Maynard Keynes, *The General Theory of Employment, Interest, and Money* [London: Macmillan, 1936], p. 158)

For more recent discussions of the importance of expectations, see Thomas Schelling, *The Strategy of Conflict* (Cambridge, Mass.: Harvard University Press, 1960), especially pp. 53–80; David Kreps, *Game Theory and Economic Modeling* (New York: Oxford University Press, 1990); Roman Frydman and Edmund Phelps, eds., *Individual Forecasting and Aggregate Outcomes: "Rational Expectations" Examined* (Cambridge: Cambridge University Press, 1983); Cristina Bicchieri and Maria Luisa Dalla Chiara, eds., *Knowledge, Belief, and Strategic Interaction* (New York: Cambridge University Press, 1992); Robert Koons, *Paradoxes of Belief and Strategic Rationality* (New York: Cambridge University Press, 1992).

though we believed that they believed these theories? We never resolved these questions, which made for enjoyable lunches. Indeed, I do not think that they permit definitive answers, but they remind us that the way each side proceeds and the outcomes that result are influenced by the theories that each has about interactions.

We may similarly ask whether the development of game theory has improved human welfare and/or advantaged those who understand its principles. Again, there is not likely to be an unconditional answer. In at least some cases, sophistication may make it harder for actors to reach their goals. For example, naive subjects can cooperate in a single-shot prisoner's dilemma, and when I ask my students to play a multiple-person stag hunt,[2] there is the most cooperation in my introductory class, less in an intermediate course, and least among the graduate students.[3] Learning the principles of microeconomics similarly seems to encourage people to be free riders, with the consequent failure to procure public goods.[4]

In many instances, it is hard to talk about a good or bad strategy in the abstract, divorced from the strategic beliefs of the target actor.[5] At the start of both World Wars, the German military plan worked only because of the strategy chosen by its French adversary. Israel's strategy for deterring what became the War of Attrition failed because Egypt's beliefs were hard to grasp, being not only wrong, but contradictory (Israel could not be defeated in a direct military confrontation, but the artillery bombardment would inflict such pain that Israel would withdraw without escalating).[6]

[2] In Stag Hunt mutual cooperation is everyone's preferred outcome, making this game more benign than prisoner's dilemma.

[3] Of course self-selection may also be at work. I was told by a colleague who taught the introductory social psychology course that almost all his students cooperated in a multiple-person prisoner's dilemma. But this was in California during the 1970s. Critics of the theory and the practice of American security policy might argue that these results indicate the unfortunate effects of teaching our students the "objective truths" about interaction among rational actors.

[4] Gerald Marwell and Ruth Ames, "Economists Ride Free, Does Anyone Else?" *Journal of Public Economics* 15 (June 1981), pp. 295–310; Robert Frank, Thomas Gilovich, and Dennis Regan, "Does Studying Economics Inhibit Cooperation?" *Journal of Economic Perspectives* 7 (Spring 1993), pp. 159–71. See Craig Parks and Anh Vu, "Social Dilemma Behavior of Individuals from Highly Individualist and Collectivist Cultures," *Journal of Conflict Resolution* 38 (December 1994), pp. 708–18, for the argument, indicated by the title, that a person's willingness to contribute to public good is influenced by his culture.

[5] For discussion in terms of communication and interpretation strategies, see Paul Watzlawick, Janet Beavin, and Don Jackson, *Pragmatics of Human Communication: A Study of Interactional Patterns, Pathologies, and Paradoxes* (New York: Norton, 1967), pp. 219–22; also see chapter 2, pp. 44–48 above.

[6] Janice Gross Stein, chapters 3 and 4 in Robert Jervis, Richard Ned Lebow, and Janice Gross Stein, *Psychology and Deterrence* (Baltimore, Md.: Johns Hopkins University Press, 1985); Jonathan Shimshoni, *Israel and Conventional Deterrence* (Ithaca, N.Y.: Cornell Univer-

Israeli decision-makers, like most people, assumed that others saw the world the way they did, which in fact usually is not the case. Indeed, some statements can be true only if most people do not believe them. A stock cannot be "undervalued" if everyone thinks it is, for in that case the price would be bid up to its "proper" level. A broker can in good conscience tell her clients to buy a stock because she can talk to only a few people, or only a few people will believe her,[7] just as only a few people can know of an "undiscovered" restaurant or vacation spot. An interesting political case arose in May 1986 when the U.S. Department of Defense condemned a peace proposal for Central America on the grounds that the Sandinista regime would cheat, resulting in the need for the U.S. to deploy 100,000 soldiers. But if the Sandinistas believed that this sequence of events would occur, the peace plan would have been sound because they would not have expected cheating to succeed.[8]

Effects Depend on Impressions

All social life is permeated by interpretations, many of which are reflective, being products of each actor's estimate of others' beliefs. States as well have to attend to the impressions they are making, impressions that are driven by the implicit theories that others hold about the connections between behavior and the internal dispositions that are thought to influence what the state will do in the future.[9] When the U.S. decided not to respond to the North Korean shooting down of an EC-121 intelligence aircraft in 1969, Secretary of State Rogers said: "The weak can be rash. The powerful must be more

---

sity Press, 1988, chapter 4; Yaacov Bar-Siman-Tov, *The Israeli-Egyptian War of Attrition, 1969–1970* (New York: Columbia University Press, 1980); for a dissent, see Elli Lieberman, "The Egyptian-Israel Rivalry and Deterrence Theory," *Security Studies* 4 (Summer 1995), pp. 878–910.

[7] Timing is crucial here: The broker and her clients assume that many others will indeed buy the stock *after* they have done so. John Kenneth Galbraith's discussion of bubbles of financial speculation stresses the role of foolishness and downplays the rationality of buying a stock of little intrinsic value in the belief that because others value it, you can later sell it for a profit: *A Short History of Financial Euphoria* (New York: Viking, 1993), especially pp. 12–13; but also see pp. 76, 83.

[8] See the stories in the *New York Times* on May 20–22, 1986, which indicate that the leak was denounced by the State Department as an attempt to kill the plan. Perhaps the State Department was not clever enough to understand the implications of the report—or perhaps my analysis is too clever.

[9] See Robert Jervis, *The Logic of Images in International Relations*, 2d. ed. (New York: Columbia University Press, 1989), and Erving Goffman, *The Presentation of Self in Everyday Life* (Garden City, N.Y.: Doubleday, 1959). Also see the discussion of yardsticks, chapter 2, pp. 87–91 above.

restrained."[10] If others indeed did interpret American behavior in this way, then retaliation might have been self-defeating as they would have inferred that the U.S. lacked the strength to ignore this minor pinprick. Even if others did not believe Rogers's rule, if they thought that the U.S. held it they might conclude that its restraint reflected self-confidence and that the U.S. would respond firmly to significant challenges.

Some of the dilemmas facing an actor in this regard are brought out by the question of whether a gesture of confidence will have the desired effect. Like the crucial qualities of credibility and reputation, confidence is inferred by observers who know that the actor is vitally concerned with the inferences they draw. But the very fact that everyone knows that these impressions are so important increases the chances that they will not be drawn in a straightforward way, thereby complicating matters for both actors and observers. Thus the latter may believe that acts which at first glance show confidence are likely to be taken only when the situation is desperate. When the leader of a government, business, or university is under attack, is he really helped by a statement that his party or board has "full faith and confidence" in him?[11] On the other hand, if audiences expect such a statement to be forthcoming, they may be even more alarmed by its absence. Furthermore, the notion of confidence itself is at least partly interactive in that the faith that one person can have in a leader is in part a function of his estimate of the confidence that others have.

These dynamics operate strongly in the financial arena: "Monetary strength is often a confidence game where perceptions create realities."[12] But because everyone knows that this is the game, assertions of confidence can backfire. For example, the fate of the Continental Illinois National Bank and Trust Company may have been sealed by the unprecedented press release issued by the U.S. comptroller of the currency:

[10] Quoted in Seymour Hersh, *The Price of Power: Kissinger in the Nixon White House* (New York: Summit Books, 1973), p. 72.

[11] It is not clear how observers, including General Colin Powell, interpreted President Bush's expression of confidence in him in the wake of the failure of the U.S. military to support an attempted coup against General Noriega in 1989: Bob Woodward, *The Commanders* (New York: Pocket Books, 1991), pp. 101–2. For the reception of an endorsement of the credentials of Judge Carswell, Nixon's nominee to the Supreme Court, by his peers, see Richard Harris, *Decision* (New York: Dutton, 1971), pp. 139–40.

[12] Diane Kunz, *The Economic Diplomacy of the Suez Crisis* (Chapel Hill: University of North Carolina Press, 1991), p. 101. For an interesting discussion of confidence in the context of trade liberalization, financial reforms, and investment in the Third World, see Paul Krugman, "Dutch Tulips and Emerging Markets," *Foreign Affairs* 74 (July/August 1995), pp. 28–44. It is not surprising that a study of the recent introduction of a skilled counterfeit $100 bill found that "the Federal Reserve and the Treasury don't fear the [forgery] itself as much as they fear a confidence problem that might result if they publicly acknowledge it and countenance a large-scale investigation": Frederic Dannen and Ira Silverman, "The Supernote," *The New Yorker*, October 23, 1995, p. 53.

A number of recent rumors concerning Continental Illinois National Bank and Trust Company have caused some concern in the financial markets. The Controller's Office is not aware of any significant changes in the bank's operations, as reflected in its published financial statements, that would serve as the basis for these rumors.[13]

Investors and depositors inferred that only very serious troubles would have prompted a statement of this sort.

Support for an endangered bank or currency may weaken it for the same reason. Thus the announcement of a \$4.5 billion credit package for Continental Illinois only accelerated the run against it; overt government efforts to stabilize financial markets and strengthen the dollar in 1973 failed as actors decided that only an extremely grave situation would have called forth this response; the Louvre Accord of February 1987 "was perceived by the market as a signal of the dollar's weakness rather than its strength, and the resulting run against the dollar brought it well below the Louvre target."[14] Understanding this danger, the British decided not to borrow from the International Monetary Fund when the pound was under great pressure in October 1956. "As Governor of the Bank of England C. F. Cobbold said, financial markets would be better reassured if the bank borrowed when reserves were on the increase, not as now when they were fast draining out of the bank's vaults."[15] Even increasing interest rates may repel rather than attract capital if investors believe the motivation was to bolster the currency.

Threats may be subject to similar interpretive traps. For an actor to threaten is to imply that there is some reason for others to doubt that he will defend his interests: A country rarely needs to announce its intentions to fight back if directly attacked because everyone knows it will.[16] Conversely, controllable and unnecessary actions that would seem to presage a surprise

---

[13] Quoted in Peter Kilborne, "The High-Stakes Scramble to Rescue Continental Bank," *New York Times*, May 21, 1984.

[14] Ibid.; John Odell, *U.S. International Monetary Policy: Markets, Power, and Ideas as Sources of Change* (Princeton, N.J.: Princeton University Press, 1982), pp. 325–26; Giulio Gallaroti, "The Limits of International Organization," *International Organization* 45 (Spring 1991), p. 195. A recent news story (whose claim is summarized in its headline) may have it backwards: Thomas Friedman, "Dollar Steadies Although U.S. Does Not Intervene," *New York Times*, June 23, 1994. The government's apparent confidence that the U.S. economy was so strong that extraordinary measures were not needed may have discouraged speculators from putting pressure on the dollar.

[15] Kunz, *Economic Diplomacy of the Suez Crisis*, p. 112. Companies that feel that their performance will be lower than expected will often release some discouraging news as soon as possible in order to avoid a more severe reaction later. But sometimes the result is a quick and drastic decrease in the stock's price: Susan Antilla, "An Unforgiving Market Punishes Laggards," *New York Times*, July 14, 1992.

[16] If the other side has disclaimed the intention of acting in the undesired way, threats also indicate a lack of faith in this assurance.

attack actually should lead to a different inference, because if the state were planning such a move, it would have behaved differently. Thus the reaction of the British foreign minister at a tense moment in the second Moroccan Crisis was a bit odd: "I have just received a communication from the German Ambassador so stiff that the Fleet might be attacked at any moment."[17]

In much the same way, a leader's statement that war between his country and another is unthinkable contradicts itself because these proclamations are not made when good relations are taken for granted—American and Canadian leaders, for example, do not tell each other that their countries will never fight. At the end of the Munich Conference, Neville Chamberlain thought it very important that he and Hitler declare: "We regard the agreement signed last night and the Anglo-German Naval Agreement as symbolic of the desire of our two peoples never to go to war with one another again. We are resolved that the method of consultation shall be the method adopted to deal with any other questions that may concern our two countries. . . ."[18] If today the American president and Japanese prime minister were to issue a similar statement, most observers would be alarmed.

Lack of Awareness of System Effects

Although behavior is influenced by beliefs about the dynamics of the system, people sometimes think that others will neither anticipate nor react strategically to what they do.[19] While this is sometimes supported by careful thought, often it is an implicit assumption that turns out to be unfounded. Much of Robert McNamara's initial thinking about how American intervention in Vietnam could be controlled rested on the premise that the North would not or could not increase its effort, and many of the American military tactics in the war failed to take account of the changes in enemy behavior they might induce.[20] Those who argue that an arms buildup will make

[17] Quoted in Winston Churchill, *The World Crisis*, abridged ed. (New York: Scribner's, 1931), p. 32.

[18] Quoted in Telford Taylor, *Munich* (Garden City, N.Y.: Doubleday, 1979), p. 62.

[19] Decision makers may also believe that trying to estimate the multiple consequences of their actions will lead to paralysis. This perhaps explains why Kissinger dismissed the attempts by lower-level officials to make him aware of the possible second-order consequences of various American responses to the North Korean shooting down of the American EC-121 electronic surveillance aircraft: see Hersch, *Price of Power*, p. 72.

[20] Deborah Shapley, *Promise and Power: The Life and Times of Robert McNamara* (Boston: Little, Brown, 1993), pp. 314–15, 320, 331 (for George Ball's disagreement on this point, see pp. 311, 314–15, 352; for McNamara's realization that he had miscalculated, see pp. 353–57); Andrew Krepinevich, Jr., *The Army and Vietnam* (Baltimore, Md.: Johns Hopkins University Press, 1986). Perhaps McNamara's later acceptance of the action-reaction explanation for arms races was based in part on his retrospective understanding of the escalatory process in Vietnam,

their country more secure often assume that the adversary will not respond, perhaps because it is already doing all it can to harm the state. In much the same way, many Americans who advocated the vigorous pursuit of defense against strategic missiles matched their proposed weapons against the existing Soviet systems, ignoring possible countermeasures.[21]

If during the Cold War conservatives were more prone than liberals to overestimate their ability to produce desired international outcomes by straightforward policies, the reverse may be the case on domestic issues. Liberals are predisposed to social engineering, with its assumption that others' responses will not nullify the reformers' intent.[22] For example, liberals have been slow to recognize that policies designed to ameliorate the plight of those in unfortunate situations also encourage people to perform antisocial acts in order to take advantage of the benefits. To put this in language that will be useful later, reformers may be prone to overestimate the extent to which people are so constrained that they can change their behavior in only one way.

In addition to not realizing that their behavior will alter what others do, actors may fail to appreciate that others as well as they will react to a changing environment. Thus many university departments take in more graduate students when they believe that many jobs will be available six years later and cut down when they believe that the future will be bleak. This may not be foolish, but the decisions do not seem to have been made with an understanding that others are likely to behave similarly, with the probable result that supply will exceed demand when there are many jobs available and that there may be shortages when jobs are few. While each department is correct to treat both the market and the behavior of others as beyond its control, the result is a boom-and-bust or "cobweb" cycle in which supply alternately

---

although from the start he acknowledged that the sizes of the American and Soviet ICBM programs were linked: Robert Art, "The United States: Nuclear Weapons and Grand Strategy," in Regina Cowen Karp, ed., *Security Without Nuclear Weapons?* (Oxford: Oxford University Press, 1991), p. 78.

[21] The propensity for designers and proponents of weapons to commit this fallacy was noted long ago: Albert Wohlstetter, "Theory and Opposed Systems Design," *Journal of Conflict Resolution* 12 (September 1968), pp. 302–12. More broadly, it can be argued that an awareness of how one's behavior affects others facilitates the development of moral norms: See David Gauthier, *Morals by Agreement* (Oxford: Oxford University Press, 1986). For some time, students of evolution also failed to appreciate the fact that change in one species that gave it a competitive advantage could lead to corresponding changes in others: See the discussion of the "Red Queen" hypothesis in L. Van Valen, "A New Evolutionary Law," *Evolutionary Theory* 1 (1973), pp. 1–30, and Geerat Vermeij, *Evolution and Escalation: An Ecological History of Life* (Princeton, N.J.: Princeton University Press, 1987).

[22] See chapter 2, pp. 61–64, 68–73. Albert Hirschman has noted that two of the main elements of the "rhetoric of reaction" are the "futility thesis" and the "perversity thesis," which are not fully compatible with each other: Hirschman, *The Rhetoric of Reaction* (Cambridge, Mass.: Harvard University Press, 1991).

overshoots and undershoots what would be required for a stable equilibrium, just as is the case when producers increase or decrease their output on the assumption that prices will remain stable, thus rendering this assumption false.

Acting in a System

Much of this book has argued that systems do not easily accommodate our desires. With so many forces responding to each other, unintended consequences abound and the direct path to a goal often takes one in a quite different direction. This seems like a gloomy picture for those who seek change. But there is more to it than that.

To start with, it is important not to exaggerate: "Everything is connected, but some things are more connected than others. The world is a large matrix of interactions in which most of the entries are very close to zero."[23] Meteorology based on chaos theory may tell us that the beating of a butterfly's wings can influence weather patterns halfway around the world, but this does not mean that each time a butterfly moves, it creates storms or sunshine. Although thinking in terms of one-way, linear, and additive processes often misleads, it is unlikely that we could have come to see the world in these terms if this was never appropriate. Indeed, my focus on systems dynamics means that I have not examined areas in which they are infrequent or unimportant. Furthermore, with the possible exception of a few cases in the physical realm, there is no such thing as a system without human intervention. No forests have been untouched by human activities; the notion of an "undisturbed ecology" makes no sense; even—or especially—the purest "free market" is a product of sustained human manipulation. Even if one wanted to, it is simply impossible to "let nature take its course" without interference.

Fortunately, the existence of system effects need not cripple human action.[24] The fact that there is no straightforward way to reach one's goal does

[23] Herbert Simon, "The Organization Complex Systems," in Howard Pattee, ed., *Hierarchy Theory: The Challenge of Complex Systems* (New York: Braziller, 1973), p. 23. For discussions of "nearly decomposable systems," see Simon, *Sciences of the Artificial*, 2d. ed. (Cambridge, Mass.: MIT Press, 1981), pp. 209–19; Albert Ando, Franklin Fisher, and Herbert Simon, *Essays on the Structure of Social Science Models* (Cambridge, Mass.: MIT Press, 1963); and Daniel Metlay, "On Studying the Future Behavior of Complex Systems," in Todd La Porte, ed., *Organized Complexity* (Princeton, N.J.: Princeton University Press, 1975), pp. 220–55; also see above, chapter 1, p. 26. For a related argument in biology, see Stuart Kauffman, *The Origins of Order: Self-Organization and Selection in Evolution* (New York: Oxford University Press, 1993), chapter 6.

[24] For a related argument, see Hirschman, *Rhetoric of Reaction*, p. 75; also see Don Lavoie, "Economic Chaos or Spontaneous Order?" *Cato Journal* 8 (Winter 1989), pp. 619–22. For a

not mean that there is no way at all to reach it. Here we will discuss three general methods of acting when interconnections are prevalent and powerful. First, people can constrain other actors and reduce if not eliminate the extent to which their environment is highly systemic and characterized by unintended consequences. Second, although we have just seen that people often fail to appreciate that they are operating in a system, understanding may enable them to compensate for the results that would otherwise occur. Third, people may be able to proceed toward their goals indirectly and can apply multiple policies, either simultaneously or sequentially, in order to correct for or take advantage of the fact that in a system consequences are multiple. None of this guarantees success, of course. Indeed, when two actors have sharply conflicting interests, both cannot succeed. But human action can be effective in the face of complex interconnections; a systems approach need not induce paralysis.

Constraining

Although an interconnected system is always in motion, the degrees of freedom are not unlimited. Sometimes systems are, or can be rendered, less than completely systemlike in their responsiveness: Situations and policies can box them in and facilitate action; constraint can be induced by foreclosing options and severing interconnections. Many military tactics use some forces to pin the enemy in its position while others surround or attack it.[25] Sometimes an actor can provide similar constraint by anticipating the other's likely reaction and either neutralizing or discounting for it. Thus when Henry Rowan donated $100 million to Glassboro State College, in order to prevent the state of New Jersey from cutting its contribution to the college and thereby taking much of the gift for itself, he specified that none of the

general discussion of how people can behave despite the prevalance of unintended consequences, see Sam Sieber, *Fatal Remedies: The Ironies of Social Intervention* (New York: Plenum, 1981), chapter 12. For parallel discussions in ecology, see the concluding chapter in Nancy Langston, *Forest Dreams, Forest Nightmares: The Paradox of Old Growth in the Inland West* (Seattle: University of Washington Press, 1995); Timothy Allen and Thomas Hoekstra, *Toward a Unified Ecology* (New York: Columbia University Press, 1992), pp. 222–29 and chapter 8; Daniel Botkin, *Discordant Harmonies: A New Ecology for the Twenty-first Century* (New York: Oxford University Press, 1990), chapter 10. Edward Tenner, *Why Things Bite Back: Technology and the Revenge of Unintended Consequences* (New York: Knopf, 1966), also is not totally pessimistic about using technology to improve human life. In international politics, Waltz is correct to note that an understanding of the dynamics of a system does not guarantee that they can be manipulated, but this does not mean that such a result is never possible: *Theory of International Politics* (Reading, Mass.: Addison-Wesley, 1979), pp. 107–11.

[25] Basil Liddell Hart, "The 'Man-in-the-Dark' Theory of War," *National Review* 75 (June 1920), pp. 473–84. In Charles Perrow's terms, these actions make the system more linear and loosely coupled: *Normal Accidents* (New York: Basic Books, 1984).

money could be used for operating expenses or capital projects.[26] The U.S. government deployed a similar approach when it realigned Medicare fees in the fall of 1991. Believing that the existing schedule provided incentives for complex medical procedures at the expense of preventive care, it did more than raise the payments for internal medicine and office visits and cut those for most kinds of surgery:

> The new fee schedule . . . . assumes that doctors losing money under the fee schedule will increase the volume of their medical services or substitute more costly services to recoup half of the income they would lose. To offset the effect of that expected increase, the Government is cutting expected increases in payments across the board.[27]

Many policies are self-defeating because they provide information that allows third parties to take advantage of them, which points toward a related path to effective action. The added proviso to Mr. Rowan's gift would have been unnecessary if the gift could have been kept secret from New Jersey. Although not possible in this case, it is in others. As noted earlier, Marc Trachtenberg argued that if Britain had given a blunt warning to Germany in 1914, the result might have been not deterrence but increased Russian intransigence.[28] But while Trachtenberg assumes that Russia would have learned of the British statement, a private ultimatum might have been possible because Germany would have wanted to keep it secret lest the knowledge produce the effect Trachtenberg foresees. Indeed, when statesmen mediate between two quarreling states, they often urge each to compromise without indicating that they are conveying the same message to the other; when dealing with an ally they may say that they will not support it if it is reckless while telling the other side that it should not assume that their country will stay on the sidelines if a war should develop.[29] Similarly, to

[26] Jerry Gray, "Glassboro State College to Receive a $100 Million Donation," *New York Times*, July 7, 1992. Similarly, a Senate anticrime appropriations bill specified "that state and local governments would not be permitted to use it to replace money that they divert from crime-fighting to other programs": Clifford Krauss, "Senate Approves Broad Crime Bill; Splits Over Guns," ibid., November 20, 1993.

[27] Robert Pear, "Government Realigning Fees Doctors Get Under Medicare," ibid., November 16, 1991.

[28] Marc Trachtenberg, "Mobilization and Inadvertence in the July Crisis," *International Security* 16 (Summer 1991), pp. 200–201. The British ambassador to Germany saw this danger at the time: see his cable in G. P. Gooch and Harold Temperley, eds., *British Documents on the Origins of the War*, vol. 11, *The Outbreak of War* (London: His Majesty's Stationery Office, 1926), p. 361. This problem also plagued Western policy in the former Yugoslavia: see, for example, Paul Lewis, "As Muslim Line Hardens, Serbs and Croats Halt Peace Talks," *New York Times*, August 5, 1993, and Elaine Sciolino, "U.S. Termed Ready to Press Bosnians to Accept Division," ibid., February 11, 1994.

[29] For examples, see Donald Kagan, *On the Origins of War and the Preservation of Peace* (New York: Doubleday, 1995), pp. 149, 393; Robert McMahon, *Cold War on the Periphery:*

meet a social need without creating a moral hazard problem, providers of a service may be able to restrict information about it, as a rock festival does when it refrains from publicizing the availability of free medical care, and when those in charge of a dangerous facility refrain from constantly reminding the operators of its redundant safety features.

Anticipating System Effects

Over fifty years ago, Carl Friedrich explained that our understanding of power had to include "the rule of anticipated reactions"—people might seem to be getting all that they wanted only because they had trimmed their demands to what they expected others to grant; a senator might always be on the winning side because she chose her position by estimating who would win; active power might not be displayed because others, fearing the consequences if it were, have preemptively complied.[30] A good deal of behavior can be similarly explained by actors' anticipation of expected system effects. Many of the common patterns can be discussed under the somewhat overlapping categories of the Lijphart effect, the Domino Theory Paradox, acting by twos, and quasi-homeostasis. They show that effective action can come as actors compensate for the dynamics that would otherwise operate.

The Lijphart Effect

Many undesired consequences cannot be foreseen. But on more than a few occasions, the belief that undesired results are likely if decision makers do not take unusual steps may lead them to take such steps and prevent the "natural" outcome from occurring. This is Arend Lijphart's explanation for why many countries are stable in spite of—or really because of—the presence of factors that predispose them toward instability. In studying democracy in the Netherlands, he found that the circumstances were not propitious. The population was divided by reinforcing cleavages of ethnicity, language, and religion. Common sense and many social-science theories predicted that the result would be violence if not civil war. The reason this did not happen, Lijphart discovered, was that the leaders understood that this was a likely outcome, did not want it to come about, and so crafted a

---

The United States, India, and Pakistan (New York: Columbia University Press, 1994), p. 296; René Albrecht-Carrié, Britain and France: Adaptations to a Changing Context of Power (Garden City, N.Y.: Doubleday, 1970), p. 115.

[30] Carl Friedrich, Constitutional Government and Democracy (Boston: Ginn and Company, 1937), pp. 589–91. For a good discussion, see Jack Nagel, The Descriptive Analysis of Power (New Haven, Conn.: Yale University Press, 1975), pp. 15–19.

policy of moderation and compromise. This happens in other countries as well.[31]

The basic dynamic is a form of what Albert Hirschman calls an "action-arousing gloomy vision."[32] If it is believed that a danger can be coped with by strenuous efforts, the anticipation of it can lead people to struggle to overcome it. Thus one study of why the horrifying forecasts of global starvation have not so far turned out to be correct argues that they "resulted in tremendous efforts to increase food output."[33] Similar logic led Walt Rostow, Johnson's national security advisor, to see a benefit in France's withdrawal from NATO's military machinery: "some European anxiety, if not excessive, could help diminish complacency about European security."[34] More generally, an awareness of the difficulty of procuring public goods can lead people to establish ingenious arrangements to secure them, even if conventional academic theories indicate that these results are not likely to succeed.[35]

People take advantage of these processes for more manipulative purposes as well. In the 1970s, one reason why "hard-line" critics of American policy argued that the U.S. was falling dangerously behind the USSR in military

[31] Arend Lijphart, *The Politics of Accommodation: Pluralism and Democracy in the Netherlands* (Berkeley: University of California Press, 1968); Lijphart, *Democracy in Plural Societies: A Comparative Exploration* (New Haven, Conn.: Yale University Press, 1977); Jurg Steiner and Robert H. Dorff, *A Theory of Political Decision Modes: Intraparty Decision Making in Switzerland* (Chapel Hill: University of North Carolina Press, 1980).

[32] Albert Hirschman, *A Bias for Hope: Essays on Development in Latin America* (New Haven, Conn.: Yale University Press, 1971), pp. 284, 350–53; also see Hirschman, *Rhetoric of Reaction*, pp. 153–54. A sociologist notes that "theories about interrupted self-fulfilling prophecies are the meat and potatoes of evaluative research": Michael Faia, *Dynamic Functionalism: Strategy and Tactics* (Cambridge: Cambridge University Press, 1986), p. 90. Often an outcome that seems inevitable in retrospect was the product of actors behaving on the premise that it was not. For a good example of a pessimistic report spurring action, see Harris, *Decision*, p. 116.

[33] Peter Drucker, "The Changed World Economy," *Foreign Affairs* 64 (Spring 1986), p. 771. Similarly, an analysis of the prospects for health reform legislation in the spring of 1994 quoted an informed observer as saying "We face the real possibility of things falling apart" and then commented: "Paradoxically, that very fear will be one of the strongest factors forcing a compromise" (Robin Toner, "Fear of Defeat Clouds Debate on Health Care Bill," *New York Times*, June 19, 1994). Sometimes the prophecy comes from an outside source: One reason why the USSR did not face an oil shortage in the 1980s may have been that it increased its investments in response to the Western predictions that production would decline.

[34] Quoted in Frank Ninkovich, *Modernity and Power: A History of the Domino Theory in the Twentieth Century* (Chicago: University of Chicago Press, 1994), p. 283. More broadly, peace in Europe may be guaranteed by the American military presence, which all parties want to see maintained so that old fears and rivalries do not reassert themselves: Robert Art, "Why Western Europe Needs the United States and NATO," *Political Science Quarterly* 111 (Spring 1996), pp. 1–39.

[35] Eleanor Ostrom, *Governing the Commons* (New York: Cambridge University Press, 1990).

power was that they hoped that those who were persuaded would join them in working for change. (But if change proved beyond reach, the argument would have made the situation worse by leading American and Soviet statesmen to believe that the prevailing distribution of power gave the latter usable advantage.) Similarly, in July 1992, U.S. officials probably were trying to put pressure on the Europeans when they said that the recent economic summit meeting had failed to produce progress toward a trade agreement.[36]

The Lijphart Effect can help transform a dangerous situation into a safer one. Whenever two actors find their relations becoming unusually tense, fear a natural cycle of escalation, and want to avoid that outcome, they may concert to change the trajectory. Thus when the U.S. Congress recessed in August 1989, one astute observer said:

> Given the way each chamber started out, it is surprising they have [produced] as much [legislation] as they have. The bitter struggles over John Tower's nomination to be Secretary of Defense and [former Speaker of the House] Jim Wright's fate have been, if not forgotten, largely subdued—through the efforts of the Democratic leaders in both chambers and acts of will on the part of many members who thought that things were getting out of hand.[37]

The point made in the last phrase explains why this result is not so surprising after all. Similarly, in international politics the awareness of being in a crisis often is a necessary condition for bringing it to a peaceful end and the belief that allies have conflicting interests can lead them to treat each other with care. A *New York Times* reporter states the commonsense view of post–Cold War Franco-American relations:

> Strains between the two countries have long existed. But while differences were mostly contained during the Cold War within the broad sense that the countries saw eye to eye on the key issues, that certainty now seems to have fallen away in a Europe that the French hope may become as powerful as the United States.[38]

A quite conflictful outcome is indeed possible, especially if French leaders see this as a way of dividing Europe from the U.S. and asserting French leadership. But if French and American statesmen understand the new situation and want American troops to remain in Europe, they will seek to keep their disputes within bounds and interrupt the natural cycle of tit-for-tat retaliation. During the Cold War France and the U.S. had no choice but to support each other if the situation became really tense; now, however, they will need to consciously modulate their relations.

[36] Keith Bradsher, "Some U.S. Officials Remain Skeptical on Trade Progress," *New York Times*, July 12, 1992.

[37] Elizabeth Drew, "Letter from Washington," *The New Yorker*, August 28, 1989, p. 81.

[38] Roger Cohen, "U.S.-French Relations Turn Icy After Cold War," *New York Times*, July 2, 1992.

A comparison of British and American intelligence organizations reveals a similar dynamic. The latter has a "strong center [which] enables it to tolerate more diversity, even encourage it." In the U.K., intelligence resides in various branches of the government and has no equivalent to the Director of Central Intelligence. One might think that this system would be more conflictful and less regulated than the American one. In fact, the expectation of this outcome means that the opposite is the case. "The British system sets considerable store by set procedures and formal consensus; as a departmental, collegial system . . . it needs procedures and cannot stand too much dissent."[39]

The Lijphart Effect can operate within actors as well. A person who knows that she is prone to lose her temper may have fewer fits of anger than someone who is generally calm because the former, knowing what will happen if she is not careful, may go out of her way to avoid situations that would make her mad and devote great energy to keeping control. President Truman often made quick and clear decisions in order to overcome his natural indecisiveness and develop the image—and perhaps the self-image—that he desired. Collectivities may similarly build on self-diagnosis to avoid behaviors that they know they would otherwise engage in. Norman Angell argued that while public opinion was often irresponsible and likely to favor the unnecessary use of force, the knowledge of this propensity could inoculate against it.

> We cannot make democracy a successful thing unless we recognize that we are prone to folly. Then we may avoid that folly. It's like a shipmaster who says, "There are no reefs I need bother about." If he takes that line he'll wreck his ship. But if he says, "Of course there are reefs . . . ," then he'll probably be safe.[40]

The Domino Theory Paradox

Students of Chinese foreign policy have noted that domestic disturbances in that country seem to lead to foreign policy belligerence. The connection is not the common hope to create domestic unity by generating a foreign threat: Rather, because PRC leaders believe that other countries will expect them to be weak during periods of domestic unrest, they need to disprove these expectations by behaving with particular firmness.[41] External events

[39] Michael Herman, "Assessment Machinery: British and American Models," *Journal of Intellligence and National Security* 10 (October 1995), p. 27.

[40] Quoted in J. D. B. Miller, *Norman Angell and the Futility of War* (London: Macmillan, 1986), p. 129.

[41] Allen Whiting, *The Chinese Calculus of Deterrence* (Ann Arbor: University of Michigan Press, 1975); Melvin Gurtov and Byong-Moo Hwang, *China Under Threat: The Politics of Strategy and Diplomacy* (Baltimore, Md.: Johns Hopkins University Press, 1980).

can also create the fear that others will see the state as weak and can similarly lead it to be particularly belligerent. Even if the U.S. did not use atomic bombs against Japan to intimidate the Soviet Union, in the following months Stalin probably felt it necessary to be recalcitrant lest the Americans believe that he was unduly concerned.[42]

The most important form of this dynamic is the Domino Theory Paradox. The domino theory holds that even small defeats produce positive feedback because the state's adversaries and allies will infer that it is weak and prone to retreat in other conflicts. But statesmen who believe the theory and who suffer limited defeats may act especially boldly to try to show that the theory is incorrect, or at least does not apply to them. In seeking to prevent the operation of the anticipated dynamics, statesmen then disconfirm the theory. Assistant Secretary of State for Southeast Asia William Bundy recalls that "the decision to compromise in Laos [in 1961] made it essential to convey by word and deed that the United States would stand firm in South Vietnam and the rest of Southeast Asia."[43] President Kennedy felt the same way: "There are limits to the number of defeats I can defend in one twelve-month period. I've had the Bay of Pigs and pulling out of Laos, and I can't accept a third."[44] According to Nixon's chief of staff, after having to make concessions to end the postal workers' strike in 1970, the president sought to "fire a bunch of [air controllers] to prove government workers can't win by striking."[45]

Henry Kissinger was particularly prone to thinking in this way, perhaps because he had studied the domino theory. After Nixon decided not to re-

[42] Fraser Harbutt, *The Iron Curtain: Churchill, America, and the Origins of the Cold War* (New York: Oxford University Press, 1986), p. 126. But also see David Holloway, *Stalin and the Bomb* (New Haven, Conn.: Yale University Press, 1994), pp. 155–58 and chapters 11–12. For the more general argument that Stalin was driven to act boldly, if not recklessly, for fear of revealing Soviet weakness, see Philip Taubman, *Stalin's American Policy* (New York: Norton, 1982), and Henry Kissinger, *Diplomacy* (New York: Simon and Schuster, 1994), pp. 439–40.

[43] Quoted in William Gibbons, *The U.S. Government and the Vietnam War*, part 2 (Princeton, N.J.: Princeton University Press, 1986), p. 41; also see pp. 23–25, 32.

[44] Quoted in Arthur Schlesinger, Jr., *Robert Kennedy and His Times* (Boston: Houghton Mifflin, 1978), p. 761. McNamara similarly reports that the Soviet pressure on Berlin was one reason he felt that the U.S. had to protect Vietnam: Robert McNamara, *In Retrospect: The Tragedy and Lessons of Vietnam* (New York: Times Books, 1995), p. 32. For a less extreme example, see Bernard Weintraub, "Airline Dispute: Rite of Passage for Bush," *New York Times*, March 3, 1989. See Glenn Snyder and Paul Diesing, *Conflict among Nations* (Princeton, N.J.: Princeton University Press, 1977), p. 189, for a discussion of the related "never again" response to a defeat. Recent quantitative analysis supports this position; Kevin Wang, "Presidential Responses to Foreign Policy Crises," *Journal of Conflict Resolution* 40 (March 1966), pp. 68–97.

[45] H. R. Haldeman, *The Haldeman Diaries: Inside the Nixon White House* (New York: Putnam, 1994), pp. 145–46. The impulse to strike back after having been humiliated can also have psychological roots, especially for people with personalities like Nixon's: Blema Steinberg, *Shame and Humiliation: Presidential Decision Making on Vietnam* (Pittsburgh: University of Pittsburgh Press, 1996).

spond strongly to the downing of the EC-121, he declared: "They got away with it this time, but they'll never get away with it again."[46] Two years later, he justified his policy in the clash between India and Pakistan in similar terms: "I told Nixon that precisely because we were retreating from Vietnam we could not permit the impression to be created that all issues could be settled by naked force."[47] Shortly after the fall of Saigon, he said that "the United States must carry out some act somewhere in the world which shows its determination to continue to be a world power,"[48] which helps explain why the U.S. was so quick to use force when the Cambodians seized the *Mayaguez*. The American intervention in Grenada may have been similarly motivated: The Reagan administration came into office believing that American credibility had been damaged by the behavior of its predecessor, particularly by its weak responses to hostage taking in Iran and the Soviet invasion of Afghanistan.[49] Eisenhower's intervention in Lebanon in 1958 also may have been driven by the fear that his inability to prevent the overthrow of the friendly regime in Iraq, coming on top of his opposition to Britain and France in the Suez crisis, had created the impression that the U.S. would not use force to protect its allies. More peacefully, one reason for Eisenhower's support for the Volta Dam in Ghana was the loss of credibility in the Third World resulting from his rebuffing Nasser over the Aswan Dam.[50]

---

[46] Quoted in Richard Nixon, *RN: The Memoirs of Richard Nixon* (New York: Grosset & Dunlop, 1978) p. 385. Kissinger's memory is parallel: "I told [Nixon] that failure to demand some redress or to engage in some retaliatory action would make it probable that he would have to act more boldly later on" (Kissinger, *White House Years*, [Boston: Little, Brown, 1979], p. 319). According to Haldeman, Kissinger went further and argued (in Haldeman's words): "If we don't retaliate in Korea we'll have to either find another similar incident in three or four weeks, or go with [the plans to bomb] in Cambodia" (Haldeman, *Diaries*, p. 51).

[47] Kissinger, *White House Years*, p. 886.

[48] Quoted in Tom Braden, "Why Are We Looking for Problems?" *Washington Post*, April 14, 1975.

[49] According to one official, "This Administration came to power with the intention of punching someone in the nose": quoted in Richard Gabriel, *Military Incompetence* (New York: Hill and Wang, 1985), p. 150.

[50] Robert McMahon, "Credibility and World Power: Exploring the Psychological Dimension in Postwar American Diplomacy," *Diplomatic History* 15 (Fall 1991), pp. 464–65; Gerald Thomas, "The Black Revolt: The United States and Africa in the 1960s," in Diane Kunz, ed., *Crucial Decade: American Foreign Relations During the 1960s*. (New York: Columbia University Press, 1994), p. 335. For examples from the Kennedy presidency see Michael Beschloss, *The Crisis Years* (New York: HarperCollins, 1991), pp. 123–24, 225, 350, and Richard Ned Lebow and Janice Gross Stein, *We All Lost the Cold War* (Princeton, N.J.: Princeton University Press, 1994), pp. 44–45. There is some evidence that one reason why Stalin approved the North Korean attack was that he believed that if the U.S. lost South Korea it would have to protect Taiwan, thereby precluding a Sino-American rapprochment: Kathryn Weathersby, "Soviet Aims in Korea and the Origins of the Korean War, 1945–1950: New Evidence From Russian Archives" (Washington, D.C.: Cold War International History Project, Woodrow Wilson International Center for Scholars, Working Paper no. 8, November 1993), p. 31.

Although the Cold War heightened concern with perceptions of resolve and although American decision-makers may be particularly preoccupied with the domino theory,[51] as long as states fear the consequences of being seen as weak, have been forced to retreat, and believe that they can regain their reputations, the Domino Theory Paradox can operate. As the German foreign minister put it in the second Moroccan Crisis: "When our prestige in foreign lands is lowered we must fight."[52] The same reasoning operated during the great power conference called to settle the Balkan War of 1913. The normal conflict arose between Russia and Austria, who respectively supported and opposed Serbian claims. After Russia was forced to withdraw its demand for a Serbian port on the Adriatic, the major remaining issue was the fate of the town of Scutari, claimed by both Montenegro, an ally of Serbia, and the newly created state of Albania. Contrary to the expectations of the domino theory, the Russian foreign minister informed his British counterpart "that, after his concession regarding Serbia's port, he could hardly give way over Scutari as well."[53] The need to compensate for previous defeats was felt in 1914, with even more serious consequences: "The Russians had backed away from war on Serbia's behalf in 1909, and failed to support the Serbs in October 1913 against the Austrian ultimatum requiring their evacuation of Albania. But precisely the memory of the past stiffened the Russians' resolve not to be humiliated again."[54] A. J. P. Taylor's explanation of British policy in the summer of 1939 is less plausible, but still has some truth:

> The British government were trapped not so much by their guarantee to Poland, as by their relations with Czechoslovakia. With her they had imposed concession; towards her they had failed to honor their guarantee. They could not go back on their word again, if they were to keep any respect in the world or with their own people.[55]

Regardless of the validity of this historical example, if our argument is correct then we should find dynamics that parallel the Domino Theory Paradox with other characteristics that the actor will feel great pressure to re-

[51] Patrick Morgan, "Saving Face for the Sake of Deterrence," in Jervis, Lebow, and Stein, *Psychology and Deterrence*, pp. 125–52.

[52] Quoted in Ima Barlow, *The Agadir Crisis* (New York: Archon, 1971), p. 327; for a similar case, see William Stueck, *The Korean War: An International History* (Princeton, N.J.: Princeton University Press, 1995), p. 231.

[53] C. J. Lowe and M. L. Dockrill, *The Mirage of Power*, vol. 1, *British Foreign Policy, 1902–1914* (London: Routledge & Kegan Paul, 1972), p. 112. In the end, Russia was forced to back down but at least was able to gain British support in a related dispute.

[54] David Stevenson, *The First World War and International Politics* (Oxford: Oxford University Press, 1988), p. 29.

[55] A. J. P. Taylor, *The Origins of the Second World War* (New York: Fawcett, 1966), p. 207. For another example, see John Offner, *An Unwanted War: The Diplomacy of the United States and Spain Over Cuba, 1895–1898* (Chapel Hill: University of North Carolina Press, 1992), p. 119.

plenish or repair when they are perceived to be depleted or damaged. Thus one scholar of the eighteenth-century British political economy notes that "the shock of the South Sea Bubble and of the painful financial reconstruction that followed helped secure a high level of financial probity thereafter."[56] Demonstrating one's trustworthiness will be especially important after an incident that reveals that, at least on occasion, one in fact cannot be trusted. Shortly after Trujillo's international standing was lowered by his massacre of Haitians, he offered to accept 100,000 Jewish refugees (although he later reneged).[57]

This dynamic can also work in reverse: If actors have established a reputation for being brave, decisive, or strong, they can afford some behavior to the contrary. A state that has prevailed in a series of confrontations may feel that it can now retreat. For example, Russia might have been able to put pressure on Serbia in 1914 if it had provided support in the previous confrontations, just as Walt Rostow told President Kennedy that once the U.S. prevailed in the conflicts over Berlin and Vietnam, it could "provide a golden bridge of retreat from their present aggressive positions for both Moscow and Peking."[58] Indeed, after the Cuban Missile Crisis, Kennedy was able to pursue a more conciliatory policy toward the Soviet Union than he had before.[59]

Intriguingly, decision makers who understand the Domino Theory Paradox may expect a country that has been forced to back down in one confrontation to stand firm in the next. It was this reasoning that led a Soviet diplomat to oppose Kim Il Sung's request to invade South Korea in the fall of 1949: "After their lack of success in China, the Americans probably will intervene in Korean affairs more decisively than they did in China and, it goes without saying, apply all their strength to save Syngmann Rhee."[60] Similarly, shortly after the American defeat in Vietnam, Brezhnev said:

[56] John Brewer, *The Sinews of Power* (New York: Knopf, 1989), p. 126. For a related case, see Stanley Kutler, *Privilege and Creative Destruction: The Charles River Bridge Case* (Baltimore, Md.: Johns Hopkins University Press, 1990), pp. 51–52; for the expectation of similar dynamics with morale, see Uri Bar-Joseph, "Israel Caught Unaware: Egypt's Sinai Surprise of 1960," *International Journal of Intelligence and Counterintelligence* 8 (Summer 1995), p. 207.

[57] Eric Paul Roorda, "Genocide Next Door: The Good Neighbor Policy, the Trujillo Regime, and the Haitian Massacre of 1937," *Diplomatic History* 20 (Summer 1996), p. 303.

[58] Quoted in Gibbons, *The Vietnam War*, p. 25.

[59] For other examples, see Thomas Schwartz, "Victories and Defeats in the Long Twilight Struggle: The United States and Western Europe in the 1960s," in Kunz, ed., *The Crucial Decade*, p. 126, and M. B. Cooper, "British Policy in the Balkans, 1908–9," *Historical Journal* 7 (June 1964), pp. 278–79. This process can be turned against the actor: In January 1963 the Soviets told Kennedy that to gain a test ban agreement he should accept their offer of only a handful of on-site inspections because thanks to the missile crisis he enjoyed "great personal strength and prestige and hence can afford to circumvent Congress" (quoted in Beschloss, *Crisis Years*, p. 577; also see p. 620).

[60] "Telegram from Tunkin to Soviet Foreign Ministry, 14 September 1949," translated by Kathryn Weathersby, *Cold War International History Project Bulletin*, no. 5 (Spring 1995), p. 7.

> The fact is that to these defeats in social battles, to the loss of colonial possessions, . . . aggressive circles of the capitalist world react by furiously unleashing military preparations. They inflate their defense budgets, . . . build military bases, and undertake military demonstrations.[61]

Almost seventy years earlier, a high-ranking member of the British Foreign Office similarly argued that a minor squabble with Germany gave "cause [for] legitimate anxiety" because "we know of the existence of a strong and pent-up feeling of rage in Germany at the want of success she has lately had in the domain of foreign policy."[62]

Statesmen who reason this way will call for caution rather than increased pressure after the other side has suffered a defeat. This means that both the state that has retreated and its adversary will behave oppositely from what the domino theory predicts as they understand that the former will have to try to disconfirm it. Furthermore, if the defending state foresees this sequence, it can safely retreat in the first instance, secure in the knowledge that this will enable it to stand firm next time. We have come full circle: The common knowledge that dominoes will fall unless strong measures are taken leads people to anticipate such measures, and this expectation both makes later resistence less risky and removes the need to prevail in the initial confrontation.[63]

Doing Things "In Twos"

A more general form of the dynamics described in the previous section is the tendency for people to act "in twos" when they fear that a single action will produce an undesired relationship or an unbalanced impression. I owe the phrase to Wallace Thies, who explains that the U.S. tried to orchestrate its policy in Vietnam by pairing coercive bombing with diplomatic overtures. In a variant of the familiar notion of combining carrots and sticks, American statesmen felt that while bombing would put pressure on the adversary, if

---

But it is also quite possible that the American refusal to intervene in China led Stalin to believe that it would not fight for Korea.

[61] *Pravda*, October 26, 1976, pp. 2–3; I am grateful to Ted Hopf for this citation and translation.

[62] Eyre Crowe, in G. P. Gooch and Harold Temperley, eds., *British Documents on the Origins of the War*, vol. 7, *The Agadir Crisis* (London: His Majesty's Stationery Office, 1932), p. 90. Crowe accurately anticipated the sentiments of the German foreign minister: see above, p. 269. Other examples can be found in Jonathan Mercer, *Reputation and International Politics* (Ithaca, N.Y.: Cornell University Press, 1996).

[63] What happens if only one side believes the domino theory or if both sides fully understand the paradox and try to take advantage of it is less clear; as noted earlier, behavior and interactions are highly sensitive to beliefs about them.

undertaken in isolation it might lead the North to believe that the U.S. would respond only to force. Diplomatic overtures carried the opposite danger of appearing weak. Proper policy, then, would combine both instruments.[64] NATO's "dual track" policy of moving to deploy Intermediate Range Forces (INF) while simultaneously seeking agreements that would make it unnecessary to do so was more successful and, like American policy in Vietnam, was designed to meet the demands of domestic as well as international audiences.

Relatedly, actors use paired moves to generate a desired impression about their general policies and future intentions. It was not a coincidence that in the spring of 1951 Truman coupled the firing of General MacArthur with the adoption of many of his proposals.[65] Three years later Eisenhower wanted the French and the Vietminh to believe that while he might provide more assistance to the former, he was not committed to doing so. So shortly after he sent Air Force mechanics to Indochina, he made a strongly anti-interventionist statement at a press conference.[66]

Countries also move in twos to try to establish the desired degree of friendship and hostility toward others. Contemporary and later observers may see the combination as vacillating and inconsistent (and sometimes it is), but often it represents the desire to strike the right balance.[67] Thus when Russia signed a convention settling Persian issues with Great Britain

[64] Wallace Thies, *When Governments Collide: Coercion and Diplomacy in the Vietnam Conflict, 1964–68* (Berkeley: University of California Press, 1980). Johnson explained to his advisors: "We've got to use both hands. It's like a prizefight. Our right is our military power, but our left must be our peace proposals. Every time you move troops forward, you move diplomats foward" (quoted in Brian VanDeMark, *Into the Quagmire: Lyndon Johnson and the Escalation of the Vietnam War* (New York: Oxford University Press, 1991), pp. 201–2; both the U.S. and the PRC adopted a similar approach at some points during the Korean War: See Steuck, *Korean War*, pp. 280, 285. As Thies explains, the policy failed in part because it could not be implemented as designed, although it seems doubtful that any feasible American actions could have produced an agreement at that time. Neville Chamberlain's approach of combining limited rearmament with the search for negotiated settlements with Nazi Germany was sometimes called a "double policy"; it could not have succeeded because no meaningful agreements could be made with Hitler. For a further discussion of the use of multiple policies where no one by itself would work, see pp. 291–94 below.

[65] Laura Belmonte, "Anglo-American Relations and the Dismissal of MacArthur," *Diplomatic History* 19 (Fall 1995), pp. 641–68; the British both welcomed his relief and "feared that [it] signified a more aggressive American policy" (ibid., p. 664).

[66] Melanie Billings-Yun, *Decision Against War: Eisenhower and Dien Bien Phu, 1954* (New York: Columbia University Press, 1988), p. 27. The American public also was a target of this mixed message.

[67] See, for example, the American analysis of Jordan's policy toward the Palestinian guerrillas in 1969–70: Douglas Little, "A Puppet in Search of a Puppeteer? The United States, King Hussein, and Jordan, 1953–1970," *International History Review* 17 (August 1995), p. 540. For an example from domestic politics, see Alan Cowell, "Germans Sentenced in Arson Killing of Turks," *New York Times*, October 14, 1995.

in 1907, a move it realized that Germany could readily interpret as hostile, it also moved to reduce some of its conflicts with that country.[68] Actors may also cooperate in one area in response to excessive levels of conflict in others. For example, Roosevelt made concessions to the Soviet Union over the Far East at Yalta not only to encourage the Soviets to enter the war against Japan "but also to preserve his now threatened overall relationship with Stalin."[69] Similarly, Soviet leaders took a conciliatory stance on the Berlin issue in 1969 to reduce the tensions they had created by invading Czechoslovakia the year before; when President Bush decided to sell F-16s to Taiwan he also waived restrictions on the export of several high-technology projects to the PRC; statistical analysis indicates as U.S.-Japanese trade friction increases, so does political cooperation.[70] Because Soviet-American tensions were high in the mid-1980s, the Stockholm conference on European security and cooperation produced "serious negotiations rather than . . . fruitless propaganda encounters. . . . The adverse political climate . . . provided a strong motivation to use the Conference to improve the East-West relationship."[71] As the French foreign minister put it when justifying discussions with the USSR after the latter's invasion of Afghanistan, "Dialogue is never more necessary than in a period of crisis."[72]

Allies, too, adjust their behavior in response to events that have created unusual frictions. As Eisenhower wrote Churchill in the wake of Suez:

[68] Glenn Snyder, "Alliances, Balance, and Stability," *International Organization* 45 (Winter 1991), p. 128.

[69] Harbutt, *The Iron Curtain*, p. 90. More recently, the U.S. dropped its opposition to relaxing the treaty restrictions on Russian military deployments in the Caucasus "in order to reduce tensions with Moscow" which had been increased by conflicts over several issues, especially the NATO bombing of Bosnian Serbs: Steven Greenhouse, "Arms Treaty Restrictions on Russia Eased," *New York Times*, September 16, 1995.

[70] Jonathan Dean, "Berlin in a Divided Germany," in Alexander George, Philip Farley, and Alexander Dallin, eds., *U.S.-Soviet Security Cooperation: Achievements, Failures, Lessons* (New York: Oxford University Press, 1988), p. 99; "Security Developments in Northeast Asia," *Asian Defence Journal*, October 1992, p. 14; Renee Marlin-Bennett, Alan Rosenblatt, and Jianxin Wang, "The Visible Hand: The United States, Japan, and the Management of Trade Disputes," *International Interactions* 17, no. 3 (1992), pp. 191–213.

[71] James Goodby, "The Stockholm Conference: Negotiating a Cooperative Security System for Europe," in George, Farley, and Dallin, eds., *U.S.-Soviet Security Cooperation*, pp. 152, 169–70. The high level of tension similarly largely explains the restarting of Soviet-American arms control talks in the mid-1980s. Janice Stein argues that calculations like this underpinned the security cooperation between Israel and Egypt in 1977: Janice Stein, "A Common Aversion to War: Regime Creation by Egypt and Israel as a Strategy of Conflict Management," in Gabriel ben-Dor and David Dewitt, eds., *Sources and Management of Conflict in the Middle East* (Lexington, Mass.: D.C. Heath, 1987), pp. 59–77.

[72] Quoted in Robert Legvold, "France and Soviet Policy," in Herbert Ellison, ed., *Soviet Policy Toward Western Europe* (Seattle: University of Washington Press, 1983), pp. 69–70. Although Carter objected, Secretary of State Vance's views were quite similar: Cyrus Vance, *Hard Choices* (New York: Simon and Schuster, 1983), pp. 394–95.

"Nothing saddens me more than the thought that I and my old friends of years have met a problem concerning which we do not see eye to eye. I shall never be happy until our old-time closeness has been restored."[73] While one may wonder if there was quite as much sentiment in it as this, the U.S. did make a number of gestures and concessions, just as Carter favored deployment of intermediate-range nuclear missiles to compensate for having cut the ground out from under NATO by his last-minute decision not to develop the neutron bomb.[74] It is not only the major partner that acts this way: Helmut Schmidt endorsed the American boycott of the Moscow Olympics after the Soviet invasion of Afghanistan although he had no faith in this gesture because he needed to reduce the frictions with America that had arisen over the previous years. Indeed, Schmidt's trip to Washington in March 1980 went well largely because he and Carter recognized that their relations were strained.[75]

The same pattern is to be found in triangular relations. In 1970–71 China moved toward a rapprochement with the U.S. and, ceteris paribus, the result would have been conflict with North Vietnam, which was fighting the U.S. Anticipating this consequence, "Chinese leaders had to adopt measures strongly supportive of Hanoi's struggle."[76] When the U.S. increased its support for Pakistan in response to the Soviet invasion of Afghanistan, it sim-

---

[73] Dwight D. Eisenhower, *Waging Peace* (Garden City, N.Y.: Doubleday, 1965), p. 681; also see McGeorge Bundy, *Danger and Survival* (New York: Random House, 1988), p. 471, and Thomas Risse-Kappen, *Cooperation Among Democracies: The European Influence on U.S. Foreign Policy* (Princeton, N.J.: Princeton University Press, 1995), pp. 98–99. One reason for the crisis was that British and American leaders thought that their countries were so close that the other would not act against the common interest. For Eisenhower and Churchill moving to repair strained Anglo-American relations created by a serious dispute over policy in Korea, see Stueck, *Korean War*, p. 324.

[74] At the same time that the Dutch government announced its willingness to accept bases for the new missiles, it also drew back other NATO commitments: Ivo Daalder, *The Nature and Practice of Flexible Response: NATO Strategy and Theater Nuclear Forces Since 1967* (New York: Columbia University Press, 1991), p. 245. For an earlier example, see R. J. Crampton, *Hollow Detente: Anglo-German Relations in the Balkans, 1911–1914* (Altantic Highlands, N.J.: Humanities Press, 1980), p. 137. Here, as in the case of the domino dynamic discussed in the previous section, Eyre Crowe anticipated that Germany would not repeat its behavior of cooperating with England at the cost of endangering its relations with Austria.

[75] Jay Speakman, "Continuity of Discord: Responses of the Western Allies to the Soviet Invasion of Afghanistan" (unpublished dissertation, Department of Political Science, Columbia University 1994), chapter 6. Furthermore, as Speakman shows, American resentment over the weak position that the Europeans had taken over Afghanistan led the latter to feel that they had to pledge sanctions against the Soviet Union if that country should invade Poland. For a later example, see John Darnton, "Clinton Tries to Make Major Feel Special," *New York Times*, March 6, 1994. For a parallel case in domestic politics, see Harris, *Decision*, pp. 30–32.

[76] John Garver, "Sino-Vietnamese Conflict and the Sino-American Rapprochement," *Political Science Quarterly* 96 (Fall 1981), p. 450. For China's similar tactics in seeking to improve its relations with India without sacrificing its ties to Pakistan, see Garver, "Sino-Indian Rapprochement and the Sino-Pakistan Entente," ibid. 111 (Summer 1996), p. 333.

ilarly sought to limit the damage to relations with India by sending a high-ranking envoy and providing nuclear materials for India's Tarrapur reactor.[77] The invasion also led East and West Germany to increase their cooperation with each other.[78]

As is true for many of the dynamics we have described, actors can take advantage of the propensity for others to do things in twos. Thus during the spring 1972 North Vietnamese offensive, Kissinger told Brezhnev that "the Soviets had an interest in preventing a North Vietnamese victory; I doubted that the President could come to Moscow [for the scheduled summit meeting] if we suffered a defeat."[79] Just as baseball players complain to the umpire about the last call in the hope of influencing the next one, in domestic politics actors may claim that because recent government decisions have gone against them, the balance should be rectified by some desired program or appointment. Anticipating this process, people may vote for a leader whose political views are different from theirs in the expectation that, secure in her hold over her natural constituency, she will have to bend toward the opposite end of the political spectrum.[80] Leaders can utilize these dynamics as well: Some conservative members of Congress from districts with active liberal groups may have voted for nuclear freeze resolutions in the early 1980s so that they could more safely vote for the new MX missile.[81]

Quasi-Homeostasis

The Lijphart Effect, the Domino Theory Paradox, and doing things in twos are manifestations of the fact that actors do not merely react but seek a particular relationship or outcome. A frequent result is "quasi-homeostasis" as one or more of them try to establish or maintain a desired equilibrium. Even though the results are neither invariant nor precise (thus the modifier "quasi"), negative feedback appears in various guises and often reduces the

[77] Speakman, "Continuity of Discord," p. 826; also see Zbigniew Brzezinski, *Power and Principle* (New York: Farrar, Straus & Giroux, 1983), p. 133.

[78] John Vinocur, "Two Germanies Moving Toward Closer Ties," *New York Times*, June 11, 1980.

[79] Kissinger, *White House Years*, p. 1144. Kissinger calls this a "startling thesis." A more apt description would be shrewd and perhaps too clever by half, but not startling.

[80] For an example see Robert Dallek, *Lone Star Rising: Lyndon Johnson and His Times, 1908–1960* (New York: Oxford University Press, 1991), p. 377.

[81] Janne Nolan, *Guardians of the Arsenal* (New York: Basic Books, 1989), pp. 145–46; for another example see Adam Clymer, "Gingrich Won't Duck Tough Medicare Vote," *New York Times*, October 18, 1995. David Baldwin's point is perhaps better understood by politicians than by scholars: The common idea "that a broken promise has no value is . . . unacceptable. Anyone with children knows that breaking last week's promise to take them to the movies makes it much harder to break this week's promise" (Baldwin, *Paradoxes of Power* [New York: Basil Blackwell, 1989], p. 125).

amount of change that occurs as actors respond to each other. For example, when Germany conquered France in May 1940, the immediate result was a drastic worsening of the British position and greatly increased Nazi strength. But for this reason, the U.S. became much more actively involved and restored the Anglo-German balance to something closer to what it had been before France fell.

Competitive power balancing is only one of the processes of this type. As we have seen, attempts at social reform can go wrong as people adapt to the changed environment by offsetting behavior that meets their goals, not those of the reformers. From this perspective, it is not surprising that the introduction of extensive "labor-saving" devices resulted, not in reducing the time women spent maintaining the house, but in increased expectations for cleanliness and amenities.[82] In much the same way, U.S. hopes that Spain would contribute more to the Western alliance once it joined NATO were defeated by Spanish preferences. Because NATO membership largely satisfied Spain's need for security, it moved to gain other values by reducing the undesired American military presence in Spain.[83] With more deadly effects, a partially effective vaccine for malaria or AIDS might increase the death rate as people respond by cutting back on other precautions.[84]

Quasi-homeostasis also operates when a state seeks to demonstrate its displeasure to another, with the implied threat to do more if the other refuses to moderate its behavior. One common countertactic is for the other to minimize or ignore the state's signal. But the state may then have to escalate in order to ensure that its message gets through. In other words, the other's attempt to lower the international temperature will not succeed if the state wants the temperature to be higher. These dynamics were at work at the end of 1983 when the Soviets terminated the discussions of INF arms control because NATO began its deployment. But the USSR was

> irritated by the relatively tranquil response of the North Atlantic Treaty Organization to the interruptions at Geneva and by the tendency to dismiss the announced Soviet countermeasures to Western deployment as long-planned military moves.
>
> The Russians appeared to be particularly incensed by Chancellor Helmet Kohl's disclosure of the details of a letter from the Soviet leader, Yuri V. Andropov, which the West German leader construed as meaning Moscow might eventually return to the . . . talks in Geneva. A standard, upbeat West German reading of the international situation has typically included a litany of other forums where East-West negotiations are continuing, including the Vienna talks.

[82] Ruth Schwartz Cowan, *More Work for Mothers* (New York: Basic Books, 1983). For a related discussion, see chapter 2 above, pp. 59, 68–70.

[83] Edward Schumacher, "Spain Insists U.S. Cut Troops There," *New York Times*, November 20, 1985.

[84] See, for example, John Maurice, "Malaria Vaccine Raises a Dilemma," *Science* 267 (January 20, 1995), p. 322.

"It will be interesting to see how far Moscow feels it has to go to show that they [sic] really are angry," a senior Bonn official said.[85]

In the event, the Soviets hinted that they might also cancel the conventional arms control negotiation in Vienna.

More generally, states often seek a certain level of conflict. If they overshoot or tensions rise more than they want, they will try to defuse the situation by concessions, diplomatic initiatives, or "peace offensives."[86] Thus the "unprecedented candor, direct personal contact, and . . . mutual respect between the chief actors" during the Cuban Missile Crisis may be explained by the understanding that ordinary behavior was excessively dangerous in these circumstances.[87] Conversely, a state can afford to offend another when their relations are good. Thus in March 1914, the British foreign secretary told his ambassador in Berlin to stiffen his position in the negotiations over the Portuguese colonies: "The way in which we had dealt with each other during the Balkan crisis had greatly improved our relations. . . . From this point of view, therefore, the thing was not so necessary as it had been as a friendly transaction between Germany and England."[88]

Quasi-homeostasis can frustrate a state's ability to woo neutrals who, wanting to maintain this status, are likely to respond to friendly gestures, not with reciprocity, but by picking a fight with the state or making a friendly move toward the state's adversary. Thus one reason why India refused to sign the American-sponsored peace treaty with Japan in 1951 was that the

[85] James Markham, "Soviet Intention Queried in Vienna," *New York Times*, December 10, 1983. For another example, see Fred Greenstein, *The Hidden-Hand Presidency: Eisenhower as Leader* (New York: Basic Books, 1982), p. 68. The other side of this coin is represented by the Palestinian claim (if it is not a rationalization) that the low turnout in response to Arafat's call for prayers in the Jerusalem mosque in protest against the Netanyahu regime was not a disappointment because it came a day after a strike that was so successful that "there was no seriousness in dealing with [the prayer]. The strike achieved its aims and had results" (quoted in Serge Schmemann, "Arafat's Call for Prayer Protest Gets Modest Response," *New York Times*, August 31, 1996).

[86] For an interesting if not fully substantiated account of such a cycle, see Frank Kofsky, *Harry S. Truman and the War Scare of 1948* (New York: St. Martin's, 1993), chapters 5 and 7. For cases of tension management before World War I, see Glenn Snyder, *Alliance Politics* (Ithaca, N.Y.: Cornell University Press, forthcoming), chapter 10. Seemingly contradictory responses in public opinion polls may similarly represent the desire for equilibrium: see Miroslav Nincic, "U.S. Soviet Policy and the Electoral Connection," *World Politics* 42 (April 1990), pp. 370–96. For a discussion of parallel processes in the behavior and self-images of individuals, see Lee Ross and Richard Nisbett, *The Person and The Situation* (New York: McGraw-Hill, 1991), pp. 51, 118.

[87] Bernard Brodie, *War and Politics* (New York: Macmillan, 1973), p. 426.

[88] Quoted in Crampton, *Hollow Detente*, p. 177. But many leaders in both Germany and Britain may have been misled by the warming of relations between them into expecting the other to cooperate in July 1914: Sean Lynn-Jones, "Détente and Deterrence: Anglo-German Relations, 1911–1914," *International Security* 11 (Fall 1986), pp. 121–50.

U.S. had just provided large amounts of food to meet the danger of drought-induced starvation.[89] The U.S. benefited from this impulse twenty years later when, in the wake of its Soviet-supported victory in the Indo-Pakistani War of 1971, India "pressed forward with arms purchases from non-Soviet sources . . . [to show that] a New Delhi victorious with Soviet assistance was not to be considered a dependency of Moscow."[90] In much the same way, after Egypt had turned to the U.S. in the aftermath of the October War, President Sadat gave an unusually cordial welcome to the Soviet foreign minister "to answer those of his critics who . . . complained that he has thrown himself into the arms of the Americans."[91]

President Eisenhower sought to take advantage of this kind of behavior when he wrote in his diary in March 1956 that it might be best to leave Egypt "with no ally in sight except Soviet Russia." In reaction, Egypt "would very quickly get tired of that prospect and would join us in the search for a just and decent peace" in the region.[92] But later that year this dynamic limited the improvement in U.S.-Egyptian relations that many observers expected to follow from America's support for Egypt in the Suez conflict. As Kissinger notes, Nasser's "radical constituency would not have permitted him to admit that he had been saved by American pressures even if he had been inclined to do so. On the contrary, to impress that very constituency, he accelerated his attacks on moderate, pro-Western governments in the Middle East."[93]

[89] H. W. Brands, *The Specter of Neutralism: The United States and the Emergence of the Third World, 1947–1960* (New York: Columbia University Press, 1989), pp. 69–71. The same dynamic may explain why India became more hostile to the U.S. after the two states cooperated on a UN resolution that the USSR strongly opposed: Stueck, *Korean War*, p. 302. For related examples, see David Sanger, "Manila Embassy Warns Americans," *New York Times*, December 5, 1989, and Jussi Hanhimaki, "Self-Restraint as Containment: United States' Economic Policy, Finland, and the Soviet Union, 1945–1953," *International History Review* 17 (May 1995), pp. 294–95. This behavior is not so different from Les Aspin's characterization of the House of Representatives: "The House doesn't want to go on one tack for too long. If it hits a couple of votes going left, the boys are then looking to tack back and go to the right" (quoted in Linda Greenhouse, "A Military Bill Like None Other," *New York Times*, May 13, 1987).

[90] Howard Wriggins, "South Asian Regional Politics," in Wriggins, ed., *Dynamics of Regional Politics* (New York: Columbia University Press, 1992), p. 108. For other examples from Indian-American relations, see McMahon, *Cold War on the Periphery*, pp. 90, 226, and 286.

[91] Henry Tanner, "Sadat, Gromyko's Host, Backs Soviet Tie," *New York Times*, March 3, 1974. Abraham Lincoln gave this advice to the general he put in charge of the deeply divided state of Missouri: "If both factions, or neither, shall abuse you, you will probably be about right. Beware of being assailed by one, and praised by the other": quoted in David Donald, *Lincoln* (New York: Simon and Schuster, 1995), p. 453. Modern newspapers are supposed to be objective, and so cover political campaigns by "equal side-by-side Democratic and Republican daily campaign stories," a practice Ben Bagdikian dubs "twinning": "The Fruits of Agnewism," *Columbia Journalism Review* 11 (January/February 1973), p. 10.

[92] Quoted in John Lewis Gaddis, *The Long Peace* (New York: Oxford University Press, 1987), p. 192.

[93] Kissinger, *Diplomacy*, p. 546.

SEEKING THE DESIRED LEVEL OF RISK

It is not only the degree of friendship and hostility between them that actors adjust. In bargaining situations that resemble a game of chicken, they often seek a desired level of risk and danger. States are not thrill seekers, but the danger that things will get out of control and the associated "threat that leaves something to chance"[94] are ways of bringing pressure to bear in a crisis, so even states that do not want war may need to see that it remains possible. In the context of quasi-homeostasis this means that at a certain point efforts to make crises easier to manage will become self-defeating as the actors adjust their behavior to increase the danger.[95] So if risk is decreased by such measures as "hot lines" and military forces that are less prone to accidents, statesmen may act more recklessly during conflict in order to show the other side that undesired war is still a real possibility. During the Cuban Missile Crisis, Khrushchev called for a disengagment of forces that "would give people the possibility of breathing calmly."[96] But until Khrushchev agreed to remove the missiles, breathing calmly was exactly what the U.S. could not permit because it would take the pressure off him.[97]

THE SEQUEL TO A GREAT VICTORY IS OFTEN A GREAT DEFEAT

As does the balance of power, quasi-homeostasis operates to limit the gains actors can make—and should seek. At the end of the missile crisis, President Kennedy pointed out that "every setback has the seeds of its own reprisal, if the [defeated] country is powerful enough."[98] He realized that victo-

---

[94] Schelling, *Strategy of Conflict*, chapter 8. Because children, unlike most statesmen, actively do seek a certain level of danger, it is not surprising that at least some of them behave more recklessly when they visit safer playgrounds: Douglas Martin, "That Upside-Down High Will Become Only a Memory," *New York Times*, April 11, 1996.

[95] See Jervis, *The Meaning of the Nuclear Revolution*, p. 96; Barry Nalebuff, "Brinkmanship and Deterrence: The Neutrality of Escalation," *Conflict Management and Peace Science* 9 (Spring 1986), pp. 19–30; Paul Bracken, "Do We Really Want to Eliminate the Chance of Accidental War?" *Defense Analysis* 4, no. 1 (1988), pp. 81–89; also see the remarks of Soviet analysts quoted in Joseph Nye, Jr., "Nuclear Learning and U.S.-Soviet Security Regimes," *International Organization* 41 (Summer 1987), p. 390. The other side of this coin is more familiar: The belief that a situation is excessively dangerous gives the actors reason to make it less so.

[96] Quoted in Beschloss, *Crisis Years*, p. 518. One reason why Khrushchev felt greater pressure than Kennedy was that only he knew that the USSR had a large ground force in Cuba, one that was equipped with nuclear weapons, which meant that an American invasion could easily lead to all-out nuclear war.

[97] For the importance of perceptions of controllability of risk, see Alexander George and Richard Smoke, *Deterrence in American Foreign Policy* (New York: Columbia University Press, 1974), pp. 527–29.

[98] Quoted in Arthur Schlesinger, Jr., *A Thousand Days* (Boston: Houghton Mifflin, 1965), p. 841. Kennedy had in mind the need not to gloat after the apparent American victory; the extent to which the outcome of the crisis led to the subsequent Soviet arms buildup remains unclear.

ries will be pyrrhic if they call up undesired reactions. In domestic society, the excesive use of a tax loophole or the abuse of a government regulation can lead to changes that make the behavior impossible.[99] In wartime, a defeat can lead the adversary to mobilize additional resources or change its tactics.[100] During peacetime, action-reaction dynamics can produce arms races. Thus Henry Kissinger argued—somewhat disingenuously—that it was foolish for either the U.S. or the USSR to pursue military advantage: "No net advantage can long be preserved by either side. A perceived inequality could shake the confidence of other countries, even when its precise military significance is difficult to define. Therefore, we certainly will not permit a perceived or actual imbalance to arise against us and the Soviet Union is likely to follow similar principles."[101] Of course the example of arms races in general and the Soviet-American competition in particular reminds us that the equilibrating process is not automatic and that advantages and victories, even unlimited ones, are possible. Dominoes sometimes fall, actors climb on bandwagons, and states can come to see that they cannot recoup previous defeats. But when they are powerful and agile, states that suffer setbacks are likely to be able to respond.

In a form of the security dilemma, putting others in danger then may not redound to the state's benefit. This point can be illustrated by imagining the likely consequences of some Cold War events that did not occur. In 1985 Michael May argued, correctly in my view, that "it would lessen, not improve, Soviet security if the Soviet Union would 'win' in the Caribbean, particularly if it won big and began to be a military factor in, say, Mexico. The extraordinary insecurity created in the U.S. would greatly overbalance whatever conventional military advantages might accrue."[102] Similarly, had

[99] When a number of states increased their federal Medicaid payments by claiming matching funds for state money that had come from donations and taxes paid by hospitals and nursing homes, the federal government changed the rules: Robert Pear, "U.S. Moves to Curb Medicaid Payments for Many States," New York Times, September 11, 1991.

[100] For example, the British naval victories at Trafalgar and Jutland, although crucial, "did not [immediately] improve the safety of British shipping. In fact, things got worse" as the enemy shifted to targeting merchant ships with privateers in the first case and submarines in the second: Jan Breemer, "The Burden of Trafalgar," Journal of Strategic Studies 17 (March 1994), pp. 46–47. For a case from World War II, see Sebastian Cox, "'The Difference between Black and White': Churchill, Imperial Politics, and Intelligence before the 1941 Crusader Offensive," Intelligence and National Security 9 (July 1994), p. 440. Also see Edward Luttwak, Strategy (Cambridge, Mass.: Harvard University Press, 1987), pp. 50–65, 210–14.

[101] Henry Kissinger, "Foreign Policy and National Security," International Security 1 (Summer 1976), pp. 186–87. A civilian Pentagon official who blew the whistle on weapons procurement abuses found that attempts to reduce the information at his disposal did not work: "Knowing that my access to official communication had been limited, my secret sympathizers stepped up their assistance" (A. Ernest Fitzgerald, The High Priests of Waste [New York: Norton, 1972], p. 109).

[102] Michael May, "The U.S.-Soviet Approach to Nuclear Weapons," International Security 9

the Soviets succeeded in pushing the West out of Berlin in the crises of 1948 or 1958–62 I doubt that the results would have been to their liking.[103] When a state goes too far, others are likely to counter; in a competitive system, moderation often serves the state well.

Kissinger argued that "the bane of Soviet diplomacy is its persistent quest for maximum advantage. . . . [which] often backfires by removing any incentive for a serious dialogue."[104] But the failing is not uniquely Soviet nor does it work only through the mechanism Kissinger noted. Overexpansion comes in many guises.[105] The Korean War supplies a series of illustrations. North Korea might have been able to dominate the peninsula if it had stopped after conquering part of the South; the U.S. could have ended the war successfully if it had been content to reestablish the status quo rather than seeking to liberate North Korea;[106] China could have spared itself enormous casualties by stopping at the 38th parallel. Indeed, the American reaction to the North Korean attack would have greatly harmed the USSR and PRC no matter what happened on the battlefield because the U.S. more than tripled its defense budget, transformed NATO into a functioning military organization, and concluded defense treaties with countries around the globe. The latter policy in turn may have harmed the U.S. by making it the target for local nationalisms and drawing it into unwise military interventions. At every stage, statesmen might have thought more about the fact that

---

(Spring 1985), p. 150. For a discussion of the virtues of moderation with special reference to nuclear weapons, see Jervis, *Meaning of the Nuclear Revolution*, chapter 7. For the ability of actors to provoke others into self-defeating behavior, see below, pp. 290–91.

[103] These cases are not unique. For American thinking about how it would react to a defeat in the first Quemoy and Matsu crisis, see Gordon Chang and He Di, "The Absence of War in the U.S.-China Confrontation over Quemoy and Matsu in 1954–1955: Contingency, Luck, Deterrence?" *American Historical Review* 98 (December 1993), p. 1519. See Stueck, *Korean War*, p. 134 for what the U.S. might have done if the PRC had pushed it off the Korean peninsula at the end of 1951. For Kennedy's speculations on what he would have had to do if the USSR had prevailed in the Cuban missile crisis, see Tom Wicker, "Kennedy Finds Prospects For Peace Better in 1963," *New York Times*, January 2, 1963.

[104] Kissinger, *White House Years*, p. 1292.

[105] For general treatments, see Paul Kennedy, *The Rise and Fall of the Great Powers: Economic Change and Military Conflict from 1500 to 2000* (New York: Random House, 1987); Jack Snyder, *Myths of Empire* (Ithaca, N.Y.: Cornell University Press, 1991); Charles Kupchan, *The Vulnerability of Empire* (Ithaca, N.Y.: Cornell University Press, 1994).

[106] Until recently, most scholars believed that the U.S. could have safely pushed to the narrow neck of North Korea, but it now appears that Chinese intervention was triggered by the crossing of the 38th parallel. See Thomas Christensen, "Threats, Assurances, and the Last Chance for Peace: The Lessons of Mao's Korean War Telegrams," *International Security* 17 (Summer 1992), pp. 122–54; also see Chen Jian, *China's Road to the Korean War: The Making of the Sino-American Confrontation* (New York: Columbia University Press, 1994), and Jian, "China's Road to the Korean War" and the accompanying documents, *Cold War International History Project Bulletin*, nos. 6–7 (Winter 1995/1996), pp. 41, 85–91.

any move that would bring their state great competitive advantage would also call up great opposition from the other side.

Indirect Approaches

Systems effects do not always thwart actors. Indeed, at times it is only by utilizing them that actors can reach their goals: When a direct approach will fail, a more circuitous one may succeed.[107] This is relatively—but only relatively—simple when the actor is dealing with nature or those who cannot anticipate its behavior. Thus in some cases pests can be controlled by destroying their breeding grounds or introducing other species that compete with or prey on them. Albeit with even greater difficulty, skillful diplomats may be able to predict the forces that will be generated by their policies and take advantage of the resulting ramifications. For example, one way in which Germany reduced French resistance to Britain's entry into the Common Market was by advocating monetary policies that both France and Britain opposed, thereby giving France reason to bring Britain in. Indeed, a great deal of diplomacy in multipolar systems employs indirect effects. States seek to reduce the menace to themselves by sowing discord among potential adversaries; they encourage others to expand in areas in which the burdens of defense will fall on third parties; they take actions aimed at calling up responses by others that will foreclose undesired paths that a target could otherwise follow. Understanding this, the memoranda of diplomats in the late nineteenth and early twentieth centuries are littered with references to the fear that their countries are being lured into "pulling others' chestnuts out of the fire" and the corresponding hope of using another as their "catspaw."

Pluralist politics, especially when it involves separation of powers, can be seen as arrangements and institutions that constitute a system to generate and deploy forces that will serve general social goals although each actor seeks only a narrower self-interest. Factions in the polity and branches

[107] In fact, the very meaning of "direct" and "circuitous" depends in part on what people believe and expect, just as unintended consequences can only be defined as a divergence from what actors intend. For example, before the mid-1930s, it was believed that the best way for the government to combat an economic depression was to cut its spending, allowing more funds to be available for the private sector. Keynes showed that this commonsense position was incorrect and that moving in the different direction of running a deficit would help restore the economy. After people became accustomed to the idea, the behavior seemed straightforward. But there is a further twist: Some economists argue that while Keynesian remedies may work when the general population and business leaders are naive—i.e., do not understand the implications of the policy—it will fail when they are sophisticated because they will discount for its expected effects. For discussions, see David Begg, *The Rational Expectations Revolution in Macroeconomics* (Baltimore, Md.: Johns Hopkins University Press, 1982), and Frydman and Phelps, eds., *Individual Forecasting and Aggregate Outcomes*.

within the government are made to contend in order to govern, with the premise not only that excessive power leads to tyranny, but also that no one person or organ could successfully integrate all the information and interests in society. By creating and structuring conflicts, the processes will sustain democracy, and over the long run the results will be better than could be achieved by mandating the direct search for the common interest.

The virtues of using the dynamics of the system are well understood here. But tactics that take advantage of the system often face special obstacles because the links between behavior and goals will be obscure to many at home (raising problems for democracies) and abroad (raising the question of whether they will be effective if they are understood). In some cases, however, the bait is so sweet that even a recognition of it may not preclude its being swallowed. This might have been the case with the policy advocated by ingenious British officials in the wake of the Boer War. To solidify British power over the Boers, they called for

> the immediate consolidation of the various areas of British South Africa into one nation. Although unification would at first place Boers in authority over all of South Africa, it would, they believed, ironically cause their eventual political decline. No matter which group stepped into power, unification would create conditions of economic prosperity and political security which had been lacking ever since the war. With prosperity and security would come British immigrants in greater and greater numbers. Assuming a constitution containing equitable franchise and constituency provisions, the result, they insisted, would be an eventual transfer of political power from the Boer population to the British.[108]

The Boers probably were more likely to act as desired if they did not grasp the British plan, but knowledge might not have led them to resist because they received great advantages and their options were limited. The media may similarly be unable to resist the strategy of candidates for office who use advertisements that are designed to be too controversial to be aired more than a few times, but for that reason will receive extensive news coverage.[109]

Indirect effects can be deployed by changing the incentives others confront, thereby steering them in a desired direction. Thus some people who are trying to preserve mahogany forests reject calls for a consumer boycott: "We should be buying tropical timber so that it remains valuable. If there's no market for the wood, the forests will be mowed down and the land

[108] Walter Nimocks, *Milner's Young Men* (Durham, N.C.: Duke University Press, 1968), pp. 75–76. A rough parallel in the economic arena is the call for "unbalanced growth" in which pushing one sector ahead creates the need and incentives for growth in other sectors: Albert Hirschman, *The Strategy of Economic Development* (New Haven, Conn.: Yale University Press, 1958).

[109] That the news organizations are generally aware that they are being used is indicated in Brett Pulley, "Zimmer Takes on Torricelli in Ad That Mimics TV News," *New York Times*, October 9, 1996.

turned to agriculture."[110] Similarly, although the most obvious way to protect an endangered species is to prohibit hunting it, a better approach may be to sell expensive hunting licenses in order to give the local population incentives to maintain the species.[111] On a larger scale, economic interdependence often gains political support not by altering the beliefs or goals of top leaders, but by strengthening groups that favor an open economic system and giving important actors a stake in foreign trade.[112] Following similar logic, in 1929 the British ambassador to Washington argued that to preserve its naval lead over the U.S., Great Britain should agree to the former's demand for parity in the arms control treaty. "This would remove the one issue which the American 'Big Navy party' brandished to garner public support. . . . Once achieved, paper parity would eliminate the poison in Anglo-American relations and . . . weaken congressional support for building up the U.S.N."[113]

A related approach is for the actor to turn over power to an agent whose incentives to stand firm are greater than his.[114] This was not done by the British when they followed the straightforward policy of negotiating the best possible deal with the PRC for the future of Hong Kong after it reverts to Chinese control. But perhaps they should have offered British citizenship to Hong Kong's residents.[115] It might seem that had they done so, people would have flocked to Great Britain, which was not Britain's goal. But because the PRC wanted a thriving economic zone, not a few miles of additional territory, it would have had to come to terms with Hong Kong's citizens, who would have had greater bargaining power because they could

---

[110] Quoted in Les Line, "Advocates of Sustainable Mahogany Harvest Counter Boycott," *New York Times*, June 4, 1996.

[111] Eliot Marshall, "Mountain Sheep Experts Draw Hunters' Fire," *Science* 248 (April 27, 1990), pp. 437–38; also see Nancy Simmons, "Make Room for Elephants," *Wildlife Conservation* 98 (July/August 1995), pp. 50–53.

[112] Helen Milner, *Resisting Protectionism: Global Industries and the Politics of International Trade* (Princeton, N.J.: Princeton University Press, 1988); Scott James and David Lake, "The Second Face of Hegemony: Britain's Repeal of the Corn Laws and the American Walker Tariff of 1846," *International Organization* 43 (Winter 1989), pp. 1–30; William Long, "Trade and Technological Incentives and Bilateral Cooperation," *International Studies Quarterly* 40 (March 1996), pp. 77–106.

[113] B. J. C. McKercher, "No Eternal Friends or Enemies: British Defence Policy and the Problem of the United States, 1919–1939," *Canadian Journal of History* 28 (August 1993), pp. 273–74. Ironically, the Anglo-American naval rivalry and treaties were based on faulty premises and it turned out to be in each side's interest for the other to have a large navy.

[114] Schelling, *Strategy of Conflict*, pp. 26–29.

[115] Christopher Patten, the British governor of Hong Kong, actually suggested this in the fall of 1995. Even though this was well after the bargain had been struck, this policy still could have affected Chinese behavior: "Hong Kong Plea to Britain," *New York Times*, September 24, 1995; also see Edward Gargan, "As China Undercuts Democracy, Hong Kong Scuffles for Passports," ibid., April 4, 1996.

depart.[116] Furthermore, their knowledge that they could leave would have decreased the danger of panic and self-fulfilling prophecies of gloom.

Liddell Hart's ingenious explication of how the British could have used system effects before World War II similarly rests on the potential for taking advantage of how others would have to respond to a move that would appear to take the actor further from his goal. In the spring of 1939 Britain guaranteed Poland's territorial integrity, hoping to avoid war by a combination of Polish concessions and pressure on Germany, which was to be increased by an Anglo-Russian alliance. But neither Poland nor Russia cooperated, in part because the British pledge had given them new opportunities. Perhaps an alternative approach could have exploited others' interests rather than being exploited by them:

> If [Britain] had not given that delusory guarantee, Poland would have been forced to accept Russia's help, as the only chance of withstanding German pressure. And Russia would have been forced to give Poland such support, because of her then existing value as a buffer State, and as an auxiliary army. Under these circumstances, it would have been much less likely that Germany would have attacked Poland.[117]

Like many indirect strategies, this might have backfired.[118] But it could not have been more of a failure than the one Britain followed.

As this case shows, states may be well advised to limit their security commitments lest they allow potential allies to reduce their own efforts, relieve third parties of the need to provide assistance, and frighten those who fear their clients. Thus there might have been greater regional opposition to the Soviet invasion of Afghanistan if the U.S. had not been so quick to supply Pakistan with arms and support, a course of action that reduced the Soviet threat and made it easier for others to pursue their narrower agendas. Similarly, less of an American commitment to West Germany during the Berlin crisis of 1958–62 might have ameliorated the conflict by moderating Adenauer's behavior and assuaging Soviet fears that German interests would dictate American policy.[119] The same ability to influence others by reducing

[116] This assumes that emigration to Britain would not have been preferred to any offer China might make.

[117] Basil Liddell Hart, *Why Don't We Learn from History?* (London: Allen & Unwin, 1944), p. 39; also see Kissinger, *Diplomacy*, pp. 342–44.

[118] Stalin may have signed the Nazi-Soviet pact primarily because he feared having to fight Germany alone, a fear that could have been reduced only by an even stronger and more unequivocal Anglo-French commitment to fight not only for Poland, but for the USSR as well: Adam Ulam, *Expansion and Coexistence* (New York: Praeger, 1968), pp. 265–75; also see Kissinger, *Diplomacy*, p. 348.

[119] Marc Trachtenberg, *History and Strategy* (Princeton, N.J.: Princeton University Press, 1990), chapter 5. For an example from the eighteenth century, see Paul Schroeder, *The Transformation of European Politics, 1763–1848* (Oxford: Oxford University Press, 1994), p. 91. For

their protection could allow the U.S. to increase cooperation between Japan and South Korea by partially withdrawing from the region, although the benefits might not be worth the risks.[120]

More generally, actors may be able to manipulate the environments in which they or others act in order to generate desired behavior.[121] Many political maneuvers have the effect—and some have the aim—of widening or narrowing the circle of those who are involved, thereby strongly influencing the outcome. Indeed, Schattschneider argues that "the expansion of the political community . . . has been the grand strategy of American politics."[122] Even with size constant, actors can affect the contours of the political landscape, in part, as Schattschneider shows, by increasing or decreasing the salience of issues that divide the community in different ways. Other manipulative strategies are familiar as well. Haldeman notes that a "fairly typical strategy on Nixon's part [was] to set up, or hope for, an external extremist view to be launched which would in turn bring counterpressure on the extremists of the other side instead of letting the current activist element dominate the debate and the action."[123] Relatedly, actors may be able to place themselves in a position where new forces will be acting on them, as politicians do when they seek to expose themselves to domestic attack if they retreat in a foreign dispute. Sometimes without following a conscious strategy, an act can have a large indirect effect by framing an issue in a certain way, placing it in a different context, and getting people to regard it differently. These processes may have been the way in which *Brown v. Board of Education* so deeply affected American politics and society: Although it did not produce much immediate desegregation, it altered the way people thought about race and about what policies and behaviors were legal, legitimate, and appropriate.[124]

---

parallel policy prescriptions for the constitutions of ethnically divided societies, see Arend Lijphart, "The Power-Sharing Approach," in Joseph Montville, ed., *Conflict and Peacemaking in Multiethnic Societies* (Lexington, Mass.: Lexington Books, 1990), pp. 491–509, especially pp. 494, 496.

[120] Victor Cha, *Alignment Despite Antagonism: The United States–Korea–Japan Security Triangle* (Stanford, Calif.: Stanford University Press, forthcoming), and Tae-ryong Yoon, "The U.S. Role in Promoting Security Cooperation" (unpublished paper, Department of Political Science, Columbia University, 1993).

[121] See George Kennan's remarks about how Roosevelt influenced public opinion quoted in Warren Kimball, *The Juggler: Franklin Roosevelt as Wartime Statesman* (Princeton, N.J.: Princeton University Press, 1991), p. 18; also see the discussion of an interaction approach to behavior in chapter 2, pp. 48–58 above.

[122] E. E. Schattschneider, *The Semisovereign People* (New York: Holt, Rinehart and Winston, 1960), pp. 99–100.

[123] Haldeman, *Diaries*, p. 129.

[124] Lawrence Tribe, "The Curvature of Constitutional Space: What Lawyers Can Learn from Modern Physics," *Harvard Law Review* 103 (November 1989), pp. 29–32; Gerald Rosenberg, *The Hollow Hope: Can Courts Bring About Social Change?* (Chicago: University of Chicago Press, 1991).

Understanding feedbacks similarly may allow actors to follow indirect routes to their goals, especially when information and beliefs are not fully shared. Small steps are psychologically, politically, and technically easier than dramatic changes and yet can have great influence. For example, if a state that wants extensive regional integration and understands the spillover process faces others who do not but who see benefit in limited cooperation, it may propose the latter in the expectation of gaining much more. Earlier we discussed Schelling's tipping dynamics, which can produce results that no one likes;[125] the extension here is that under some circumstances it is only by utilizing them that an actor can succeed. A small group may be able to set off a chain reaction by altering others' environments, if not their preferences. Thus in the negotiations leading to the Montreal Protocol of 1987, it proved politically impossible to set a date for the prohibition of chlorofluorocarbons (CFCs), in part because substitutes were not available. But under U.S. prodding the participants agreed to cut their production in half by 1999. In so doing "the protocol was in fact tipping CFCs toward obsolescence. U.S. negotiators had reasoned that, when substitutes were developed to such an extent, the remaining CFC market could probably not be sustained. By providing CFC producers with the certainty that their sales were destined to decline, the protocol unleashed the creative energies and considerable resources of the private sector in a search for alternatives."[126] Stalin used a similar approach in 1929 to malign ends. He did not demand the immediate collectivization of farms but rather established compulsory grain delivery quotas. As he expected, the result was a drastic decrease in production because the peasants lacked incentives to grow as much as they could. When this became clear, there was little choice but to undertake more radical collectivization if the cities were not to starve.[127]

Moving in the Opposite Direction

Actors may be able to reach their goals by proceeding in the opposite direction and utilizing the reactions to produce the desired results.[128] The conditions that permit such an approach are fairly stringent, however—strategies

[125] Chapter 4, pp. 150–52.

[126] Richard Benedick, *Ozone Diplomacy* (Cambridge, Mass.: Harvard University Press, 1991), p. 105. This was much of the strategy of the senators who worked to defeat the elevation of Judge Carswell to the Supreme Court: Harris, *Decision*.

[127] Robert Tucker, *Stalin in Power* (New York: Norton, 1990), pp. 131–45.

[128] As with indirect effect, what constitutes "the opposite direction" cannot be objectively determined. To their proponents, deterrence theory, whose basic logic can be summarized by the old saying "If you seek peace, prepare for war" and the spiral model, whose motto could be "If you seek security, cut your arms and make the adversary more secure," seem to advocate direct approaches. But those who disagree, or who find the posited causal relations obscure, would see these policies as heading backwards.

that require outsmarting the other are likely to be short-lived, as parents discover when they try to get their children to stop noxious activities by telling them that it is perfectly all right.

Nevertheless, this approach can operate through several mechanisms. Most obviously, an actor may be able to deceive the adversary: Making a feint toward attacking at point A may enable a successful attack at point B. Thus Sun Tsu's aphorisms included:

> When capable, feign incapacity; when active, inactivity. When near, make it appear that you are far away. . . . Offer the enemy a bait to lure him; feign disorder and strike him. When he concentrates, prepare against him; where he is strong, avoid him. Pretend inferiority and encourage his arrogance. . . . Attack where he is un-prepared; sally out when he does not expect you.[129]

Politicians often try to mislead others about which of their rivals is the strongest,[130] are careful not to indicate their support for a preferred con-tender in a hostile country,[131] gain partisan advantage by appearing nonpar-tisan, and often make claims like the one made by New York's Mayor Giu-liani when he cut the budget of an office headed by a rival: "I recognize the fact that that could be conceived as political, so I think it is quite courageous that I'm doing it because it's quite substantive."[132] On occasion, preferences as well can be induced in the adversary by expressing a desire that the other will feel called upon to oppose.

Even shared goals may be reachable only by moving in the opposite direc-tion. Earlier we saw that denying that a bank was in serious difficulties could accelerate a run on it. Perhaps it would be better to tell depositors that they should feel no hesitation in withdrawing their money. This proposition is not hypothetical: During the first stages of the Berlin blockade allied authorities

---

[129] Sun Tzu, *The Art of War*, translated by Samuel Griffith (New York: Oxford University Press, 1963), pp. 63–64.

[130] For example, in the spring of 1972, Nixon ordered the release of fake polls showing that McGovern would be difficult to defeat: Haldeman, *Diaries*, p. 449.

[131] Hitler was careful to see that the German press did not support American isolationists: Saul Friedlander, *Prelude to Downfall: Hitler and the United States, 1939–1941*, translated by Aline Werth and Alexander Werth (New York: Knopf, 1967), pp. 49–56; during the 1960 presi-dential campaign Harriman, Kennedy's unofficial emissary, "reminded Khrushchev to be tough on both candidates: the surest way to elect Nixon was to praise Kennedy": Beschloss, *Crisis Years*, p. 35; Russia's foreign minister Andrei Kozyrev may have been hurt at home by expres-sions of support abroad: Alessandra Stanley, "Yeltsin's Foreign Minister Stays in Office, For-lornly," *New York Times*, October 21, 1995.

[132] Quoted in Alison Mitchell, "For Giuliani and Green, It Might As Well Be 1997," ibid., June 11, 1994; also see Iver Peterson, "Whitman Denies Forcing Official Out," ibid., Septem-ber 28, 1995. For a good example of the political advantages of appearing nonpolitical, espe-cially when such behavior is not expected, see Lyndon Johnson's handling of the 1957 space hearings: Robert Devine, *The Sputnik Challenge* (New York: Oxford University Press, 1993), pp. 60–68.

feared a water shortage because much of the supply came from Soviet-controlled territory. When the West Berliners, who knew this, started to fill their tubs, the authorities assured them that supplies were ample and that they could use all the water they wanted. As a result, the demand dropped to manageable levels.[133]

More subtle psychological processes can permit reverse strategies as well. Because people are prone to feel that objectives that are easy to achieve lack value, playing "hard to get" may increase one's attractiveness and, conversely, setting too low a price on an object may make it harder to sell as potential buyers fear that it is defective or doubt their initially high subjective valuations of it. The belief that if the action was for the best we would not have to be told to do it and a concern for the inferences that will be drawn similarly mean that an action may be shunned if the person believes that others—or he—will see him as having responded to pressures.[134] The instinctive desire to preserve our autonomy also enters in when we no longer desire activities we are told to undertake. This may explain why some people who resist standard psychotherapies respond to "paradoxical intervention," for example telling a procrastinator to spend a half hour sitting at his desk daydreaming.[135]

Lyndon Johnson both used and was vulnerable to this tactic. In his 1948 campaign he spread the rumor that his opponent, Coke Stevenson, was in favor of the unpopular Taft-Hartley bill. Johnson then pressed Stevenson to declare his position, and when he refused denounced his "pussy-footing and fence-straddling." Johnson was able to do this because he knew that while Stevenson favored the bill, even more Stevenson hated giving in to demands and so would keep silent once people insisted on knowing where he stood.[136] Johnson may have employed this tactic because he himself did not want others to believe that they could influence or even predict his behavior. When he was president, an accurate press account of what he was about to do often became a self-denying prophecy, as he would reverse himself.

[133] Frank Howley, *Berlin Command* (New York: Putnam, 1950), pp. 202–3.

[134] Knowing this, those who do not want the action may tell the actor that they believe he would only behave this way if he were pressured into doing so: See, for example, the arguments of an official who was trying to stave off the elimination of his agency: Jeffrey Richelson, "Task Force 157: The U.S. Navy's Secret Intelligence Service, 1966–77," *Intelligence and National Security* 11 (January 1996), p. 128.

[135] Leon Seltzer, *Paradoxical Strategies in Psychotherapy* (New York: Wiley, 1986); Daniel Goleman, "Prescribing the Symptom: Psychologists Say Its Power Lies in the Paradox," *New York Times*, November 30, 1989. The underlying theory of "reactance" is discussed in Jack Brehm, *Responses to Losses of Freedom: A Theory of Psychological Reactance* (Morristown, N.J.: General Learning Press, 1972); Paul Watzlawizk, John Weakland, and Richard Fisch, *Change* (New York: Norton, 1974), pp. 89–90, 134–36. For the related phenomenon of "enticement—the forbidden fruit effect," see Sieber, *Fatal Remedies*, pp. 136–39.

[136] Robert Caro, *The Years of Lyndon Johnson: Means of Ascent* (New York: Knopf, 1990), pp. 223–28, 271–72.

Moving in the opposite direction can also be effective against a target who is extremely suspicious. The Truman administration then may have made a mistake by being honest with the USSR in the spring of 1948. "To counter any false impressions and deductions the Soviets might draw from the [upcoming presidential] election, Ambassador Smith made a confidential *démarche* to [Foreign Minister] Molotov. . . . The Russians were told not to believe any stories that American foreign policy was paralyzed and irresolute in an election year; the course was set firmly and with the backing of both major parties."[137] The result may have been to reinforce the impression that Smith and his superiors wanted to erase. Perhaps "admitting" that little could be done during an election year and that a new administration might follow a different policy might have yielded better results. But this tactic depends on an unstable asymmetry: The target has to be highly suspicious of the actor, but not to believe that the actor is aware of this and is seeking to manipulate it.[138] On occasion, this combination is to be found. One country may "turn"—i.e., bring under its control—an agent who is spying for the enemy. The enemy may learn this and so assume that most of the source's reports are false. But if the state understands that this is the case, it can send correct information through the channel, knowing that the enemy will infer the opposite.[139]

Several of these mechanisms come into play when one actor provokes another, which means seeking a certain response—usually a belligerent one—from the target which is not in the latter's interest.[140] This tactic requires that the other lacks either an understanding of the situation or the ability to control itself. I suspect that both were at work when the Bosnians talked about—and probably undertook—actions that were designed to lead the Serbs to shell Sarajevo and perhaps when Churchill bombed Berlin in 1940, which led Hitler to switch his bombing from RAF airfields to London, a move that saved Britain from invasion.[141] Almost by definition, terrorism works not by the direct damage it does, which in all cases so far has been minor, but by overreactions of public opinion and the government. More subtly, an actor may follow the example of Br'er Rabbit and protest against a policy that it believes is actually in its interest. Thus in 1791 when Spain invited foreigners to settle in Florida, Secretary of State Jefferson wrote to Washington:

---

[137] Adam Ulam, *The Rivals* (New York: Viking, 1971), p. 145.

[138] If conflict of interest is complete, an actor will only talk or listen to another if he thinks he can outsmart him.

[139] Jervis, *Logic of Images*, pp. 55–64.

[140] For a survey from a sociological perspective, see Sieber, *Fatal Remedies*, chapter 6.

[141] John Burns, "Bosnia 1992: New Puzzles in the Jigsaw of Violence," *New York Times*, December 31, 1992; George Quester, *Deterrence Before Hiroshima* (New York: Wiley, 1966), pp. 113–22—but the evidence for British intention is ambiguous at best: see Frederick Sallagar, *The Road to Total War* (New York: Van Nostrand, 1974), pp. 179–87.

I wish a hundred thousand of our inhabitants would accept the invitation. It will be the means of delivering to us peaceably, what may otherwise cost us a war. In the meantime we may complain of this seduction of our inhabitants just enough to make [the Spanish] believe we think it a very wise policy for them, and confirm them in it.[142]

Provocation can also work through the reactions of third parties. Guerrillas often seek to provoke a violent reaction by the authorities in the belief that repression will alienate the general population and mobilize support for the guerrillas. More peacefully, the NAACP may have invited Louis Farrakhan to its 1994 leadership conference at least in part to generate vocal opposition from whites, which in turn would help draw dissenting blacks back into the organization.[143] When John Foster Dulles's "diplomatic bluster" at Geneva in 1954 "threatened . . . [to lead to] the breakdown of the conference, [Anthony] Eden redoubled his efforts to promote a compromise."[144] Perhaps this was Dulles's goal.

Doing More Than One Thing

Effective action is often made possible by employing multiple policies that constrain and work with the dynamics of the system. In chapter 2, I noted that when we are dealing with a system "we can never do merely one thing."[145] This means not only that behavior rarely has only one effect, but, more importantly here, that in order to produce a desired change, the actor must do several things.[146] Garrett Hardin, to whom I owe the phrase, provides a good example. Family planning will not be effective if many children

[142] Quoted in Stephen Knott, "Thomas Jefferson's Clandestine Foreign Policy," *International Journal of Intelligence and Counterintelligence* 4 (Fall 1990), p. 330. More generally, George Kennan is not alone in arguing "that there may be times when there can be advantages as well as disadvantages in luring your adversary into the assumption of responsibilities and commitments far afield" (quoted in Gaddis, *Long Peace*, p. 175; Gaddis also notes that, contrary to the common impression, Dulles agreed with this view).

[143] Joe Klein, "Grieving for the NAACP," *Newsweek*, June 27, 1994, p. 37.

[144] George Herring, "'A Good Stout Effort': John Foster Dulles and the Indochina Crisis, 1954–1955," in Richard Immerman, ed., *John Foster Dulles and the Diplomacy of the Cold War* (Princeton, N.J.: Princeton University Press 199), p. 223.

[145] Garrett Hardin, "The Cybernetics of Competition: A Biologist's View of Society," *Perspectives in Biology and Medicine* 7 (Autumn 1963), p. 80.

[146] I think this is what W. Ross Ashby means when he argues that for a system to be stable, the variety in the disturbance must be matched by the variety in the regulator: W. Ross Ashby, *Design for a Brain* (1st ed., New York: Wiley, 1952; 2d ed., London: Chapman & Hall, 1965); Ashby, "Variety, Constraint, and the Law of Requisite Variety," in Walter Buckley, ed., *Modern Systems Research for the Behavioral Scientist* (Chicago: Aldine, 1968), pp. 129–36. To put it in terms used earlier, some acts may constrain the target, thereby permitting other behavior to have the desired effects.

die young, and while improving public health in poor countries saves lives, it also increases population and so may lead to massive starvation. But health care plus family planning may produce healthy, small families and a stable society.[147] Other examples are not hard to find: A disease that defeats any single medication may be controlled by a combination of treatments; pests can be controlled—if they can be controlled at all—only by multiple lines of attack; where a social reform that relies on either incentives or regulation fails, one that utilizes both may succeed; sending food aid to a country where people are starving often can and must be accompanied by measures to spur indigenous production;[148] after World War II, West German reconstruction, let alone rearmament, would have been rejected by the West Europeans had it not been coupled with the continued presence of American troops and economic integration that tied Germany tightly to the West; when Chancellor Kohl moved toward rapid German unification in 1989–90, he simultaneously increased his support for European integration.

Critics of social reform are correct to note that welfare can decrease incentives to work, that providing housing for the homeless will increase their number, and that building new highways is not likely to decrease traffic congestion. For related reasons, subsidized flood insurance can encourage people to live in areas that are prone to flooding and systems to warn people of tornadoes may lead them to take fewer precautions. In foreign policy, critics of a policy of deterrence point out that increasing defense spending often makes the adversary more belligerent. But this does not mean that nothing can be done, just that no single policy will be effective. Thus welfare programs can be coupled with education, job training programs, and work incentives; highway programs need to be accompanied by taxes on cars, lanes for car pools, and support for mass transit; flood insurance can be conditioned on requiring that homes be built to minimize water damage; warning systems can be coupled with educational programs stressing that they can never be perfect; deterrence often must be combined with reassurances. As Paul Streeten notes in his discussion of economic and political development:

> Scientists may have a solution to every problem, but development has a problem for every solution. . . . Single actions, which look technically correct, can be worse than useless if they are not accompanied by supplementary actions. . . . To be effective, several actions must be taken together, in the right order; rural educa-

[147] Hardin, "The Cybernetics of Competition," pp. 80–81; also see Hardin, "The Tragedy of the 'Unmanaged' Commons," in Robert Andelson, ed., *Commons Without Tragedy* (London: Shepheard-Walwyn, 1991), pp. 166–67; William Stevens, "Green Revolution Is Not Enough, Study Finds," *New York Times*, September 6, 1994.

[148] This is why the U.S. and CARE sold rather than gave away some of the food sent to Somalia: Alison Mitchell, "A New Question in Somalia: When Does Free Food Hurt?" ibid., January 13, 1993.

tion has to be combined with the improvement of rural amenities or the educated will leave the countryside. The new seeds have to be applied with fertilizers and water at the right time; there must be extension services and roads to get the food to the market.[149]

In some cases, perhaps including those mentioned by Streeten, we know enough to specify the actions that will combine to produce the desired outcome. But more frequently we have only limited ability to anticipate what will happen. Multiple policies must then be applied sequentially and actors must be ready to alter their behavior to cope with unintended consequences and the novel strategies that others employ.[150] Flexibility and resilience are necessary for effective action. The policymaker who is psychologically and politically unprepared for surprises is almost certain to fail; good generals not only construct fine war plans but also understand that events will not conform to them; doctors must shift medications as bodies and microbes react to treatments; many parasites change their "signature proteins just often enough to stay one step ahead of the host antibodies aimed against them."[151]

It is then not surprising that programs that freeze their elements from the beginning and leave little slack for changes will require difficult adjustments. Thus the attempt to develop technologically ambitious weapons systems through a "concurrent" development strategy that starts building before testing is completed invites cost overruns, delays, and performance deficits.[152] But it is alluring to try to get everything right the first time, and so in the 1950s the U.S. Air Force reacted to the pressures to quickly produce very advanced bombers by ignoring this precept. As one aircraft manufacturer explained:

> In an airframe designed to achieve the extreme performance of the B-58, a high degree of design efficiency must be achieved. The airplane must be designed with

[149] Paul Streeten, "The United Nations: Unhappy Family," in David Pitt and Thomas Weiss, eds., *The Nature of United Nations Bureaucracies* (London: Croom Helm, 1986), p. 187. I have rearranged the order of some of the sentences in this quotation.

[150] I am drawing on a slightly different formulation by Aaron Wildavsky, *Searching for Safety* (New Brunswick, N.J.: Transaction Press, 1988), especially pp. 77–79 and 118–20; also see Sieber, *Fatal Remedies*, pp. 23–26. For an application to international politics, see Phil Williams, "Crisis Management in Europe," in Alexander George, ed., *Avoiding War* (Boulder, Colo.: Westview, 1991), pp. 500–502. The need for adaptability is a theme of Charles Lindblom: see *The Intelligence of Democracy* (New York: Free Press, 1965); Lindblom and David Cohen, *Usable Knowledge: Social Science and Social Problem Solving* (New Haven, Conn.: Yale University Press, 1979); and Lindblom, *Inquiry and Change: The Troubled Attempt to Understand and Shape Society* (New Haven, Conn.: Yale University Press, 1990).

[151] Natalie Angier, "Malaria's Genetic Game of Cloak and Dagger," *New York Times*, August 22, 1995.

[152] Michael Brown, *Flying Blind: The Politics of the U.S. Strategic Bomber Program* (Ithaca, N.Y.: Cornell University Press, 1992).

a minimum of duplication of function, with no unnecessary design features, and with complete marrying to the airframe of the various systems required to perform the mission. As a result, the operating systems in the aircraft must be integrated closely from a functional standpoint.[153]

This sounds sensible, but a well-integrated system can neither take advantage of unforeseen opportunities nor cope with unexpected difficulties. When an element underperforms or one part of a policy fails, other parts must be added or improved; when unforeseen interactions appear, several alterations are likely to be necessary. The tighter the design of the system, the greater the ramifications of these disruptions. Only if complete predictability and control is possible can actors afford to follow a blueprint.

While policy makers need to try to anticipate what others will do and how the environment will be changed by their actions, they must also leave themselves room to respond if their anticipations are incorrect. Problems are almost never solved once and for all; initial policies, no matter how well designed, rarely can be definitive; solutions will generate unexpected difficulties. In the domestic arena, while American political campaign reform laws have had some of the consequences that their sponsors sought, they have had others as well, such as the creation of political action committees.[154] Similarly, even the most sophisticated health care reform is certain to increase costs somewhere or produce some undesired behavior by patients, doctors, or companies. This does not mean that reforms must fail or that directed change is impossible, but that the game does not end after one or two plays and that new measures will be needed to cope with the new problems. So in criticizing the quotation with which I began this book, I do not mean to imply that it is a mistake to require tankers to have double hulls, but only that doing so would have multiple consequences, some of which could defeat the purpose unless other actions are taken. They can be, however: Special instructions and training could be given to ships' captains, additional taxes might be levied on pipelines, and officials could be ready to respond to the undesired consequences of these supplementary policies.

The idea that social action forms and takes place within a system is familiar. In the study of international politics the term *system* is commonplace, the most important book of the past decade propounds a systems approach, and basic notions of game theory are staples of discourse. Nevertheless, scholars and statesmen as well as the general public are prone to think in non-

[153] Quoted in ibid., p. 176; for parallel discussions in ecology and biology, see Allen and Hoekstra, *Toward a Unified Ecology*, pp. 277–28, and Kauffman, *Origins of Order*, p. 36.

[154] See, for example, Edwin Epstein, "Business and Labor Under the Federal Campaign Act of 1971," in Michael Malbin, ed., *Parties, Interest Groups, and Campaign Finance Laws* (Washington, D.C.: American Enterprise Institute, 1980), pp. 107–51, and Nelson Polsby, *The Consequences of Party Reform* (New York: Oxford University Press, 1983).

systemic terms. This is often appropriate, and few miracles will follow from thinking systemically because the interactive, strategic, and contingent nature of systems limits the extent to which complete and deterministic theories are possible. But we need to take more seriously the notion that we are dealing with systems and to look for the dynamics that drive them. A distinguished student of genetics summarized his perspective in the phrase: "Nothing in biology makes sense except in the light of evolution."[155] Very little in social and political life makes sense except in the light of systemic processes. Exploring them gives us new possibilities for understanding and effective action; in their absence we are likely to flounder.

[155] Theodosius Dobzhansky, "Nothing in Biology Makes Sense Except in the Light of Evolution," *American Biology Teacher* 35 (March 1972), pp. 125–29.

Index

About the author

ROBERT JERVIS is Adlai E. Stevenson Professor of International Politics at Columbia University. He is the author of numerous books, including *Perception and Misperception in International Politics*.